Understanding E-Government in Europe

This volume critically explores the contentions in the emerging debate surrounding new media technologies and the extent to which they are challenging traditional political and government models.

Examining a range of citizen/government interactions which together form E-Government in different contexts, this book assesses the potential of new media technologies to facilitate new institutional patterns for governance and participation, as experienced primarily, but not only, across Europe. Analysing a range of challenges spanning from those of a technological and conceptual nature to those of a more political and legal nature, the authors scrutinise the central policies at governmental and organisational levels and consider the following questions:

- Is society driving or responding to E-Government and is it ready to cope with it?
- What implications does E-Government have for the power/democracy relationship?
- Is the technology right for E-Government? What is needed to ensure government services are delivered optimally?
- How is E-Government perceived and is it trusted?
- How are the sensitive issues of identity, privacy and social inclusion dealt with?
- How are management and safety dealt with when one considers issues such as activism, cyberterrorism, biometrics, and new implications for international relations?

This comprehensive text will be of interest to students and scholars of public policy, politics, media and communication studies, sociology, law and European studies. It will also offer insights of relevance to practitioners and policy-makers in regional, national and transnational governance, reform and innovation.

Paul G. Nixon is Senior Lecturer of Political Science at The Hague University of Applied Sciences, the Netherlands.

Vassiliki N. Koutrakou is Director of the Centre for Research in European Studies (CREST) at the University of East Anglia, Norwich, UK.

Rajash Rawal is a Lecturer in European Politics at Academy of European Studies & Communication Management, at The Hague University of Applied Sciences, the Netherlands.

Understanding E-Government in Europe

Issues and challenges

**Edited by Paul G. Nixon,
Vassiliki N. Koutrakou and
Rajash Rawal**

Routledge
Taylor & Francis Group

LONDON AND NEW YORK

First published 2010
by Routledge
2 Park Square, Milton Park, Abingdon, Oxon OX14 4RN

Simultaneously published in the USA and Canada
by Routledge
270 Madison Avenue, New York, NY 10016

Routledge is an imprint of the Taylor & Francis Group, an informa business

© 2010 Selection and editorial matter, Paul G. Nixon, Vassiliki N.
Koutrakou and Rajash Rawal; individual chapters, the contributors

Typeset in Baskerville by
Keystroke, Tettenhall, Wolverhampton
Printed and bound in Great Britain
by CPI Antony Rowe, Chippenham, Wiltshire

The publisher has no responsibility for the persistence or accuracy of URLs
for external or third-party internet websites referred to in this book, and
does not guarantee that any content on such websites is, or will remain,
accurate or appropriate.

British Library Cataloguing in Publication Data
A catalogue record for this book is available from the British Library

Library of Congress Cataloging in Publication Data
Understanding e-government in Europe : issues and challenges / edited by
Paul G. Nixon, Vassiliki N. Koutrakou, Rajash Rawal.
     p. cm.
    Includes bibliographical references and index.
  Internet in public administration – Europe. 2. Communication in
politics – Europe. I. Nixon, Paul G. II. Koutrakou, Vassiliki N.,
1962– III. Rawal, Rajash.
JF1525.A8U53 2009
352.3′802854678 – dc22   2009019699

ISBN10: 0-415-46799-3 (hbk)
ISBN10: 0-415-46800-0 (pbk)
ISBN10: 0-203-86609-6 (ebk)

ISBN13: 978-0-415-46799-5 (hbk)
ISBN13: 978-0-415-46800-8 (pbk)
ISBN13: 978-0-203-86609-2 (ebk)

To Patrick and Ingrid
Paul G. Nixon

To Ismini and to my lost little boys Steffy and Jason
Vassiliki N. Koutrakou

To my mother and father
Rajash Rawal

Contents

Figures

Tables

Notes on contributors

Michael Blakemore is Professor of Geography, University of Durham. His recent publications include (with R. Longhorn) 'Re-visiting the valuing and pricing of digital geographic information', *Journal of Digital Information*, 2004; 'Communicating Information about the World Trade Center Disaster: Ripples, Reverberations, and Repercussions', *First Monday*, 2001; and (with M. Craglia) 'Access to Public-Sector Information in Europe: Policy, Rights, and Obligations', *The Information Society*, 2006.

Cristiano Codagnone is Aggregate Professor at the Faculty of Political Science of Milan State University. He teaches comparative social and administrative systems. He is a partner in a research and consulting company, Tech4i2 Limited, which specialises in helping define and evaluate innovative and inclusive public policies in the field of the information society (E-Government, E-Inclusion, E-Health). Cristiano graduated in economics from Bocconi University in 1988 (MA equivalent) and has a Ph.D. (1995) in sociology from New York University. Since 1997 he has combined academia, consulting and policy-making, mostly focusing on the Information Society and on the topic of public sector modernisation. He has also served as Project Officer within the UN E-Government for Development Programme (2003–2004). Since 2005 he has been working as an adviser to the DG INFSO in several studies and projects.

William H. Dutton is Director of the Oxford Internet Institute, Professor of Internet Studies, University of Oxford, and Fellow of Balliol College, Oxford. He was previously a professor in the Annenberg School for Communication at the University of Southern California. He was National Director of the UK's Programme on Information and Communication Technologies (PICT) (1993–1996). He is also Co-Director of the e-Horizons Institute and Director and Principal Investigator of the Oxford e-Social Science Project, a node within the UK's National Centre for E-Social Science. Among his numerous publications on the social aspects of information and communication technologies are *Society on the Line* (Oxford University Press, 1999); (edited with Brian D. Loader) *Digital Academe* (Routledge, 2003); and (edited with Brian Kahin, Ramon O'Callaghan and Andrew W. Wyckoff) *Transforming Enterprise* (MIT Press, 2005).

Arthur Edwards is Senior Lecturer at the Department of Public Administration, Erasmus University, Rotterdam. His research fields are ICTs and democracy, local democracy and the public sphere. He also researches interactive policy-making in Dutch municipalities and new forms of local democracy in European countries. He is widely published in these areas. He is Secretary for the Centre of Public Governance.

G. Honor Fagan is based at the National University of Ireland, Maynooth. Recent publications include 'Changing a Mindset: From Recognition of Qualifications towards Embedding Ethnic Reflexivity and Transnational Positionality', *Translocations*, 2007; and (with D. R. Newman *et al.*) 'Final Report: E-Consultation: Evaluating Appropriate Technologies and Processes for Citizens' Participation in Public Policy', 2006, *www.e-consultation.org*.

Olivier Glassey heads the research unit at the Science Policy and Society Observatory at the University of Lausanne, Switzerland. Recent publications include (with Thomas F. Gordon) 'A Case Study on Taxpayer Segmentation' (ICEGOV, 2008); 'Feasibility Study for a Legal Knowledge System in the County of Herford' (EGOV, 2005); and 'PETALE: Case Study of a Knowledge Reengineering Project' (KMGov, 2004).

Antje Grebner is a lecturer in the Academy of European Studies and Communication Management at The Hague University of Applied Sciences (de Haagse Hogeschool). In parallel, she is completing a Ph.D. at the School of Political, Social and International Studies at the University of East Anglia. Her main research interests are Russian politics, civil society, non-governmental actors and political cybercultures.

Nicola Hall works with ECOTEC Research and Consulting Limited, Birmingham, UK. Her recent publications include (with S. Coleman and M. Howell) 'Hearing Voices: The Experience of Online Public Consultations and Discussions in UK Governance' (Hansard Society, 2002); (with S. Coleman) 'Spinning on the Web: E-Campaigning and Beyond', in S. Coleman (ed.) *2001: Cyber Space Odyssey: The Internet in the UK Election* (Hansard Society); and (with A. Collinge *et al.*) 'The Pensions Services' Interactive Digital Television Pilot: A Qualitative Evaluation' (DWP, 2003).

Rasa Jucuite is a Ph.D. student in management and public administration at Mykolas Romeris University, Lithuania and a research student at Kingston University in London. She has worked as a research fellow at Mykolas Romeris and also as a trainee at the Department of European Integration, Ministry of Foreign Affairs and the Department of Regional Development, Ministry of Public Administration and Reform and Local Authorities, contributing in particular to preparatory work for Lithuania's accession to the EU.

Vassiliki N. Koutrakou is a lecturer in European Studies and Director of the Centre for Research in European Studies (CREST) at the University of East Anglia, Norwich, UK. Publications include the book *Technological Collaboration for Europe's Survival* (Avebury, 1995) and the edited collections *European Union and Britain: Debating the Challenges Ahead* (with L. A. Emerson) (Macmillan, 2000), *Contemporary Issues and Debates in EU Policy – The EU and International Relations* (MUP, 2004) and *E-Government in Europe* (with Paul G. Nixon) (Routledge, 2007).

Miriam Lips has recently been appointed the inaugural Chair in E-Government at Victoria University of Wellington. She is a Research Fellow at Oxford University's Internet Institute. Her research and teaching interests include identity management, digital citizenship, personalisation, Internet governance, regulation in the information society and public management. She has been responsible for a number of funded European research projects and has published widely in the field of E-Government.

Juliet Lodge is Director of the Jean Monnet European Centre of Excellence, Institute for Communication Studies, University of Leeds, UK, where she is also Professor of European Union politics and European Integration. European Woman of Europe 1992, she has written numerous books on EU politics and EU responses to international terrorism. She is series editor of the Euro-elections to the European Parliament for Palgrave and has published extensively on EU reform, openness, internal security, pillar III and E-Judicial co-operation. Co-convenor of the eJustice ethics committee in the UK, she has contributed to EU publications on biometrics and accountability, openness, Euratom, the Hague programme and the draft Constitution.

Paul McCusker is a lecturer at Letterkenny Institute of Technology. He has worked on collaborative research looking into the procedures of E-Consultation and its implementation in Ireland and across Europe. He has attended numerous international conferences and is published widely in the field. Recent publications include (with S. Stephens *et al.*) 'On the Road from Consultation Cynicism to Energising E-Consultation' in Dan Remenyi, *6th European Conference on E-Government – Proceedings* (2006); and (with G. H. Fagan *et al.*) 'Final Report: E-Consultation: Evaluating Appropriate Technologies and Processes for Citizens' Participation in Public Policy' (www.e-consultation.org, 2006).

Neil McDonald is Senior Consultant, ECOTEC Research and Consulting Ltd, working on public policy development and evaluation across a range of themes, including energy and environment, economic development and the information society at EU, national and regional levels and across a number of thematic areas including information society, E-Government, energy and environment, and competitiveness. He was Project Manager for a DG INFSO study to assess the contribution of EU information society activities to the Lisbon Agenda. He is currently managing the DG INFSO study on organisational change for citizen-centric E-Government.

Michael Margolis is Professor of Political Science at the University of Cincinnati. He was co-author (with the late David Resnick) of *Politics as Usual: The Cyberspace 'Revolution'*. His scholarly and popular publications include books, chapters and articles on political parties, elections, public opinion, mass media and democratic theory. He has held visiting appointments in Scotland, at the Universities of Strathclyde and Glasgow, and in Korea at Hankuk University of Foreign Studies Seoul.

Gianluca Misuraca is Managing Director of the Executive Master in e-Governance at the Chair of Management of Network Industries (MIR) of the

College of Management of Technology (CdM) of the Ecole Polytechnique Fédérale de Lausanne (EPFL). He is also an independent adviser and researcher in E-Governance and public administration for international public and private organisations. Recent publications include 'LOG-IN Africa local governance and ICTs research network for Africa' (DG.O, 2006), and (with M. Finger and P. Rossel) 'E-Governance as a Global Knowledge-Enabling Platform' (DG.O, 2006).

Filipe Montargil is an associate researcher at CIES/ISCTE, Portugal. He lectures at ISCTE in Lisbon. He also collaborates with the Department of Communications and Performance Studies of the University of Milan and the Portuguese Catholic University. His international co-operation in European research networks brought him to work with the Internet Interdisciplinary Institute (IN3) in Barcelona. Example of publication: 'Electronic Democracy and Public Participation in Portugal: an Exploratory Analysis', in *Public Participation and Information Technologies* (ICPPIT 99 – CITIDEP – DCEA-FCT-UNR, 2002).

Gerson Moreno-Riaño is based at Regent University. His areas of expertise include the history of political philosophy with a special emphasis on early modern political ideas, postmodern political philosophy, natural law philosophy and political ethics. His publications include four authored/edited books as well as numerous chapters and journal articles in peer-reviewed books and academic journals. He is a member of the American Political Science Association, the Medieval Academy of America, the Association for Political Theory and the National Association of Scholars.

John Morison is Professor at Queen's University Belfast School of Law. He has worked on various empirical projects funded by government, research councils and the European Commission. He has published extensively on governance, democracy, constitution and human rights. Recent publications include 'Modernising Government and the E-Government Revolution: Technologies of Government and Technologies of Democracy', in P. Leyland and N. Bamforth (eds) *Public Law in a Multi-layered Constitution* (Hart Publishing 2003); 'Models of Democracy: From Representation to Participation?', in J. Jowell and D. Oliver (eds) *The Changing Constitution*, 6th edition (Oxford University Press, 2007); and 'Governance and Democracy: From E-Consultation to E-Participation', in S. Flogaitis *et al.*, 'E-Government and E-Democracy/E-Gouvernement et E-Démocratie'. *European Public Law Series* (Esperia, 2006).

Michael Murray is based at the National University of Ireland, Maynooth, Department of Adult and Community Education. His recent publications include (with C. Collier) *Northern Ireland after the Troubles? A Society in Transition* (Manchester University Press, 2008); 'Cosmopolitans versus the Locals: Community-Based Protest in the Age of Globalisation', *Irish Journal of Sociology* (2007); 'Multi-level "Partnership" and Irish Waste Management: The Politics of Municipal Incineration', *Economic and Social Review* (2006); and (with H. Fagan) 'Urban Governance and the Environment: An Irish Case Study', *Journal of Irish Urban Studies* (2004).

D. R. Newman is based at the Queen's University Belfast Management School. He is a member of the Information Systems Research Cluster. Recent publications include (with G. H. Fagan) 'Final Report: E-Consultation: Evaluating Appropriate Technologies and Processes for Citizens' Participation in Public Policy' (www. e-consultation.org, 2006).

Paul G. Nixon is Senior Lecturer in Political Science at the The Hague University of Professional Education, The Hague, the Netherlands. He has contributed chapters to many edited collections on the use of ICTs, particularly in the fields of political parties, electronic democracy and social welfare. He has co-edited three previous collections for Routledge (with V. Koutrakou): *E-Government in Europe* (2007); (with S. Ward and R. Gibson) *Political Parties and the Internet* (2003); and (with Wim Van De Donk, B. Loader and D. Rucht) *Cyberprotest* (2004). He has also published in the fields of culture and literature, including editing a collection entitled *Representations of Education in Literature* (Edwin Mellen Press, 2000). He has recently been appointed as an editorial member for the Routledge journal *Information, Communication and Society*.

David O'Donnell is based at the Intellectual Capital Research Institute of Ireland. His recent publications include 'Why Humanistic Approaches in HRD Won't Work', *Human Resource Development Quarterly* (2005); 'Theory and Method on Intellectual Capital Creation: Addressing Communicative Action through Relative Methodics', *Journal of Intellectual Capital* (2004); and 'Exploring Human Resource Development: A Levels of Analysis Approach', *Human Resource Development Review* (2004).

Joe Organ is a researcher at the Oxford Internet Institute. His research explores the UK E-Government landscape, comparing Cabinet Office policy with departmental projects and programmes. At present, he is primarily working on the ESRC e-Society project Personal Identification and Identity Management in New Modes of E-Government.

David Osimo joined Tech4i2 Ltd in 2008 as Managing Partner, after 15 years working on EU innovation policies and projects. Up until 2005 he worked in the Institute for Prospective Technological Studies, based in Seville and part of the Joint Research Centre of the European Commission, where he was co-ordinating research activities on E-Government. Previously, he worked as an adviser and a project manager on public policies for innovation and information society in Milan (Italy), Brussels (Belgium) and Bologna (Italy). His current interests cover the role of government in the innovation system, the impact of technology on future models of government and, in particular, the impact of Web 2.0 on public services.

Dimitra Petrakaki is a postdoctoral researcher in the Department of Organization, Work and Technology, Lancaster University. Her research specialisation centres on the impact of E-Government and its implementation and applicability. She has presented a number of papers at international conferences.

Rajash Rawal is a lecturer in European Politics at HEBO, Haagse Hogeschool, the Netherlands. He is a visiting lecturer at the Fachhochschule, Eisenstadt, Austria and the Department of European Studies, Budapest Business School. He is a research fellow within the European Public Management Research Group. He specialises in the impact of media on political agents in the modern era, and has written a number of papers around this theme.

Pierre Rossel is based at the Ecole Polytechnique Fédérale de Lausanne, Switzerland. Among his numerous publications are: (with Matthias Finger) 'Conceptualizing e-Governance' (ICEGOV, 2007); and (with T. Zwahr and M. Finger) 'Towards Electronic Governance: A Case Study of ICT in Local Government Governance' (DG.O 2005).

Joseph Savirimuthu is Law Lecturer at the University of Liverpool and co-editor of the *Journal of International Commercial Law and Technology*. His recent publications include 'P2P@softwar(e).com: Or the Art of Cyberspace 3.0', in F. Macmillan (ed.) *New Directions in Copyright Law* (Edward Elgar, 2007); and 'DRMs, RFID and Disruptive Code: Architecture, Dystopia and Eunomics', in S. Kierkegaard (ed.) *Legal, Privacy and Security Issues in Information Technology* (Institutt for Rettsinformatikk, 2006).

Savvas Savvides studied Computer Science at the University of East Anglia before completing an M.Sc. at the London School of Economics. He is currently completing a 'stage' traineeship at the European Commission while also pursuing a remote postgraduate course in health research at Lancaster University.

Simon Stephens is based at the Letterkenny Institute of Technology. His recent publications include (with O'Donnell *et al.*) 'Navigating between Utopia and Dystopia in the Public Sphere through eParticipation: Where Is the Value?', International Critical Management Studies Conference in Manchester (2007); and (with G. H. Fagan *et al.*) 'Final Report: E-consultation: Evaluating Appropriate Technologies and Processes for Citizens' Participation in Public Policy' (2006), www.e-consultation.org.

Laura Sudulich is a Ph.D. student in the Department of Political Science, Trinity College Dublin. Her research interests include e-democracy, political parties, e-participation and political philosophy. She has presented several papers at international conferences.

John Taylor is Professor of Government and Information Management at Caledonian Business School, Glasgow. He has worked on a number of major UK research programmes including the ESRC's Programme on Information and Communications Technologies (PICT) and the Virtual Society Programme, focusing on the diffusion and uptake by governments and NGOs of information and communication technologies. He has published widely in the areas of E-Government and E-Democracy. He is the editor of the international journal *Information Policy*.

Acknowledgements

The editors would like to express their sincere thanks to everyone at Routledge, particularly Heidi Bagtazo and Lucy Dunne, for their guidance, commitment and patience.

We must next congratulate and thank our amazing range of contributors for their inspired contributing chapters, which have made this a rich volume of which we can all be proud. We hope this volume will prove a useful resource for scholars and students in the field, and for practitioners alike. We hope too that we have done justice to their generosity and not committed any mistakes in the editing process which might compromise in any way the top quality of their contribution.

On a personal level, Paul would like to thank Joy for her assistance with American issues, Rayne for providing invaluable moments of levity, Ben van der Sluijs for being Ben and the crew at Xieje for providing inspiration.

Vassiliki is grateful to her father for his patience and sacrifices, especially at a very difficult time, as well as all good friends, human and feline, for their support along the way.

Rajash would like to thank Nayna Rawal, who made this possible, Claudia Bulnes, who made him believe, and Andrés and Laura, who make everything worthwhile. He would not, however, wish to leave out Berry Minkman, Mohamed Bouras and Marjo van den Haspel, who supported and put up with him during the process of editing this book (and beyond).

Last but not least, we would all like to thank our generous funders: the British Academy, whose grant facilitated the planning phase of the project, as well as the Academy of European Studies and Communication Management of The Hague University and the Centre for Research in European Studies (CREST) of the University of East Anglia Norwich, who co-sponsored the seventh CREST Conference in 2007 in Norwich, which served as an invaluable melting pot of ideas for contributors and a springboard without which this volume would not have materialised.

Acknowledgements

Introduction

Rajash Rawal, Vassiliki N. Koutrakou and Paul G. Nixon

As more and more governments seek to implement E-Government mechanisms in order to reform their government and public administration, questions abound as to how successful this can be. Indeed, it has even been mooted that E-Government has become an integral component of public sector reform. Moreover, on an ever-increasing basis, citizens and governments alike use information and communication technologies (ICTs) to interact on a wide range of matters with increasing frequency. E-Government is no longer the exception but is becoming the norm, the familiar, *the* way to 'do' modern government. The importance of E-Government public services seems to be beyond reasonable doubt and its place on the policy agenda often unchallenged. This edited collection endeavours to chart, explain and assess the challenges that governments face and the various roles that factors play before we can even begin to speak of successful transferral to E-Government.

This volume takes a multi-disciplinary approach, analysing a range of challenges which spans from those of a technological nature to those of a more legal nature. It brings together a wide range of divergent views from established experts and new academic voices, all of which are at the cutting edge of E-Government research. It melds these contributions into a coherent and convincing explanation of the challenges and difficulties experienced in E-Government implementation, understanding and use. Notably, the contributions take a global perspective rather than focus on particular countries or geographical areas.

Structure and contents of this volume

This book analyses the following challenges, among others, faced by E-Government, its implementers and its users in all spheres:

*   Is society ready for E-Government? How is society being informed/trained to cope?
*   What implications does E-Government have for the power/democracy relationship?
*   Is the technology right for E-Government? What is needed to ensure government services are delivered optimally?
*   How is E-Government perceived in the media?

- How are the sensitive issues of identity, privacy and social inclusion dealt with?
- How is the issue of safety dealt with when one considers the threats of activism, cyberterrorism and biometrics?

The purpose of this book is to examine and critique the central policy and then to see how this is interpreted at member-state level in actions towards service delivery and E-Government.

In Chapter 1 Dutton focuses on the growing use of the Internet and related digital technologies that are creating a space for networking individuals in ways that enable a new source of accountability in government, politics and other sectors. The chapter explains how this emerging 'Fifth Estate' is being established and why it could challenge the influence of other, more established bases of institutional authority. It discusses approaches to the governance of this new social and political phenomenon that could nurture the Fifth Estate's potential for supporting the vitality of liberal democratic societies.

Chapter 2 sees Blakemore *et al.* examine the challenge for governments that wish to become citizen-centric, which is to deliver cost-effective, personalised and relevant E-Services that simultaneously enhance democratic dialogue. From their study of over 24 months for the European Commission E-Government Unit, they assessed the ways in which organisations are changing to deliver E-Government services. They found that a simple focus on the organisation was not sufficient. It is the way in which the organisation mediates a critical relationship between government and citizen that matters, and it is this aspect which forms the focal point of the chapter.

In Chapter 3 Codagnone and Osimo present a selective and critical re-elaboration of insights from several policy studies that the authors have conducted on the topic of E-Government, current challenges and possible future needs and scenarios for the Directorate General Information Society and Media of the European Commission. The chapter partially reflects the detailed analysis of a report Codagnone and Osimo wrote on the needs for future E-Government services. It examines the supply and demand of E-Government, identifying gaps that they feel need attention. It then goes on to identify differing groups of users and their divergent needs. It is felt that for too long users have been thought of as a homogenised group when, as is shown here, nothing could be further from the truth. The chapter concludes by examining the need for future research and identifying areas of research – not just specifically those designed for E-Government purposes but also others – that may contribute to a more holistic research effort in the pursuit of better governance in Europe.

Montargil argues in Chapter 4 that E-Government services have been the subject of theoretical elaboration and regular evaluation surveys since around 2000. He argues that the theoretical paradigms used for methodology design in these surveys (and, therefore, also its main results) tend to neglect political influence as an analytic dimension and consider citizen return as resulting from technical interactivity. A critique is offered based on the assumptions underlying this paradigm and a complementary criterion is presented for the analysis of E-Government services.

Margolis and Moreno-Riaño consider in Chapter 5 that differing versions of the democracy notwithstanding, governments tend to use representative democracy as a way to realise popular government. In order to decide whether to retain or replace their representatives, therefore, citizens need information about both the impact of governmental policies on people like themselves and the government's future policy priorities. The Internet represents one solution to this problem. Citizens can use it to acquire information about public policy, not only from the established interests and media of their own nation, but also from less familiar sources. One side effect of the process has been the transferral of status of the citizen to customer or consumer. Chapter 5 challenges this notion by suggesting that as citizens of a democracy exercise the ultimate authority to choose or dismiss those who decide the great political issues, shouldn't their role in governance be more than that of customer?

In Chapter 6 Petrakaki addresses the question of what constitutes accountability in the context of E-Government. Accountability is embedded in the traditional bureaucratic public sector because of the principles that underpin, at least ideally, its function. By contrast, E-Government initiatives are surrounded by different principles such as technological orientation, joining up, re-engineering of administrative procedures, customer orientation and contractualisation. These principles are supposed to engender accountability and responsibility by standardising officials' behaviour and eliminating their discretion. Yet, when put into effect, these principles open up a field of multiple possibilities for officials to act. Petrakaki argues that within this context, accountability cannot be established, as it is, at least ideally, in the bureaucratic public sector. Rather, it becomes an individualistic, political and contingent issue that is dependent upon officials' personal values and ethics.

One of the key elements often mooted in the ongoing debates on E-Government is the possibility of using ICT to widen and deepen public consultation processes in decision making, hence improving policy outcomes. Chapter 7, by O'Donnell *et al.*, draws on the findings of eight focus group discussions on 'real world' consultation processes in both Northern Ireland and the Republic of Ireland to map out how the early history of ICT-engendered participation may not illustrate such a smooth and uncontested road.

The implications of the convergence of communication technologies for the resolution of civil disputes are explored by Savirimuthu in Chapter 8. Enabling parties to make informed decisions, using third parties and technology to help identify key issues and presenting disputants with realistic solutions can only serve to enhance the quality of the administration of justice. The convergence of information communication technologies and mechanisms for resolution of civil disputes provides us with an invaluable opportunity to re-think orthodox conceptualisations of access to justice, particularly in the light of Article 6 of the European Court of Human Rights. Savirimuthu describes and explains the transformative capabilities of new technologies for traditional methods of dispute resolution and identifies the key policy priorities for E-Justice.

In Chapter 9 Lips *et al.* present how identity management (IDM) has come to the heart of E-Government policy agendas throughout the world. Considering how E-Government is evolving to transactional service applications, government needs new digitised personal identification and authentication to solve the emerging identity question online: How can we know the individual wanting to access online transactional public services? How can we make sure that that individual is indeed entitled or authorised to access these services? These are the poignant questions posed in this chapter.

Lodge, in Chapter 10, argues that in the context of E-Government, biometrics are not a problem per se. However, the different ways of defining them and the use made of them are problems. Why is securitising borders using biometric tools stored by ICTs a problem? Three reasons for this are explored: (1) the definition and use of biometrics; (2) the practices of E-Government information sharing and inter-operability; and (3) the nature of political controls. Making accountable and securitising access to space within and beyond territorially defined borders highlight the intangibility and elusiveness of the frontiers of new digi-spaces.

In another sectoral case study, as crucial as that of E-Justice, this volume explores the European Commission's high-calibre aims for the adoption of E-Health in the near future. The benefits promised, including patients taking advantage of online processes, health portals and physician web pages and becoming partners in their own health management, redefining the physician–patient management, are already realised by medical professionals and citizens. There are, nevertheless, still many barriers posed on their part that limit its rapid adoption. The most prominent ones are fears about spending on technology over health, reach and privacy and, more importantly, trust. Savvides and Koutrakou, in Chapter 11, explore existing literature and build on Fountain's Technology Enactment Framework in an attempt to suggest ways in which E-Health can be implemented so that the finalised applications both fulfil user requirements and answer the medical professionals' concerns. Thus the reality of E-Health's many useful applications can override concerns and promote trust in E-Health.

In Chapter 12 Misuraca *et al.* use Switzerland as a country case study to revise traditional models of E-Government and substantiate the various datasets and rankings that have marked the battle for situating, stimulating and evaluating Swiss progress in E-Government. They illustrate a series of real measures, programmes and innovative evolutions hiding behind those datasets and rankings. They then reconsider the notion of barriers, re-thought in the Swiss context. They then draw some lessons for general use in the area of E-Government at large. Finally, they suggest some new – and hopefully more meaningful – avenues for future E-Government developments.

Edwards, in Chapter 13, investigates the key role of elected politicians in the evolution of E-Democracy. He presents a theoretical framework for explaining politicians' use of online tools for communication with citizens. This framework includes such factors as politicians' role perceptions, their views on democracy and citizenship, their personal dispositions and competences in using online tools, and political system factors. In their daily work, politicians are facing various challenges and dilemmas. In addition to ambiguities, signs of reluctance and resistance, experiences also show potentially important positive changes.

In Chapter 14 Nixon *et al.* begin by indicating that it has been clear for some time that, particularly in Western democracies, there is a crisis of confidence in the ability of traditional political systems to be able not just to deliver desired services, but to match the changing aspirations of an ever-increasingly articulate, media-savvy and demanding public and thus to shape society in a modern reflexive, albeit inherently complex, form. That public has been seen to at least partially reject traditional fixed political party positions, seeking instead numerous outlets to meet their wishes and aspirations. Those wishes and aspirations are more fluid and fragmented, and indeed being continually re-fragmented, along with changing lifestyle issues and concerns. Therefore, it is impossible to ignore both the new forms of interaction facilitated in cyberspace and the threats and opportunities that these offer existing civil society.

Rawal, in Chapter 15, considers the threats of cyberterrorism. While campaigning for office of President of the United States in 2008, Barack Obama famously referred to a 'net attack' as being as serious and grave a problem as any potential nuclear or biological threat. These concerns echo long-standing criticisms of the Internet and its capacity. Such criticisms include the Internet's openness and lack of a regulatory power. Governments have readily highlighted that terrorists have been quick to utilise the potential that the cyberworld has to offer terrorists. As a result, efforts to curb and contain have often trampled over human rights, privacy and civil liberties. This chapter examines the developments by looking at what the actual threats of cyberterrorism are and what threats are posed by the use of the Internet by terrorists. It analyses the trends in government measures to attempt to control hyperspace, question the nature of these measures and present how these measures threaten E-Democracy, while at the same time highlighting the need for legitimate E-Identity mechanisms to be created.

Chapter 16 sees Nixon examine the links between trust and perceptions of ICTs and E-Government and how they may be affected by media coverage. The introduction of E-Government has often been heralded as the beginning of a bright new future, modernising government and its interactions with citizens. However, the very nature of most E-Government processes and procedures does not always entail a harmonious and happy user interface. Facilitation of communication channels has little impact upon the quality of information provided and experiences of E-Government are not often shared and pooled in quite the same way that traditional experiences of government traditionally have been shared and pooled.

The use of E-Government as a tool for communication is the subject of Chapter 17. Koutrakou explores future challenges for E-Government mechanisms and techniques to improve connectivity not only within state and/or regional organisation boundaries, but also between international organisations. The benefits of such a development in a multi-lateral world, still evidently embryonic in its deployment, can be massive in terms of the improvement of awareness, consultation and even co-ordination of action, especially in matters of conflict and development. Regional and international organisations in the developed world are only just beginning to fumble through the potential uses of ICTs in this manner; regional organisations in the developing world are not yet at this stage. Rather than losing valuable time waiting and replicating the bottom-up growth of accessibility approach which has applied in much of the Western world, regional organisations in the developing world could be the ones which stand to benefit the most from this fast-track, high-level deployment.

In the Conclusions, the editors argue that there can be little doubt that, as in so many facets of our lives, the Internet has, at least in part, changed the way in which we interact with governments at all levels. It has moved from being some bizarre technical toy to becoming an accepted part of mainstream life in many countries.

A clear conclusion we can draw is that Internet-enabled government will play a role in the delivery of services in a bundle of practices and procedures that is commonly described as E-Government. The shape of E-Government and the component parts of it will no doubt change. The potential of this is explored here.

Part I

The fundamentals of E-Government in Europe

1   The Fifth Estate

Democratic social accountability
through the emerging network
of networks[1]

William H. Dutton

Summary

The rise of the press, radio, television and other mass media has enabled the development of an independent institution: the 'Fourth Estate'. The Fourth Estate is central to pluralist democratic processes. The growing use of the Internet and related digital technologies is creating a space for networking individuals in ways that enable a new source of accountability in government, politics and other sectors. This chapter explains how this emerging 'Fifth Estate' is being established and why this could challenge the influence of other, more established bases of institutional authority. It discusses approaches to the governance of this new social and political phenomenon that could nurture the Fifth Estate's potential for supporting the vitality of liberal democratic societies.

The emergence of a new pluralist democratic institution

The historical conception of feudal societies being divided into estates of the realm, as reflected in France, England and Scotland, can be updated in a way that is useful for understanding developments in contemporary network societies. In pre-revolutionary France and England, for example, these estates were identified as the clergy, nobility and commons.[2] In the eighteenth century, as explained by Thomas Carlyle, Edmund Burke identified the press as a Fourth Estate:

> Burke said there were Three Estates in Parliament; but, in the Reporters' Gallery yonder, there sat a Fourth Estate more important far than they all. It is not a figure of speech, or witty saying; it is a literal fact – very momentous to us in these times.[3]

Since then, radio, television and other mass media have been enfolded with the press into the important independent democratic institution of the Fourth Estate. The passing of feudal society has led many to redefine the estates, as in the US, where these have come to be most often linked to the separation of powers in legislative, executive and judicial branches of government. But the press remains identified as a Fourth Estate in many liberal democratic societies.

However, in the twenty-first century, a new institution is emerging with some characteristics similar to the Fourth Estate, but with sufficiently distinctive and important features to warrant its recognition as a new Fifth Estate. This is being built on the growing use of the Internet and related information and communication technologies (ICTs) in ways that are enabling 'networked individuals'[4] to reconfigure access to alternative sources of information, people and other resources. Such 'networks of networks'[5] enable networked individuals to move across, undermine and go beyond the boundaries of existing institutions, thereby opening new ways of increasing the accountability of politicians, press, experts and other loci of power and influence. These are neither personal nor institutional networks, but networked individuals that reflect many attributes of Manuel Castells's conception of a 'network society'[6] and which are similar to what have been called 'Internet-enabled networks'.[7]

This chapter explores the nature and implications of the Fifth Estate, highlighting why it has the potential to be as important in the twenty-first century as the Fourth Estate has been since the eighteenth century. It begins by placing the notion of the Fifth Estate within a wider conception of the societal implications of the Internet. It then sketches more details of its characteristics and uses, as based on evidence across a range of research findings. It concludes by looking at the main threats to the vitality of the new estate and the governance approaches that could help to maintain and enhance its role.

The Internet as distinct from the mass media

Some have argued that computer-based communication systems like the Internet are essentially a new medium, building on traditional media.[8] This media-centric view has led to the Internet being seen as simply an adjunct of an evolving Fourth Estate. Many of those who acknowledge that some aspects of the Internet compose something distinctive also have a limited notion of new digital media as being essentially a complementary form of news publishing – a blogosphere or online digital add-on to the mass media.[9]

The politics of the Internet in society

The Internet's broad social roles in government and politics have similarities with those of traditional media. However, the Internet differs from traditional media, particularly in opening up other institutional arenas, from everyday life to science, and to greater social accountability. This needs to be understood in the context of three common views on the political role of the Internet for society at large as irrelevant, deterministic or socially shaped:

1   *An emphasis on technical novelty.* A view of the Internet as a 'passing fad'[10] focused on the supposed ephemeral nature of the Internet in comparison with other institutions and previous media. For a time, this included major players in the field of information technology,[11] who were slow to recognise the increasing importance of this form of networking. With time, this passing fad thesis has become less credible as Internet use has continued to grow and diversify around the world, but it continues to arise around particular themes, such as the Internet as simply a novelty in political campaigns and elections.

2   *Technologies of freedom v. control.* One claim is that the Internet tends to democratise access to information and undermine hierarchies. For example, de Sola Pool[12] saw Internet-based networks as inherently democratic 'technologies of freedom' through which individuals can network with people, information, services and technologies in ways that follow and reinforce their personal self-interests. In contrast, others (e.g. Schiller[13]) contend that institutions will adopt, design and use the Internet to enhance their control of existing institutional structures and organisational arrangements (e.g. in E-Government initiatives that enhance existing institutional arrangements) or in the dystopian vision of a 'surveillance society' based on pervasive networks of closed-circuit television (CCTV) cameras and other digital means of monitoring and controlling citizens' behaviour (e.g. Surveillance Studies Network[14]).

3   *The Internet as a 'network of networks'.* This conception moves on from the largely technologically deterministic freedom v. control debate to accept that the Internet can support and reinforce many different forms of network,[15] each shaped by its stakeholders to reinforce or challenge the interests of individuals or organisations that form the Fifth Estate. These networks connect not only in the one-to-many pattern of the mass media, but also one-to-one, many-to-one, many-to-many and so on patterns.

The Fifth Estate: interplay between individual and institutional networks

Enhancing citizens' communicative power

The view outlined here of the social shaping of ICTs by developers, users and regulators highlights why technologically deterministic thinking that extrapolates the societal implications of a technology from knowing some of its key features has been a major factor contributing to the generally poor track record of many forecasts in this field.[16] However, as explained in this chapter, the social shaping view enables the implications of technical change to be revealed by observing patterns of Internet use and impact over time. For example, networks can be designed to operate as horizontal peer-to-peer communications or for much more hierarchical and centralised structures. Their aims can be to emphasise broad social objectives or to bolster a more individualist viewpoint from which to serve up entertainment for a 'daily-me'.[17] Networks comprising the Fifth Estate have two key distinctive and important characteristics:

1   *The ability to support institutions and individuals to enhance their 'communicative power'.* This is the use of ICTs to form networks that can then lead to real-world power shifts, which, however, does not mean the Internet on its own can give new real power to its users.[18] This enhancement of communicative power is achieved by affording individuals opportunities to network within and beyond various institutional arenas.

2   *The provision of capabilities that enable the creation of networks of individuals which have a public, social benefit* (e.g. through social networking websites).

The self-selected, Internet-enabled individuals who have a primarily social aim in their networking activities often break from existing organisational and institutional networks, which themselves are frequently being transformed in Internet space. For example, local government officials can engage with individuals on community websites within and beyond their constituencies.

Reconfiguring access to the Fifth Estate

The Internet and related ICTs can play a central role in 'reconfiguring access'[19] to people, information, services and other resources. This helps to explain how patterns of digital divides and choices can change the communicative power of individuals, groups and nations, although this understanding cannot be used to forecast the societal implications of the Internet. Instead, it indicates that outcomes are inherently unpredictable at micro and macro levels because they depend on the interaction of numerous strategic and non-strategic choices made by actors about how they seek to shape access to and from the outside world in what I have called an 'ecology of games'.[20] Think, for instance, of the strategies of government agencies, politicians, lobbying groups, news media, bloggers and others trying to gain access to citizens over the Internet.

The Internet can reconfigure access in two fundamental ways. First, it can change the way we do things, such as how we get information, how we communicate with people and how we obtain services and access technologies. Second, and perhaps more fundamentally, its use can alter the outcomes of these activities. It changes what we know, whom we know, with whom we keep in close touch and what services we obtain (e.g. through E-Government), as well as what technologies we use and what know-how we require to employ them. ICTs can also reconfigure access by changing cost structures, eliminating or introducing gatekeepers and expanding or contracting the geography of access. (As well as overcoming geographical barriers, the Internet could also make geography more important because it could enable people to be where they need to be to have face-to-face communication.)

Particular attention in the context of the Fifth Estate needs to be given to the ability of digital networks of networks to reconfigure access by giving greater or lesser control to users (i.e. citizens, viewers, readers and consumers). An appreciation of how the use and diffusion of technologies is socially shaped reveals why the development of any particular platform, including those supportive of a Fifth Estate, has not been inevitable. Instead, platforms have developed over time through the unpredictable interaction of strategic or unintentional choices by many actors with many different competing and complementary objectives. The outcomes of decisions in this ecology have opened up opportunities for individuals to network in varied ways.

These networks can blur the boundaries of households, organisations, institutions and nations. They enable not only institutions but individuals to create local and global networks, as illustrated by the mobilisation of political and financial support around the world for causes as varied as climate change, promotion of terrorism and struggles against state control.

Related conceptions

There are alternative but related conceptions to my formulation of the idea of the Fifth Estate. For instance, the seminal idea of the 'public sphere' articulated by Jürgen Habermas[21] offers valuable insights, but is too closely tied to a romantic view of the past and therefore unable to capture the rise of an entirely new sphere of influence. The notion of an 'information commons' and its many variants is often used by many others to characterise aspects of the new virtual Internet space, especially open sharing of information for free or at low cost.[22] However, although the Internet and Web may be packed with material that is free, they also contain much that is owned and trademarked, copyrighted, proprietary, licensed, etc. For example, the personal computer is a key component of the Internet's infrastructure[23] and is normally owned by individuals or organisations.

My description of this new space is anchored in a social science perspective, but has been supported across other disciplines. Leading computer scientists and engineers have made similar observations, for example, in the way a key creator of the Web, Tim Berners-Lee, and his Web science colleagues speak of the Web as an 'engineered space' that creates a distributed 'information space'.[24] However, they realise this space is being engineered by an increasingly diverse set of actors, including users, and for a wide range of purposes. They also acknowledge that many of these emergent outcomes were not those originally engineered for the Web by its designers. This has led them to call for more multi-disciplinary collaboration with the social sciences.

Evidence of the Fifth Estate

The following sections give a glimpse of the mounting evidence from studies around the world that are identifying patterns of use of the Internet which lend substance to the establishment of a Fifth Estate. After a discussion on background trends in everyday use of the Internet, specific institutional spheres are explored. Important sources of data used include the internationally collaborative World Internet Project (WIP)[25] covering more than twenty countries, such as the Oxford Internet Surveys (OxIS)[26] in Britain.

Everyday use of the Internet

Digital choices and the diffusion of the Internet

Evidence for the basis for a Fifth Estate can be seen in changing patterns of everyday Internet use around the world, as indicated in WIP studies. Internet use continues to grow in number, variety of applications and spread around the globe, pointing to the weakness of the proposition that the Internet is a passing fad. In the UK, for instance, the proportion of the population over 14 years old using the Internet rose from about one-third in 2000 to two-thirds in 2007. This is reflected worldwide to greater or lesser degrees. Countries in Scandinavia and North America have more of their population online, but many more have far less, such as across the global South.

Nevertheless, there are still important divides in Internet access within and between nations and regions, and within and between groups within them. Generally, along the access divide the economic 'haves' get more access to the Internet than the 'have-nots'. This underpins concerns that the Internet reinforces socio-economic inequalities in society. Despite these continuing digital divides, the Internet has achieved a critical mass that enables networked individuals to become a significant force, indicating that the existence of a Fifth Estate is not dependent on universal access.

Studies such as WIP have also shown that social and economic status does not explain all patterns of adoption and use.[27] In addition, the making of 'digital choices'[28] (i.e. about whether or not to use the Internet) also comes into play. For instance, many people choose not to use the Internet even when they have opportunities to do so. It may be generally understandable that the more senior citizens are significantly less likely to use the Internet than younger generations who have appropriate skills and greater familiarity with the technology. However, many older people in homes with access to the technology and other support still do not find the motivation to go online. The Internet plays such a critical role in society that these disparities and lack of interest should not be seen as simply an example of consumers making different choices about products.

Trust in the centrality of the Internet as a new 'space of flows'

The Internet has become central to everyday life for many people in many societies. The core of Internet uses has been communication, as shown by the continuing key role of email. It also rivals the traditional media, government and business as the prime place to go not only for information and services, but also conviviality and entertainment. More recently, what is known as 'Web 2.0' has become an important tool for social networking and meeting new people through services like Facebook, SecondLife, YouTube and MySpace.

As the use of broadband grows,[29] so does the Internet as a popular venue to go to for entertainment (e.g. for downloading music or video, playing online games, viewing television and listening to the radio). Frequency of use of the Internet has also increased rapidly, with a significant majority of users accessing the Internet as a routine part of their daily life.

As well as becoming a critical infrastructure of everyday life, the Internet is networking information and people in ways never before possible. For example, OxIS found that in 2007 in the UK the Internet was the first or second most common place users would first choose to go for information across a range of tasks, such as looking for the name of their MP, getting information about taxes or looking for information about local schools. People increasingly go to the Internet instead of going to a place or institution.

This is illustrative of what Castells[30] calls a new 'space of flows'. Users usually do not go to a particular place on the Internet, but increasingly rely on search engines to find information or to find what could be located anywhere in the world. This is significant because governments, libraries, newspapers, universities and other institutions are just beginning to realise that an increasing number of people are choosing not to come to them specifically for information and some services, but instead are going to a search engine on the Internet.

A frequent response from traditional institutions, such as the Fourth Estate, is to suggest that that they will retain their central position because of the trust they have built over the years. However, users trust what they find on the Internet about as much as, or more than, they trust broadcast news or newspapers.[31] Generally, the more experience people have with the Internet, the more they develop a learned level of trust in the information they can find and the people they can meet online. People remain sceptical; more educated individuals are relatively more sceptical, but the most distrustful are those who have never used the Internet. This suggests the Internet is an 'experience' technology.[32] As experience online continues to build, more users are likely to develop such a learned trust in the Internet. This will make the Internet as a space of flows even more the place to go for finding information, making contact with other people and finding services and entertainment.

Use of the Internet in key institutional spheres

There are complementary patterns to the use of the Internet in everyday life across various other institutional arenas, such as those identified in Table 1.1. In all of these, existing institutional actors are trying to use the Internet and Web in various E-Initiatives designed to reinforce and enhance the effectiveness of their operations and services.

The Internet is crucially enabling individuals in each arena to network in new ways that reconfigure and enhance their communicative power as a type of Fifth Estate. This is achieved by those involved in a sphere (e.g. political constituencies) going outside their respective institutional sphere to reach alternative sources of information

Table 1.1 A categorisation of networked institutions and individuals

Arena	Networked individuals of the Fifth Estate	Networked institutions of the other estates
Governance and democracy	Web-based political movements (e.g. moveon.org)	E-Government, E-Democracy
Press and media	Bloggers, online news aggregators, Wikipedia contributors	Online journalism, radio, TV
Business and commerce	Peer-to-peer file sharing (e.g. music downloads), collaborative network organisations	Online business-to-business, online business-to-consumer (e.g. E-Shopping, E-Banking)
Work and the organisation	Self-selected work collaborations, open-source software creation and distribution, wikis for co-creation	Flatter networked structures, networking to create flexible work location and times
Education	Informal learning via the Internet, checking facts and information, teacher assessment	Virtual universities, multi-media classrooms, online courses
Research	Collaboration across disciplinary, institutional and national boundaries	Institutional IT services, online grant and proposal submissions

and services over the Internet. Institutions rooted in the other estates are also being networked in new ways, such as through the opening of new online communication channels by print and broadcast media. In addition, institutional networking is supporting strategic organisational shifts in activities such as E-Government, E-Commerce and E-Learning.

There is growing overlap and interaction between these networks, with individuals in institutions participating in networks that enable them to connect to networked individuals outside their institution. In public, private and voluntary sectors, organisations must begin to understand that people will not necessarily go directly to their organisation for the information or services they want, even when that organisation is the responsible body. People go to the Internet, where they can search a network of information distributed around the world. For instance, this enables some patients to visit a doctor armed with much background information gathered from the Web.

Government, business and non-governmental organisations (NGOs) – alongside individual users – can contribute to this distributed network of networks, but it is becoming increasingly separate and independent from any single government department, agency, NGO, business or other entity. For such reasons, all organisations need to consider how they can reconfigure services in ways that allow them to be provided more efficiently online. Organisations should also identify what services and information they need to provide, taking account of what capabilities and resources they are best positioned to provide and what information is already being provided well by others, including over the Internet.

The following sections discuss the implications of the Fifth Estate in key arenas identified in Table 1.1.

Government and democracy on the line

Many administrations have made major strides in putting public information and services online, even though they have not generally kept up with the commercial sector.[33] This means, for instance, that citizens and businesses can go online to complete tax returns, apply and pay for some local services or licences and much more. Important initiatives to develop E-Government services are gaining momentum.[34] The growth in this kind of Internet use is evident in the way, between 2005 and 2007, significantly more Britons – although still not a majority – started to go to the Internet for information about local or central government, to pay taxes, to learn about government policy or to contact a politician.[35]

In political campaigns, elections and democratic engagements, many still view the Internet as largely irrelevant or marginal, while others argue that it is likely to undermine democratic institutions.[36] Some critics view E-Democracy primarily as an innovation that could erode traditional institutions of representative, deliberative democracy by offering direct point-and-click participation in public policy-making. Others see E-Democracy initiatives like gathering and delivering signatures for online E-Petitions as an ineffectual, minor technical novelty. However, each era has its own version of this threat, such as the way interactive cable communication raised concerns over so-called 'push-button democracy'.[37]

The Fifth Estate's network of networks can enable political movements to be orchestrated among opinion leaders and political activists in Internet time, which can be far quicker than real-world time. This provides a novel means for holding politicians and mainstream institutions accountable through the online interaction between ever-changing networks of individuals, which form and re-form continuously depending on the issue that is generating the particular network. A dramatic example is the use of texting after the 11 March 2004 Madrid train bombings to alert people to anti-government rallies, which challenged the government's claims and contributed to unseating José María Aznar's Partido Popular (PP) administration.[38] In the UK, the many E-Petition signatures posted to the Prime Minister opposing the expansion of road charging schemes may not have changed policy, but they forced the Government to reconsider and explain its case for moving ahead on this issue.[39]

Politicians are increasingly seeking to use the Internet and Web to engage with citizens, including finding new sources of funding.[40] Some are entering Fifth Estate spaces, for instance, by creating a presence on Facebook or Second Life. In addition, numerous individual political activists[41] are posting their own opinions on blogs, websites or social networking sites.

The press and mass media

The traditional media of the Fourth Estate has sometimes criticised the Internet for eroding the quality of the public's information environment and undermining the integrative role of the media in society. One concern is that the individuals who use the Internet to produce much online content are amateurs who are spewing misinformation or trivial non-information while marginalising high-quality journalistic coverage.[42] Another critique is that, despite having a vast array of content at their fingertips, Internet users will choose to access only a narrow spectrum related to what most interests them, creating 'echo chambers' in which their own personal prejudices will be reinforced rather than challenged.[43]

However, these views ignore the degree to which all communication technologies are double-edged swords. For instance, they dismiss some of the same weaknesses of the traditional mass media, such as the focus on negative news stories. More importantly, there is also often an unjustified assumption that the Internet will substitute for, rather than complement, traditional media. Many Internet users read online newspapers or news services, although not always the same newspaper as they read offline. In these ways, the Internet can be realistically seen as a source of news that, in part, complements, or even helps to sustain, the Fourth Estate. At the same time, citizen journalists, bloggers, politicians, government agencies, researchers and other online sources provide a related, but independent, and often competing, alternative.

For instance, Salam Pax, the 'Baghdad Blogger',[44] helped to change the media agenda on the war in Iraq by using his enhanced communicative power to present to a worldwide audience a local Iraqi perspective that could not find a strong voice in the mainstream Fourth Estate, which later gave him a platform. In contrast, the press ignored a long, complex blog on the counter-insurgency in Iraq that lent support to keeping Coalition forces in Iraq for a time, although this view became increasingly visible through a grassroots movement using email and other blogs.[45]

Work and the boundaries of the firm

The Fifth Estate has a crucial transformative potential in the workplace, the business firm and other organisations. Internet-enabled networks allow networked individuals to address a variety of problems through collaborative network organisations (CNOs), also known as distributed problem-solving networks.[46] Successful examples of CNOs include Wikipedia, which has become widely used and trusted despite the controversy over the merits of its creation through open inputs from Internet users,[47] and open source software produced by creative arrangements of distributed expertise.[48] Internet users not only read Wikipedia and use open source software, but exercise their Fifth Estate communicative power to help to co-produce these and a host of other products, services and information.[49]

Most firms do not choose to use these networks because they may blur the boundaries and operations of the firm. Instead, individuals are choosing to join CNOs to enhance their own productivity, performance or esteem. Organisations are trying to understand how such innovations can be exploited for the benefit of the enterprise as a whole, and not simply the individual user.[50]

Education and research

E-Learning networks can move beyond the boundaries of the classroom and university. However, many follow and reinforce existing institutional structures (e.g. with the teacher as the primary gatekeeper in a multi-media classroom or virtual learning environment). At the same time, students are linking with one another worldwide through e-mail lists, social networking sites, etc. in ways that enable them to challenge their teachers by bringing in other authorities and views. When done in real time, this can be a positive force or a disruption in the classroom, depending on how well preparations have been made to harness these learning networks.

Likewise, universities are building campus grids, digital library collections and institutional repositories to maintain and enhance the productivity and competitiveness of the institution. At the same time, researchers are collaborating more than ever before through Internet-enabled networking,[51] often across institutional and national boundaries.[52] In general, they are more likely to go to an Internet search engine before they go to their library; as likely to use their personal computer to support network-enabled collaboration as to meet their colleagues in the next office; and post work on their websites and blogs rather than in institutional repositories. Indeed, freely available social networking sites offer tools for collaboration that could be as, or more, useful to researchers than systems for collaboration in which universities and governments have invested much money.

Academics are engaged in their own emerging Fifth Estate through, for instance, online mobilisation around local issues (e.g. university governance) as well as more international topics (e.g. copyright and open science). Checks and balances on more established academic institutional structures are being broadened on the Internet with a growing sense of accountability to the often anonymous blogosphere of fellow academics, for instance.

Conclusions: Sustaining democratic vitality through the Fifth Estate

A new space of flows: implications for governance and democracy

The conceptualisation of the Fifth Estate in this chapter builds on Castells's [53] depiction of the Internet as a 'space of flows', in contrast to a space of places. When you go to the Internet, you enter this new space that connects with people and places. This is significantly different from a physical place, although they complement each other in shaping the quality of our information environment.

This space of flows enables a multitude of actors to reconfigure access to information, people, services and technologies. This can reinforce existing institutions, such as when the government posts information and documents online. This can also enable individuals to be at the centre of their own personal networks, such as when students are at the centre of their own learning network, including friends, school or university resources and the treasury of Web knowledge. Individuals can also network in ways that constitute the Fifth Estate as an independent source of social accountability across multiple arenas.

The evidence highlighted in this chapter – the tip of a larger and growing research base – indicates that the Fifth Estate is a robust concept which can flourish despite a digital divide in access and with only a minority of users actively producing material for the Internet, as opposed to simply using it. It allows networked individuals to employ the Internet to increase the accountability of the other estates, for instance by challenging government policies and Fourth Estate sources. And the Fifth Estate can be deployed as an alternative source of authority to professional expertise by offering alternative sources of information, analysis and opinion to citizens, patients, students, etc.

Threats to the Fifth Estate

The Fifth Estate faces a number of threats, related to each of the other estates. Its Internet-enabled networks therefore need to be identified and better understood if they are to be protected and fostered as a means for realising the growing potential of the Internet.

The Internet's role in networking individuals is a double-edged sword. The Internet opens gates to allow in those aspects of the outside world which are of benefit to the Internet user. This also brings in those causing harm by intent or accident. Just as environmental or positive political movements can exploit the Internet, extremist groups can establish a strong Internet presence as a resource for recruiting, funding and magnifying their image. The Fifth Estate could undermine valuable institutions or become a conservative force by establishing more checks and balances. Although such dangers are offset by a similarly long list of advantages, the thrust of the critique remains that the Internet can empower both the malicious and the well intentioned.

This double-edged nature of the Internet is the source of some of the main threats to the Fifth Estate from the established estates (and the lay public, which Burke might have called the mob). The modern equivalent of the First Estate clergy could be seen as the public intellectuals and critics who undermine the value of the Internet by depicting it as a space over-occupied by an ill-informed, ill-disciplined 'cult of the amateur'.[54] The power base of twenty-first-century nobility is reflected in economic elites. These include, for example, global corporations competing to dominate and commercialise Internet spaces, such as the 'Edisons of the digital age',[55] who seek to create vertically integrated 'clouds' of 'giant information utilities' equivalent to the power utilities of an earlier era.

Government, which is the Third Estate, is increasingly aware of the potential power of the Fifth Estate to challenge its authority. In some countries, the response has been to develop various techniques of filtering, regulating and otherwise using controls to constrain and block Internet access.[56] As discussed above, the Fourth Estate overlaps with the Fifth Estate in some complementary ways. But traditional media are also competing with, co-opting and imitating the Internet's space of flows. Finally, the communicative power of the mob of citizens, audiences and consumers, as well as spammers, virus writers and hackers, is enhanced by entering the new space of flows. Table 1.2 summarises these threats.

Governance of the Fifth Estate space

The risks and hazards intrinsic to an open technology like the Internet have increasingly led for calls from citizens, governments, business and industry and others to introduce online gatekeepers and other controls to govern what was originally conceived by the Internet's designers as an open, end-to-end network allowing a free flow of content.[57] Questions about the governance of the Fifth Estate are likely to become more prominent as people realise that the Internet is a social phenomenon with broad and substantial societal implications. Appropriate forms of governance of Fifth Estate social and political processes, not just technical Internet and infrastructure aspects, will be required to ensure that public debate and accountability are supported by finding a balanced governance approach. This should minimise the risks without

Table 1.2 Threats to the Fifth Estate from established institutions

Traditional Estate	Modern parallel	Type of threat
First: Clergy	Public intellectual	Internet seen as a space for amateurs unable to challenge the knowledge and analytical rigour of experts
Second: Nobility	Economic elites	Centralisation of information utilities and commercialisation of Fifth Estate spaces
Third: Commons	Government	Filters, regulations and other controls to constrain and block Internet access
Fourth: Press	Mass media	Co-opting, imitating and competing with the Fifth Estate space of flows
Mob	Citizens, audiences, consumers, spammers, hackers	Malicious and accidental uses of the Internet undermine trust and confidence

damaging the openness of the Internet that supports the users' ability to generate innovative applications and content.[58]

Fifth Estate governance includes topics that have become well understood in other Estates, such as freedom of expression, protection of minorities and media ownership and concentration. A right to anonymity is a key issue since governments and other estates could threaten networked individuals they could identify, but many, such as some service providers, are asking for authentication of the identity of users for safety and security purposes.

The vitality of Internet-enabled Fifth Estate networks rests less on new policy initiatives than on preventing excessive regulation or inappropriate regulation of the Internet. An intriguing avenue to explore could be to hold Internet users more accountable through the development of innovative approaches to encourage more Fifth Estate self-regulation, such as by what has been called the 'peer production of Internet governance'.[59] These are typified by self-governing processes developed for successful, novel online applications, such as Wikipedia and the eBay online auction service, where users participate in establishing and monitoring governance rules. These could stimulate ideas for approaches to governance of the space of flows in ways that protect and enhance its vitality to ensure that, using Burke's observation on the Fourth Estate, the Fifth Estate continues to be not 'wishful thinking, but a literal fact'.

Key points

- The Internet as a Fifth Estate is distinctive and opens up other institutional arenas in that it has proven to be more than a technical novelty, is viewed as enhancing both individual freedom and government control and is ultimately a network that supports and reinforces networks.
- The Internet enhances citizens' communicative power by supporting individual and institutional networking, leading to possible real power shifts, and enabling social networking.
- The Internet reconfigures access to people, information, services, etc. by altering how we do things and, potentially, the outcomes of these activities.
- Evidence of the Fifth Estate includes both the change of patterns and growth of daily Internet use despite the digital divide and the trust in the centrality of the Internet as a new 'space of flows' which increasingly supersedes that in traditional information sources (libraries, traditional media, etc.).
- The Internet is used in key institutional spheres (E-Government, E-Commerce, E-Health, etc.), enabling communicative power with the following implications for traditional estates: access to government and democracy is transformed; the Internet is a news source which partly complements and partly sustains traditional media; the Internet has a transformative potential in the workplace; the Internet revolutionises education and research.
- The Internet is a social phenomenon and the Fifth Estate is a robust concept.

Notes

1 This chapter builds on the author's Inaugural Professorial Lecture, Examination Schools, University of Oxford, 15 October 2007. See Dutton, W. H. (2007) 'Through the Network of Networks – The Fifth Estate' (15 October). Available at http://ssrn.com/abstract= 1134502.

2 Fitzsimmons, M. P. (2003) *The Night the Old Regime Ended: August 4, 1789 and the French Revolution*. Philadelphia, PA: Pennsylvania State University Press, provides an account of the estates of pre-revolutionary France.

3 Carlyle, T. (1905) *On Heroes: Hero Worship and the Heroic in History*, pp. 349–350. London: H. R. Allenson.

4 The notion of networked individuals corresponds to the term 'networked individualism' used by Barry Wellman (2001) to break old dichotomies between the individual and place-based communities. Wellman, B. (2001) 'Physical Place and Cyberplace: The Rise of Personalized Networking', *International Journal of Urban and Regional Research* 25/2, June: 227–252.

5 Craven, P. and Wellman, B. (1973) 'The Network City', *Sociological Inquiry* 43/1: 57–88. Craven and Wellman (1973) coined the concept of a 'network of networks' in the early years of the Internet, when it was founded as the US Department of Defense's ARPANET. See also Dutton (2007) op. cit.

6 Castells, M. (1996) *The Rise of the Network Society*. Oxford: Blackwell Publishers.

7 Hamel, G. (2007) *The Future of Management*. Cambridge, MA: Harvard University Press.

8 e.g. Rogers, E. M. (1986) *Communication Technology: The New Media in Society*. New York: The Free Press.

9 For example, one blogger calls his blog 'The Fifth Estate'. See: http://at5thestate. blogspot.com/.

10 e.g. Wyatt, S., Thomas, G. and Terranova, T. (2002) 'They Came, They Surfed, They Went Back to the Beach: Conceptualising Use and Non-use of the Internet', in Woolgar, S. (ed.) *Virtual Society? Technology, Cyberpole, Reality*, pp. 23–40. Oxford: Oxford University Press.

11 Gates, B. (1995) *The Road Ahead*. London: Viking.

12 de Sola Pool, I. (1983) *Technologies of Freedom*. Cambridge, MA: Belknap Press of Harvard University Press.

13 Schiller, D. (1999) *Digital Capitalism: Networking the Global Market System*. Cambridge, MA: The MIT Press.

14 Surveillance Studies Network (2006) *A Report on the Surveillance Society for the Information Commissioner*. Wilmslow, UK: Office of the Information Commissioner, September.

15 Dutton, W. H. (1999) *Society on the Line: Information Politics in the Digital Age*. Oxford and New York: Oxford University Press.

16 Dutton, W. H. (1995) 'Driving into the Future of Communications? Check the Rear View Mirror', in Emmott, S. J. with Travis, D. (eds) *Information Superhighways: Multimedia Users and Futures*, pp. 79–102. New York: Academic Press; Dutton, W. H. (1999) *Society on the Line: Information Politics in the Digital Age*. Oxford and New York: Oxford University Press.

17 Negroponte, N. (1995) *Being Digital*. London: Hodder and Stoughton; Sunstein, C. R. (2007) *Republic.com 2.0*. Princeton, NJ: Princeton University Press.

18 Garnham, N. (1999) 'Information Politics: The Study of Communicative Power', in Dutton (1999) op. cit. pp. 77–78; Dutton, W. H. and Peltu, M. (2007a) 'Reconfiguring Government–Public Engagements: Enhancing the Communicative Power of Citizens', *OII Forum Discussion Paper No. 9*. Oxford: Oxford Internet Institute. Available at http://www.oii.ox.ac.uk/research/publications.cfm.

19 Dutton, W. (2005) 'The Internet and Social Transformation', in Dutton, W. H., Kahin, B., O'Callaghan, R. and Wyckoff, A. W. (eds) *Transforming Enterprise: The Economic and Social Implications of Information Technology*, pp. 375–398. Cambridge, MA: The MIT Press.

20 Dutton, W. (1999) op. cit. pp. 14–16. The term 'game' is used here not in a strict game-theoretic sense, but more generally to indicate an arena of competition and co-operation structured by a set of rules and assumptions about how to act to achieve a set of objectives.

21 Habermas, J., translated by T. Burger (1991) *The Structural Transformation of the Public Sphere*. Cambridge, MA: The MIT Press.

22 Cahir, J. (2003) 'The Information Commons'. Queen Mary Intellectual Property Working Paper, 23 July. Available at http://ssrn.com/abstract=428584 or DOI: 10.2139/ssrn.428584.

23 Zittrain, J. (2008) *The Future of the Internet and How to Stop It*. London: Allen Lane.

24 Berners-Lee, T., Hall, W., Hendler, J. A., O'Hara, K., Shadbolt, N. and Weitzner, D. J. (2006) 'A Framework for Web Science', *Foundations and Trends in Web Science*, 1 (1): 1–134. Online. Available at http://www.nowpublishers.com/product.aspx?product=WEBanddoi=1800000001.

25 See http://www.worldinternetproject.net.

26 See http://www.oii.ox.ac.uk/research/ and Dutton, W. H. and Helsper, E. J. (2007) *The Internet in Britain: 2007*, from which UK statistics in this paper have been taken.

27 Rice, R. E., Shepherd, A., Dutton, W. H. and Katz, J. E. (2007) 'Social interaction and the Internet: A Comparative Analysis of Surveys in the US and Britain', in A. N. Joinson, K. Y. A. McKenna, T. Postmes and U.-D. Reips (eds) *Oxford Handbook of Internet Psychology*, pp. 7–30. Oxford: Oxford University Press.

28 Dutton, W. H., Shepherd, A. and di Gennaro, C. (2007) 'Digital Divides and Choices Reconfiguring Access: National and Cross-national Patterns of Internet Diffusion and Use', in Anderson, B., Brynin, M., Gershuny, J. and Raban, Y. (eds) *Information and Communication Technologies in Society: E-Living in a Digital Europe*, pp. 31–45. London: Routledge.

29 Broadband access had become the norm for Internet access in many countries. By 2007, 85 per cent of Internet households in the UK accessed the Internet through broadband connections, which is over half of all households (Dutton and Helsper (2007) op. cit. p. 10).

30 Castells, M. (1996) op. cit.

31 Dutton, W. H. and Shepherd, A. (2006) 'Trust in the Internet as an Experience Technology', *Information, Communication and Society*, 9/4: 433–451; Dutton and Helsper (2007) op. cit. p. 8.

32 Dutton, W. H. and Shepherd, A. (2006) op. cit.

33 Dunleavy, P., Margetts, H., Bastow, S. and Tinkler, J. (2006) *Digital Era Governance*. Oxford: Oxford University Press.

34 European Commission (2006) '2010 e-government Action Plan: Accelerating e-government in Europe for the Benefit of All Brussels: European Commission'. Available at http://europa.eu.int/information_society/activities/e-government_research/doc/highlights/egov_action_plan_en.pdf; Hood, C. C. and Margetts, H. Z. (2006) *The Tools of Government in the Digital Age*. London: Palgrave. See also the Breaking the Barriers to e-government project led by the Oxford Internet Institute (http://www.egovbarriers.org).

35 Dutton, W. H. and Helsper, E. J. (2007) op. cit. p. 73.

36 Coleman, S. and Norris, D. F. (2005) 'A New Agenda for E-Democracy', *OII Forum Discussion Paper No. 4*. Oxford: Oxford Internet Institute. Available at http://www.oii.ox.ac.uk/research/publications.cfm.

37 Laudon, K. (1977) *Communication Technology and Democratic Participation*. New York: Praeger.

38 See: http://info.interactivist.net/article.pl?sid=04/09/02/1821228&mode=nested&tid=12.

39 Blair, T. (2007) 'The E-petition Shows that My Government Is Listening', *Observer*, 18 February. Online. Available at http://observer.guardian.co.uk/politics/story/0,,2015871,00.html.

40 In the Democratic primaries for the US presidential election in 2008, for instance, Barack Obama raised more money, more quickly than anyone had done before, mainly by Internet-enabled networking among a large number of supporters, each of whom contributed relatively small amounts. According to Green, J. (2008) 'How Silicon Valley Made Barack Obama This Year's Hottest Start-up', *Atlantic Monthly*, 301 (5), June. Available at http://www.theatlantic.com/doc/200806/obama-finance: 'To understand how Obama's war chest has grown so rapidly, it helps to think of his website as an extension of the social-network boom'.

41   For example, the Drudge Report (http://www.drudgereport.com) and Guido Fawkes (http://www.order-order.com).
42   Keen, A. (2007) *The Cult of the Amateur: How Today's Internet is Killing Our Culture*. New York: Doubleday.
43   Sunstein, C. R. (2007) *Republic.com 2.0*. Princeton, NJ: Princeton University Press.
44   See: http://dear_raed.blogspot.com/.
45   See 'The Anatomy of a Tribal Revolt' at: http://smallwarsjournal.com/blog/.
46   Dutton, W. H. (2008) 'The Wisdom of Collaborative Network Organisations: Capturing the Value of Networked Individuals', *Prometheus* 26/3: 211–230.
47   Giles, J. (2005), 'Internet Encyclopedias Go Head To Head', *Nature* 438, 900–901. Online. Available at http://www.nature.com/nature/journal/v438/n7070/full/438900a.html.
48   Weber, S. (2004) *The Success of Open Source*. Cambridge, MA: Harvard University Press.
49   For example, the system called 'Sermo' enables licensed physicians in the USA to ask questions of one another, post replies and answer and create surveys (http://www.sermo.com), and a Swarm of Angels is an internal open-content film production collaboration (http://aswarmofangels.com).
50   Hamel, G. (2007) op. cit.
51   The Access Grid is one major initiative (http://www.accessgrid.org).
52   Wuchy, S., Jones, B. F. and Uzzi, B. (2007) 'The Increasing Dominance of Teams in Production of Knowledge', *Science*, 316/18, May: 1036–1039.
53   Castells, M. (1996) op. cit.
54   Keen, A. (2007) op. cit.
55   Carr, N. (2008) *The Big Switch: Rewiring the World, From Edison to Google*. New York and London: W. W. Norton.
56   Zittrain, J. L. and Palfrey, J. G. (2007) 'Access Denied: The Practice and Policy of Global Internet Filtering', *OII Research Report No. 14*. Oxford: Oxford Internet Institute. Available at http://www.oii.ox.ac.uk/research/publications.cfm; Deibert, R. J., Palfrey, J. G., Rohozinski, R. and Zittrain, J. (eds) (2008) *Access Denied: The Practice and Policy of Internet Filtering*. Cambridge, MA: MIT Press. See the OpenNet Initiative (http://opennet.net), which identifies and documents Internet filtering and surveillance.
57   Dutton, W. H. and Peltu, M. (2007) 'The Emerging Internet Governance Mosaic: Connecting the Pieces', *Information Polity* 12: 63–81.
58   Zittrain, J. (2008) op. cit.
59   Johnson, D. R., Crawford, S. P. and Palfrey, J. G. (2004) 'The Accountable Net: Peer Production of Internet Governance', *Virginia Journal of Law and Technology* 9 (9). Online. Available at http://ssrn.com/abstract=529022.

Further reading

Blumler, J. G. and Coleman, S. (2001) *Realising Democracy Online: A Civic Commons in Cyberspace*. London: Institute for Public Policy Research.
Castells, M. (1996) *The Rise of the Network Society*. Oxford: Blackwell Publishers.

2 Delivering citizen-centric public services through technology-facilitated organisational change

Michael Blakemore, Neil McDonald, Nicola Hall and Rasa Jucuite*

Summary

Governments that wish to become citizen-centric face a challenge to deliver cost-effective, personalised and relevant E-Services that simultaneously enhance democratic dialogue. Over 24 months, for the European Commission E-Government Unit, the authors assessed the ways in which organisations are changing to deliver E-Government services. They found that a simple focus on the organisation was not sufficient. It is the way in which the organisation mediates a critical relationship between government and citizen that matters. They observed a complex interplay of issues, and in this chapter they focus on actions which, in combination, can help deliver public value where citizen-centric E-Government services are created to deliver increasingly cost-effective, personalised and relevant services to citizens. They can serve to enhance the democratic relationship and build better democratic dialogue between citizens and their government, which in turn enhances the practice of citizenship within society. The research findings are presented under a series of themes: ensuring access; making the front office fully customer-focused; achieving a lighter and smarter back office; understanding your customers – building relationships; becoming a flexible and stable organisation; and learning beyond the organisation.

Introduction

The challenge for governments that wish to become citizen-centric is to deliver cost-effective, personalised and relevant E-Services that simultaneously enhance democratic dialogue. From our study over 24 months for the European Commission Unit[1] we assessed the ways in which organisations are changing to deliver E-Government services. We found that a simple focus on the organisation was not sufficient; it is the

---

* The opinions expressed in this study are those of the authors and do not necessarily reflect the views of the European Commission. Reproduction is authorised, provided the source (E-Government Unit, DG Information Society and Media, European Commission) is clearly acknowledged, save where otherwise stated.

way in which the organisation mediates a critical relationship between government and citizen that matters.

We have observed a complex interplay of issues, and in this chapter we focus on actions which, in combination, can help deliver public value where:

Citizen-centric E-Government services are designed to deliver increasingly cost-effective, personalised and relevant services to citizens, but also serve to enhance the democratic relationship, and build better democratic dialogue, between citizens and their government, which then enhances the practice of citizenship within society.

Our research findings are presented under a series of themes: ensuring access; making the front office fully customer-focused; achieving a lighter and smarter back office; understanding your customers – building relationships; becoming a flexible and stable organisation; and learning beyond the organisation.

Ensuring access

It is a truism that access is strongly linked to availability of services (e.g. an appropriate ICT infrastructure at an appropriate price). However, the issue of access is also closely related to managing citizens' expectations in the sense that speed and convenience of access is increasingly important to people as they become accustomed to online transactions.

Sometimes co-ordinated provision of access can occur. This is the case in the community of Neunen in the Eindhoven area of the Netherlands, where high-speed fibre – 100 megabits speed (symmetrical) – has been provided to every home.[2] Increased access also provides opportunities to deliver a wider service portfolio such as that provided by Rabobank in the Netherlands. Rabobank goes beyond its core service delivery of banking and finance to provide online health checks and advice to citizens via video as well as services targeted on the elderly. Investing in IT literacy and skills at a national level has been undertaken in the Czech Republic.[3] Integrated access to information about government services has been widely undertaken at national levels, for example in Austria[4] and France,[5] and at a more local level in the Service Birmingham partnership in the UK.

The approach taken by the France Internet Accompagne initiative has been to simplify ICT equipment and connectivity, and make sure that all French citizens can master ICT through government support, mentorship and encouragement. Availability of cost-effective Internet access supports these efforts. Since the deregulation of telecoms in 2002, French citizens have benefited from low subscription rates for Internet access and 99 per cent broadband coverage.

Making the front office fully customer-focused

Multi-channel

Ensuring that citizens have a number of channels through which to access public services is perhaps one of the most common principles or goals that inform the development of E-Government services. The Netherlands e-Citizen Charter[6] explicitly embodies the channel-choice principle: 'As a citizen I can choose myself in which way to deal with government. Government ensures multi channel service delivery, i.e. the availability of all communication channels: visit, letter, phone, e-mail, and internet.'

Another example is the Scottish Government's Customer First[7] programme, which is based on an 'all channels open' approach, focusing on re-engineering the back office rather than reducing customer-facing channels. There are also many examples where specific services benefit from it. For example, in the modernised Ireland,[8] new customers may interact via the Internet, touch-tone phone, text message and so on as part of a more customer-focused service. Another example is RDW, the Netherlands' Vehicle Licensing Agency,[9] which has a multi-channel focus maintained through modernisation; although there are 25 million visits a year to the website, one million telephone enquiries are still supported.

Multi-channel strategies imply the desire not to deny users the options to use traditional means of interaction (e.g. telephone or face-to-face interaction) with their public service provider, but to encourage people to use the online option in order to achieve efficiency savings. The UK's Transformational Government Strategy[10] emphasises choice and multi-channel delivery, but the initial focus was on monetary savings. The answer may be that it is possible to maintain traditional channels, but this requires government to work flexibly and in partnership with industry and the voluntary sector[11].

Procedural services

In many cases, particularly where the service is relatively routine, simply using ICT to make processes more efficient provides significant benefits to delivery organisations and customers. The Irish Tax Office[12] is an example of a fully automated online service with rapid automatic responses relating to rebates – the phrase used is 'efiling not efilling'. Repayments of up to €5,000 are made automatically and customers can check their account details for the last seven years. Monthly use of the service in early 2007 was about 490,000 accesses and about 70 per cent of business returns were processed online.

In another example, the Finnish Finance Ministry[13] operates a system where pre-filled tax forms are sent, and if you accept the details you do not even need to sign it. Information is collected automatically from employers, banks and insurance companies. The trust in the electronic process is underpinned by proactive and ongoing work on data and network security.

In the Netherlands, both the Kadaster[14] and RDW provide examples where a routine service has been re-configured to achieve efficiency gains, provide an improved service and deliver cost reductions to customers. RDW switched from using post offices for notification of change of car ownership (which took six to seven days) to online notification at 20,000 garages. The process is instant and the fee is retained by RDW. The garages are happy to see the business benefit of online registration, valuing the convenience of the service above revenue sharing. The Netherlands Kadaster collects information about registered properties. Investment in IT has resulted in efficiency gains that have been passed on to customers in the form of reductions in tariffs of nearly one-quarter over the three-year period.

Emotional services

One of the main differences between the public and commercial sectors is the emotionally charged nature of certain public services, such as health services. This means that 'citizens' and 'customers' are not directly and simply interchangeable terms, for people tend to regard the public sector as 'important and different from the private sector', referring in particular to important life events such as birth, health, education and death.[15] The provision of consistent and robust integrated health information in Lithuania[16] and Poland[17] aims to help build an underpinning infrastructure for better health provision to citizens.

We saw how the UK Health Service is developing the concept of 'patient choice',[18] but choice is constrained by two factors: first, most people wish to go to a local hospital because, for example, relatives and friends can visit them more easily; second, performance targets and financial restrictions may mean that their first-choice hospital does not have capacity and will therefore reject their choice. Here we saw how organisational behaviour, focused on being efficient and in delivering customer choice, failed to effectively research the customer behaviours.

One of the most significant examples of the delivery of emotionally laden services is the Crossroads Bank in Belgium.[19] To deliver proactive social security services for citizens, it has sought to provide reassurance in areas of privacy and to change behaviour in stakeholders. For example, it has focused on the construction sector, where historically many people did not pay contributions. Instead of a large-scale data surveillance activity, it changed the regulations. Now an organisation that employs a construction company becomes liable for contributions of the construction company employees if it is found to be avoiding social security payments. Therefore the users of the social security services have a greater interest in ensuring compliance throughout their employment chain.

Healthcare has emerged as one of the most sensitive areas of emotional services, and any successful delivery of such services links technical efficiency and security with trusted relationships. For example, there have for long been concerns (e.g. quality of information, accuracy, liability, etc.) about online health sites, but emerging arguments indicate a possible joint approach:

> Patients who live with chronic diseases such as epilepsy often know more about them than their doctors, contends Daniel Hoch, a professor at Harvard Medical School who helped to found BrainTalk. Many doctors, he says, 'don't get the wisdom of crowds.' But he thinks the combined knowledge of a crowd of his patients would be far greater than his own. A wiki capturing the knowledge of, say, 300 epileptics could be invaluable not only to others with epilepsy, but also to the medical professionals who care for them.[20]

Achieving a lighter and smarter back office

Information: integration, interoperability and sharing

One of the key messages of our research[21] is the importance of integrating information across a range of hitherto administrative silos. Public authorities have been quick to recognise that in sharing information between departments and service actors, the internal users have to deal with a huge amount of information, much of which is not directly required for their own service tasks.

Structuring and searching information now involves techniques such as information mark-up (e.g. XML, an extensible mark-up language), also known generically as 'metadata', which encodes content so that external users and processes may know what is contained there. An example of this is the RISER project,[22] which has created a European registry information service. The service offers an online one-stop shop providing uniform, centralised access to the registries of a number of European countries. Importantly, the integration of information is not through a single integrated database, but through protocols that interoperate between existing information silos at national and regional levels. As with the Crossroads Bank[23] in Belgium, the fact that sensitive data are not held by the application is an important reassurance for citizens about their privacy and security being protected.

Information sharing through interoperability is also evident in the Estonian E-Government Strategy, which emerged from a strong desire to build up governance from the ground level and to build on existing departments and delivery channels (silos) using ICTs. Rapid prototyping was possible given the relatively small size of the country, whose population is 1.3 million. Local and departmental autonomy meant that municipalities and departments could design and develop systems and services rapidly, and the integration of these systems has been achieved through a secure system of interoperability, known as the X-Road.[24] In early 2006, 355 agencies and 50 state databases were operating within the X-Road, which also permits interoperability between public and private services, such as finance and banking.

In Denmark, the Borger.dk[25] web portal brings together different government services to make it easier for people to use them. This means, however, that the different administrations need to work together to provide the kind of easy access to services that people want. The project has therefore resulted in what is described as an 'internationally unusual' arrangement,[26] where representatives from all three levels of government (i.e. local, regional and national) are brought together to collaborate on the implementation of the project.

Sharing services, facilitated by new back-office IT systems, is one way to achieve greater cost-efficiency while improving service delivery.[27] Local accountability can be retained while sharing services to achieve economies of scale. There are many examples of this across Europe. For example, as part of the Customer First[28] programme in Scotland, a citizens' portal being deployed across multiple channels underpins the delivery of the whole programme. Although service delivery is the responsibility of 26 different local authorities (and other bodies), the model adopted has a single underlying infrastructure built on customer data, allowing access to different services via one account.

An example where responsibility is shared across government organisations was examined by the UK's National Audit Office, which acknowledged the need for shared service delivery but noted that 'People are, however, most interested in services, such as how to obtain support or care for an elderly relative, which is often the shared responsibility of a number of organisations'.[29] In fact, our case study on the UK Transformation[30] strategy highlighted some mixed messages about the joined-up services requiring joined-up data. The messages ranged from the sharing of Council Tax information[31] to the paradox that people increasingly share personal information online through virtual communities,[32] yet often react adversely to the integration of personal information on identity cards.[33] Concerns are often expressed by citizens even though there is clear public value in the use of electronic identity management in the health services (e.g. avoiding errors in hospitals by identifying patients and linking them to the correct treatment[34]).

ICT strategy

Our research explored the paradoxes between service delivery expectations from the public and private sectors. Although it is easy to demonise businesses such as Ryanair,[35] the business model works well in short-term service relationships that are generally and largely devoid of emotion. Furthermore, some of the business processes being used by governments indicate a strong cross-over of strategies, ranging from flexible working to creating new agencies and market-testing service delivery.

An example is the organisational change resulting from the Bremen.online[36] initiative. It is the creation of a private limited company which is owned by the City of Bremen and charged with running Bremen.de on its behalf. The approach seems to combine the ethos of the public sector (i.e. citizen service, non-discrimination for reasons of profit, etc.) with the efficiencies that can be gained from private sector working practices and financial independence.

Partnership with the private sector – whether it is contracting out a service or sharing risk through a public–private partnership (PPP) – more explicitly acknowledges the need of the private sector to make a profit. The controversial cost benefit justification for such approaches assumes that the profit for the business will be more than offset by the combination of hard financial efficiency gains and the softer, more intangible benefits for the customers. This is possibly one of the most controversial areas in government service delivery. There is a rich literature that, on one hand, warns governments that they need to be more businesslike when developing large-scale IT projects[37] and, on the other hand, shows that there are detailed concerns that business-led IT projects can also fail[38] and that some initiatives, such as PPP, may risk deferring, not avoiding, costs.[39]

Security is a concern that consistently appears high on the E-Government agenda. It is prompted by fears that privacy is compromised when data is provided to the government. Overcoming these fears is a central process for successful citizen-centric E-Government. In particular, attention to both privacy and security in data sharing and integration and the natural oligopoly (i.e. single dominant sources of information) that exists with public sector information providers is needed. The use of verifiable identity in electronic services requires robust trust and security mechanisms so that 'Trust enables security' and 'security enables trust'.[40]

Estonia's E-Government strategy includes the development of a fully integrated identity card that can be used for a wide range of services from social security to transportation. Underpinning the identity card is a dramatic act of transparency. An Estonian citizen can log onto a secure Web service and see which civil servant in which ministry has used their data, and for what purposes, on a daily basis. The citizens now accept that the ICTs allow them to verify and audit government services and employees in a way that maintains trust through transparency. Participation also encourages trust, and this is maintained through the interactive citizen portal[41] and the specific linking of rights to consume public services with the obligations of being a citizen.

The same process of trust and intervisibility is championed by the Netherlands eCitizen programme; the Netherlands OV public transport chip-card[42] is a particular example of this. Concerns over privacy are balanced by the utility and flexibility – in particular, time saved purchasing individual tickets for journeys and a guarantee that the lowest fare will be charged for your journey – that the card gives a user. This is similar to the London Oyster card,[43] of which there also is an over-the-counter version that does not require any personal identification.

Organisational knowledge, skills capacity and learning

Public sector organisations do have characteristics that make them distinct from business. Successful organisational change therefore does not rely on the mere one-to-one transfer of tried and tested concepts from the private sector to government, but rather translating concepts across sectors, testing their practical usefulness in context, and at times transforming them. Developing knowledge, skills and learning can therefore be critical determinants of success.

In Norway it has been the experience of the eHandel[44] electronic procurement initiative that the key is to change the focus away from paper handling and re-allocate time to improving supplier lists and making the contracting process efficient. By increasing performance in these more strategic areas, E-Procurement actually increases the number of people dealing directly with procurement. This suggests a need to analyse the whole system to reveal impacts in a chain. Efficient procurement online is a feature of many E-Government strategies such as in Germany,[45] Latvia,[46] France[47] and Austria.[48]

Revenue Online in Ireland[49] was initially created as a high-interaction customer service, but, subsequently, the reduction in the need for staff–client interaction allowed organisational restructuring to take place. However, this was achieved without staff job losses, an issue described as an important 'comfort factor' when dealing with workplace changes. However, there was an expectation that staff become broader in their skills and be able to move roles within Revenue.

The experience of the Crossroads Bank in Belgium shows that there is a middle ground between IT staff inflexibility with people on normal civil service contracts, the potentially high costs of PPP projects and the short-termism of commercial contract staff. This is achieved through the establishment of an intermediary skills organisation that provides services to a range of IT-rich projects. We could term this combination of stability and flexibility as being what Jens Rose terms 'flextability'.[50]

The Netherlands Kadaster gained agency status in 1994. With more business being undertaken online, it is logical to plan for fewer staff. Every person in Kadaster was interviewed about goals, competences and the need to go through change and job mobility programmes. This process allowed organisational change to occur, but with a business focus on the dignity of employees. Some people may develop particular skills relevant to new projects, such as digitising the archives. The organisation is focused on retaining knowledge and developing skills, rather than just dispensing with a target number of people.

Understanding customers – building relationships

Customer relationship management and customer engagement

We reviewed how business manages customer relationships and the transferability of commercial approaches to the public sector. Commerce seeks to retain customers and generate customer loyalty, whereas government service delivery, such as social and health services, ideally wants fewer customers who will make reducing demands. For this and a range of other reasons, it seems unlikely that governments can become customer-centric in the business sense, but will often remain product-centric where services remain delivered through silo-based organisations. Customer-centricity can be achieved through integrated and personalised packages of service, support, education and consultation. Examples include the integrated assessment and proactive payment of benefits in Belgium and Andalucia[51] and in the formal adoption of enterprise-wide customer relationship management by the Scottish Executive.[52]

We also considered the dominance of customer handling in many discussions about making public services more citizen-centric. It is the essential non-discriminatory aspect of service delivery that differentiates a citizen-customer from a commercial customer.[53] Nevertheless, without a detailed understanding of customers (by which we mean the customer as a person with many needs, not just a consumer of one particular service), it is difficult to deliver services effectively and efficiently. A range of methods is available to understand citizen needs better and feed this knowledge into service development. Citizens' Services in Aarhus[54] delivers a one-stop service for citizens including services for taxes, passports, drivers' licences, child care, social security and notifications of moving house. In developing the strategy, a tool called 'personas' (i.e. profiles relating to the needs and characteristics of various typical citizens) has been used to provide a better understanding of citizen behaviour.

Participation, engagement and E-Democracy

We noted that, in the context of participation, administrations can learn from the citizen and vice versa in an environment of mutual enrichment. This is increasingly being facilitated through online tools and mechanisms such as online consultations and online petitions, although there are associated concerns about the extent to which such activities widen representative participation[55] or amplify existing uneven participation.[56] We identified four main types of citizen behaviour: the disengaged, the expert, the activist and the excluded.

In the eDialogos initiative in Greece, the Access2democracy[57] system acts as a trusted intermediary and supports a holistic E-Democracy approach, not just the online forum.[58] It facilitates mediation between national, regional and local government and ICT companies to help them understand each other. Importantly, it shows that E-Democracy must be clearly linked to changing policy outcomes, otherwise it can be counterproductive by facilitating unstructured and noisy debates.

The DenmarksDebatten[59] initiative is an online discussion forum designed to allow citizens and elected representatives in Denmark to contribute to debates on current topics which affect them locally and nationally. Local authorities and other government bodies can use the system to instigate debates based around a current issue which faces citizens in a locality. Citizens are then able to engage in an exchange with their elected representatives by submitting their views through DanmarksDebatten. As elsewhere in Europe, Denmark experienced a declining interest among the population in political engagement.

A range of other cases illustrate democratic participation initiatives at the national level (e.g. Slovenia,[60] the Netherlands,[61] the UK,[62] Scotland[63] and Italy[64]) and at more local levels (e.g. Madrid[65] and Issy-les-Moulineaux[66]), where there is a stronger opportunity to retain and strengthen traditional place-based relationships between government and citizens.

Trust and transparency

We noted that while organisations need to change, the impact of the change is strongly mediated through the trust relationship between citizens and government. Therefore, culture matters because the extent of trust varies across European countries. Another component of the process is transparency – most evident in Estonia, where the comprehensively integrated information that underpins the ID card and enables joined-up services is linked to full transparency. As we have seen, citizens in Estonia can log onto a secure website and see which civil servants have accessed their data, and for what purposes. This nicely inverts the rights and obligations argument, implying that if government has rights to use citizen data, it has associated obligations to inform the citizen when data have been used.

Trust is a central underpinning to the development of services for citizens and businesses in the Nordic countries in particular. In Finland,[67] for example, we found that trust in government is not the same as trust in politicians. Furthermore, the levels of trust are also maintained by high levels of openness and transparency, for example being able to see the salaries of government employees. Trust in government has enabled the Nordic welfare state model to operate with high levels of taxation. There is high acceptance by citizens, who receive services that are citizen-centric and comprehensive.[68]

The approach that underpins the Netherlands eCitizen project is that citizens cannot expect to receive services unless they are also aware of their obligations to society. Transparency reduces suspicion in emotional areas such as planning decisions, where citizens may expect insider deals and corruption. Malta[69] has a planning system in which there is transparency of information, as does local government in Ireland,[70] where online mapping that allows citizens to rapidly pre-test the potential feasibility of their own development intentions is provided.

Out of all the countries studied, Estonia is an individual model that maximises investment in trust and public value. It ranks low on the cost of government and medium on trust and peace. However, it ranks strongly on sophistication and availability of services, network readiness and ICT spend per head. Although levels of service use by citizens and business rank only medium, the conditions are in place for continuing and effective uptake of services, as was evident in the use of E-Voting in 2007,[71] participatory governance[72] and the integrated ID card[73] with very transparent use by government.

Estonia is significant because it provides a pathway through the dilemma of how other countries could produce and sustain a high-cost, highly trusted Nordic government model. It would be a brave, indeed foolhardy, government that expected to be re-elected on the basis of a dramatic increase in taxation in order to reach the Nordic levels of funding. Furthermore, the challenge for Nordic countries now is how they can maintain trust and service levels in an atmosphere of pressure on taxation levels. Keeping the citizen both engaged and committed to governance is crucial, and trust and transparency therefore emerge as central enabling factors for citizen-centric E-Government.

Becoming a flexible and a stable organisation

To be flexible, agile and knowledgeable, an organisation needs to have strong autonomy in its ability to reform and refocus, while still maintaining a focus on the higher-level public service goals of delivering citizen-centric services. There is a difficult challenge of moving away from centralist bureaucracy that is easily critiqued as being big, slow, costly and ineffective,[74] with confrontational situations over a need for major reform at all levels,[75] towards organisational strategies that combine the strengths of flexibility with security: 'Flexicurity combines active labour market policies, flexible contractual arrangements, lifelong learning and modern social protection systems.'[76]

Structure, 'ownership' and leadership

One common outcome of modernisation or transformation is to move responsibility for service delivery from a government department to an agency. The Dutch vehicle licensing authority (RDW), prior to receiving agency status, was a small part of the Ministry of Transport and Water Management, with only 8 per cent of all employees in that Ministry. Agency status led to a big change in emphasis, with independence in budget and strategic autonomy proving major enablers for culture change. RDW could now start to understand its own performance; there was a move from focusing on inputs (i.e. staff and allocated budget) to outputs (i.e. service quality, income levels, etc.).

A similar case is that of Netherlands Kadaster, which has been a 'self-administering state body' since 1994. The first ten years involved cost-cutting, raising income while reducing prices (and making the pricing policy open and transparent) and developing a business approach to customers. Financial flexibility has been provided because Kadaster no longer operates within traditional civil service budgets of yearly budgets and 'revolving funds',[77] and one-third of a yearly balance can now be kept as a strategic reserve.

Performance management

Crucially, how do we measure the success of an organisation in delivering public value through E-Government services? Measuring the impact of non-emotional services is far easier than measuring the impact of emotional ones as cost savings for procurement for example can be stated clearly.[78] Furthermore, Hodgson *et al.* warn of the risk that measurement 'studies are more concerned with improvements in processes rather than improvements in services in the form of outputs or outcomes for consumers'.[79]

Measurement also needs to be trusted and transparent. It needs to be a process which operates within a 'corporate framework for management and accountability of data quality, with a commitment to secure a culture of data quality throughout the organisation'.[80] The Crossroads Bank does not measure performance itself; this is carried out independently by the Federal Planning Bureau. Most of the direct cost savings are experienced by the companies, which now provide information electronically to the Social Security system.

A final approach is more collaborative and qualitative, moving towards what Picci terms 'reputation-based governance' that links customer feedback (the customer relationship management issues noted in earlier sections) with formal metrics that allow comparison between service deliverers. The key lessons about measurement are, first, that it should be simple and elegant (long sets of prescriptive measures risk changing organisational behaviour towards the activities that are measured); second, that it should be clearly linked to policy aims and public value outcomes; and third, that it should be standardised to allow for comparisons or benchmarking. Finally, measurement is designed to inform the organisation, not to be a central controlling activity.[81]

Learning beyond the organisation

The wider literature is well populated with examples in which both public and private sectors' large IT projects and organisational change processes have been problematic.[82] However, that has been the case throughout history.[83] The important context is provided by Jane Fountain's research,[84] which shows that the people in organisations are 'central enactors of technology in the state', and it is through their 'organisational networks' that they integrate the delivery of public services and deliver public value. Put simply, people matter more than the technologies, and the maxims that have emerged advise us to:

- work with citizens to build and maximise their trust;
- develop an open and quality-controlled information strategy (allow people to see their data and encourage them to be quality controllers of their data);
- be transparent about what you are doing with their data (tell them who is using it and why);
- inform people clearly about the security and data protection procedures you used to protect their data, privacy and identity;
- be very clear about the complex demands of emotional services such as health and social security;

- understand that transforming an organisation and delivering an emotional E-Service will not guarantee that all citizen demands will be met;
- work with citizens to build a mutual understanding of the importance of both their rights to access a service and their obligations as citizens to use the services acceptably and ethically;
- do not undertake organisational change simply to reduce bottom-line costs;
- develop strategies to maximise the engagement of staff in organisational change so that knowledge is retained within the organisation;
- maximise staff flexibility through a combination of performance management linked to job security.

In our research we have seen that organisational change has been used best where it has helped to mediate the challenging trust relationships between citizens and government. We have also found that organisational change, even where it uses the latest technologies and management practice, can fail to deliver public value because there is a lack of transparency – this is seen most in the integration and sharing of citizen information for emotional services such as health services and in the context of security and terrorism.

Organisational change will rightly continue to be centre stage in the delivery of public value to European citizens. For countries in Scandinavia used to relatively high-cost government, there are challenges of ageing populations and a declining tax base. Organisations will need to be smarter and more efficient, while still retaining the core trust of citizens through transparency of process. In larger nations such as France,[85] governments have been elected on platforms of organisational change and reform; citizens are giving clear messages that they want public value, but that they also expect it to be delivered in a cost-effective manner. In nations such as Greece,[86] the investments in technology and E-Government services must also be accompanied by dramatically increased trust in government if they are to deliver public value. In November 2007 the UK suffered a major setback to citizen trust in E-Government security[87] when confidential information about 25 million citizens was lost when one agency transferred it to another agency on disks through unsecured postal channels.

Many new member states in Eastern and Southern Europe face difficult challenges:[88] how can you increase tax income to deliver public value while not diminishing fragile trust relationships that exist because public value is not presently being delivered? Organisational change will therefore be essential in reducing the costs of government and in delivering more value for the money that is available. As this project has shown, the reduction of costs and the associated efficiency gains are best translated into public value when citizen trust is placed at the heart of the transformation process.

Conclusions

Our research has shown that it is not enough just to implement organisational change. Change, in itself, will not guarantee services that deliver public value. Progress can be made in E-Government through modernisation and the effective use of IT. Processes that improve the trust of citizens in government can also be worked on. To make real progress on transforming government services, the aim should be to positively transform the relationship between government and citizens. In particular, we note a key conclusion of our investigation into the relationship between service delivery and service uptake. While investment in infrastructure and E-Government service development is fundamental to service delivery, the governance characteristics of transparency and trust are critical in legitimating the investment and in creating the conditions for widespread usage of services.[89]

We have argued in detail that public value is not a process, but a relationship built on participation,[90] organisational transparency and trust.[91] Set within the European E-Government policy context,[92] the interplay of efficiency (i.e. administrative burden reduction), organisational transformation, use of integrated information (eID) within interoperable systems built on open standards, operation on a pan-European basis, trust and transparency have become more important than ever.

Being citizen-centric is a crucial challenge for three groups[93] which produce and/or consume E-Government services:

1   politicians and policymakers, who set the policy and regulatory environment;
2   producers, who are tasked with enabling the policy through organisational and business strategy;
3   users, who are the recipients/consumers of services. (In this particular study these are citizens.)

For politicians and policymakers, E-Government is a central action in achieving two important goals: reducing the cost of government and delivering quality services to customers (i.e. businesses and citizens). The cases we have studied encourage them to reform the legislative and regulatory frameworks to maximise accessibility of services through relevant ICT channels; to provide sustainable investment and business models for agencies that are tasked with building E-Government services; and to set out a new vision of government that combines the characteristics of being lighter, simpler, swifter, available and trusted. These actions deliver the E-Government environment – in essence, the producer dimension. To maximise the consumption dimension (i.e. the uptake, use and impact of E-Government services) requires more than just the availability of infrastructure and services, no matter how well the services are designed. What helps to really maximise consumption is a healthy and trusted relationship with citizens: to be transparent with citizens (e.g. be open about what is being done with citizen information) and to build their trust in the custodianship of their information, as citizens need to be confident that their data are not being misused and that their data are securely held.

For producers of E-Government services, we note that the successful organisations we studied combine characteristics such as strong independence in financial and staff planning, flexibility in the development of the E-Government service strategy and constructive relationships with citizens and businesses.

The relationship with customers is critical. It is mediated through two major processes. First is the process of understanding the needs and behaviours of customers. Second is the process of developing customer trust in the use of electronic services. Here the case studies can provide guidance about understanding what is meant by citizen-centric design and using personas and segmentation to identify and understand citizen needs. Many successful projects emphasise building and maintaining the trust of citizens and businesses, utilising cost-effective and relevant ICT security strategies and aligning channels to multiple user needs (multi-channel strategies, using familiar channels as well as new ones).

There are also some important messages for users of E-Government services, who are not passive in the construction of efficient E-Government services. There are important considerations for individual citizens, the important intermediary organisations which represent and help citizens and groups of citizens to be included in E-Government service consumption. Citizens should understand the relationships between their rights to receive services from government and their obligations when using them, and understand the important relationship that exists between the use of their personal information and delivering the right services to them. After all, it is our money, contributed through taxes, that is re-invested in services, and we should no more waste that money than you would do our own.

Key points

- For governments to become citizen-centric, they must deliver cost-effective, personalised and relevant E-Services that simultaneously enhance democratic dialogue.
- This two-year study for the European Commission E-Government Unit, which assessed ways organisations are changing to deliver E-Government services, found that a simple focus on the organisation was not sufficient and it is the way in which the organisation mediates a critical relationship between government and citizen that matters.
- Suggested solutions and examples from different European national strategies include ensuring access (i.e. availability of services, speed, convenience, simplification of ICT equipment and connectivity); making the front office fully customer-focused (with multi-channel strategies, procedural services and emotionally charged public services); achieving a lighter and smarter back office (via integration, interoperability and sharing of information, ICT strategy based on lessons from the public and private sectors, organisational knowledge, skills capacity and learning); understanding customers (i.e. building and managing customer relationships and customer engagement, participation, engagement, E-Democracy, trust and transparency); becoming a flexible and stable organisation (in structure, 'ownership', leadership and measuring performance management); and learning beyond the organisation (i.e. working with citizens to build and maximise trust).
- Being citizen-centric is a crucial challenge for politicians and policymakers, producers enabling policy through organisational and business strategy and users and citizens.

> • While investment in infrastructure and E-Government service develop-
> ment is fundamental to service delivery, the governance characteristics of
> transparency and trust are critical in legitimating the investment and
> creating the conditions for widespread usage of services.

Notes

1 http://ec.europa.eu/e-government.
2 http://www.onsnet.tv/.
3 http://www.epractice.eu/cases/1042.
4 http://www.epractice.eu/cases/289.
5 http://www.epractice.eu/cases/1941.
6 http://www.epractice.eu/cases/1034 and Annex A (an internal document).
7 Annex A.
8 Ibid.
9 Ibid.
10 Annex A and http://www.epractice.eu/cases/1029.
11 In 2007 the review of Transformational Government noted ongoing underpinning activities
   of website rationalisation and shared services/information. CABINET (2007b)
   Transformational Government: Enabled by Technology. Annual Report 2006. London: Cabinet Office.
   January. http://www.cio.gov.uk/documents/annual_report2006/trans_gov2006.doc.
12 Annex A.
13 Annex A.
14 http://www.epractice.eu/cases/1805 and Annex A.
15 McDonald, N. (2006) *Think Paper 5: Is Citizen-centric the Same as Customer-centric?* (October)
   Ccegov Project, [accessed 22 November 2006]. http://www.ccegov.eu/thinkpapers.asp.
16 http://www.epractice.eu/document/289.
17 http://www.epractice.eu/document/244.
18 Blakemore, M. (2006a) *Think Paper 2: Customer-centric, Citizen Centric. Should Government Learn
   Directly from Business?* (October) Ccegov Project [accessed 22 November 2006]. http://www.
   ccegov.eu/thinkpapers.asp.
19 http://www.epractice.eu/cases/1908.
20 Economist (2007a) 'Health 2.0' *Economist* (6 September) [accessed 16 September 2007].
   http://www.economist.com/science/tq/displaystory.cfm?story_id=9719054.
21 Wilson, F. (2006). *Think Paper 3: Trends in Technology for Citizen Centricity* (October) Ccegov
   Project [accessed 22 November 2006]. http://www.ccegov.eu/thinkpapers.asp; Wilson, F.
   and Blakemore, E. M. (2007) *Think Paper 8: Technology Futures – and Why Government Should Care.*
   (May) European Commission [accessed 1 June 2007]. http://www.ccegov.eu/Downloads/
   Paper%208%20-%20Technology%20Futures%20v2.pdf.
22 http://www.epractice.eu/document/1425 and now a business at http://www.riserid.eu/
   magnoliaPublic/en.html.
23 http://www.epractice.eu/cases/268.
24 http://www.ria.ee/?id=27309&&langchange=1.
25 Annex A.
26 http://www.e.gov.dk/english/egov_projects/citizen_portal/index.html.
27 Europe (2007b) *Ministerial Declaration: Interoperability and Reduction of Administrative Costs are
   the Objectives* (20 September) European Commission [accessed 20 September 2007].
   http://www.epractice.eu/document/3928.
28 Annex A.
29 Commons (2002) Public Accounts – Sixty-Sixth Report: Progress in Achieving
   Government on the Web. (December) House of Commons, Public Accounts Committee,

[accessed 14 December 2002]. http://www.publications.parliament.uk/pa/cm200102/cm select/cmpubacc/936/93602.htm.

30 Annex A.

31 Kablenet (2007d) 'ICO Approves Council Tax Data Share' *Kable Government Computing* (31 January) [accessed 31 January 2007]. http://www.kablenet.com/kd.nsf/Frontpage/E456485EBEEAFCA0802572720061F411?OpenDocument.

32 Anon. (2007f) 'Web Information-Sharing the New Force for Social Progress Says Cabinet Office' *Public Technology* (8 February) [accessed 8 February 2007]. http://www.public technology.net/modules.php?op=modload&name=News&file=article&sid=7689.

33 This issue became politicised, with the Conservative Opposition party proposing to abolish moves to create identity cards. See: Higgins, J. (2007) 'ID Cards: IT Trade Association Blasts Conservative Pledge to Kill ID Cards' *Public Technology* (8 February) [accessed 8 February 2007]. http://www.publictechnology.net/modules.php?op=mod load&name=News&file=article&sid=7696.

34 BBC (2007e) 'Hospitals Pick Hi-tech Clipboard' (21 February) BBC [accessed 21 February 2007]. http://news.bbc.co.uk/2/hi/technology/6383035.stm.

35 Blakemore, M. (2007) *Think Paper 7: 'Consumizens': Taking Ryanair to the Public Sector?* (February) Ccegov Project [accessed 18 February 2007]. http://www.ccegov.eu/Downloads/Paper%207%20%20-%20Consumizens%20-%20Taking%20Ryanair%20to%20the%20Public%20Sector%20v2.pdf.

36 Annex A.

37 Jackson, W. (2007) 'IT Security: Too Big for Government' *Government Computer News* [accessed 19 August 2007]. http://www.gcn.com/print/26_21/44843-1.html; Anon. (2007b) 'Gartner Highlights Massive Future Risks in Large Scale Enterprise IT Projects' *Public Technology* (21 September) [accessed 22 September 2007]. http://www.public technology.net/modules.php?op=modload&name=News&file=article&sid=11620.

38 Anon. (2007d) 'IT Managers Hugely Cynical & Fearful of Large-Scale Transformation Projects' *Public Technology* (6 September) [accessed 10 September 2007]. http://www.public technology.net/modules.php?op=modload&name=News&file=article&sid=11293; Carvel, J. (2007). 'Concern over NHS's IT Systems after 50 View Celebrity's Details' *Guardian* (London) (19 September) [accessed 20 September 2007]. http://www.guardian.co.uk/uk_news/story/0,2172039,00.html.

39 For example, Standard and Poors' survey noted, 'Some of the 161 respondents said PPPs performed no better than the most efficient public sector procurement processes, which incorporated many of the stringent standards and penalty regimes that PPPs tended to employ'. Griggs, T. and Timmins, N. (2007) 'PPPs "No Magic Bullet for Public Sector"' *Financial Times* (London) (12 April) [accessed 13 April 2007]. http://www.ft.com/cms/s/6a57952c-e893-11db-b2c3-000b5df10621.html.

40 Wilson, F. (2007) *Think Paper 11: Trust and Identity in Interactive Services: Technical and Societal Challenges* (November) Ccegov Project [accessed 12 November 2007]. http://www.ccegov.eu/?Page=ThinkPapers.

41 http://www.eesti.ee/est.

42 http://www.ov-chipkaart.nl/.

43 https://sales.oystercard.com/oyster/lul/entry.do.

44 http://www.epractice.eu/cases/1894.

45 http://www.epractice.eu/cases/2261.

46 http://www.epractice.eu/cases/2238.

47 http://www.epractice.eu/cases/1945.

48 http://www.epractice.eu/cases/1939.

49 Annex A.

50 http://www.amazon.com/Weiterbildung-Besch%C3%A4ftigter-Arbeitskr%C3%A4 fte-Wissenspool-FlexStAbility/dp/3825503437.

51 http://www.epractice.eu/cases/2222.

52 http://www.epractice.eu/cases/1792.

53 We did explore more the blurring of this difference. For example, public services can use discriminatory filters such as eligibility tests, means tests (i.e. tests against your financial well-being) and the most frequently used of all, the waiting list (i.e. you are eligible for a service, but you can only obtain it at some time in the future).

54 http://www.epractice.eu/cases/2384.

55 Tempest, M. (2007) 'E-Petitions Could Undermine Democracy, MPs Warned' (8 March) *Guardian* (London) [accessed 29 April 2007]. http://society.guardian.co.uk/e-public/story/0,2029433,00.html.

56 Scotland (2007) *Review of the Renewing Local Democracy Project* (27 July) Scottish Executive [accessed 31 July 2007]. http://www.scotland.gov.uk/Publications/2007/07/26144456/0.

57 Annex A.

58 Note also other platforms that are available such as the Local Channel. Local (2006) *The Local Channel.* The Local Channel [accessed 16 August 2006]. http://tellmeabout.thelocalchannel.co.uk/home.aspx?p=1&m=130.

59 www.danmarksdebatten.dk and Annex A.

60 http://www.epractice.eu/cases/2007.

61 http://www.epractice.eu/cases/1034.

62 http://www.epractice.eu/cases/1021.

63 http://www.epractice.eu/cases/1812.

64 http://www.epractice.eu/cases/1035.

65 http://www.epractice.eu/cases/1012.

66 http://www.epractice.eu/cases/1019.

67 Annex A.

68 Finland (2006) *A Renewing, Human-Centric and Competitive Finland.* (September) Information Society Programme, Prime Minister's Office, Finland [accessed 2 May 2007]. http://www.tietoyhteiskuntaohjelma.fi/esittely/en_GB/introduction/_files/76222690188788831/default/Strategia_englanti_181006final.pdf.

69 http://www.epractice.eu/cases/1036.

70 Annex A.

71 BBC (2007d) 'Estonia Claims New E-Voting First' (1 March) BBC [accessed 4 May 2007]. http://news.bbc.co.uk/2/hi/europe/6407269.stm.

72 ePractice (2007b) *New Website Gives Estonians Their Say in Government Issues* (13 July) European Commission [accessed 9 August 2007]. http://www.epractice.eu/document/3708.

73 ePractice (2006b) *Estonian eID Card Passes 1 Million Threshold* (23 October) European Commission [accessed 25 October 2006]. http://www.epractice.eu/document/295.

74 Bain, B. (2007) 'Giuliani: Federal Workforce Is Too Big' (21 September) *Federal Computer Week* [accessed 23 September 2007]. http://www.fcw.com/article103822-09-21-07-Web; ePractice (2006e) *Minister Calls for Reform of State Administration to Facilitate E-Government* (4 December) European Commission [accessed 5 December 2006]. http://www.epractice.eu/document/232.

75 BBC (2007f) 'Sarkozy Announces Huge Job Cuts' (19 September) BBC [accessed 20 September 2007]. http://news.bbc.co.uk/2/hi/europe/7003866.stm.

76 Europe (2007a) *European Partners Join Lively Debate on Flexicurity* (20 April) European Commission [accessed 24 April 2007] http://europa.eu/rapid/pressReleasesAction.do?reference=IP/07/519&format=HTML&aged=0&language=EN&guiLanguage=fr.

77 Revolving funds have featured strongly in traditional civil service structures. Any income received by a Department is not kept, but is sent to the Treasury – hence the revolving door analogy. This process damages any process of developing markets, since resources are diverted in the Department to develop a service, and the income received is not then used to offset those costs.

78 Kablenet (2007g) 'Record E-Auction Saves £100m' *Kable Government Computing* (29 June) [accessed 30 June 2007]. http://www.kablenet.com/kd.nsf/Frontpage/76EE5DCF16B7F69D8025730800594115?OpenDocument; Kablenet (2007e) 'IT Overhaul Saves

Council £5m' *Kable Government Computing* (3 September) [accessed 4 September 2007] http://www.kablenet.com/kd.nsf/Frontpage/830C45CBE1688C0E8025734B00353BA 6?OpenDocument.

79 Hodgson, L., Farrell, C. M. and Connolly, M. (2007) 'Improving UK Public Services: A Review of the Evidence', *Public Administration* 85: 355–382.

80 Audit (2007) *Improving Information to Support Decision Making: Standards for Better Quality Data* (9 November) Audit Commission [accessed 10 November 2007]. http://www.audit-commission.gov.uk/reports/NATIONAL-REPORT.asp?CategoryID=&ProdID=AE 298947-73F0-4dcb-AF77-D2520EECBCFB&fromREPORTSANDDATA= NATIONAL-REPORT.

81 Picci, L. (2007) 'Reputation-Based Governance', *First Monday* 12/9 (September) [accessed 22 September 2007]. http://firstmonday.org/issues/issue12_9/picci/index.html.

82 ePractice (2006c) *European Project to Banish Dumb Call Centres in Public Administrations.* (28 August) European Commission [accessed 31 August 2006]. http://www.epractice.eu/document/363; *Economist* (2006a) 'Never Doubt the Power of Bureaucrats to Waste Your Money', *Economist* (23 November) [accessed 23 November 2006]. http://www.economist.com/world/britain/displaystory.cfm?story_id=8329090; Economist (2007c) 'Toughing Out a Rethink', *Economist* (29 March) [accessed 10 April 2007]. http://www.economist.com/world/britain/displaystory.cfm?story_id=8934853; Griggs, T. and Timmins, N. (2007) 'PPPs No Magic Bullet for Public Sector', *Financial Times* (London) (12 April) [accessed 13 April 2007]. http://www.ft.com/cms/s/6a57952c-e893-11db-b2c3-000b5df 10621.html; BBC (2007b) 'Complacency "Rife" in IT Projects', (4 June) BBC [accessed 5 June 2007]. http://news.bbc.co.uk/1/hi/business/6720547.stm.

83 Whittaker, B. (1999) 'What Went Wrong? Unsuccessful Information Technology Projects', *Information Management and Computer Security* 7: 23–29.

84 Fountain, J. E. (2001) *Building the Virtual State: Information Technology and Institutional Change.* Washington, DC: Brookings Institution.

85 Cole, A. and Jones, G. (2005) 'Reshaping the State: Administrative Reform and New Public Management in France', *Governance* 18: 567–588; BBC (2007f) 'Sarkozy Announces Huge Job Cuts', (19 September) BBC [accessed 20 September 2007]. http://news.bbc.co.uk/2/hi/europe/7003866.stm.

86 Hahamis, P., Iles, J. and Healy, M. (2005) 'e-Government in Greece: Bridging the gap between Need and Reality', *Electronic Journal of e-Government* 3/4, December[accessed 6 January 2007]. http://www.ejeg.com/volume-3/vol3-iss4/v3-i4-art4.htm; ePractice (2007a) *New On-Line Services for Greek Enterprises through the Citizen Service Centres (KEP)* (6 February) European Commission [accessed 19 February 2007]. http://www.epractice.eu/document/167; *Economist* (2007b) 'School for scandal', *Economist* (4 April) [accessed 10 April 2007]. http://www.economist.com/world/europe/displaystory.cfm?story_id=8972460.

87 BBC (2007g) 'UK's Families Put on Fraud Alert', BBC (20 November) [accessed 20 November 2007]. http://news.bbc.co.uk/1/hi/uk_politics/7103566.stm; Houlder, V. (2007) 'HMRC Chairman Resigns after Loss of Records', *Financial Times* (20 November) (London) [accessed 20 November 2007]. http://www.ft.com.

88 For more detail refer to: Blakemore, M. and Lloyd, P. (2007). *Think Paper 10: Trust and Transparency: pre-requisites for effective e-government.* (August) Ccegov Project [accessed 1 September 2007]. http://www.ccegov.eu/Downloads/Paper%2010%20Trust,%20 Transparency,%20Efficiency%20and%20e-government%20v2.3.pdf.

89 Ibid.

90 Hall, N. (2007) *Think Paper 6: The Participative Citizen* (January) Ccegov Project [accessed 31 January 2007]. http://www.ccegov.eu/Downloads/Think%20Paper%206%20v2%200%20Jan%202007%20Final.pdf.

91 Blakemore, M. and Lloyd, P. (2007) op. cit.

92 Europe (2007b) *Ministerial Declaration: Interoperability and Reduction of Administrative Costs Are the Objectives* (20 September) European Commission [accessed 20 September 2007]. http://www.epractice.eu/document/3928w.

93 We stress that the three are not discrete groups. For example, politicians are citizens, and citizens work in the organisations that are delivering services to other citizens.

Further reading

McDonald, N. (2006). *Think Paper 5: Is Citizen-centric the same as Customer-centric?* (October) Ccegov Project [accessed 22 November 2006]. http://www.ccegov.eu/thinkpapers.asp.

Wilson, F. (2006) *Think Paper 3: Trends in Technology for Citizen Centricity.* (October) Ccegov Project [accessed 22 November 2006]. http://www.ccegov.eu/thinkpapers.asp.

Wilson, F. & Blakemore, M. (2007). *Think Paper 8: Technology Futures – and why Government should Care* (May) European Commission [accessed 1 June 2007]. http://www.ccegov.eu/Downloads/Paper%208%20-%20Technology%20Futures%20v2.pdf.

3 Beyond i2010

E-Government current challenges and future scenarios

Cristiano Codagnone and David Osimo

Summary

This chapter is a selective and critical re-elaboration of insights from several policy studies that the authors have conducted on the topic of E-Government and current challenges and possible future needs and scenarios for the Directorate General Information Society and Media of the European Commission.[1] Due to word limitations this chapter only partially reflects the detailed analysis of a report we wrote on the needs for future E-Government services.[2] The chapter examines the supply and demand of E-Government, identifying gaps that we feel need attention. It then goes on to identify differing groups of users and their divergent needs. We feel that for too long users have been thought of as a homogenised group when, as we show, nothing could be further from the truth. The chapter concludes by examining the needs for future research and identifying areas of research, not just those specifically designed for E-Government purposes, but also others that may contribute to a more holistic research effort in the pursuit of better governance.

Introduction

As the current Information Society policy framework, i2010,[3] comes to a close, policymakers at both the European Commission and member state levels are taking stock of what E-Government has achieved, what the key challenges are and in which directions policy efforts and public money for deployment of technology and/or for E-Government research should go.

Summarising these discussions, and especially the main goals of the Commission, it can be stated that the aim is to identify the key future scenarios and related technological solutions and research directions with a high potential to positively impact both back and front-office operations, thus improving E-Government performance.[4]

Government spending is financed through taxation, which can create distortion in resource allocation. It is thus important to measure results in terms of efficiency and effectiveness to ensure that they foster both economic growth and social cohesion and contribute to the Lisbon agenda.[5] This is even more salient today. Given the conditions of financial turmoil and socio-economic crisis, governments are going to face increasing budget constraints which are likely to squeeze resources available for ICT investments.

ICT can produce impacts only inasmuch as citizens, firms and governments incorporate them into their daily practices in an effective and efficient way. Impact depends on patterns of appropriation and consumption of ICT-supported services. The future contribution of the Information Society to prosperity and social cohesion in Europe will depend on effective and efficient appropriation of ICT by all: across value chains by firms of different size and in different sectors, in the provision of public services, in the revitalisation of the public sphere and participatory processes and in citizens' everyday life (including working, learning, staying in contact with friends, entertaining themselves and buying goods and services).

It is thus evident that, in the future, investments of public funds in IT should be optimised and deliver more benefits to the constituencies directly as they become consumers of E-Government or indirectly if E-Government improves the design of policies and services. In this respect it is of key importance to identify the policy actions and the research funding decisions that can, in the future, help fill the gap between supply and demand of E-Government services and increase their economic and social impact in terms of benefits delivered to the constituencies.

This is what we aim to do in this chapter by looking at the gap existing between the supply and demand sides of E-Government in the first section from which, in the second section, we extract the key users' needs and supply-side gaps that need to be addressed in the future to improve the level of consumption of E-Government. Next we review areas of ICT deployment and research traditionally considered as lying outside of E-Government. We discuss possible future scenarios and their implications. We conclude by identifying the key direction of technological deployment and E-Government research to be the focus of policy efforts and investments beyond the timeframe of i2010.

E-Government supply and demand: the gap

The various policy frameworks agreed between the Commission and member states between the end of 1999 and 2002[6] reflected the heyday of the dot-com boom. The dominant idea at the time was that everything would be about E-Commerce and transactions,[7] and it worked well as a catalyser for the supply side of E-Government. Very rapidly, a large number of public services were made available online and became fully transactional, as measured by the supply-side benchmarking of online public services carried out since 2001 by Capgemini on behalf of the European Commission (Figure 3.1).

Yet the growth of the supply side is in stark contrast with that of the demand side.[8] Considering that in 2007 regular Internet users in Europe constituted 51 per cent of the total population[9] and that the latest Eurostat data shows that in 2008 this percentage has reached 56 per cent, there are about 278 million adult Europeans who could potentially be E-Government consumers. The latest data available from the Eurostat Survey of Households and Enterprise (Figure 3.2) indicates that in 2008 in EU27 (i.e. the EU, comprising 27 states):

- 41.8 per cent of regular Internet users accessed the Internet to find government-related information (116 million vis-à-vis 162 million who did not do so);

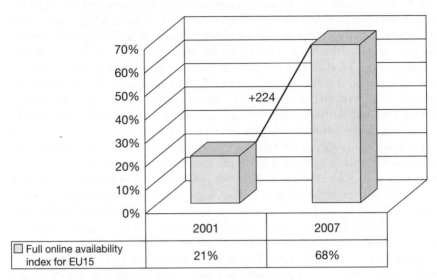

Figure 3.1 Online availability index EU15: 2001 and 2007

Source: Authors' elaboration on data from various editions of Capgemini benchmarking.

- 26.2 per cent of regular Internet users accessed the Internet to download government forms (73 million vis-à-vis 205 million who did not do so);
- 19.2 per cent of regular Internet users accessed the Internet for sending filled-in forms to government (53 million vis-à-vis 225 million who did not do so).

Evidence from other EU-wide research[10] and from country-specific studies[11] corroborates the finding that E-Government consumption in general is very moderate and that citizens mostly use the Internet to search for information about government services, and to a much lesser degree to perform transactions. Yet it could be argued that since citizen interactions with government are infrequent, an appraisal of the actual penetration would need to ask citizens how many interactions they had with government in a given time period, and ask only those who had such interaction whether they used E-Government. The earlier-cited user satisfaction study has done this, and the findings are comparable to those of the Eurostat data (see Figure 3.4).[12]

Now going back to data on regular Internet usage, which can be considered as a proxy indicator of the level of digital inclusion, we must also consider the 44 per cent of adult Europeans who do not use the Internet and to a large extent include social groups at risk of exclusion (i.e. those who are low-educated, unemployed, inactive, living in rural areas, aged 55–64, aged 65–74, women, marginal youth, immigrants and ethnic minorities).[13] Recent studies on the issue of digital inclusion show that individuals and/or communities facing conditions of multiple social disadvantage are very unlikely to become proficient digital users and use online services, including E-Government.[14] These same individuals, however, are those most in need of government services such as education, healthcare, job opportunities and access to welfare entitlement. Empirical studies show that many individuals eligible for welfare

Online availability index for citizens: 2001 (EU15) and 2007 (EU27)

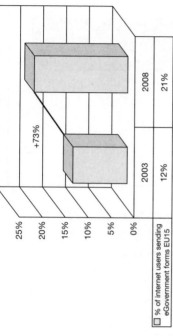

Online availability index Austria: 2001 and 2007

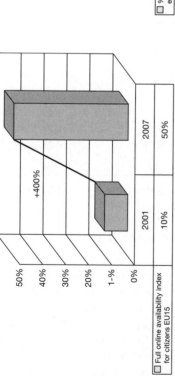

% of internet users sending eGovernment forms EU 15: 2003 and 2007

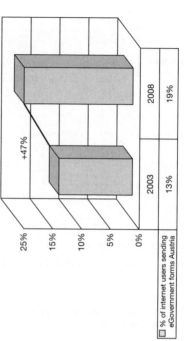

% of internet users sending eGovernment forms Austria: 2003 and 2007

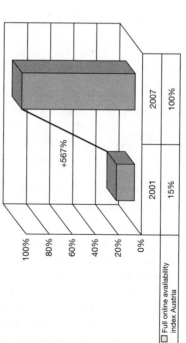

Figure 3.2 Impressionistic comparison: supply-side and demand-side improvements

Source: Authors' elaboration on Eurostat Information Society Statistics and Capgemini benchmarking.

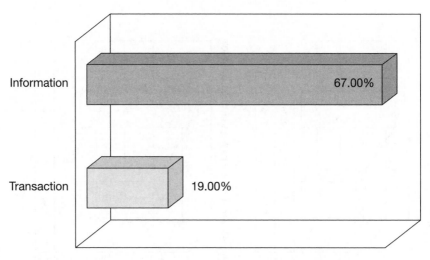

Figure 3.3 E-Government 'consumption' by online users: 2005–2008 (EU 27)
Source: Authors' elaboration on Eurostat Information Society Statistics.

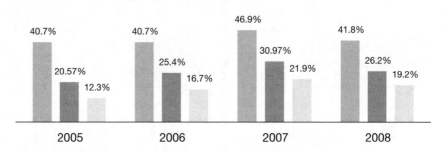

Figure 3.4 Citizens' weighted consumption of E-Government
Source: Authors' elaboration on data from User Satisfaction Study.

entitlement do not apply for them for two reasons: lack of information and the 'social stigma' effect.[15] Not accessing such entitlement prevents them from increasing their disposable income and relatively improving their conditions, which could remove them from poverty and contribute to inclusion.[16] Inclusive E-Government services, enabling groups at risk to benefit indirectly from support by eEnabled care givers and social workers, multi-channel Web-centred delivery and use of ICT to optimise policy and service design (even when delivery does not occur online), could greatly impact these problems by increasing information and removing the stigma with a set of integrated measures. Such measures include E-Enabled frontliners who visit people in their homes, benefits buses to spread information and awareness, online benefit calculators, online-enabled smart cards to enable socially excluded groups receive school meals or attend leisure centres without stigma, and online advice and support to the unemployed. Many of these non-users of ICT may never become autonomous consumers of E-Government, and this calls for a change in policy focus from traditional efforts to help them use ICT to new approaches aimed at using ICT to help them.

It is our contention that the focus on transactional services in the definition of policy targets and especially in the benchmarking of E-Government has outlived its initial purpose and should be abandoned. Since 2004 numerous critiques of supply-side benchmarking have emerged.[17] The stages model (from information to transaction) is called into question and doubts are raised on two counts: 1) as to whether the stages fully reflect the actual functioning/usage of E-Services, and 2) the validity of the assumed linear progression, with transaction being scored as more important than information with respect to actual user needs and interests. Most importantly, the focus of the benchmarking on transaction is sidetracking governments, leading them to invest in benchmarking compliance even if the services benchmarked may not be the most relevant to achieve take-up and impact. Raising the score in the EU benchmarking will surely contribute to the rise of institutionally perceived quality, but not necessarily the real quality and utility of the services. Keeping the transactional stage as the highest goal is old-fashioned, reflecting an outdated emphasis of the 1990s dot-com boom on E-Commerce and of New Public Management with its exclusive focus on efficiency. New trends emerging in the use of the Internet show how the importance of the medium goes beyond transactions (i.e. Web 2.0), while the New Public Management vision is being superseded by concepts such as digital governance and public value.[18] The value of information is coming to the fore. In this respect Osimo[19] has proposed that, if the measurement of online availability and sophistication (aimed at transaction) functioned as the flagship of E-Government 1.0, the focus must now change to information and transparency, the measurement and benchmarking of which need to become the flagship of E-Government 2.0.

Users' needs and supply gaps

We now proceed to identify the main users and their needs in order to increase (direct or indirect) E-Government usage and delivery of benefits to the public, as well as the supply-side gaps which need to be filled in order to do that.[20]

We propose the following heuristic and theory-driven typology of users:

- *Dropouts.* Digitally excluded and lacking intellectual and material resources to use ICT. Comprising mostly individuals with multiple and acute social disadvantages.[21] Examples include youngsters excluded from school, the unemployed, etc. The main target of inclusive E-Government and approaches that use ICT to help them rather than help them use ICT.

- *Digitally reluctant.* 'Self-excluded', for they potentially have the material resources to access and use ICT but choose not to due to a lack of motivation, confidence and/or trust.
- *Potential climbers.* Less socially disadvantaged relative to dropouts and with some limited exposure to digital means. Could possibly catch up and become E-Government consumers. Require simple, usable and intuitive interfaces and well-targeted ad hoc content and services. Examples include immigrants and ethnic minorities.
- *Basics.* Centrally positioned with respect to digital and social inclusion. Utilise E-Government services mostly to search for information. Need simple, usable and intuitive interfaces, more and better-quality information, and reassuring solutions for security, privacy and exchange of data issues.
- *Trendy and mobile.* Positioned high on the social ladder with a fairly high degree of digital confidence and sophistication. Examples may include time-starved professionals, managers, entrepreneurs who are possibly highly mobile and in need of advanced and automatic pushed services and of cross-border services.
- *Digitally native.* Individuals who have grown up with ICT and cut across the social inclusion dimension. They are the evidently undershot and would require radically innovative services including co-design and co-production of services, as well as virtual reality interaction platforms.

Looking at these groups in a simplified way: a) the first two ('dropouts' and 'digitally reluctant') are the 'ICT never use'; b) the second two ('potential climbers' and 'basics') are the actual and potentially less sophisticated consumers of E-Government for whom easy-to-find and clear information would do it; c) the last two ('trendy and mobile' and 'digital natives'), though in different ways, are the sophisticated users most likely undershot and in need of new innovative services. The corresponding more salient needs are reported in Figure 3.5.

Among the main supply-side gaps which we identify are:

- *Need for cost-effective technologies to sustain innovation under budget constraints.* The low level of take-up of transactional E-Government services did not produce the expected savings. On the contrary, it has produced an additional channel without

Non-users of ICT	• Targeted and pre-emptive policies and services designed with ICT support • Indiret benefits from ICT (multi-channel, eEnabled frontliners) • Easy-to-find and simple targeted information
Basic users	• Better-targeted and easy-to-find information services • Better-targeted and easy-to-find accessible and usable content and services • New user-friendly and reassuring solutions for privacy and authentication
Advanced users	• Personalised pushed services • Cross-border multi-language services • Radically innovative interactive services • Service co-production

Figure 3.5 Users' needs to be addressed to increase E-Government consumption

Source: Authors' elaboration.

entirely relieving the workload on other existing channels. This situation is worsened by the current financial and socio-economic crisis, which will result in severe cost-containment measures, likely to reduce operational and IT budgets.

- *Need for infusing collective intelligence into policy and service design through new ICT tools.* We interpret the clear imbalance between the supply of E-Government services and their consumption as being due to a lack of understanding of the context of demand and a failure to use appropriate analytical, ICT-supported tools to tailor services to needs. However, the realisation of intelligent policy and service modelling and design is not merely a matter of technological development as it requires multi-disciplinary social science expertise and joined-up approaches across policy silos.

- *Need for architectures enabling composability[22] and re-use of content and services.* There is a need to improve the supply of quality information and content and easy-to-find integrated services at a single point of contact. New innovative architectures are needed to improve the design and re-use of content and services, both across governments and between government and civil society (private and third sector). Opening up the delivery of government information and services to third-party players, who would use government information and services to deliver them to the public, would lower the pressure on governments. This is fully in line with the public sector information (PSI) legislation (i.e. EU Directive 2003/98).

- *Need for small footprint, strong authentication and federated E-ID management.* There is a need for innovative E-ID federated solutions with delegation functions which enable intermediation. These innovative solutions also need to be user-friendly and re-assuring in order for citizens to overcome problems of trust in and resistance to the use of online public services.

- *Need for integrated multi-channel delivery connected to E-Enabled frontliners and caregivers.* The issues of E-Exclusion (i.e. dropouts) that should be addressed by inclusive E-Government policies and services have not yet produced a widespread adoption of truly multi-channel strategies or the deployment of eEnabled frontliners (e.g. social workers, caregivers, etc.).

- *Need for innovative and intuitive interfaces which maximise human and computer interaction.* Currently, despite the existence of some exemplary practices, the provision of public online services is still characterised by poor content quality, including low conformity to legal and professional standards, difficult language, inconsistent navigation, unstable reliability of the interface, lack of multi-language content, unsatisfactory level of usability in terms of human and computer interaction and embarrassingly by low levels of conformity to international accessibility standards.

Research, technologies and future scenarios

We now look at areas of technological development outside what has been traditionally regarded as E-Government research. Starting from the Strategic Research Agendas proposed by the European Technology Platforms[23] and reviewing the EU database's ICT results,[24] the database of FP7 projects[25] and insights from premium market research data,[26] we consider the following seven challenges (using 'C' and numbering abbreviation):

- C1 = secure infrastructures;
- C2 = cognitive systems, robots and interaction;
- C3 = components and systems engineering;
- C4 = digital content;
- C5 = ICT for health;
- C6 = ICT for mobility, sustainability and energy efficiency;
- C7 = ICT of independent living and E-Inclusion.

We have mapped the technological developments and results achieved in these areas against the traditional E-Government building blocks (Figures 3.6 and 3.7) and then assessed to what extent they can be leveraged to address users' needs and the supply-side gap identified earlier.

In all of the seven areas there are relevant insights and research findings for E-Government, including:

- identity management;
- Internet services and innovative architectures;
- language-based interaction;
- machine-readable data;
- personalisation of content and knowledge;
- intuitive user-friendly interfaces.

	Citizens and business			
INTERFACES	3D, immersive reality	Language-based interaction	Assistive technologies	Flexible interfaces
AUTHENTICATION	Secure, lightweight and federated ID management			
ACCESS CHANNEL	Web	Mobile	Pervasive computing, Internet of things	
SERVICE/CONTENT	Personalized content	Knowledge management	Semantics, automatic reasoning	
BACK OFFICE	Internet of services	Software as a service	Collaborative technologies	Semantic interoperability
INFRASTRUCTURE	Trusted networks			
	Government			

Figure 3.6 Traditional E-Government building blocks

Source: Authors' elaboration.

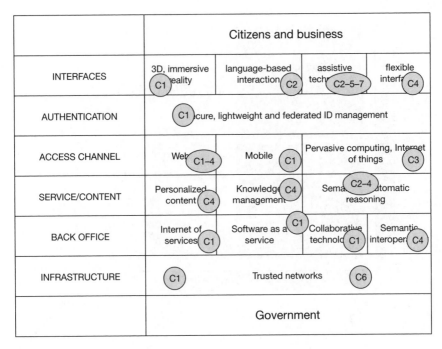

	Citizens and business			
INTERFACES	3D, immersive reality **C1**	language-based interaction **C2**	assistive tech **C2-5-7**	flexible interf **C4**
AUTHENTICATION	**C1** cure, lightweight and federated ID management			
ACCESS CHANNEL	Web **C1-4**	Mobile **C1**	Pervasive computing, Internet of things **C3**	
SERVICE/CONTENT	Personalized content **C4**	Knowledge management **C4**	Sema **C2-4** tomatic reasoning	
BACK OFFICE	Internet of services **C1**	Software as a service **C1**	Collaborative technolo **C1**	Semantic interoper **C4**
INFRASTRUCTURE	**C1**	Trusted networks		**C6**
	Government			

Figure 3.7 Mapping current research issues against E-Government building blocks
Source: Authors' elaboration.

An additional area of research that is already identified by the Commission and confirmed by this study as highly relevant for the identified users' needs and supply-side gaps is 'ICT for Governance and Policy Modelling'.

Technological requirements of government can thus be to some extent covered by activities in other areas of ICT deployment and research. It is our view that this fact suggests the need for some form of collaborative platform that ensures consistency of the different technological developments and the respondence of the specific needs of government. One could think of dedicated testbeds or living labs devoted to piloting the results of the ICT research effort in government. In a way, our analysis shows a major gap in research funding: a silo approach reducing integration and cross-fertilisation among different areas and preventing a better understanding of the functional and logical relation between the different research fields.

The future of E-Government

In the final step we used consolidated foresight techniques[27] to envision possible future scenarios and match them with their corresponding service platforms. The elaboration of future scenarios in foresight and road-mapping studies is not an end in itself, but it is instrumental to both eliciting divergent and out-of-the-box thinking and envisioning contrasting possible future directions. This is done, however, knowing

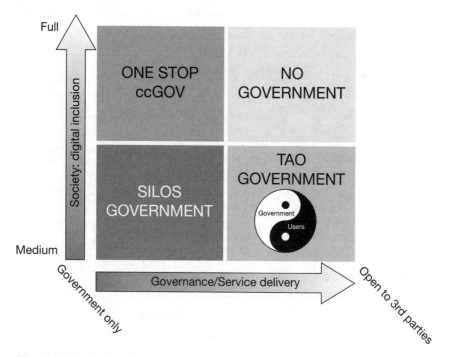

Figure 3.8 Scenario snapshot
Source: Authors' elaboration.

that the future will never occur exactly as imagined in any of the scenarios taken separately as a self-contained picture, but will rather contain elements from all scenarios. Envisaging several contrasting scenarios and associating with each of them the possible challenges maximises the likelihood of anticipating as many of those that will actually occur as possible.

The two axes used to identify the four scenarios (Figure 3.8) are:

1 the degree of digital inclusion in societies ranging from the two extremes of a moderate level of digital inclusion up to a situation of full digital inclusion;
2 the level of engagement of governments in the delivery of digital service ranging from the two extremes of government continuing to be the only provider of digital public services to that of government entirely delegating such delivery to third parties (from the private or the third sector).

Apart from the less interesting scenario of silos government, to each of the other three scenarios a future services platform has been associated. Figure 3.9 provides the intuitive characterisation of the three relevant scenarios and the associated services platforms, which are further summarised below.

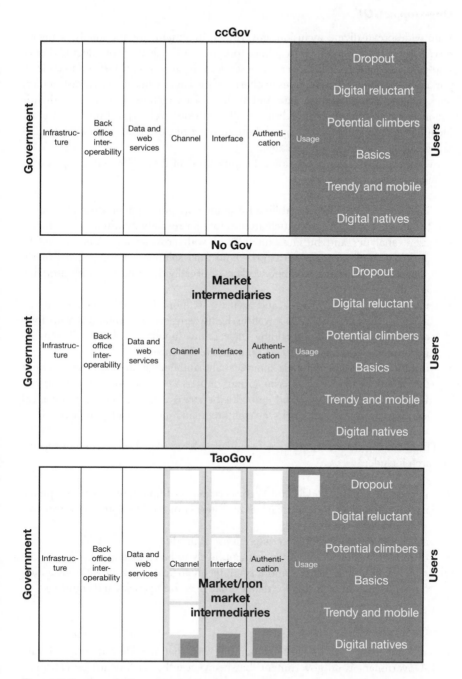

Figure 3.9 Services platform roles for the three scenarios

One-stop ccGOV

With widespread digital inclusion, government maintains the monopoly of digital service delivery and manages to achieve progress in the delivery of integrated one-stop shop, citizen-centric E-Government services, mostly through a few national-level portals. Government thus remains in charge of the entire value chain: infrastructure, back-office inter-operability, data and Web services, channel, interface, authentication and direct interaction with usage. (The various archetypical profiles of users identified in the study, from top to bottom, go from the least to the most technologically confident or sophisticated.)

Synthetically, the key technological components of the ccGov services platform include:

• integration and interoperability for joined-up government through shared services based on Web-oriented architecture for re-usability within government;
• users analytics and business intelligence with cross-agency data sharing to anticipate and meet user demands – innovative solutions should be particularly aimed at empowering frontline workers, especially those dealing with dropouts and digital reluctants;
• innovative identity, privacy and security solutions for data exchange across agencies and the country as well as lightweight security solutions with low-technology footprint-embedding delegation functions which will enable government frontline staff to act on behalf of the citizens;
• flexible solutions for channels, interfaces and authentication, taking into account the different capacity of differing groups of users as well as non-computer-based IT channels (e.g. mobile and embedded systems with the latest technological solutions in terms of channel synchronisation and interface adaptability).

The technological challenges to be potentially addressed by E-Government-specific research include:

• new collaboration models and Web services exposition mainly between public agencies based on the paradigm of an Internet of services with a government-wide enterprise architecture;
• adaptable interfaces suited to different users' needs;
• own solutions for identity management, likely to be re-used also by the private sector, combining security and a small technological footprint with delegation functions built in, allowing for data exchange across agencies and countries.

No government

On the one hand, let us start by pointing out that the view that 'the future of E-Government is no government' has been recently put forward by Gartner's analyst, Andrea Di Maio,[28] who also argued that by 2013, more than 70 per cent of citizen-centric (or E-Government or transformational) government strategies will fail. On the other hand, the idea of increasingly less government in the delivery of online public services is also mirrored in the current debate on the 'invisible hand' of civil society and Web 2.0 in delivering public services which build on the availability of public data. The scenario narrative we developed is as follows. With most users fully confident digital players owning their personal data, governments entirely delegate the delivery of online public services to third-party intermediaries (from either the private or the third sector), remaining in charge of governance matters such as policies and services design, strategic control, measurement of outcomes and accountability issue, as well as infrastructure and the back office, ensuring the re-usability of its data and contents. Issues from channel to direct interaction with users are managed by third parties.

Synthetically, the key technological components of the No Gov services platform include:

- interoperable architecture ensuring good data quality and data availability to third parties and other government departments;
- horizontal business processes managed as shared services, with infrastructure and services increasingly provided as 'cloud computing' and also often provided privately;
- Web 2.0 E-Participation platforms ensuring accountability and legitimacy, since service delivery channels, interfaces and authentication will be fully managed by intermediaries;
- personal identity management systems and privacy-enhancing technologies mainly dealt by the private sector with governments playing a monitoring role;
- strong intelligence layer (i.e. policy and service modelling and monitoring) as governments need to steer and oversee a networked/blurred governance model (to monitor social trends, quality of service provision and universal service compliance).

The technological challenges to be potentially addressed by E-Government-specific research include:

- definition of secure architecture for the composability and re-use of services and information;
- the mining and monitoring of a large amount of users' feedback;
- intelligence: 'ICT for governance and policy modelling' (models for understanding societal trends and challenges and regulatory impact);
- no research on identity management, but rather adaptation of identity management solutions from the private sector and monitoring data repositories by the private sector and their impact;
- research on embedded systems, sensors, mesh and resilient networks for emergency situations.

Tao Gov

The Tao metaphor is used to characterise an E-Subsidiarity scenario. It differs from both the ccGOV and No GOV scenarios in that it does not foresee a dichotomy between the two extremes of the axis, but rather a flexible approach where, in the case of the most advanced users, government delegates delivery to third parties and achieves savings, and the resources thus released are invested to deal directly with the less sophisticated users. E-Subsidiarity is flexibly adapted to different user profiles, and is dynamic across time. Most of all, it rejects the zero-sum paradigm, aiming at a positive-sum situation, arguing that government and civil societies are complementary, fully co-penetrated and requiring one another to succeed. Tao Gov indeed requires government efforts in two directions (both characterised in ccGOV and No GOV), yet it potentially promises gains while at the same time presenting a more realistic institutional solution.

Synthetically, the key technological components of the Tao Gov services platform include:

- the same components as the previous two (as in ccGOV, deliver services to some groups of users and as in NO GOV, enable and facilitate third-party provision of services);
- higher customisation for advanced users and third-party intermediaries (i.e. co-design and delivery by digital natives);
- highly intuitive content and service provision, including gesture-recognition and multi-touch solutions, for less sophisticated users serviced directly by governments (including, for dropouts, the possibility for frontline workers to actually use the service on behalf of users to deliver services across multiple online and offline channels);
- strong but lightweight authentication methods, including federated ID-management solutions, available across multiple channels;
- scalable and flexible solutions within the approach of an Internet of services, which enable the necessary flexibility to serve different users in different ways;
- knowledge management and intelligent mobile tools that empower frontline staff and social workers to deliver services and even act as intermediaries on behalf of users such as dropouts.

The technological challenges to be potentially addressed by E-Government-specific research include:

- absorption/integration through the living labs model, incorporating users' needs and ecosystem requirements from the early stage of development;
- user involvement in service co-delivery through configurable interfaces;
- technologies for governance and orchestration of processes, intelligence and modelling and aggregation and analysis of large amount of qualitative feedback by citizens.

Besides these scenarios, specific technological components and research challenges, we identified cross-cutting elements leading to a set of potential recommendations for the future regardless of the scenarios or platforms from which they originate. We discuss them below.

Conclusions

We argue that there are three main directions of development for future technologies supporting a new E-Government services platform capable of increasing consumption of services:

1 Highest strategic level
   i.   technologies harnessing collective intelligence and mass collaboration to better design and model policies and services, which are designed and developed taking into account the needs of governmental employees as a specific user group;
   ii.   technologies gathering, mining and extracting knowledge from large-scale users' qualitative feedback and using it for constituent relationship management, which is developed and designed taking into account the needs of (particularly local) governmental employees as a specific user group;
   iii. technologies supporting the steering, monitoring and evaluating of multi-layer and multi-player processes of service delivery, cutting across the boundaries between government and civil society (i.e. individual end-users, online networks, private sector organisations, third sector organisations, etc.).
2 Operational level
   i.   technologies enhancing composability and re-usability of services and content to improve collaboration both within government and between government and civil society;
   ii.   small-footprint strong authentication with delegation functions allowing multiple identities and intermediation.
3 Front-office level
   i.   futuristic human-and-computer interaction applications;
   ii.   virtual and augmented realities.

In addition, given increasing constraints on the public finances, the future imperative will be to look for relatively inexpensive solutions which enable innovation to continue in a cost-effective way – in other words, technological solutions that do more with less.

Moving to the possible topics of future E-Government-specific technological research, we also propose three directions:

First, 'ICT for Governance and Policy Modelling', which was a theme included in the ICT Call 4 of FP7 2009 Work Programme.[29] We can only add that the findings of this study strongly support its relevance for the future of E-Government in that it promises to feel the supply-side gaps in terms of intelligence in the design of services and policies, as below.

Policy modelling, simulation and visualisation requires instruments to assess options based on the simulated behaviour and wishes of individuals, groups or communities (at local, regional and national levels) to understand the possible outcomes of government proposals, decisions and legislation; and tools and techniques to understand, model, simulate and validate the next generation of public services as complex service systems in the environment of social networking and collaborative society, including the needs of the younger generation.

The participation toolbox includes advanced tools embodying structural, organisational and new governance models to empower and engage all types of societal groups and communities, enable them to utilise mass co-operation platforms and allow governments to incorporate their input while safeguarding against misuse. These tools will enable the creation, learning, sharing and tracking of group knowledge that cuts across language and cultural interpretation. They should also facilitate transparency and tracking of inputs in the policy-making process. The toolbox must include security, identity and access controls to ensure privacy and, where appropriate, the delineation of constituency domains according to the specific needs of government applications.

Second, 'ICT for Orchestration of Multi-layered and Multi-players Service Delivery', meaning technological solutions for the implementation of a multi-layered, overall service architecture which supports the steering, monitoring and evaluation of output and outcome of the services delivered by a variety of non-governmental players, thus ensuring the delivery of services meets agreed standards of quality as well as the overall monitoring, control and evaluation of the multi-layer processes of service production and delivery. The need here is for research on developing technological solutions that integrate operational back-office solutions and infrastructure, enabling composability and re-usability between all possible involved actions with tools in support of the orchestration of complex service production and delivery processed (i.e. a service co-produced by individual final users and/or organisations). One concrete example is the development through ad hoc research of a platform which enables the processing and analysing of very large amount of direct qualitative and unstructured feedback from users. We envisage distributed and multi-layered systems which provide differing kinds of analysis and intelligence to different public sector players in order to support their monitoring and evaluation activities on the output and outcome of the services delivered.

Third, ICT for invisible and/or augmented human and computer interaction, meaning research for the development of E-Government-specific futuristic human-and-computer interaction applications (to lower barriers for users and increase consumption for all individuals with some level of digital inclusion and through ICT-enabled intermediation extending access also to the so-called 'dropouts') and innovative virtual and augmented reality solutions for so-called 'digital natives'.

Finally, while we understand the need of E-Government-specific research and we have proposed the three directions above, we are also convinced of the importance of integration into E-Government of findings and insights from the other areas of research. We further stress the promising potential of the living lab concept.

In particular, we suggest that on the one hand FP7 could support new E-Government-specific research, whereas the Competitiveness and Innovation Framework Programme (CIP) and Information and Communication Technologies Policy Support Programme (ICTPSP) pilots could finance initiatives which help government agencies at various levels increase their capacity to absorb research results. Moreover, such absorption could be facilitated through the direct involvement of users, thus facilitating appropriation and its understanding in a dynamic and interactive fashion, including real-life experimentation in terms of service co-production by users and/or delivery by third parties, for instance, at the local level.

Key points

- Examine the supply of and demands for E-Government. Identify differing groups of users and their divergent needs.
- Discuss possible future scenarios and their implications.
- Consider the need for future research. Identify areas of research that may contribute to a more holistic research effort in the pursuit of better governance.
- Identify the key direction of technological deployment, E-Government research and investments beyond the timeframe of i2010. Propose three directions such research can take.

Notes

1 In particular, in 2008 both Codagnone and Osimo worked on the study 'Future Technology Needs for Future E-Government Services' (see all the study deliverables at: http://82.187.13.175/eGEP/static/E_FutureofE-Government.asp?ST=0&page=1). In addition also in 2008 Codagnone was part of the team that delivered the study on 'Users' Satisfaction' with E-Government (see Draft Final Report of the study at http://ec. europa.eu/information_society/activities/E-Government/studies/docs/user_ satisfaction_draft_final_report.pdf) and also conducted a pilot study finalized at improving the traditional supply-side EU benchmarking of E-Government which critically reviewed the main pillars of this exercise (this study has not yet been made public at the time of writing this chapter). Insights and data from these studies are used in this chapter. Needless to say, the opinions expressed in this chapter are those of the authors and do not necessarily reflect in any way the views of the European Commission.
2 The interested reader can download the full report at: http://82.187.13.175/eGEP/ static/Contents/FutureTechnology/service%20platform%20report.pdf.
3 European Commission (2005), *i2010 – A European Information Society for Growth and Employment*, COM(2005)229 final, Brussels: EC.
4 For further information see Codagnone, C. and Wimmer, M. (eds) (2007) *Roadmapping E-Government Research Visions and Measures towards Innovative Governments in 2020*. Milan: eGovRTD2020 Project Consortium, also available online at http://www.unikoblenz.de/ FB4/Contrib/EGOVRTD2020/FinalBook.pdf [last retrieved January 2008]; Missikov, M. (2006) *New Trends in Technologies and Enablers for Applications for the Future Government in 2020*, Prepared for European Commission. Seville: DG JRC, IPTS; Osimo, D., Zinnbauer, D. and Bianchi, A. (eds) (2007) *The Future of E-Government: An Exploration of ICT-Driven Models of E-Government for the EU in 2020*. European Commission, DG JRC, IPTS Seville JRC. [online] Available at http://ftp.jrc.es/eur22897en.pdf [retrieved April 2008]
5 Mandl, U., Dierx, A. and F. Ilzkovits (2008), *The Effectiveness and Efficiency of Public Spending*, European Commission, Economic and Financial Affairs, Economic Papers, 301. [online] Available at http://ec.europa.eu/economy_finance/publications/publication11902_en. pdf [last retrieved January 2009].
6 (1999), *eEurope, an Information Society for All*, Communication on a Commission Initiative for the Special European Council of Lisbon, 23–24 March 2000, COM(1999)687 final, Brussels, European Council and Commission; (2000), *eEurope 2002, an Information Society for All*: Action Plan prepared by the Council and the European Commission for the Feira European Council, Brussels. European Commission (2002); eEurope 2005, *An Information Society for All: An Action Plan to be Presented in View of the Sevilla European Council*, COM(2002)263 final, Brussels, European Commission.

7 Osimo, D. (2008b) 'Benchmarking E-Government in the Web 2.0 Era: What to Measure and How', *European Journal of ePractice* 1/4: 33–43. [online] Available at http://www. epracticejourna.eu/volume/4/document/4972 (last retrieved January 2009).

8 Besides the aggregate data for the EU, we also report those for Austria, for it is the best performer on the supply-side benchmarking.

9 European Commission (2008) Volume 1: i2010 — Annual Information Society Report 2008, *Benchmarking i2010: Progress and Fragmentation in the European Information Society*, COM(2008)199 final, Brussels, pp. 33–36.

10 eLost (2008) Deliverable D4.3:Final report – findings from the foresight process and recommendations, eLOST Consortium. [online] Available at http://www.elost.org/ D4-3.pdf [last retrieved January 2009]; eUser (2006), D5.2: Report on current demand/supply match and relevant developments, Part D (E-Government), eUser Consortium. [online] Available at http://www.euser-eu.org/ShowDocument.asp?Focus AnalysisDocumentID=27 [last retrieved January 2008].

11 AGIMO (2008), Australians' use of and satisfaction with E-Government services, AGIMO. [online] Available at http://www.finance.gov.au/publications/use-of-E-Government-services-2007/docs/31576_AGIMO_Satisfaction-ALL.pdf [last retrieved January 2009]; Dutton, H. and Helsper, E. (2007), *The Internet in Britain: 2007*, Oxford Internet Institute, Oxford. [online] Available at http://www.oii.ox.ac.uk/microsites/ oxis/ [last retrieved December 2008]; Underhill, C. and Ladds, C. (2006) *Connecting with Canadians: Assessing the Use of Government On-Line*, Statistics Canada, Ottawa. [online] Available at http://www.statcan.gc.ca/pub/56f0004m/56f0004m2007015-eng.pdf [last retrieved January 2009].

12 Draft Final Report, p. 124 (http://ec.europa.eu/information_society/activities/E-Government/studies/docs/user_satisfaction_draft_final_report.pdf).

13 See the periodic report produced by the Commission Services and called 'Riga Dashboard' (http://ec.europa.eu/information_society/activities/einclusion/docs/i2010_ initiative/rigadashboard.pdf).

14 Codagnone, C. (2009) *Vienna Study on Inclusive Innovation for Growth and Cohesion: Modelling and Demonstrating the Impact of eInclusion*. Brussels: Information Society and Media Directorate. Also available at http://ec.europa.eu/information_society/activities/einclusion/library/ studies/docs/eco_report.pdf.

15 Blank, R. and Ruggles, P. (1996), 'When Do Women Use Aid to Families with Dependent Children and Food Stamps? The Dynamics of Eligibility Versus Participation', *Journal of Human Resources* 31: 57–89; Manski, C. (2004) 'Social Learning from Private Experiences: The Dynamics of the Selection Problem', *Review of Economic Studies* 71: 443–458; Cohen-Cole, E. and Zanella, G. (2008) *Welfare Stigma or Information Sharing? Decomposing Social Interactions Effects in Social Benefit Use*. Wisconsin: Department of Economics, University of Siena WP 531.

16 de Haan, A. (1997) 'Poverty and Social Exclusion: A Comparison of Debates on Deprivation'. Working Paper No. 2. Brighton: Poverty Research Unit at Sussex, University of Sussex; D'Ambrosio, C., Papadopoulos, F. and Tsakloglou, P. (2002) 'Social Exclusion in EU Member-States: A Comparison of Two Alternative Approaches', Working Paper. Milan, Italy: Bocconi University; Tsakloglou, P. and Papadopoulos, F. (2002a) 'Aggregate Level and Determining Factors of Social Exclusion in Twelve European Countries', *Journal of European Social Policy* 12: 209–223; Tsakloglou, P. and Papadopoulos, F. (2002b) 'Identifying Population Groups at High Risk of Social Exclusion', in Muffels, R., Tsakloglou, P. and Mayes, D. (eds) *Social Exclusion in European Welfare States*. Cheltenham: Edward Elgar; Sen, A. (2000) 'Social Exclusion: Concept, Application and Scrutiny', *Social Development Papers* 1, Oxford: Office of Environment and Social Development, Manila Asian Development Bank.

17 For a review see Codagnone, C. and Undheim, T. (2008) 'Government Efficiency and Effectiveness: The Theory and Practice of Benchmarking and Measurement', *European Journal of ePratice* 1/4, August: 4–18. pp.6–7.

18 Dunleavy, P., Margetts, H. *et al.* (2006) 'New Public Management Is Dead – Long Live Digital-Era Governance', *Journal of Public Administration Research and Theory* 16: 467–494.

19 Osimo, D. (2008a) *Web 2.0 for Government: Why and How?* Technical Report. JRC, EC JRC [online] Available at www.jrc.es (last retrieved January 2009). Osimo, D. (2008b) op. cit.

20 These paragraphs only briefly summarise the analysis contained in the various deliverables of the aforementioned EC-funded study 'Future Technology Needs for Future E-Government Services'. For the full analysis of users' needs and supply-side gaps see the study report on trends and needs (http://82.187.13.175/eGEP/static/Contents/FutureTechnology/D2supply_and_demand_trends_and_needs.pdf, chap. 4, pp. 36–57) and the study final report (http://82.187.13.175/eGEP/static/Contents/FutureTechnology/service%20platform%20report.pdf, chap. 2, pp. 11–30).

21 Although we cannot rule out that socially excluded groups may be users of the Internet (i.e. counter-culture use by marginalised youth).

22 'Composability' refers to the possibility for Web services to be re-assembled in different compositions to deliver new services.

23 ftp://ftp.cordis.europa.eu/pub/technology-platforms/docs/etp3rdreport_en.pdf.

24 http://cordis.europa.eu/ictresults/.

25 http://cordis.europa.eu/fp7/ict/projects/home_en.htm.

26 See full analysis in the report delivered for the EC-funded study 'Future technology needs for future E-Government Services' on disclosure of concealed R&D (http://82.187.13.175/eGEP/static/Contents/FutureTechnology/disclosure_of_concelead_R&D.pdf) and in its accompanying compendium (http://82.187.13.175/eGEP/static/Contents/FutureTechnology/disclosure_of_concelead_R&D_annex.pdf).

27 See for instance Codagnone and Wimmer (eds) (2007) op. cit.

28 See Di Maio's blog at http://blog.gartner.com/blog/government.php?itemid=3558.

29 See WORK PROGRAMME 2009, COOPERATION THEME 3: ICT – Information and Communication Technologies, p. 74, but also: a) the Report of FP7 Consultation Workshop on ICT for Governance and Policy Modelling, Brussels, 28 May 2008 (http://ec.europa.eu/information_society/activities/E-Government/research/fp7/fp7_workshop/documents/report_fp7_online.pdf); b) the 'ICT for Governance and Policy Modelling' ePractice community (http://www.epractice.eu/community/egovernance/blog/182), where a discussion document is also available (http://www.epractice.eu/resource/2462).

Further reading

Christensen, C. (1997) *The Innovator's Dilemma.* Boston: Harvard Business School Press.

Codagnone, C. (2007) 'Measuring E-Government: Reflections from eGEP Measurement Framework Experience', *European Review of Political Technologies* 4: 89–106. (Further reading on the topic of how to measure the outcomes of E-Government is mentioned at the beginning of the chapter.)

Dunleavy, P., Margetts, H. *et al.* (2006) 'New Public Management Is Dead – Long Live Digital-Era Governance', *Journal of Public Administration Research and Theory* 16: 467–494.

European Commission (2004) 'Facing the Challenge: The Lisbon Strategy for Growth and Employment', in Kok, C. B. W. (ed.) *Report of the High Level Group*, Brussels, http://ec.europa.eu/growthandjobs/pdf/kok_report_en.pdf. (A general discussion of delay and bottleneck toward the Lisbon goals in relation to the information and knowledge society.)

Foley, P. (2008) 'Government Realising the Transformation Agenda: Enhancing Citizen Use of E-Government', *European Journal of ePractice* 1/4, August. [www.epracticejournal.eu] (Analysis of data on use of E-Government by citizens in the UK and extraction of policy recommendations.)

Mayo, E. and Steinberg, T. (2007) *The Power of Information: An Independent Review.* [online] Available at: www.cabinetoffice.gov.uk/media/cabinetoffice/strategy/assets/power_information.pdf (last retrieved January 2009).

Osimo, D. (2008a) *Web 2.0 for Government: Why and How? Technical Report.* JRC, EC JRC [online] Available at www.jrc.es (last retrieved January 2009).

Osimo, D. (2008b) 'Benchmarking E-Government in the Web 2.0 Era: What to Measure and How', *European Journal of ePractice*, 1/4: 33–43. [online] Available at http://www.epractice journal.eu/volume/4/document/4972 (last retrieved January 2009).

Robinson, D. *et al.* (2008) 'Government Data and the Invisible Hand', *Yale Journal of Law & Technology*, Vol. 11 [online] Available at: http://papers.ssrn.com/sol3/papers.cfm?abstract_id=1138083 (last retrieved January 2009).

Part II
Conceptual challenges

4 E-Government and government transformation

Technical interactivity, political influence and citizen return

Filipe Montargil

Summary

E-Government services have been the subject of theoretical elaboration and regular evaluation surveys since around 2000. It is argued in this chapter that the theoretical paradigms used for methodology design in these surveys (and, therefore, their main results too) tend to neglect political influence as an analytic dimension and consider citizen return as resulting from technical interactivity.

A critique is carried out of the assumptions underlying this paradigm and a complementary criterion is offered for the analysis of E-Government services. Available results from existing surveys are re-examined in light of this reflection. Findings reveal an indisputable growth in coverage (i.e. a larger percentage of services are available online) and in technical interactivity of government services online. However, a more careful look at the same surveys also supports the hypothesis that their results should not be taken as automatically meaning an increase in citizen engagement or that services are being developed from a starting point of the user's needs and expectations. On the contrary, data suggests that sophistication is increasing faster in the technical interactivity dimension than in citizen participation features. Simultaneously, services more closely related with the extractive activity of the state (e.g. that imply revenue or income generation) are placed online sooner and with more technical sophistication than services in other areas. Some data also suggests that these trends are not imperceptible to citizens. According to one survey, citizens expect from E-Government more consequences in state efficiency and cost reduction than in government transparency or accountability.

Introduction

Public administration agencies and national governments have a strong online presence, providing a large range of content and services for citizens and companies. This presence started at the beginning of the 1990s, after the creation of the World Wide Web (WWW) in 1991, and we can chart a progressive proliferation of activity throughout the decade. The diffusion of Internet use, through the WWW, has created the opportunity and indeed, one might argue, the need for governments to provide information and services through this new channel. Many countries adopted objectives during the second half of the 1990s, and put into practice strategies for services provided through the Internet (eventually in conjunction with other technologies). These strategies involved an increasing range of departments, agencies and services, and were often the object of public debate through national information society strategies or specific policy documents. The discourse around these policies, by both public officials and scholars, was transformist and sometimes hyperbolic with words like 'revolution' or 'transformation' abounding.

Each new technology has its government enhancement, transformation or revolution enthusiasts. We can find these expectations and arguments associated to virtually all emerging technologies. This is true for the printing press,[1] radio,[2] personal computer and computer networks[3] and cable television.[4] So, in this sense, there is nothing new in the expectations of government transformation and political potential ascribed to the Internet. Some conceptual lenses have been, however, developed to analyse the specific reality of the Internet, and several surveys have been conducted with this purpose. Let us now examine one or two of them.

The green paper on public sector information: Technical influence in E-Government

References in public policy documents at the European or national level, in EU member states, regarding government enhancement or transformation through WWW use appear early on.[5] The first typology classifying these possibilities included in a public policy document appears in the *Green Paper on Public Sector Information in the Information Society*.[6]

This Commission document adopts a typology of E-Government services previously presented by a team of Austrian researchers[7] at the Conference of the Information Society Forum held in Vienna in November 1998. According to the green paper,

> [t]he use of Information and Communication Technologies does not only smoothen public administration internal operations, but also strongly supports the communication between different administrations as well as the interaction with citizens and businesses. This is one of the key elements of 'Electronic Government': it brings public sector bodies closer to citizens and businesses and leads to better public sector services.[8]

This typology combines two dimensions. The first dimension regards the functions served by E-Government services, including three functions. The first, most basic function is information, through which services retrieve sorted and classified information on demand (e.g. WWW sites). The second function, referred to as communication, concerns interaction with other individuals or groups of people, whether private or corporate (e.g. via email or discussion fora). The third function, transaction, corresponds to the online acquisition of products, services or the sub-mission of data (e.g. government forms or voting).

These functions highlight the way communication channels are used: in the informational level, the flow of information is unidirectional; in the transactional level, flows are bidirectional and the Internet is able to fully replace other traditional channels to manage citizen relationships in an interactive way. Since this interactivity is technically assured, through the use of hardware and software, I also call this the 'technical interactivity dimension'.

This first dimension is considered central for E-Government. Its several functions are considered as levels in an ordinal scale, where the next level reaches a higher technical interactivity degree than the previous one. The existence of these differences from level to level justifies the fact that 'transaction services are generally seen as the future of electronic government'.[9]

The second dimension in this typology regards the application areas[10] of resources identified in the first dimension. The first area (Table 4.1) is oriented to everyday life needs, where electronic services cover information necessary to the pursuit of everyday life (e.g. housing, education, work, etc.). The electronic support for the citizens' or businesses' interaction with public administration through, for instance, a public service directory or electronic forms (i.e. tele-administration) is a second area of application. The third area consists of political participation, where services provide electronic support for processes of political opinion formation and decision making (e.g. discussion fora or electronic voting).

These different areas imply different political influence levels; having access to information useful in everyday life does not represent a political influence comparable to the participation in an election. I also refer to this dimension, for this reason, as the 'political influence dimension'.

Political influence does not receive the same attention in the analysis of E-Government services and is not conceived, curiously, as being organised in an ordinal scale: the reading of both texts suggests it is considered as a nominal variable.[11]

Table 4.1 The typology of E-Government services in the *Green Paper on Public Sector Information in the Information Society*

	Information services	*Communication services*	*Transaction services*
Everyday life	Information on work, housing, education, health, culture, transport, environment, etc.	Discussion for a dedicated to questions of everyday life; jobs or housing bulletin boards	Ticket reservation, course registration
Tele-administration	Public service directory, guide to administrative procedures, public registers and databases	Email contact with public servants	Electronic submission of forms
Political participation	Laws, parliamentary papers, political programmes, consultation documents. Background information in decision-making processes	Discussion fora dedicated to political issues, e-mail contact with politicians	Referenda, elections, opinion polls, petitions

Source: Aichholzer *et al.* (1998: 4) (see p. 76, note 7) and European Commission (COM(1998)585: 8).

This green paper had some impact on EU member states over the coming years and was considered in the formulation of their own policy documents.

The first typology of E-Government included in public policy documents for information society includes, thus, two dimensions. The first concerns the technical interactivity of services. The second relates to the level of political influence citizens can achieve through those services.

Gartner's model of E-Government: transformation and citizen return as resulting from technical interactivity

In 2000, IT research and consulting firm Gartner published a series of papers presenting its E-Government model.[12] This model is influenced by the approach presented in the Commission's green paper, and is similar in approach to the methodology adopted in regular surveys about E-Government services.

The first phase, presence, is the most elementary level of E-Government. In this phase, services passively present generic information on their website, containing, for instance, information about an agency, such as its address, hours of operation and contact numbers. In this phase, the Internet does not replace existing delivery channels in any step of the process.

The second phase is interaction. In this phase, websites provide basic search capabilities, links to other relevant sites, email addresses or forms to download. Downloaded forms must, however, be printed, filled in by hand and mailed or faxed to the agency. Services in this phase replace existing delivery channels, at least partially, in the first flow of information from the public agency to the citizen (e.g. downloading a form). The subsequent flow of information, from the citizen to the public agency, needs to adopt other channels.

The third phase is that of transaction. This stage allows users to conduct and complete entire tasks online. Services in this phase are based on self-service applications where a task can be undertaken and concluded online. Operations in this phase have a greater complexity, not being limited to the simple provision of information, but allowing the conclusion of tasks electronically without interruptions in service provision. Applications for the payment of contributions or taxes, licence renewals or submission of candidacies are examples of services in this phase. This phase represents maturity for E-Government. The Internet can be considered, at this point, as a full delivery channel, side by side with existing channels.

The fourth and final phase in Gartner's model corresponds to transformation. Services in this level use technology to transform the way governments' functions are conceived, organized and executed. These services should have a high standard of customer relationship management, should be applicable to a large range of situations and should be based in resources shared between different administrative levels and agencies. Changes in the government's modus operandi could occur in this phase, due to technology use. It can be assumed that information flows must be bidirectional but there are no explicit or defined rules that establish what is specific to this phase.

Information in the communication process between the citizen and a public agency flows, in the first phase (assuming the first phase implies a communication process), only from the agency to the citizen: information about the address, contact or the agency's working hours is displayed to the citizen. In the second phase, the flow still follows the same direction: a form available to download is sent to the citizen. Their feedback, however, has to be returned through another channel (e.g. mail, fax, delivery in person, etc.). In the third phase there is, for the first time, a flow of information originating with the citizen and oriented towards the public agency. In the fourth phase flows are indeterminate, even though it can be assumed that they should, normally, be bidirectional. A scheme for information flows in each phase is presented in Figure 4.1.

These phases are considered by the authors as different, subject to variation, according to three dimensions: cost and technical complexity, time and constituency value. If cost and complexity increase over time, and from phase to phase, it is also argued that constituency value should increase from one phase to the next: 'as the government progresses through each phase, it should become increasingly constituent-focused. By the time it reaches Transformation, it should be completely remade to best fit the needs of the constituent'.[13] The association between the transformation phase, considered as 'the long-term goal of almost all national and local E-Government initiatives',[14] and constituency value is assumed as automatic. This association assumes that technical interactivity implies constituency value.

Differences between Gartner's several phases refer, essentially, to the technological dimension and to the use of its capabilities. Differences in constituency value are, however, mainly cultural and not technological. These are two independent dimensions with different sociological worlds and values. It is argued here that technical interactivity and constituency value (or citizen return) are independent dimensions, not necessarily related in its beginning, its process or its finale. Citizen return does not result, it is argued, from technical interactivity. One can find services with high technical interactivity levels and residual citizen return and, likewise, low technical interactivity associated with high citizen return.

Comparing this model with the previous one, political influence is eliminated as an analytic dimension and citizen return is considered as resulting from technical interactivity. Gartner's model is closer to the methodology adopted in the analysis of E-Government services since the beginning of the decade. It can be considered, for

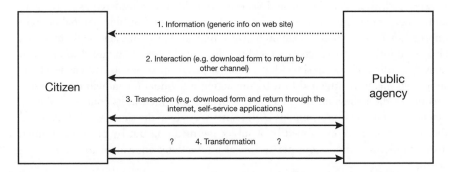

Figure 4.1 Flows of information in citizen–public agency communication according to Gartner's four phases of E-Government services

this reason, as a sort of paradigm: Gartner's paradigm. This expression does not necessarily imply a direct influence from Gartner's model over regular survey methodology. There are, however, some common elements: the first regular surveys were inaugurated by other consulting firms[15] and, as we have the opportunity to analyse ahead, political influence is not an analytic dimension in existing surveys,[16] and citizen return is frequently seen as resulting from technical interactivity.

Assumptions in the Gartner paradigm

This paradigm for the analysis and evaluation of E-Government services, which has shaped our understanding and vision of its evolution, lies on some debatable assumptions.

First, the key driver for transformation is understood to be technology. It is necessary to wait for technology to settle in, to be embedded in administrative and bureaucratic processes, and when mature it will give place to transformation. Transformation is assumed as only occurring when electronic service maturity is reached – that is why transformation is the final phase. Transformation is expected when E-Government services can replace or fully compete with other delivery channels. It is not considered as a possibility in earlier phases. It is only possible to find transformation in the final phase of the model because it is seen as depending solely on technology.

This assumption overlooks the possibility of service transformation when transition to online use is in its infancy, in primary socialisation. This is a technocratic vision of change and transformation that neglects the cultural factors determining organisational, political and social change.

A second assumption is the idea that technical interactivity is equivalent to social interaction and to democracy. The adoption of technology to manage information flows in the communication process between the citizens and public agencies is frequently considered as equivalent to some form of social interaction. This is why, for instance, a form download (e.g. a flow of standardized information from the public agency to the citizen) can be called interaction in Gartner's paradigm.

This association between the two concepts confuses the 'technical mechanisms of interactivity between humans and machines with the social mechanisms of interaction between individuals', as Proulx and Sénécal argued.[17] It is considered as a necessary and sufficient condition for perfect technical interactivity that bidirectional flows of information exist in communication between man and machine. Although this could also be considered as a necessary condition for social interaction and democracy, it does not suffice if we consider that action is social 'in so far as, by virtue of the subjective meaning attached to it by the acting individual (or individuals), it takes account of the behaviour of others and is thereby oriented in its course'.[18] Since a machine always reacts to stimulus in the same way given the same set of stimuli and the reaction is not conditioned by a subjective meaning but by pre-programmed instructions, we cannot consider technical interactivity equivalent to social interaction.

According to a third assumption, citizen return, or constituency value, is seen as resulting from technical interactivity. Establishing communication with a machine using technical interactivity features is considered to intrinsically imply citizen return; this is why, in Gartner's model, constituency value is considered to increase automatically from phase to phase. It increases not because of additional criteria or features that are mobilised in E-Government services, but because the channel is more sophisticated, with higher technical interactivity. Citizen return does not result, in this model, from better meeting the citizen's needs and expectations, but from gradual advances in the provision of the same service through a new channel. Value is not, in the end, in the service, but in the channel.

This assumption reduces citizen return to user convenience. Paying taxes on-line, for instance, can be more convenient, but it does not necessarily represent more value for the citizen, as an agent of civil, political and social rights and duties.

Two main differences can be found between the previous typology of E-Government and Gartner's model. First, the political influence dimension is non-existent in the latter model. Including it could even seem somehow redundant: if technology is seen as the key driver for change and technical interactivity is considered as equivalent to social interaction, technical interactivity exhausts the analytic needs. Second, citizen return is considered to be a consequence of technical interactivity – something that does not happen in the first model. Thus, Gartner's model stresses the 'electronic' dimension of 'E-Government', omitting the 'government' component.

This model can be considered useful for assessing the level of website development as a delivery channel and to assist the purchase of technology and technology services. However, it does not after the possibility of evaluating the kind of political influence or citizen return from such services.

A concept of government and some implications: Service development based on the state v. service development based on the user

Accepting the definition of government as 'the utilisation of public authority by some subset of elected or appointed actors, backed by the coercive power of the state and (sometimes) the legitimate support of the citizenry to accomplish collective goals',[19] one implication is that procedures must be defined to establish the collective goals that government activity seeks to accomplish. The definition and delimitation of these procedures leads to the debate around the notions of government, governance and democracy. Schumpeterian definitions of democracy, for instance, accept elections as the central mechanism for the expression and establishment of these collective goals.

As for the development of E-Government services, the establishment of collective goals can be viewed as corresponding to the definition of resources available, and the way in which they may be allocated. We can conceive of two different ways to establish these goals: internally, based on the State; and externally, based on the user.

The first stage implies that E-Government services are developed having public agencies in a leading role, as the central unit for the establishment of goals and its subsequent evaluation. This process places the agency itself at the starting point, along with a set of internal expectations and needs. In the second stage, services that somehow involve users are the object of intervention and transformation, through the use of technology in some part of the communication process. In the end, it is expected that the objectives initially defined will be reached, eventually giving place to evaluation and benchmarking. This is an internal perspective on E-Government services development.

There is also the possibility of conceiving the process as having the citizen at its centre. We can call this an external perspective since it implies that an agency including the process of intervention in its services places at the centre an external entity – the user.

The development of citizen-driven services, oriented to citizen return and based on their expectations and needs, implies adopting a starting point based on the citizen. The objectives established must assume the citizen as the unit of analysis for the process. In the following stage attention is turned to the processes and resources used by the agency in its activity. In the last phase, the process focuses again on the end user and on its return. Evaluation and benchmarking are also centred on the user. A scheme of both perspectives is presented in Figure 4.2.

It is possible to conceive the use of Internet resources based on a complex model of communication embedded in E-Government services that does not adopt objectives particularly valued by citizens or imply a relevant positive return. Conversely, it is possible to conceive, in an elementary way, the use of technology, not benefiting totally from its communication capabilities (with flows of unidirectional communication, for example), but applied to services pursuing objectives valued by the users, or that imply a relevant return.

These are mutually exclusive possibilities: it is not possible to start the process departing simultaneously from the agency's and the user's expectations and needs. Additionally, phases in the development of a service are path dependent, being conditioned by the previous phase.

The mutual exclusivity does not imply that the adoption of an internal point of view necessarily corresponds to an output with no benefits for the user. The user may also

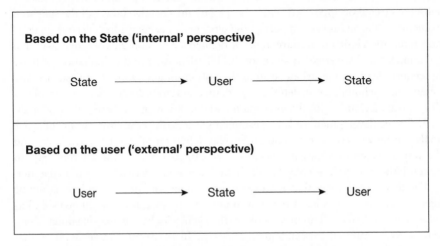

Figure 4.2 Perspectives in the development of E-Government services

obtain some kind of return, even from services developed in an internal perspective. This distinction between the two perspectives respects, in the first place, the motivations of public agencies. When trying to address internal issues, public agencies can also collaterally address citizens' issues. This result is logically possible since different motivations and paths can lead occasionally to roughly the same result. This is not, however, a necessary result of the adoption of different perspectives in the development of E-Government services.

Historically, the use of information and communication technologies (ICT) by the State is oriented by internal objectives. Public use of ICT appears, in a first stage, mainly in academic research and military applications. Beyond the limits of these two restricted circulation areas, which imply limited consequences in the interaction between the State and the remaining social actors, the use of ICT also seems predominantly aimed at internal State objectives rather than at the development of its responsiveness. The role of the State and of public administration in computer development has been the object of scarce interest.[20] However, available sources seem to point in the direction of the development and use of computers as being influenced by internal matters more than by external motivations.

An example illustrating this point in the first stages of personal computer use in public administration is the memorandum prepared by the Treasury of the United Kingdom in response to a request of the Fulton Committee. This committee, created with the objective of reflecting on the organisation of public administration, requested the Treasury, in 1966, to evaluate the possible impact of computers in public administration.[21] More specifically, the Fulton Committee intended to evaluate the possibility of using personal computers to slow down, stabilize or even invert the trend of growth for civil service staff.

The answer of the Treasury to this initial question is delivered through two memoranda.[22] The first memorandum describes what was then called 'automatic data processing' in government departments, and investment in computers was justified by staff cost reduction. The second memorandum suggested that this reduction would be more significant in the initial stages of the adoption of computers, since the most probable trend would be the growing use of computers as the capabilities were further developed. The framing of the question by the Fulton Committee, the choice of the Treasury to address it and the answers provided are evidence of an internal perspective.

The relationship between ICT use and the fiscal efficiency of the State determines the relevant role the Treasury assumes in global information society policies in several countries. This is the case in two of the countries that inaugurated early public policy documents on information society in Europe: Finland and Denmark. Finnish governments (mainly between 1992 and 1996) and the Danish governments, in the initial stage of their policies for the information society, between January 1993 and September 1994, handed responsibility for policy development on the information society to the Treasury.[23]

Thus, it is necessary to bear in mind that motivations behind the development of ICT use by government institutions were not related to intra-societal environments, to other spheres of society or to communication improvement with external agents. ICT adoption by the State was oriented, on the contrary, towards internal goals such as efficiency in data processing, resource management, tax collection and public expenditure reduction. ICT was first considered by public authorities as information technology and only subsequently seen, potentially, as being a communication technology. This reality can correspond to a source of tension with the citizen's perspective, which is more focused in the communication dimension of ICT.

The historic relevance of internal perspectives, frequently underestimated in the analysis of information society policies, allows one to formulate the hypothesis that agents responsible for information technology in public administration also value internal public administration users, to the detriment of external users.[24] However, much of the discourse about E-Government services creation and development uses the citizen as an argumentative category. Gartner, for instance, defined E-Government as 'the transformation of public-sector internal and external relationships through Net-enabled operations, IT and communications to optimize service delivery, constituency participation and governance'.[25]

The Finnish government, in an information society policy document called *Finland as an Information Society*, published by the Ministry of Finance, defines the aim of its E-Government project as being the improvement of 'the availability, quality and customer-orientation of the services of public administration'.[26]

The European Commission defined 'electronic government' as 'the use of information and communication technology in public administrations combined with organisational change and new skills in order to improve public services and democratic processes and strengthen support to public policies'.[27]

These are just a few examples of reference to 'citizen-centric', 'customer-oriented', 'customer participation' or 'citizen engagement'-like expressions in the initial period of E-Government initiatives. The discourse around the creation and development of E-Government services valued, right from the beginning, the citizen, including the citizen in its rhetoric.

At the beginning of the twenty-first century, several surveys on E-Government services were inaugurated. In 2000 Accenture launched its first E-Government survey. Accenture undertakes regular surveys on E-Government services, trying to identify trends and good practices in the area. Soon after, several other surveys appeared. Capgemini Ernst & Young launched a benchmark survey for an eEurope action plan, under a contract with the European Commission, in 2001. The Center for Public Policy of Brown University started a global E-Government survey in 2001. In 2002 the United Nations also launched its own E-Government survey.[28]

All these surveys adopt indicators methodologically coherent with the Gartner paradigm. Accenture calculates overall maturity scores for electronic services in each country included in the survey using two indicators: service maturity breadth and service maturity depth.[29] The first is about universal service, the second about interactivity underlying the flows of information in the service. The first is an indicator for coverage (percentage of services that are online) and the second for technical interactivity, considering three levels: publication, interaction and transaction. By combining these two indicators into an overall maturity score, Accenture calculates a ranking for each of the twenty-two countries sampled. In 2005 these two indicators were joined in one dimension, service maturity, and combined with a new dimension: customer service maturity. This component is intended to evaluate how governments address four dimensions in customer service: citizen-centred, multi-channel, cross-government service delivery and proactive communication.[30]

The Capgemini survey was, initially, a benchmark for the achievement of eEurope's plan of action objectives, adopted by the European Commission.[31] This evaluation, focused on European Union member states,[32] analyses coverage (number of basic public services that are entirely available through the Internet) and sophistication. Sophistication levels correspond, in this case, to information, interaction, two-way interaction and transaction. Capgemini, unlike Accenture, does not calculate a global index combining coverage and technical interactivity. Instead it predominantly uses, in the initial reports, figures for online sophistication and in the later reports includes figures for both sophistication and for full online availability, not combining them into one final index.

The Center for Public Policy at Brown University has, since 2001, published a global E-Government survey including about 200 countries. Although it does not explicitly use a typology with levels similar to those considered in the Gartner paradigm, its variables are oriented to the measurement of technical interactivity. Issues covered include existing online information (with the offering of publications and databases; electronic services; privacy and security (with the existence of privacy or security policy visible in the site); disability access, considering the existence of some form of disability access in the website (with standards such as that proposed by the World Wide Web Consortium (W3C) or similar); the existence of foreign language features, allowing access to non-native-speaking individuals; the existence of restricted areas that require username and password for accessibility for security reasons or to personalise service delivery (this feature was discontinued from the 2003 to the 2004 edition); and the existence of public outreach resources, as features that would help citizens contact government officials and make use of information on websites (features such as email, search engines or areas to post comments).

The United Nations inaugurated its survey in 2002. It is often considered as the survey with the richest and most diverse set of methodological options. This survey included three dimensions, in its first edition: Web presence, ICT infrastructure and human capital. The first is an interpretation of technical interactivity.[33] The second includes variables related to telecommunications infrastructure, where higher values correspond to higher availability of equipment, networks and services. The third concerns human capital and is based in indicators used by the United Nations Development Programme in its Human Development Index.[34] In 2003, a fourth dimension was added. It regards the extent of citizen participation, including three levels: E-Information, E-Consultation and E-Decision making.

Results of these four surveys reveal a consistent trend in the development of coverage (i.e. a larger percentage of services available online) and technical interactivity (Table 4.2).

This evolution represents an indisputable commitment to the creation of more and more sophisticated E-Government services. But the same results can also be explored according to other concerns, beyond coverage and technical interactivity.

First, these survey results should not be considered as necessarily implying an increase in citizens' political influence. For example, the positive evolution Singapore

Table 4.2 Coverage and technical interactivity in regular surveys

	Coverage			Technical interactivity				
	Accenture	Capgemini		Accenture	Capgemini		UN	
	EU12*	EU15	EU25	EU12*	EU15	EU25	EU15	EU25
2000	—	—	—	—	—	—	—	—
2001	—	21%	—	—	47%	—	—	—
2002	—	36%	—	—	62%	—	—	—
2003	—	44%	—	—	67%	—	56%	50%
2004	—	48%	39%	—	73%	65%	66%	60%
2005	92%	—	—	62%	—	—	69%	65%
2006	—	54%	49%	—	79%	75%	—	—
2007	—	67%	61%	—	82%	77%	68%	64%
Compound annual growth rate		21.5%	15.8%		9.6%	6.1%	4.9%	6.2%

Sources: Accenture, Capgemini and UN (adpated). Limitations in evolution analysis apply in some cases, due to changes in methodology.

Coverage: Accenture: service maturity breadth; Capgemini: availability. Technical interactivity: Accenture: service maturity depth; Capgemini: online sophistication; UN: web measure or web presence.

* Accenture's survey includes 10 EU members in 2000 and 12 since 2001. Despite contacts with Accenture, it was not possible to obtain country values for other years.

registers in E-Government surveys and its stable classification as a partly free system, in regard to political rights and civil liberties, can be used to support this argument. Singapore comes second in Brown University's 2007 ranking, among 198 countries; twenty-third in the UN's E-Government readiness 2008 survey, among 189 countries; and fourth in the 2005 Accenture leadership in customer service rankings.[35]

Singapore formally is, according to its Constitution, a representative democracy. The existence of a dominant party raises, however, reservations about its democratic nature.[36] Singapore is, for these reasons, considered only a partly free system in the Freedom in the World Survey carried by Freedom House.[37] Despite this, its level of E-Government maturity is high and rising. The existence of E-Government services with high technical interactivity seems to be, therefore, independent of the citizens' political influence. It is, for this reason, doubtful that the evolution of technical interactivity in E-Government services is necessarily associated with citizen engagement in the political system.

Second, these results should not be automatically taken as meaning that E-Government services are being developed from the user's needs and expectations (i.e. from an external perspective). On the contrary, data suggests that technical interactivity is increasing faster than the citizen participation component in E-Government websites. UN's E-Participation index registered a compound annual growth rate, between 2003 and 2007, in EU 15, of –0.6 per cent (while technical interactivity growth reached 4.9) and, in EU 25, of –0.1 per cent (while technical interactivity registered 6.2). In both cases, growth in the E-Participation index was negative or near zero, contrasting with technical interactivity growth.

Data also suggests that services implying revenue or income generation (e.g. the State's extractive function) are placed online earlier and with more technical sophistication than services in other areas. Overall maturity for revenue services reached, according to Accenture's survey, an average of 70 per cent for all 22 countries included, while overall maturity including all services was 54 per cent.[38] Capgemini's results also show evidence of the same trend. In 2006, coverage and technical interactivity registered values in the 80–100 range for almost all income-generating services. In contrast, other services, like social security benefits, health-related services or environment-related permits, reach much lower values.[39]

This seems to be a sign that public administrations are more concerned with income generation than with direct citizen return. E-Government services are reaching universal service and getting more sophisticated, but mostly when income generation is at stake. Some data suggests this trend is not imperceptible to citizens. According to one survey, citizens expect more consequences in cost reduction and state efficiency than in government accountability from E-Government initiatives. In Accenture's 2004 survey, the results of a questionnaire to regular Internet users carried out in twelve countries[40] included a group of sentences with which the respondent could agree or disagree. Three of the propositions included in the questionnaire relate directly to E-Government consequences: 'e-government will save the economy money in the long term', 'e-government will make government departments and agencies more efficient' and 'e-government makes government more accountable to its citizens'.[41] While the first two sentences are related to the perceptions of the

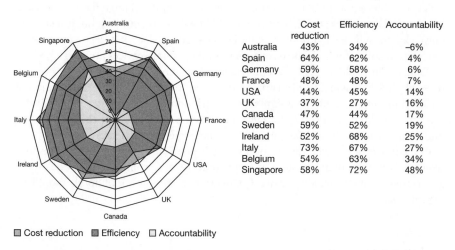

	Cost reduction	Efficiency	Accountability
Australia	43%	34%	–6%
Spain	64%	62%	4%
Germany	59%	58%	6%
France	48%	48%	7%
USA	44%	45%	14%
UK	37%	27%	16%
Canada	47%	44%	17%
Sweden	59%	52%	19%
Ireland	52%	68%	25%
Italy	73%	67%	27%
Belgium	54%	63%	34%
Singapore	58%	72%	48%

□ Cost reduction ■ Efficiency □ Accountability

Figure 4.3 Agreement with sentences related to E-Government services

Source: Adapted from Accenture (2004: 30–31) (see note 38).

Note: Values presented correspond to the difference between the total number of respondents agreeing with one statement and the total number of respondents disagreeing with the same statement. Values in the table are approximate since they were estimated from figures included in the original publication.

respondent about internal motivations for E-Government, the third can be considered as related to one kind of citizen return that can be expected from this process. Results suggest that citizens expect more relevant consequences in cost reduction and state efficiency than in government.

The percentage of people agreeing with any of the two first statements is higher, in all countries, than the percentage of people who agree with the third sentence. Respondents in all countries considered that the development of the E-Government would more probably lead to cost reduction or a more efficient administration than to more transparent government activity.

E-Government and government transformation

Technical interactivity in E-Government is not conceptually equivalent, it was argued, to citizen's political influence or citizen return. If one analyses regular surveys, there are also signs that, besides being different theoretical notions, technical interactivity does not necessarily result, in practice, in political influence or in citizen return. On the contrary, despite a transformist discourse since the adoption of E-Government policies in the mid-1990s, there are reasons to believe that growth in technical interactivity has predominantly served the internal interests of the public administration machine more than the citizen's needs and expectations. This seems to configure more a transition of government to electronic, or digital, form than a transformation or a revolution, as is sometimes argued in official discourse.

Government transformation is taking the place of E-Government in some documents[42] and is frequently seen as an updating of the concept.[43] It is necessary, in order to achieve government transformation, to culturally change the way services are conceived and developed. This process will be slow and gradual, but it seems the only way to achieve naturally qualitative change. It does not seem credible to introduce change dramatically or overnight in the way all services are developed.

Changes in evaluation also seem crucial. The introduction of citizen opinion research, just like qualitative research in the development process or the creation of satisfaction surveys, could be a significant contribution to the ongoing debate.[44] But this is not, in itself, a warranty for citizen return; research can also easily be turned into research about the satisfaction with technical interactivity features.

In a context of growing disaffection towards political agents and lack of responsiveness from the political system, it seems that the opportunity to introduce some government transformation, before E-Government reaches adulthood, should be regarded as valuable.

Key points

- The European Commission-accepted typology of E-Government (i.e. green paper) combines function (i.e. information, communication and transaction) and application areas (i.e. everyday life, tele-administration and political participation).

- Public policy for information society typology for E-Government has two dimensions: technical interactivity of services and political influence of citizens.
- Gartner's model of E-Government envisages four phases: presence (one-way); interaction (one-way); transaction (two-way); and transformation (two-way).
- While differences between Gartner's several phases refer to the technological capabilities, differences in constituency value are mainly cultural, not technological, so there are two independent dimensions to consider.
- Assumptions in the Gartner paradigm: *key driver for transformation is technology* – overlooking possible service transformation when transition to online use is in its infancy in primary socialization; *technical interactivity is equivalent to social interaction and to democracy*, but does not suffice as action is social and takes into account the behaviour of others; *citizen return, or constituency value, results from technical interactivity* – reduces citizen return to user convenience.
- A concept of government: E-Government service development based (internally) on the State v. service development based (externally) on the user.
- Four surveys on E-Government in the last decade (Accenture, Capgemini, CPP at Brown University and United Nations) reveal consistent growth in coverage and technical interactivity. But they do not necessarily imply an increase in citizens' political influence and cannot be taken as meaning that E-Government services are being developed from the (external) perspective of the user's needs and expectations; indeed, the contrary is evident.
- Technical interactivity in E-Government is not conceptually equivalent to citizen's political influence or citizen return.
- Government transformation is taking the place of E-Government in some discourse.

Notes

1 de Tocqueville, Alexis (2003) [1835 and 1840] *Democracy in America* and *Two Essays on America*. London: Penguin.
2 Brecht, Bertold (1983) [1930] 'Radio as a Means of Communication: A Talk on the Function of Radio', in Armand Mattelart and Seth Siegelaub, *Communication and Class Struggle. 2: Liberation, Socialism*. New York: International General.
3 Henderson, Hazel (1970) 'Computers: Hardware of Democracy', *Forum 70* 2/2, https://frontpage.auburn.edu/tann/hazel/forum.html (accessed 15 April 2008).
4 See Etzioni, Amitai (1971) 'Cable TV: Instant Shopping or Participatory Technology', *Social Policy* 2/4: 52–55; Smith, Ralph Lee (1972) *The Wired Nation – Cable TV: The Electronic Communications Highway*. New York: Harper & Row; Pool, Ithiel de Sola (ed.) (1973) *Talking Back: Citizen Feedback and Cable Technology*. Cambridge, MA and London: The MIT Press.
5 Denmark 1994, 1995, 1997; European Commission 1996, 1996a; Luxembourg 1996; Portugal 1997; France 1997, 1997a.

6   European Union [European Commission] (1998) *Public Sector Information: A Key Resource for Europe*. Green paper on public sector information in the Information Society, COM(98)585, Brussels: European Commission.

7   Aichholzer, Georg, Schmutzer, Rupert and Hochgerner, Josef (1998) *Bringing Public Administration Closer to the Citizens*. Background Paper to 'the Information Society, Bringing Administration Closer to the Citizens Conference', November 1998 (organised by the Centre for Social Innovation on behalf of the Information Society Forum/Work Group 5/Public Administration), Vienna, 12–13 November 1998, http://www.oeaw.ac.at/ita/ebene5/isbacc98.pdf (accessed 15 April 2008).

8   European Union [European Commission] (1998) op. cit. pp. 585–588.

9   Aichholzer, Georg, Schmutzer, Rupert and Hochgerner, Josef (1998) op. cit. p. 4.

10 Ibid. p. 3.

11 Ibid. p. 4; European Union [European Commission] (1998) op. cit. p. 585.

12 e.g. Baum, Christopher and Di Maio, Andrea (2000) *Gartner's Four Phases of E-Government Model*. Stamford, CT: Gartner; Baum, Christopher (2000) *The Four Phases of E-Government: Phase 2 – Interaction*. Stamford, CT: Gartner; Keller, Bill (2000) *Four Phases of E-Government: Phase 4 – Transformation*. Stamford, CT: Gartner; Kreizman, Gregg (2000) *The Four Phases of E-Government: Phase 3 – Transaction*. Stamford: Gartner.

13 Baum, Christopher and Di Maio, Andrea (2000) op. cit. pp. 3–4.

14 Ibid. p. 3.

15 e.g. Accenture (2000) 'Implementing E-Government – Rhetoric and Reality', *Insights*, Issue no. 2; Capgemini Ernst & Young (2001) *Web-based Survey on Electronic Public Services. Results of the First Measurement – October 2001*.

16 Except for United Nations (2003) *UN Global E-Government Survey 2003*. New York: UN Department of Economic and Social Affairs.

17 Proulx, Serge and Sénécal, Michel (1995) 'L'Interactivité technique, simulacre d'interaction sociale et de démocratie?', *Technologie de l'Information et Société* (TIS) 7/2, July: 239–255, p. 240.

18 Weber, Max (1997) *The Theory of Social and Economic Organisation*. New York: The Free Press, p. 88.

19 Schmitter, Philippe (2001) 'What is There to Legitimize in the European Union and How Might This be Accomplished?', Contribution to the Jean Monnet Working Paper No. 6/01, *Symposium: Mountain or Molehill? A Critical Appraisal of the Commission White Paper on Governance*, http://www.jeanmonnetprogram.org/papers/01/011401.rtf (accessed 15 April 2008), p. 4.

20 See, for an exception, Agar, Jon (2003) *The Government Machine: A Revolutionary History of the Computer*. Cambridge, MA: The MIT Press.

21 Bellamy, Christine and Taylor, John A. (1998) *Governing in the Information Age*. Maidenhead: Open University Press.

22 Ibid. p. 33.

23 In Denmark, this Department shared this role with the Communication and Tourism Department, in which the former assured the information technologies area and the latter the telecommunications.

24 As can be illustrated by a public officer affirmation in a research interview: 'as we well know, the main client for public agencies information services are other public agencies'.

25 Baum, Christopher, Di Maio, Andrea and Caldwell, French (2000) *What is E-Government? Gartner's Definitions*, Research Note TU-11-6474. Stamford, CT: Gartner.

26 Finland (2000) *Finland as an Information Society – The Report of the Information Society Advisory Board to the Government*. Helsinki: Ministry of Finance, p. 4.

27 European Union [European Commission] (2003) *The Role of E-Government for Europe's Future*. Communication from the Commission to the Council, the European Parliament, the European Economic and Social Committee and the Committee of the Regions, COM(2003)567 final, Brussels: European Commission, p. 4.

28 Several other surveys were published in this period. But, as far as I was able to identify, none of them kept a regular basis.

29 Accenture (2004) *E-Government Leadership: High Performance, Maximum Value*, The Government Executive Series, p. 107. http://www.accenture.com/NR/rdonlyres/D720 6199-C3D4-4CB4-A7D8-846C94287890/0/gove_egov_value.pdf.
30 Accenture (2005) *Leadership in Customer Service: New Expectations, New Experiences*, The Government Executive Series, p. 9. http://www.accenture.com/Global/Services/By_ Industry/Government_and_Public_Service/LeadershipExperiences.htm.
31 Until 2004, the institution carried the designation Capgemini Ernst & Young (CGE&Y), due to the acquisition of the consultancy business of Ernst & Young by Capgemini, in 2000. Its designation changed, however, to Capgemini in 2005.
32 Iceland, Norway and Switzerland are also in the survey. In Switzerland's case, since the second measurement, in 2002 (Capgemini Ernst & Young, 2002: 3).
33 United Nations and American Society for Public Administration. (2002) *Benchmarking E-Government: A Global Perspective – Assessing the Progress of the UN Member States*. New York: UN Division for Public Economics and Public Administration and American Society for Public Administration.
34 In the 2002 edition the human capital index also included data from Transparency International (www.trasparency.org) and Freedomhouse International (www.freedom house.org) annual surveys. Since 2003 the index has only included UN data.
35 Accenture (2006) *Leadership in Customer Service: Building the Trust*, http://www.accenture. com/Global/Services/By_Industry/Government_and_Public_Service/PS_Global/R_ and_I/BuildingtheTrustES.htm
36 See, for this issue, Grace: 'Singapore has a functioning democratic system in which voters are freely able to elect their preferred representatives. However, tight government control of the electoral process, combined with other tactics designed to harass opposition parties, results in these elections being less than free and fair.' http://aceproject.org/ace-en/ topics/bd/bdy/bdy_sg.
37 www.freedomhouse.com.
38 Accenture (2004) *e-government Leadership: High Performance, Maximum Value*, The Government Executive Series. http://www.accenture.com/NR/rdonlyres/D7206199-C3D4-4CB4- A7D8-846C94287890/0/gove_egov_value.pdf
39 Capgemini (2006) *Online Availability of Public Services: How Is Europe Progressing?* Web Based Survey on Electronic Public Services. Report of the 6th Measurement – June 2006.
40 Australia, Belgium, Canada, France, Germany, Ireland, Italy, Singapore, Spain, Sweden, United Kingdom and the United States. Fieldwork was performed, in all countries, between 5 and 23 January 2004. Regular Internet use was defined as weekly access at least (Accenture 2004: 108). There were 600 interviews by telephone, selected by RRD (Random Digit Dialing), in the United States, and a sample of 400 in the remaining countries.
41 Accenture (2004) op. cit. pp. 30–31.
42 e.g. United Kingdom (2005) *Transformational Government – Enabled by Technology*, London: Cabinet Office.
43 Di Maio, Andrea (2006) *What Does Technology Mean to Government Transformation?* Stamford, CT: Gartner.
44 As recently annouced, for instance, by the Information Society and Media Directorate-General of the European Commission. See http://www.epractice.eu/document/4433 (accessed 15 April 2008).

Further reading

Agar, Jon (2003) *The Government Machine: A Revolutionary History of the Computer*. Cambridge, MA: The MIT Press.
Chadwick, Andrew (2006) 'E-Government', in *Internet Politics: States, Citizens, and New Communication Technologies*. New York: Oxford University Press.
Schmitter, Philippe and Alexander Trechsel (Coord.) (2004) *The Future of Democracy in Europe – Trends, Analyses and Reforms. A Green Paper for the Council of Europe*. Strasbourg: Council of Europe.

5 E-Government, customers and citizens[1]

Michael Margolis and Gerson Moreno-Riaño

Summary

Democracy today has become an ideal that practically everyone claims to embrace. Differing versions of the democracy notwithstanding, governments tend to use representative democracy as a way to realise popular government. In order to decide whether to retain or replace their representatives, therefore, citizens need information about the impact of governmental policies on people like themselves and also about the government's future policy priorities. The Internet represents one solution to this problem. Citizens can use it to acquire information about public policy, not only from the established interests and media of their own nation, but also from less familiar sources. Civic life, of course, extends beyond matters of governmental policy. Citizens interact with one another over a variety of matters, most of which have no direct connection to governance. Indeed, one thing that political scientists can say with confidence is that most people don't know and don't care very much about questions of public policy. Despite the Internet's facilitation of citizen participation in determining policy, few are willing and able to commit the time and effort required to assume the responsibilities that direct democracy requires. This has led theorists to extend the idea of democratic responsiveness to the administration of governmental policies. Citizens are not only franchise holders who ultimately exercise political power, but also the government's clients and customers. The idea of citizen as client or customer, combined with burgeoning worldwide access to the Internet via new ICTs, has led theorists and practitioners to advocate E-Government as the modern form of representative democracy.

Advocates of E-Government see the Internet as a way to modernise the public sector and democratise the relationship between citizens and their government in much the same manner as the Internet has brought dramatic improvements to E-Commerce. Critics of E-Government, however, suggest that this new or representative democracy model tends to ignore a critical question: Should governments employ new ICTs to encourage citizens to deliberate and determine which policies and services government *should* provide? Using ICTs to encourage greater deliberation is not the same as demanding that citizens decide policy by means of direct democracy. Nevertheless, if citizens of a democracy exercise the ultimate authority to choose and to dismiss those who decide the great political issues, shouldn't their role in governance be more than that of customer? Customers, after all, are largely concerned with transactions that satisfy their personal private demands and those of persons or groups they hold dear. They generally do not raise questions about how their private transactions might help or hinder the resolving of broader problems that affect the quality of life – perhaps even the survival – of society as a whole.

Introduction

Democracy today has become an ideal that practically everyone claims to embrace. Where dictionaries generally define 'democracy' as government by the people, exercised directly or through elected public officials, most people and most public officials invoke democracy to represent whatever they consider good or desirable for a modern secular society. It's nearly impossible to find a nation whose government boasts of institutions that eschew democracy. Indeed, nations love democracy so much that they perform extraordinary deeds to protect their versions of it. For example, China suppresses Tibetans who oppose the constitutionally prescribed democratic and socialist reforms that develop and unify the autonomous Tibet region with the motherland. The USA topples an Iraqi tyrant who was said to underwrite and train radical Islamists bent on destroying democracy through terrorist attacks upon the American homeland and upon America's allies and interests. Singapore bankrupts or locks away citizens who criticise the ruling party's policies or actions as overstepping its constitutionally defined powers as a parliamentary democracy.

In spite of this almost universal agreement about the good of democracy, the practical upshot of the concept seems to elude us. As John Dunn reminds us in his book *Democracy: The Unfinished Journey*, the 'old but vigorous idea' that 'ordinary people . . . and not extra-ordinary people' should rule is 'devastatingly obvious, but also tantalizingly strange and implausible'.[2] Dunn notes that such an idea 'is not a very plausible description of how things are in the world in which we live' though it is the 'reigning conception . . . of how they ought to be'.[3] This disjuncture between democratic practice and democratic theory has facilitated a large body of scholarly work that seeks to understand as well as remedy the gap between our democratic ideals and realities. Regardless of the different projects advanced, most scholars in what may be called the 'democracy improvement project' agree that a common element in the solution to this gap must encompass more substantive citizen involvement in democratic policy and decision making. Obviously, the call for a more robust democratic citizenship raises a number of related questions.[4] But if Dunn is correct that defining democracy as the rules of 'ordinary people' is 'obvious' but 'implausible', then a more robust political engagement of the 'ordinary' is the sine qua non of twenty-first-century democracy.

In this chapter, we consider the obstacles to a more robust political engagement for today's democratic citizens despite the rapid advances of ICTs that pervade the political landscape. Since Benjamin Barber's *Strong Democracy*[5] and Robert Dahl's *Democracy and Its Critics*,[6] there have been growing expectations that rapidly changing communication technologies would revolutionise political participation in democratic societies. The Internet was hailed as one of these technologies, perhaps *the* technology to rescue democracy from flagging citizen participation, elitism and poor information pools, thus embodying the calls for more reasoned discourse as outlined by such deliberative democrats as James Fishkin, Amy Gutmann, Dennis Thompson and Cass

Sunstein.[7] Even though the Internet has had political ramifications, the scholarly consensus is that it falls far short of meeting these expectations.[8] A number of factors account for this gap between E-Democratic theory and its practice. We focus upon three in particular. First, the use of the Internet in democratic politics has fostered the model of the citizen as consumer or client in contradistinction to that of the citizen as policy-making participant. Democratic governments increasingly use the Internet in a market-based E-Commerce sense, thereby reducing the functions of democratic citizens to those of consumers of governmental services. Second, and equally troublesome, are the rapid changes in communication styles and the increasing degradation of communicative content. The new communication dynamics foster a climate of rhetoric, demagoguery and pre-packaged information that socialises citizens into passive and unthinking receptors of political data. Third, is whether or not electronic democracy is sustainable given the global economic struggle of everyday citizens to maintain basic standards of living, a struggle that has prevented many from participating in traditional 'bricks and mortar' democracy. Given the destructive effects of these obstacles upon traditional and electronic versions of democracy, we consider whether governments should utilise ICT features mainly to implement policies expeditiously and provide services efficiently (citizens as customers) or whether governments should utilise them mainly to encourage citizens to deliberate and determine which policies and services governments should provide (citizens as democratic participants).

Even though the latter appears preferable at first sight, we must recall Dunn's caveats concerning the disjuncture between democratic theory and democratic practice. Indeed, one thing that political scientists can say with confidence is that most people do not know and do not care very much about questions of public policy. Except when a political problem obviously impinges upon their day-to-day lives, ordinary citizens are more concerned about pursuing personal, family or group interests than about participating directly in public policy-making. Despite the Internet's facilitation of citizen participation in determining policy, few are willing and able to commit the time and effort required to assume the participatory responsibilities that substantive deliberation requires.

In what follows, we first consider the phenomenon of the citizen as consumer. In doing so, we discuss two dominant theories of democracy – deliberative and aggregative democracy – and the corresponding citizen models these advance. We argue that aggregative democracy is the most common form of democratic governance and suggest that its brand of market-style politics has fostered a political consumerism that is part of a larger cultural shift towards a society of consumers. This shift is also replicated within most examples of E-Government and democracy where E-Citizens are primarily conceptualised as consumers seeking information and purchasing products and services. Thereafter, we consider the persistent inequalities within and among societies that keep citizens focused on the daily struggle of living with little time for political engagement. We call attention to the elitist nature of the global economy and the manufacturing of wants and needs rather than the creation of markets to satisfy needs. We argue that free trade and the fluid movement of capital tends to enslave a relatively sedentary labour force to broader forces of production and consumption, and to perpetuate groups of people that live only to work. Lastly, we consider the rapid transformation of communication styles and outlets. The convergence of print and electronic technologies, along with the consumer nature of contemporary politics, leads to more pre-packaged soundbites and the degradation of substance from political information. We conclude the chapter with some observations and suggestions for future action.

Theories of democracy, consumerism and E-Government

Just what embodies a more robust political engagement of the citizenry is a contentious question. Different 'on the ground' versions of democracy notwithstanding, however, governments tend to use similar procedures to realise democracy. Except for the smallest units of government, direct democracy gives way to various forms of representative democracy. Ordinary citizens express their choices by electing representatives who govern directly or who go through additional steps to select those who govern. The governors are responsible to the people through formal mechanisms, such as constitutionally defined powers, limited terms of office, periodic elections and legislative or judicial oversight. In spite of its popularity, it would seem that a more robust political engagement would necessitate the rejection of the form of representative democracy that Amy Gutmann and Dennis Thompson call 'aggregative democracy'.[9] Simply defined, aggregative democracy uses expressed individual political preferences as the raw material for democratic policy-making and decision making, regardless of their merit or justification. In its most popular form, aggregative democracy is majoritarian in nature and is usually mediated through representatives.[10] While this form of democracy is widely practised, such extensive use should not cloud its deficiencies. At its most basic level, aggregative democracy operationalises the political engagement of citizens as the summed expression of atomised political preferences through periodic elections and opinion polls. As Gutmann and Thompson suggest, this process bears an uncanny resemblance to a consumer market of buyers, sellers, products and advertisements. We return to this notion of democracy and consumerism later. But for now, it is instructive to note that aggregative democracy is minimalist in nature, requiring only a modicum of citizen engagement.

Beyond a rejection of simple aggregative democracy, no clear scholarly consensus exists regarding what constitutes a robust political engagement for democratic citizens. The scholarly literature most commonly proposes more citizen participation, but the character of this participation is at times chimerical. For example, Kevin O'Leary argues that better participation means more effective and substantive representation.[11] O'Leary proposes that such representation entails the rejection of the current American constitutional order and the creation of 435 discursive and advisory assemblies of 100 people each to work with Congress, as well as a People's House, of 100 delegates from each congressional district, which could vote on bills passed by Congress and initiate legislation in Congress. Others, such as Nancy Love, contend that no conception of democracy takes into account the mystical and metaphysical dimension of human life, and therefore none can accurately communicate our deepest longings. It follows that all versions of democracy must be rejected for a more 'agonist' or 'musical' one.[12] Even though these imaginative proposals are unrealistic, they are united in their belief that truer participation requires more effective discourse and deliberation. Indeed, it is this theme of discourse and deliberation that embodies the more sophisticated calls for a participatory democracy that realises a government of the people – namely, deliberative democracy.[13]

In the contemporary era, Jürgen Habermas has done more than any other theorist to connect the notion of deliberation with democratic government. Habermas's theory of communicative rationality suggests that democratic legitimacy arises out of a communicative inclusiveness and rationalisation of all of the 'lifeworlds' within modern society. For Habermas, communicative rationality does not provide normative direction for actors. It is not an 'immediate source of prescriptions'.[14] Rather, it provides a communicative structure that is widely inclusive and enables actors to reach consensus through the provision of acceptable justifications for one's moral claims. This structure facilitates social discourses from which 'the matrix' of 'democratic authority emerges.' As Habermas argues,

> From this perspective, the forms of communication that confer legitimacy on political will-formation, legislation, and the administration of justice appear as part of a more encompassing process in which the lifeworlds of modern societies are rationalized under the pressure of systemic imperatives.[15]

Habermas's theory of communicative rationality is reminiscent of the ancient legal principle *quod omnes tangit debet ab omnibus approbari* (what touches all should be approved by all) and is firmly rooted not only in the principle of popular sovereignty, but in the collective judgment of citizens.[16] For Habermas, democratic policy-making and decision making must arise out of an inclusive process of deliberation that is democratic at heart.

This notion of deliberation is obviously at the core of deliberative democracy. Deliberative democracy, as Gutmann and Thompson suggest, 'affirms the need to justify decisions made by citizens and their representatives'.[17] It is

> [a] form of government in which free and equal citizens (and their representatives), justify decisions in a process in which they give one another reasons that are mutually acceptable and generally accessible, with the aim of reaching conclusions that are binding in the present on all citizens but open to challenge in the future.[18]

Deliberative democracy acknowledges three important facts of civic life. First, co-operation is essential for humans to flourish. Human beings need the contributions of others to realise a variety of human goods. Second, deliberative democracy engages the fact that moral disagreement is an intrinsic part of human life. Reasonable people often have good reasons for disagreeing with each other – reasons that ought to be considered and discussed, not merely glossed over. Third, deliberative democracy emphasises the importance of open flows of information for sound governance. If legitimate government is based on a high degree of deliberation and consensus, then information is essential for civil and political discourse. Deliberative democracy, then, is a co-operative process of collective decision making that is dynamic, inclusive, information-based and, as some argue, vital for invigorating the waning democracies of the twenty-first century.[19]

The suggestion that deliberation is essential for democratic government and citizenship is not new. Since ancient Athens, deliberation among rulers and the ruled has been considered as central to politics in general and to democracy in particular. Substantive deliberation fosters a spirit of co-operation, tolerance and mutual respect, strengthening social and political bonds. The strength of a democratic society depends upon the quality of social trust and co-operation exhibited in the deliberative practices of its citizens. If democratic citizenship, as some scholars have argued, is the 'aptitude of ordinary people to take part in political life and to exert influence upon it',[20] then deliberative democracy seems to be one of the strongest candidates for the robust political engagement of ordinary citizens.

In spite of the strong argument for the importance of discursive co-operation, contemporary democratic politics is far removed from substantive deliberation. As Gutmann and Thompson argue, the aggregative model of democracy is most popular.[21] In a telling analogy, Gutmann and Thompson argue that the electoral process in aggregative democracies resembles the market. In such democracies,

> [p]oliticians and parties, [like producers], formulate their positions and devise their strategies in response to the demands of voters who, like consumers, express their preferences by choosing among competing products (the candidates and their parties). Whatever debate takes place in the campaign serves a function more like that of advertising (informing the voters about the comparative advantages of the candidates) than like that of argument (seeking to change minds by giving reasons).[22]

Aggregative democracy, by its very nature, furthers a non-deliberative spirit and a weak democratic citizenship. It enshrines a democratic politics where citizens are socialised as political consumers. In such market-style politics, information and deliberation are also important, but for different reasons. Whereas in a deliberative democracy open information and discourse are essential pieces of collective judgement and do not presuppose any normative closure, in aggregative politics they are centrally pre-fabricated and designed to elicit wide acceptance and rapid closure.[23] Transforming citizens into consumers is part of a larger cultural shift from a market economy to a market society. This shift nurtures a perilous propensity to reduce civil society's human goods and desires to simple economic goods and desires.[24]

The commodification of everything, or what Jürgen Habermas has termed 'the colonisation of the lifeworld', is the rapid and seemingly unending transition from a market economy to a market society.[25] In such a scenario, 'the market and its categories of thought . . . dominate ever more areas of our lives', areas such as 'our most intimate relationships . . . [and] our understanding of what it means to be human'.[26] In a similar vein, Zygmunt Bauman has called our current era a 'society of consumers', by which he means a 'society that "interpellates" its members primarily . . . as consumers; and a society that judges and evaluates its members mostly by their consumption-related capacities and products'.[27] Such a phenomenon, he argues, leads to the perception and treatment of virtually all the parts of the social setting and of the actions they evoke . . . by the 'consumerist syndrome' of cognitive and evaluating predispositions. 'Life politics,' containing Politics with a capital 'P' as much as the nature of interpersonal relations, tends to be reshaped in the likeness of the means and objects of consumption and along the lines implied by the *consumerist syndrome*. [italics original][28]

Call them what you will: 'the commodification of everything', 'the colonisation of the lifeworld' and 'the society of consumers' all transmogrify political life into a state of affairs where 'citizens are consumers, and politics are economics by other means'.[29]

The citizen as consumer syndrome represents a broader cultural shift towards a market society. Such a society and its accompanying politics are antagonistic to the classical democratic view of citizenship and politics: the citizen as policy-making participant. In short, the market society is antithetical to the deliberative conception of democracy that we previously described. But as things stand, the citizen as consumer currently characterises democratic politics due as much to the dynamics of a market society as to the habits of an aggregative democracy. The question we now consider is the extent to which this same tendency has been replicated in the practice of E-Government and E-Democracy.

The practice of E-Government and E-Democracy

Giovanni Sartori's notion of 'confused democracy' is as applicable to conceptions of E-Government and E-Democracy as it is to brick and mortar democratic theories and practices. The confusion surrounding the meaning of E-Government and E-Democracy and their brick and mortar versions stems from the dynamism of digital ICTs and the shortsightedness of their advocates. As Bekkers has suggested,

> E-government is a policy and managerial concept with minimal theoretical foundation but supported by a large amount of empirical research focused on the effects of ICT on the functioning of public administration. Due to this nebulous variety of practices, the concept of e-government is ill defined and based on pragmatic experiences and visions.[30]

As we argue below, a broad conception of E-Government largely dominated by an E-Commerce model has encapsulated considerations of E-Democracy. Attempts to define E-Democracy apart from E-Government do not fare any better. While most of these focus upon broader political participation, the definitions are extremely vague. Consider, for example, the understanding of E-Democracy advanced by the UK Hansard Society, which has an important E-Democracy research centre. In 2003, the Society provided a clear definition of E-Democracy as the 'efforts to broaden political participation by enabling citizens to connect with one another and with their representatives via new information and communication technologies'.[31] More recently, the Hansard Society has suggested that E-Democracy is

> more likely to be many small, independent projects, each engaging a handful of people on focused, topical issues. Technology is matched to the nature of the issue

and local forums emerge so that people can think things out and get to know each other offline as well as online . . . This is long tail democracy in action; hundreds, even thousands, of micro-projects, issued based, choosing the right technology. They're temporal; projects come and go. Growth is viral, dynamic, evolutionary and sites have a natural, short lifecycle – mayfly not tortoise. People have multiple and varied roles in many campaigns or consultations and so it doesn't just become noise, all of this is aggregated and listened to where it counts.[32]

Whereas the former definition is theoretical and the latter is more representative of politics on the ground, there are few differences between how the two are operationalised. While both definitions contain deliberation, in the end decisions will result from the aggregative character of modern democracy. Such ambiguity has perhaps led scholars to argue that the term 'information government' best encapsulates 'the significant changes of governing and governance that occur in part facilitated by new technologies'.[33] Information government, 'the flows of information within government as well as between government and citizens',[34] encompasses most accounts of E-Government and E-Democracy. Considerations of E-Democracy are usually couched within the broadest definitions of E-Government. Such definitions consider the provisions of online services to citizen-consumers, the increased efficiency, automation and storage of information within public agencies and the incorporation of more democratic processes in the policy-making process. Narrow conceptions of E-Government or information government focus solely on the provision of online services to citizen-consumers.[35] Broader understandings of E-Government include this transactional account as well as considerations for a more efficient and automated public sector where 'the Internet [is used] as an instrument to improve government structures and processes and to foster the culture and values of public administrations'.[36] The broadest accounts of E-Government add the implementation of some forms of democratic processes to encourage more robust political participation.[37] Just as all versions of E-Government can be conceptualised through the lens of information flows, so too can they be conceptualised in terms of the syndrome of citizen as consumer rather than the citizen as policy-making participant. To put it differently, we argue that for the foreseeable future, E-Government in its broadest sense will further the citizen-consumer model of democratic politics – in its aggregative sense as well as in its online services provision model – rather than the citizen as an active policy-making co-producer.

The continuance of the syndrome of citizen as consumer is as much due to the commodification of politics as it is to the fact that the main theoretical model on which to build E-Government has been that of E-Commerce. E-Government has been seen as a natural outgrowth of the use of computers, the Internet and other ICTs to conduct business transactions. In its most generic sense, the definition of E-Commerce is readily applicable to any E-Activity, including politics. As some scholars suggest, E-Commerce is 'a technology-mediated exchange between parties (individuals or organisations) as well as the electronically based intra- or inter-organisational activities that facilitate such exchanges'.[38] If one considers E-Commerce from a number of different perspectives (e.g. those of communications, commerce, business, service, learning, collaboration and community), one finds a great deal of similarity and overlap between electronic commerce and E-Government. As Turban *et al.* suggest, electronic commerce within any perspective is about the buying, selling, exchanging and distributing of goods, services and related information over computer networks or by other electronic means.[39] This implies automated business processes, efficiency and effectiveness, quality measures for products and services and inter- and intra-organisational collaboration and communication.

In many ways, E-Government is a replication of E-Commerce practices and procedures extended to government–citizen interactions. The assumptions are in many ways the same; online transactions are about goods and services within businesses (government agencies), between businesses (agency to agency) and between businesses and consumers (government agencies and citizens). This replication of assumptions and procedures between E-Commerce and E-Government is evidenced in some of the latest E-Democracy scholarship. Berthon and Williams,[40] for example, propose a re-conceptualisation of E-Democracy based upon the rapid changes in electronic business and marketing practices (e.g. Linux and open-source software) that are affecting the interaction between producers and consumers. The authors suggest that political consumers (i.e. citizens) should be re-conceptualised as coducers (i.e. co-producers) and no longer simply as consumers. Regardless of their analyses and suggestions, many scholars continue to consider E-Government, broadly understood, through the categories of commercial society.

Beyond the commodification of politics and the prevalence of E-Commerce practices within E-Government, the syndrome of citizen as consumer has also been furthered by a lack of citizen interest in and concern for politics and policy. Even in aggregative democracies, citizens need information about the impact of governmental policies and service on people like themselves, as well as information about the government's policy priorities for the future. They can acquire first-hand information about the former from personal experience and they can get additional information from trusted friends, neighbours, relatives and co-workers. But for most information about policy priorities they must rely upon what established political parties, interest groups, government officials and familiar candidates provide to them, often via the mass media. The Internet represents a prospective solution to this problem since it increases the avenues and flows of information citizens can acquire. Such information flows come not only from the established interests and media of their own nation, but also from less familiar (foreign and domestic) sources, including upstart, independent and dissenting political parties, candidates, bloggers, interests and publications as well as a broader range of established organisations and media. As each user can function as both a receiver and an originator of information, the Internet makes it feasible for new political agendas to emerge through interaction among users and for virtual communities to arise among those who share these agendas, as well as for political entrepreneurs to transform these virtual communities into real world political organisations.

Civic life, of course, extends beyond matters of governmental policy. Citizens interact with one another over a variety of matters, most of which have no direct connection to governance. As we previously observed, ordinary citizens are more concerned about pursuing personal, family or group interests than about participating directly in public policy-making, except when a political problem obviously impinges upon their day-to-day lives. Thomas and Streib,[41] for example, show that more individuals use the Internet to seek information about government than to communicate with government. More disconcerting is the finding that traditional socio-economic patterns of political participation are replicated on the Internet – a situation that portends the emergence of elite E-Citizens who are more engaged and more powerful than their ordinary compatriots. A parallel finding leads Hindman to argue that open-source politics has 'quickly produced its own set of political elites':[42]

> A small number of people on a small number of projects thus wield a hugely disproportionate influence in open-source software – and similar patterns can be seen in the most widely cited examples of open-source politics.[43]

It appears that representative institutions remain viable means of achieving a minimalist democratic rule even when a large political digital divide exists along with technical possibilities for online communities and information acquisition. Even if we could entice millions of citizens to research, debate and vote on public policies via networked devices, where is the (theoretical or empirical) evidence that they actually would improve democratic governance?

This is not to say that employing new ICTs should have no significant effect on governance. Citizens in a democracy are both rulers and subjects. As rulers they hold the ultimate authority to choose and to dismiss those who decide great political issues of the day. Simultaneously, they have obligations to the authority they wield collectively (i.e. the legitimate rule of the officials they have chosen). Governments enforce laws and implement public policies. Democratic citizens should expect their government to be responsive to them in their everyday transactions with it. Considerations such as these have led theorists to extend the idea of democratic responsiveness to the administration of governmental policies. Citizens are not only franchise holders who ultimately exercise political power; citizens are also are the government's clients and customers. As has been suggested, the idea of citizen as client or customer, combined with burgeoning worldwide access to the Internet via new ICTs, has led theorists and practitioners to advocate E-Government as the modern form of representative democracy.

Advocates of E-Government, basically defined as the provision of governmental information and services online, see the Internet as a way to modernise the public sector and democratise the relationship between individual citizens and their government[44] in much the same manner as the Internet has brought dramatic improvements to E-Commerce. Information can be accessed and services can be delivered at the convenience of the citizen – no more having to visit a government office, no more trying to reach a bureaucrat by telephone, no more waiting for forms to arrive in the mail. E-Governments will realise modern representative democracy by employing ICT features to implement policies expeditiously and to provide services efficiently. With transparent organisation and user-friendly programming, elected officials and bureaucrats can employ ICTs to exchange relevant information with their peers, as well as with their citizen clientele, individually or in groups. As a bonus, these exchanges should increase efficiency by reducing duplication of records and services among governmental agencies and by giving administrators better feedback from citizens regarding the effectiveness of the policies and services they provide.

Critics of E-Government, however, suggest that this bureaucratic E-Democracy model tends to dodge a critical question: To what extent ought democracies to encourage their citizens to employ new ICTs to deliberate and determine which policies and services governments *should* provide? Using ICTs to encourage greater deliberation that leads to citizens deciding policies would be the very embodiment of a more robust political engagement. If citizens of a democracy are supposed to exercise the ultimate authority to choose and to dismiss those who decide the great political issues, shouldn't their role in governance be more than that of customer? Customers, after all, are largely concerned with transactions that satisfy their personal private demands and those of persons or groups they hold dear. They generally do not raise questions about how their private transactions might help or hinder the resolving of broader problems that affect the quality of life – perhaps even the survival – of the society as a whole.[45]

Obstacles to achieving Internet-based deliberative democracy

In addition to discussing the commodification of politics, citizens' reluctance to devote the time and energy required for serious deliberation of governmental policy as well as business, civic and political leaders' penchant to have E-Government's procedures imitate E-Commerce's models of efficient customer service, we have alluded to other socio-political, economic and technological factors that hinder taking advantage of Internet-based ICTs to improve democratic political participation. Among these are the digital divide within and among nations, international corporations' growing domination of the global economy, the manufacture of artificial material wants and needs, the denigration of public goods, the privatisation and consolidation of Internet-based ICTs and the fragmentation of traditional communities as audiences migrate from print to electronic media. Although a full discussion of all these factors is beyond the scope of this chapter, we shall explain how they impede efforts to achieve realistic increases in deliberative democratic participation.

For a problem that could not have existed before popular usage of the Internet ballooned in the mid- to late 1990s, the digital divide within and among nations has received enormous attention.[46] As the phrase suggests, citizens of more affluent and technologically advanced nations have far more opportunities to access the Internet than their counterparts who live in poorer, less technologically advanced nations. Most members of the European Union and the Organisation for Economic Co-operation and Development (OECD) have much higher rates of exposure to and usage of the Internet. The entire continent of Africa has approximately 14 per cent of the world's population, but as of December 2007 (Nigerian-based business solicitations notwithstanding) fewer than 5 per cent of its people could access the Internet, and their usage represented less than 3.5 per cent of world traffic. Asia and the Middle East are similarly – though less drastically – underrepresented. Canada and the USA are particularly overrepresented, having 5 per cent of the world population but accounting for 18 per cent of the world's usage.

If you have access to the Internet, it is best to be fluent in English, Chinese or Spanish. Respectively, these languages account for approximately 30, 15 and 9 per cent of all users. Add Japanese, French, German, Portuguese, Arabic, Korean and Italian (between 7 and 3 per cent in descending order), and you have nearly 85 per cent of the world's users. While English users still predominate, Arabic, Portuguese, Chinese, French and Spanish speakers are growing at better than twice the rate of English speakers.[47]

Even though the distribution of Internet users who speak each major language is becoming more representative of the distribution of these speakers in the real world, global Internet access remains a rather meagre 20 per cent. Moreover, a digital divide is manifest within nations: more affluent citizens not only have more widespread access than their less well off compatriots, but they are also more likely to enjoy better-quality high-speed access. In capitalistic nations this latter inequality is exacerbated by international corporations' progressive domination of access to the Internet and ownership of its routers. While public funds largely underwrote the Internet's initial development, its operations have largely been privatised. Most users view the Internet as a publicly accessible resource which, like the telephone, is open to all as a common carrier. The business models of private companies, however, are generally designed to create profits rather than to provide service to those who have little to spend. Among other things, profits are made through selling Internet access with differing tariffs for various speeds of transmission between the users' devices and Internet service providers (ISPs), charges for transmitting data between ISPs and fees involving advertising, user responses and sales. Additional profits arise from fees for use of intellectual property, such as copyrighted material or proprietary rather than open-source software. Increasingly, those who own and operate most of the Internet's routers are seeking ways to charge for prioritising messages instead of treating all packets of information alike.[48]

If the corporate owners succeed in changing priorities of messages that move between routers, they would abandon the common carrier notion of 'net neutrality'.[49] If this were to occur, the future Internet would be drastically different than its creators envisioned. As Goldsmith and Wu[50] have suggested, the Internet was designed upon an open, minimalist and neutral framework. As the authors argue, such a design was unprecedented because

> it was willing to accept almost any kind of computer or network to join in one universal network-of-networks . . . it required very little of the computers that wanted to join . . . [and] treated e-mail, downloads, and every other type of early application the same. This allowed new and better applications . . . to evolve and replace the old.[51]

Network neutrality has become a highly contentious issue in the US and the EU. While the matter remains unsettled, it seems likely some sort of neutrally tiered system in which owner-operators promise not to discriminate against users regarding content or devices used to assemble information will be adopted. Critics suggest that if the past is any indicator, businesses will use their privileged relationships with governments to expand their control over content and to favour messages of allies and supporters over those of competitors and dissenters.[52]

The growing commercialisation of the Internet exemplifies what we have discussed as the commodification of everything. It inevitably involves the denigration of public goods because they do not fit into business models. Moreover, critics like Benjamin Barber see the Internet's commercialisation as contributing to both the manufacture of artificial wants and needs and the infantilisation of the citizenry:

> Digitalization encourages and facilitates both speed and nonlinearity, the latter a kind of artificial rupture in temporalities in which our 'normal' linear experience of time is deconstructed into nonsequential fragments. Ruptures in temporality may catalyze art and creative innovation . . . but are corrupting to normal consciousness and to responsible and predictable behavior of the kind traditionally associated with mature adulthood.[53]

Slow is replaced by fast; books and newspapers are replaced by videos; complex is replaced by simple. If a problem cannot be solved quickly, it is hardly worth pondering. There are close to 100 million websites online. One might expect not only a fragmentation of audiences but also a great variety of paths those audiences would take to diverse websites of interest. If one runs through Alexa.com's most trafficked websites of OECD nations, however, there is a surprising commonality among the top 25. Familiar names like Google, Yahoo, YouTube, eBay, MySpace, Facebook, Flickr, Friendster, Wikipedia, Msn.com, blogger.com and Youporn.com repeatedly appear. There are relatively few news media sites and few, if any, governmental ones.[54] In sum, the obstacles to realising the Internet's potential to encourage more enlightened citizen participation in deliberative democratic politics are formidable. In our concluding section we offer no solutions for overcoming these obstacles, but we do have some observations and suggestions that may bear fruit over the long term.

Concluding thoughts on deliberative democracy

Give a child a hammer and s/he will find an amazing number of things that need hammering. As political scientists who teach and do research, we face the danger of falling back on the traditional recommendation of providing our students with more and better education for citizenship. We would love to see a global commons, where citizens deliberate questions of world social and economic policy using relevant information gleaned from the Internet. Our modest hope, however, is that we, as educators and researchers, will utilise Internet-based ICTs to learn to change ourselves even as we work to educate our students and perhaps the general public at large. Most faculty are what Marc Prensky (and others) have called 'digital immigrants', while most of our students are 'digital natives'. In contrast to Barber, Prensky argues that educators should accept the fast-paced, non-linear world of short attention spans that digital natives share. A gaming specialist, he hammers away at building video games from which students (and others) can gain information – perhaps even wisdom – through play. He argues that psychological research provides some support for the proposition that using logical linear lesson plans tends to retard rather than help digital natives to learn.[55]

Our suggestions for change are not as radical as Prensky's suggestions. We believe that new ICTs must be incorporated into our teaching methods if we are to communicate effectively not only with our students, but with increasing portions of the public at large. We place our hopes on new programmes that use ICTs to illustrate and enhance the knowledge we intend to impart and the values we intend to encourage. Questions of citizens' roles in achieving just, orderly and democratic societies have been around for a long time because they are difficult to answer and because events beyond a society's control may require those roles to change.

We need to adopt two strategies that lessen the likelihood that the Internet's content and its ICTs can quickly degrade the information contained in any book or article's tables, figures and exhibits. First, this means establishing conceptual themes that lend a logical order or context to any data or arguments we present. (It also means teaching logic early in a curriculum.) Previously introduced concepts help readers to place new developments into a broader picture. Second, we need to develop companion websites, where students and others will find not only updated material for each section of our syllabi, but also PowerPoint presentations, videos, blogs and links to other online sources. We need to realise a convergence of print and electronic technologies, possibly making this convergence the norm for scholarly publication. Indeed, the skills required for multimedia publication (e.g. writing, audio, video, graphics, animation, etc.) are becoming increasingly common as core courses in the arts and sciences and as concentrations in interdisciplinary degree programs, often under the rubric of informatics.

If deliberative democracy is to survive, let alone improve, citizens need to appreciate Max Weber's maxim that 'politics is a slow boring of hard boards'.[56] Solving political problems by rational democratic means takes time, patience and effort. Instantaneous solutions grabbed from the Internet via ICTs are unlikely to succeed.

Key points

- Even though the Internet has had political ramifications, the scholarly consensus is that it falls far short of meeting these expectations.
- There is a gap between E-Democratic theory and practice. The use of the Internet in democratic politics has fostered the model of the citizen as consumer or client rather than policy-making participant. Changes in communication styles are rapid and degradation of communicative content is increasing.
- The syndrome of citizen as consumer exists in the context of two dominant theories of democracy: deliberative and aggregative.
- Obstacles to a more robust political engagement for today's democratic citizens despite the rapid advances of ICTs that pervade the political landscape include the persistent inequalities within and among societies, the elitist nature of the global economy and the rapid transformation of communication styles and outlets.
- Is electronic democracy sustainable given the global economic struggle of everyday citizens to maintain basic standards of living? Is this struggle

preventing many from participating in traditional 'bricks and mortar' democracy?

- Should governments utilise ICT features mainly to implement policies expeditiously and provide services efficiently (citizens as customers) or should they utilise them mainly to encourage citizens to deliberate and determine which policies and services government *should* provide?
- Solving political problems by rational democratic means takes time, patience and effort. Instantaneous solutions grabbed from the Internet via ICTs are unlikely to succeed.

Notes

1 Paper presented for delivery at the Seventh International Conference of the Centre for Research in European Studies, University of East Anglia, England, 17–18 April 2008.

2 Dunn, John (1992) *Democracy: The Unfinished Journey*. Oxford: Oxford University Press, p. v.

3 Part of this dilemma may be related to what Giovanni Sartori has called the 'problem of confused democracy' – the fact that in the contemporary world most claim to approve of democracy though they 'no longer know (understand, agree) what it is'. Sartori, Giovanni (1987a) *The Theory of Democracy Revisted* Vol. 1. Chatham, NJ: Chatham House Publishers; Sartori, Giovanni (1987b) *The Theory of Democracy Revisted* Vol. 2. Chatham, NJ: Chatham House Publishers.

4 One such question is how to foster a culture of engagement among citizens amidst rapid demographic and technological changes. On this point consider Calvert, Robert E. (2006) *To Restore American Democracy: Political Education and the Modern University*. Lanham, MD: Rowman & Littlefield; Zukin, Cliff, Andolina, Molly, Jenkins, Krista and Delli-Carpini, Michael X. (2006) *A New Engagement? Political Participation, Civic Life, and the Changing American Citizen*. New York: Oxford University Press. Another important question, one that is addressed below, is that of the socio-economic preconditions for democratic citizenship. As Dunn rightly notes, this interactive relationship between democracy and development forms the 'central questions of modern politics, defining what is at stake in that politics, and indicating by their answers what real options it offers'. Dunn, John (1999) 'Democracy and Development?' in I. Shapiro and C. Hacker-Cordón (eds), *Democracy's Value*. Cambridge: Cambridge University Press, pp. 132–140.

5 Barber, Benjamin R. (2004), (1984). *Strong Democracy*. Berkeley: University of California Press.

6 Dahl, Robert (1991) *Democracy and Its Critics*. New Haven, CT: Yale University Press.

7 Fishkin, James (1995) *The Voice of the People: Public Opinion and Democracy*. New Haven, CT: Yale University Press; Fishkin, James S., Director, Center for Deliberative Democracy, Stanford University. http://ccc.stanford.edu (accessed 4 November 2008); Gutmann, Amy and Thompson, Dennis (2004) *Why Deliberative Democracy?* Princeton: Princeton University Press; Sunstein, Cass R. (2007) *Republic.com 2.0*. Princeton, NJ: Princeton University Press.

8 Margolis, Michael and Resnick, David (2000) *Politics as Usual: The Cyberspace 'Revolution'*. Thousand Oaks, CA: Sage Publications; Bimber, Bruce (2003) *Information and American Democracy*. New York: Cambridge University Press.

9 Gutmann and Thompson (2004) op. cit.

10 It should be noted that not everyone agrees that a more robust engagement constitutes a rejection of aggregative representative democracy. For example, numerous scholars defend the relationship between democracy and representation, viewing the latter as intimately related to a sound democratic life. Consider Urbinati, Nadia (2006) *Representative Democracy:*

Principles and Genealogy. Chicago: University of Chicago Press; and Mansbridge, Jane (2003) 'Rethinking Representation', *American Political Science Review* 97: 515–528.

11 O'Leary, Kevin (2006) *Saving Democracy: A Plan for Real Representation in America.* Stanford, CA: Stanford University Press.

12 Love, Nancy (2006) *Musical Democracy.* Albany, NY: State University of New York Press.

13 While we define deliberative democracy below, there are other similar, if not identical, democracy models in the literature. Deliberative democracy is a part of the broader theoretical category of participatory democracy. As Sartori (1987a) suggests, the 'notion of participatory democracy remains fuzzy' (p. 111). However, there are some characteristic trademarks. Dryzek, John S. (1990) *Discursive Democracy.* New York: Cambridge University Press contends that participatory democracy models advance a politics that is 'increasingly discursive, educational, oriented to truly public interests, and needful of active citizenship' (p. 13). Thus, models such as contestatory democracy (Parijs, Philippe van (1999) 'Contestatory Democracy versus Real Freedom for All', in I. Shapiro and C. Hacker-Cordón (eds) *Democracy's Value.* New York: Cambridge University Press, pp. 191–198), discursive democracy (Dryzek) and strong democracy (Barber, Benjamin R. (2004, 1984) *Strong Democracy.* Berkeley: University of California Press) all advance an ethic of substantive political engagement predicated upon a thick account of deliberation.

14 Habermas, Jürgen (1998) *Between Facts and Norms: Contributions to a Discourse Theory of Law and Democracy.* Cambridge, MA: The MIT Press.

15 Ibid.

16 This dictum appeared first as a Roman legal principle and was later incorporated into medieval canon law. In its essence, the principle suggested how a body of individuals should operate. It was at the centre of debate concerning where legislative power was rooted – in the sovereign or in the people.

17 Gutmann and Thompson (2004) op. cit. p. 3.

18 Ibid., p. 7.

19 Deliberative democracy is a highly debated concept and not all agree that it represents the solution to democracy's ills. For example, van Mill, David (2006) *Deliberation, Social Choice, and Absolutist Democracy.* New York: Routledge, argues that deliberation cannot overcome the problem of cycling and should thus be rejected. Social choice theorists (e.g. Riker, William (1982) *Liberalism against Populism.* New York: Waveland Press) consider more participatory notions of democracy not only as ill conceived but also 'inconsistent and absurd' (p. 241). Mackie, Gerry (2003) *Democracy Defended.* New York: Cambridge University Press, provides a vigorous critique of Riker and social choice theory democratic critiques and ardently defends representative democracy.

20 Hadenius, Axel (2001) *Institutions and Democratic Citizenship.* Oxford: Oxford University Press, p. 12.

21 Dryzek (1990) considers this model part of liberal democracy, a category of politics that is 'dominated by voting, strategy, private interests, bargaining, exchange, spectacle, and limited involvement' (p. 13).

22 Gutmann and Thompson (2004) op. cit. p. 14.

23 Although it was thought that neither candidate was likely to have a clear majority of delegates, witness the prominent Democratic Party officials, contributors and commentators who urged either Senator Clinton or Senator Obama to withdraw from the presidential nominating contest before the national convention met or even before the Pennsylvania primary took place – all for the good of the party, of course.

24 *The Hedgehog Review*, an influential contemporary journal of culture and ideas, devoted an entire issue to this serious problem. See 'The Commodification of Everything', *The Hedgehog Review* 5/2 (2003).

25 For an excellent discussion of this concept see P. H. Sedgwick (1999) *The Market Economy and Christian Ethics.* Cambridge: Cambridge University Press. Also consider S. K. White (1988) *The Recent Work of Jürgen Habermas.* Cambridge: Cambridge University Press.

26 See 'The Commodification of Everything: Editorial Introduction', p. 5.

27 Bauman, Z. (2005) *Liquid Life.* Cambridge: Polity Press, p. 83.

28   Ibid. pp. 83–84.
29   Sandel, Michael (2003) 'What Money Shouldn't Buy', *The Hedgehog Review* 5/2: 96.
30   Bekkers, Victor (2005) 'E-Government and the Emergence of Virtual Organisations in the Public Sector: An Exploration of the Interplay between ICT and Socio-organisational Networks', in V. Bekkers and V. Homburg (eds) *The Information Ecology of E-Government.* Amsterdam: IOS Press, p. 74.
31   As cited in Chadwick, A. (2006) *Internet Politics.* New York: Oxford University Press from http://www.hansard-society.org.uk/edemocracy.htm (accessed 3 April 2003).
32   Hansard Society (2008) 'Mayfly Politics – e-Democracy', The Hansard Society website at http://hansardsociety.org.uk/blogs/edemocracy/archive/2008/03/19/mayfly-politics.aspx (accessed 7 April 2008).
33   Mayer-Schönberger and Lazer (2007) op. cit. p. 5.
34   Ibid. p. 6.
35   West, Darrell (2005) *Digital Government: Technology and Public Sector Performance.* Princeton, NJ: Princeton University Press.
36   OECD Observer (2003) *Virtual Revolution: The E-Government Imperative.* Paris: Organisation for Economic Co-operation and Development (http://www.oecdobserver.org/news/full story.php/aid/1096/Virtual_revolution.html) (accessed 6 April 2008).
37   Thomas, John C. and Streib, Gregory (2003) 'The New Face of Government: Citizen-Initiated Contact in the Era of E-Government', *Journal of Public Administration Research and Theory* 13: 83–102.
38   Rayport, Jeffrey F. and Jaworski, Bernard J. (2002) *Introduction to e-Commerce.* New York: McGraw-Hill.
39   Turban, Efraim, King, David, Lee, Jae K. and Viehland, Dennis (2004) *Electronic Commerce: A Managerial Perspective.* Upper Saddle River, NJ: Pearson Prentice Hall.
40   Berthon, Pierre and Williams, Christine B. (2007) 'Stages of e-Democracy: Towards an Open-Source Political Model', *International Journal of Information Technology and Management* 6/2–4: 329–342.
41   Thomas, John C. and Streib, Gregory (2003) 'The New Face of Government: Citizen-Initiated Contact in the Era of E-Government.
42   Hindman, M. (2007) 'Open Source Politics Reconsidered: Emerging Patterns in Online Political Participation', in V. Mayer Schönberger and D. Lazer (eds) *Governance and Information Technology: From Electronic Government to Information Government.* Cambridge, MA: The MIT Press, p. 184
43   Ibid., p. 198.
44   Bekkers, Victor (2005) 'E-Government and the Emergence of Virtual Organisations in the Public Sector: An Exploration of the Interplay between ICT and Socio-Organisational Networks'; Esterling, Kevin, Neblo, Michael and Lazer, David (2005) 'Home (Page) Style: Determinates of the Quality of House Members' Websites', *International Journal of Electronic Government Research* 1: 50–63.
45   See, for example, Clift, Steven (2002) 'The Future of E-Democracy – The 50 Year Plan.' http://www.publicus.net/articles/future.html#E-Citizens (accessed 14 April 2008); Slevin, James (2000) 'Publicness and the internet', in James Slevin, *The Internet and Society.* Malden, MA: Blackwell Publishers, (Chapter 7) pp. 181–197.
46   Chadwick (2006) provides an excellent analysis of the global digital divide. See in particular pp. 53–79. Googling the phrase 'digital divide' returned 3.28 million references in contrast to 1.19 and 1.04 million references to 'world literacy' and 'world hunger', respectively. Using the same phrases for a keyword search of all higher education libraries in Ohio affiliated with Ohiolink produced 354, 1,088 and 896 documents, respectively (13 April 2008).
47   Arabic currently has the fastest growth rate. Figures presented in the last two paragraphs are drawn from pages within the Internet World Statistics website: www.internetworld stats.com (accessed 13 April 2008).
48   Lessig, Lawrence (2001) 'The Internet under Siege', *A Foreign Policy*, (Nov/Dec): 56–65. Online: http://lessig.org/blog/ForeignPolicy.pdf; Wakefield, Jane (2008) 'BBC and ISPs

Clash over iPlayer.' BBC News Online 9 April 2008. http://news.bbc.co.uk/2/hi/technology/7336940.stm (accessed 13 April 2008) .

49 As Wikipedia (2008) defines it, 'Network neutrality (equivalently net neutrality, Internet neutrality, or simply NN) refers to a principle that is applied to residential broadband networks, and potentially to all networks. Precise definitions vary, but a broadband network free of restrictions on the kinds of equipment that may be attached, on the modes of communication allowed, which does not restrict content, sites or platforms, and where communication is not unreasonably degraded by other communication streams, would be considered neutral by most observers.' Wikipedia, 2008. 'Network Neutrality.' http://en.wikipedia.org/wiki/Network_neutrality#cite_note-BERNDEF-0 (accessed 13 April 2008).

50 Goldsmith, Jack and Wu, Tim (2006) *Who Controls the Internet? Illusions of a Borderless World.* New York: Oxford University Press.

51 Ibid. p. 23.

52 Lindblom, Charles E. (1977) *Politics and Markets: The World's Political-Economic Systems.* New York: Basic Books; Head, Brian (1993) 'Lindblom on Business Power and Public Policy', in Harry Redner (ed.) *An Heretical Heir of the Enlightenment: Politics, Policy and Science in the Work of Charles E. Lindblom.* Boulder, CO: Westview Press; Save the Internet (a project of the Free Press Action Fund) www.savetheinternet.com (accessed 14 April 2008).

53 Barber, Benjamin R. (2007) *Consumed: How Capitalism Corrupts Children, Infantilizes Adults, and Swallows Citizens Whole.* New York: W. W. Norton.

54 www.Alexa.com (accessed 10 April 2008).

55 Prensky, Marc (2001a) 'Digital Natives, Digital Immigrants', *On the Horizon* 9/5 (Oct.): 1–6; Prensky, Marc (2001b) 'Do They *Really* Think Differently?' *On the Horizon* 9/6 (Dec.): 1–7.

56 Weber, Max (1919) *Politik als Beruf* (lecture delivered before the Freistudentischen Bund of the University of Munich) (s.h. transl.) In: *Gesammelte politische Schriften*, p. 560.

Further reading

Sunstein, Cass R. (2007) *Republic.com 2.0.* Princeton, NJ: Princeton University Press.

Margolis, Michael and Resnick, David (2000) *Politics as Usual: The Cyberspace 'Revolution'.* Thousand Oaks, CA: Sage Publications.

West, Darrell (2005) *Digital Government: Technology and Public Sector Performance.* Princeton, NJ: Princeton University Press.

6 Accountability in the context of E-Government

Dimitra Petrakaki

Summary

The chapter addresses the question of what constitutes accountability in the context of E-Government. Accountability is embedded in the traditional bureaucratic
public sector because of the principles that underpin, at least ideally, its function. By
contrast, E-Government initiatives are surrounded by different principles such as
technological orientation, joining up, re-engineering of administrative procedures,
customer orientation and contractualisation. These principles are supposed to
engender accountability and responsibility by standardising officials' behaviour and
eliminating their discretion. Yet, when put into effect, these principles open up a
field of multiple possibilities for officials to act. We argue that within this context
accountability cannot be established, as it is, at least ideally, in the bureaucratic public
sector. Rather, it becomes an individualistic, political and contingent issue that is
dependent upon officials' personal values and ethic.

Introduction

E-Government emerged as a concept and practice in the 1990s. It first appeared in
the 1993 US document *National Performance Review* by Al Gore under the Clinton
administration.[1] It was subsequently adopted by various governments around the
globe. Despite the popularity of the term, there is not, to date, a clear definition of
what does and what does not constitute E-Government.[2] Rather, E-Government is
conceptualised and deployed in a different way in each country.[3] However, there is a
prevalent definition, according to which E-Government is defined as the mediation of
information and communication technologies (ICTs) between government processes
and officials for the distribution of public services to citizens.[4] Yet E-Government is
more than the deployment of information technology (IT) in the public sector.[5] Rather,
it brings about various changes in the function of the public sector, the relationship
between the government and citizens and also in the way in which we conceptualise
the role of government in contemporary society. This is perhaps why Ho described
E-Government as 'a paradigm shift ... a transformation in the philosophy and
organisation of government'.[6]

E-Government has an internal and an external orientation. Internally, it intends to
reorganise and streamline government procedures.[7] Externally, E-Government aims
to improve public service provision and citizens' interactions with government,

increase citizens' awareness about governments' function and results, and achieve transparency and accountability.[8] However, if E-Government radically transforms the function, role and organisation of the public sector then we anticipate that it similarly changes the conditions that ensured accountability in the bureaucratic public sector. In line with this, the aim of this chapter is to examine accountability in the context of E-Government by looking at the means that accompany E-Government initiatives and their consequences for officials' practices.

The chapter is structured as follows. In the next section I draw upon Max Weber's work in order to describe the principles that underpin the function of the bureaucratic public sector and account for how accountability is ensured in this context. Then I proceed to review the literature on the means that are deployed, at least in principle, in E-Government initiatives. We consider the use of ICTs, joining up, re-engineering of administrative procedures, customer orientation, contractualisation and involvement of the private sector in the functions of the public sector. The final section draws upon the previous sections in order to discuss the consequences of E-Government for public service accountability. The chapter ends with some concluding remarks.

The bureaucratic public sector

The Weberian bureaucracy constitutes the prevalent mode of organising the public sector. In this section we review the principles that underpin the function of the ideal type of bureaucracy. Then we draw upon the principles in order to present the source of accountability that is embedded, at least ideally, in the bureaucratic public sector.

The principles of the ideal type of bureaucracy

According to Weber, the ideal type of bureaucracy is conditioned upon some general principles. To begin with, bureaucracies are formal in nature.[9] They comprise offices, each of which is allocated certain designated jurisdictions and duties.[10] Also, they are governed by rules and sanctions, which are relatively stable and exhaustive.[11]

Another characteristic of bureaucracies is their hierarchical structure. Hierarchy suggests differences in status, expertise, jurisdictions and responsibilities and illustrates authority relations of super- and subordination. Position in the hierarchy presupposes certain responsibilities. Officials in lower hierarchical levels are responsible for the execution of policy, whereas those in the upper hierarchical levels are liable for both policy setting and the outcomes of its execution. Generally, officials are liable for their subordinates' actions and are loyal to their superiors.[12]

Moreover, the Weberian bureaucracy presupposes impersonality. This implies that officials are disconnected and detached from the authority that their job position entails.[13] This, in further reflection, means that the authority which derives from a job position belongs to the hierarchy rather than to the person who holds it. Impersonality therefore creates a distinction between the subject who holds an office and its subject position. Overall, the bureaucracy operates like a machine that is guided by the law and the hierarchy.[14] In that way, it ensures homogeneity, coherence, synergy and efficiency.[15]

Furthermore, appointments to the bureau follow a merit procedure. Each office is held by people with specific qualifications. Qualifications are judged against educational certificates, training and performance in examinations.[16] As soon as they are employed, officials have the right to job stability. Lifelong employment is exchanged for faith and responsibility for the tasks that officials undertake.[17] Finally, the office is not exploited for rents. Rather, salaries and promotion are disconnected from outputs and are mostly dependent upon seniority, position in the hierarchy and status of the office.[18]

In line with these principles and their potential consequences, bureaucracies have been considered as being both dehumanising machines and virtuous organisations. Yet, as Weber argued, the dehumanising character of the bureaucracy is pre-supposition for its virtuous function: '[Bureaucracy's] specific nature, which is welcomed by capitalism, develops the more perfectly the more the bureaucracy is "dehumanised" . . . This is the specific nature of bureaucracy and it is appraised as its special virtue'.[19] Similarly, for Hoggett bureaucracy is the place where technicalities meet ethics.[20] It is to this issue that we now turn.

Accountability in the bureaucratic public sector

As Weber argued, the bureaucratic mode of organising renders the job within a bureaucracy vocation[21] an ethical commitment to one's duties.[22] The law and the hierarchy constitute for officials their two sources of accountability. On the one hand, the law requires compliance from officials and ensures the legality of their actions. On the other hand, the hierarchy presupposes officials' compliance with the procedures[23] and eliminates their responsibility for the outcomes of their practices. Therefore, the bureaucracy, apart from being a form of organising the public sector, opens up for officials a specific field of being and acting or, as du Gay says, a 'way of conducting oneself within a given life order'.[24]

Further, the principle of impersonality obstructs officials from usurping the authority of their subject position and acting opportunistically. Impersonality differentiates the private from the public interest, and renders officials guards of the latter.[25] Also, it obstructs any kind of dependencies that could possibly arise between officials and citizens.[26] In addition, impersonality diffuses into officials a rationale that is formal in type and normative in character. In accordance with this rationale, officials' actions need to be guided by the bureaucratic norms, rules and laws and/or serve well-defined and desirable ends.[27] In turn, impersonality constitutes a 'non-inclusive mode of human involvement',[28] which is productive because it promotes a specific ethos that is necessary for the just functioning of public organisations.

Additionally, adherence to rules and abstinence from personal emotions eliminates discrimination and favouritism and ensures equal and democratic public service provision.[29] Political, economic and social differences among citizens do not affect the quality of services offered to them. Rather, citizens are treated impartially, as if they were cases, and equally before bureaucracies' laws.[30] At the same time, the quality of services offered is not sacrificed because services are provided based upon pre-established criteria.[31] Rules become, in other words, the condition for citizens' equal and fair treatment. Even in the cases when laws become contestable, the formally rational bureaucratic environment suffices to guide officials' actions since it leaves little room for personal discretion.[32]

The bureaucratic public sector and the rise of E-Government

From what has been stated thus far, one can imply that accountability is embedded in the bureaucratic public sector because of the principles that underpin its function. Yet these principles are ideal and not essential. In other words, bureaucracies develop according to social needs and cultural differentiations. Consequently, they can deviate from the ideal type that was described above. For instance, various authors have criticised bureaucracies as being ineffective, inflexible towards change and irresponsive to citizens' needs.[33] Further, bureaucracies have been accused of having dehumanising aspects, which in turn condition alienation, arbitrariness and irresponsibility.[34] These claims against bureaucracies called for new modes of organising the public sector. E-Government, one of these new modes, is supposed to address these concerns by achieving both internal and external efficiencies and engendering transparency and accountability in officials' practices.

The principles that surround the orchestration of E-Government

In this section I present the means that orchestrate, at least in principle, E-Government projects. I argue that E-Government projects are initiated by the deployment of ICTs and are imperative for joining up, customer orientation, the re-engineering of administrative procedures, development of internal markets, contractualisation and public–private partnerships.

Technological orientation

E-Government initiatives are often reduced to the type of IT that accompanies them. Indicative of this is the fact that E-Government is often presented in the literature as an incremental process which consists of certain stages that are presented in Table 6.1. Each stage illustrates the type of information technology that is deployed and its purpose.[35]

First, IT is deployed for broadcasting information to citizens (government to citizens (G2C)), governmental agents (government to government (G2G)) and business (government to business (G2B)).[36] At this stage, IT refers to the development of

Table 6.1 The stages of E-Government development

Stages	Implications
Information provision	Broadcasting of information mainly through websites
Interaction	G2C, G2G and G2B (e.g. email, downloadable forms, data-transfer technologies)
Transaction	Online transactions and exchanges
Integration	Vertical and/or horizontal joining up

websites. Second, IT is used in order to enable interaction between government and citizens and/or business.[37] Email accounts, search engines and downloadable forms are typically used for this purpose.[38] Third, sophisticated technology like, for instance, electronic and digital signatures is used in order to secure the information that is transferred via the Internet.[39] In this way, IT enables synchronous online transactions and exchanges such as online payments and E-Voting. Finally, sophisticated technology is deployed for the dissolution of governmental boundaries and integration and re-organisation of governmental processes so that they are provided by a single point.[40] An example of this is the creation of (some physical but mainly electronic) one-stop shops and portals.

Information technology is also used for automating administrative procedures. Automation implies the transformation of administrative processes from manual to electronic. Typically, in the case of automation, processes remain intact, whereas information technology handles large amounts of data and performs mundane tasks.[41] This, in turn, is supposed to increase predictability, enable quantification and assist central decision making.[42] The ultimate objective of automation is to simplify administrative procedures so that they can be followed by any person, independently of his/her knowledge. Further, automation is supposed to eliminate human error, thereby achieving transparency and accountability.

Joining up government

As Table 6.1 illustrates, one of the ultimate objectives of E-Government is integration among governmental agents or development of joined-up government (JUG).[43] The latter is often defined as the 'coordination or integration of services from more than one department and potentially from other levels of government and community groups to achieve a better result than their acting separately'.[44] Joining up occurs when governmental departments and private and volunteer organisations have achieved a high degree of interoperability and have equal access to information so that they function as if they were one and not multiple departments.[45]

Joining up can take place at strategic or operational levels.[46] At a strategic level, integration implies that different policies are re-designed and re-cast into a single policy. At an operational level, joining up means the integration of procedures and practices so that public services are provided in a holistic way.[47] Integration could also be vertical or horizontal.[48] Vertical joining up cuts across government levels (e.g. between central and local government). Horizontal joining up cuts across sectors (e.g. public, private and volunteer sectors) and departments.[49]

Joining up is perceived as being a means to establish, among other things, transparency and accountability in the public sector.[50] This is for three reasons. First, governmental integration requires interdependence between departments or public service providers. Such interdependence encourages co-operation and obstructs self-serving behaviours. Second, joined-up government presupposes that jurisdictions are clearly allocated so that overlapping activities are reduced and interactions are carried out in a transparent way.[51] Third, joining up strengthens responsibility by reducing silo mentality (which is caused by the existence of multiple autonomous and separate departments) and setting common policies and objectives for all.[52]

Re-engineering of administrative procedures

Another practice that accompanies and often presupposes E-Government is the re-engineering of administrative procedures. Re-engineering implies the radical transformation of organisational procedures so that they become responsive to citizens' needs.[53] Re-engineering presupposes examination of current processes; identification of those processes that can be streamlined or re-designed or should be considered as being problematic; identification of the necessary technology to assist their transformation; and re-definition and re-design of the administrative procedures.[54] Re-engineering intends to obliterate outmoded tasks, eliminate unnecessary processes and dissolve departmentalism.[55] Also, its deployment re-orients public organisations towards outputs and customers' needs. This requires working horizontally (i.e. across boundaries rather than vertically) and backwards (i.e. from citizens' needs to organisational processes).[56] In this way, processes serve citizens rather than departments' interests, reduce time lags and increase productivity.[57] At the same time, officials acquire a holistic view of the process within which they participate and become empowered and responsible for their outcomes.[58]

Re-engineering is also a strategy to re-organise, apart from processes, public information. Re-engineering removes information from departmental terrains and disseminates it across boundaries.[59] ICTs play an important role in this by transforming information from print into electronic form.[60] As long as information takes a digital form, it can be integrated into central locations, such as databases, and disseminated across organisational departments.[61] With the use of IT, information can also be analysed, tracked and transferred back to officials.[62] The double centralisation and decentralisation of information that IT allows enables transparency and ensures officials' accountability.

Customer orientation

The E-Government agenda goes hand in hand with the imperative for customer orientation.[63] A manifestation of this is the organisation of public services around life events. Life events represent situations that frequently occur in citizens' lives or in businesses' operations (e.g. birth, marriage, army service, submission of VAT, etc.).[64] Each life event is decomposed to the relevant services that constitute it, and each service is decomposed to the necessary procedures. These are then allocated to specific departments, which have the jurisdiction to provide a part of the service and collaborate with other departments so that the end service is provided to citizens.

Customer orientation influences officials' practices. First, officials are supposed to know who their customers are and how they can be best satisfied. Typically, they learn this by collecting information about customers' attitudes, preferences and needs.[65] In addition, officials are required to both maintain and expand their clientele, acting as sellers or marketers of public services. Second, the customer orientation implies that officials need to prioritise the needs of their customers at the expense of the requirements of the public sector or the clauses of the law and regulations.[66]

Often, customer centricity is engendered by partitioning officials between those who provide and those who purchase public services.[67] Such division of roles constructs an internal market by rendering each public department or organisation a customer of the other. The division of public services into their component parts is a prerequisite for the creation of internal markets.[68] Then each public department or organisation undertakes a part of the service and competes with others in the internal market as either provider or purchaser.[69] Both parts are held responsible for making cost-effective decisions with the aims of minimising costs, increasing budgets and securing future viability. With the creation of internal markets, citizens are re-defined as customers and their needs and preferences are prioritised by public service organisations.[70] Citizens are given choices as they can turn to various officials whose in-between competition ensures the high quality of the public services being offered.[71] Internal markets are also intended for achieving responsiveness and accountability.[72] The partitioning between provider and purchaser eliminates role conflicts and opposing targets because it unites departments under specific objectives. It also obstructs opportunistic behaviours since it binds officials to common objectives such as future viability and effectiveness.

An indicative example of an internal market in E-Government initiatives is the establishment of one-stop shops. One-stop shops can provide multiple services from a single point or access points that bring together multiple organisations.[73] In their ideal form, one-stop shops are organised with a front and a back office. The front office is responsible for coming into contact with citizen-customers and submitting any requests or enquiries they might have, whereas the back office is liable for processing citizens' information and issuing the final public document.[74] Therefore, the front and the back offices constitute an internal market. The front office needs to collaborate with the back office in order to provide public services to citizens, while at the same time each office is a customer of the other. One-stop shops do not substitute for, but rather supplement, public organisations. They are established as alternative public service providers and consequently constitute competitors of the traditional public organisations.

Contracting out and the involvement of the private sector

E-Government initiatives are usually orchestrated by the development of contractual relationships with the private sector.[75] Du Gay[76] defines contracting out as the practice that

> consists of assigning the performance of a function or an activity to a distinct unit of management – individual or collective – which is regarded as being accountable for the efficient (i.e. economic) performance of that function or conduct of that activity.

Additionally, contracts do not solely transfer duties, but rather delegate public power to third parties. Contracts are typically signed between the government and IT vendors. The latter undertake the responsibility to develop and maintain the necessary infrastructure for the provision of public services through ICTs or consult the government on a number of public services.[77] Also, contractual relations are developed between governments and individuals, who undertake duties of public officials.

The development of contractual arrangements presupposes informed consent, negotiation by mutual adjustment and mutual accountability.[78] Individuals are, so to speak, free to get involved in a contract relationship and are, at least ideally, aware of contracts' terms, implications and consequences. Contracts also delegate jurisdictions and render contractors personally responsible for carrying out contracts' specifications.[79] Characteristically, contractual specifications refer to performance targets that contractors need to meet. Performance targets may refer to inputs, outputs, outcomes, efficiency, effectiveness or quality standards.[80] Input indicators represent the amount of resources that are used for public service provision.[81] Those related to outputs indicate workload (e.g. number of services provided or citizens served).[82] Indicators of efficiency calculate outputs in relation to inputs, whereas indicators of effectiveness estimate outcomes in relation to objectives (e.g. citizens' satisfaction).[83] Contracts are signed as soon as the implicated parts give their consent and comply with the contracts' terms.[84] Finally, although legally binding, contracts cannot ensure effectiveness because many of their specifications – and even the most crucial ones – are abstract and implied and therefore not of legal standing.

Discussion: accountability in the context of E-Government

As illustrated, E-Government initiatives are accompanied by various technological, organisational and managerial means. In this section we discuss what constitutes accountability in E-Government by looking at the forms of agency that these means condition. I argue that E-Government influences officials in two opposing ways. On the one hand, it eliminates officials' autonomy and conditions standardised and mechanised forms of agency. On the other hand, it conditions autonomous forms of agency by rendering officials personally responsible for the outcomes of their practices.

Accountability and standardisation

First, the technological orientation of E-Government rationalises the role of officials in public service provision. In the E-Government context, officials' work is reduced to processing citizens' data, managing their requests and complaints and handling the public sector's interfaces with citizens (i.e. maintaining websites, call centres, one-stop shops, etc.).[85] Officials are expected to be computer literate, able to handle ICTs on a 24/7 basis and able to work without coming into contact with citizens. IT is therefore intended to bring impersonality into the work practices of public officials. Yet, in comparison to the bureaucratic public sector, impersonality here does not mean officials' disengagement from personal concerns.[86] Rather, it implies mediated and mechanistic public service provision. Accountability is similarly supposed to be an outcome of the impersonal public service provision that partitions the official, who processes and issues the public service, from the citizen, who requests it.

Second, and perhaps more importantly, the deployment of sophisticated information technology is intended to delimit officials' discretion. As we saw, E-Government initiatives are often characterised by the type of IT they use. Yet the deployment of IT is not without consequences. Rather, IT is embedded with rules, which are intended to guide individuals' decisions.[87] ICTs, for instance, predict the essential prerequisites for an action in advance. By rendering officials' work a 'pre-processing activity',[88] officials' judgements and actions become predictable and transparent. Similarly, differentiation, idiosyncratic modes of behaviour and unwanted behaviours are eliminated.[89] In this way, accountability becomes a technical objective because it is assumed to be an outcome of the deployment of ICTs rather than an outcome of officials' discretion.

Similar to this, re-engineering of administrative procedures intends to standardise officials' practices. Re-engineering intervenes in officials' work by simplifying procedures and cognitive prerequisites. Through simplification, officials' work becomes a mundane, procedural task that requires no expertise or professional values. Thus, it can be undertaken by anyone, independently of his/her capacities, experience and knowledge. This marks a sharp contrast with the bureaucratic public sector, in which accountability was an outcome of officials' practices that were respectively part and parcel of their knowledge and qualifications.

The above suggests that E-Government initiatives are underpinned by the assumption that ICTs and process re-engineering can intervene in and rationalise officials' roles, practices and knowledge, eliminate their discretion and standardise their behaviour. It is therefore assumed that making officials manageable also renders them more accountable. Nevertheless, this assumption has two limitations; the first is related to the concept of accountability and the second is related to manageability. First, discretion, autonomy and improvisations are not negative aspects but necessary ingredients for providing public services in a responsible way.[90] This is because accountability does not mean blind compliance with the law, the constitution and the hierarchy; under specific circumstances, accountability means bending the law and re-formulating policy so that it fits into the situation that officials need to address. This leads us to two conclusions. On the one hand, officials' freedom to exercise discretion is not a threat to accountability but is co-constitutive of it. On the other hand, accountability cannot be ensured by IT but is an outcome of the circumstances.

Second is the limitation that E-Government initiatives are driven by the idea that officials are passive recipients of the changes that are imposed on them. Yet, as I show below, E-Government sets a field of multiple possibilities for officials to act. It provides both responsibility and autonomy, thus reducing accountability to officials' personal values and ethic.

Accountability and autonomy

To begin with, joining up intends to construct a knowledge base that makes officials' knowledge publicly available and accessible by other government agents, citizens, corporations and NGOs. In this way, anyone, independently of their expertise in the function of the public sector, can draw upon this knowledge base in order to process or provide public services. Joining up is driven by the assumption that where knowledge resides, irresponsibility flourishes. Hence, by intervening in officials' knowledge, their power to undertake illegitimate actions is limited and consequently responsibility is engendered. Leaving aside the difficulties that surround such attempts, joining up intends to extract from officials their knowledge and expertise, which, at least in principle, legitimise their authority and ensure their responsibility for their jurisdictions.[91] In this way, joining up separates officials from the commitments that accompany their role. By doing so, joining up renders accountability dependent upon the personal values of the individuals who hold public posts. Accountability becomes, in other words, not an institutionalised outcome, but a possible outcome of the responsible self.

Moreover, the development of contractual relationships with private agents conditions self-seeking attitudes and diffuses into contractors an output orientation. This is, first, because contracts specify the outputs which officials need to meet but leave aside all those qualities that prospective officials need to possess (e.g. morality, loyalty, fairness and equity).[92] Second, because of their constant risk to job stability, contracts trigger self-serving behaviours that undermine accountability. For instance, contractors may intend contract renewal by prioritising outcomes over processes or by providing unlimited public services to ineligible citizens.[93] Contracts therefore open up a series of risks concerning public service accountability, which bureaucracies successfully addressed through lifelong employment.[94]

Further, temporal employment in the public sector, due to contracts, attributes to the office an ephemeral character. The office is perceived not as a vocation, but rather as a temporary possession that, for a limited period of time, can be exchanged for several purposes, not least personal purposes.[95] For instance, the office may condition favouritism and lead, in that way, to rationing of services, 'cream-skimming' or 'two-tier service' provision.[96] So, the transient character of the office that E-Government conditions distances officials from the consequences of their practices and causes them to take an apolitical stance towards something which is political by definition (i.e. public service).

Furthermore, customer orientation is, as presented earlier, one of the basic rationales that trigger E-Government. Officials are supposed to know their customers and their needs and the way in which these needs can be satisfied. Further, they are expected to show their competence not only to maintain, but also to expand their clientele. This presupposes that officials are expected to act neither as providers of public services[97] nor as civil servants, but rather as sellers of public services. By attributing this role to officials, we need to anticipate similar entrepreneurial behaviours. As sellers of public services, officials are likely to go to various extremes that may undermine the constitution and the laws.[98] Also, the effort to serve one citizen may turn against the rights of another, thereby endangering the public interest. Further, improving the quality of one public service might mean lowering the quality of another.[99] The above indicates that the imperative to customer orientation presupposes political decision making and requires officials to think carefully and act responsibly. This, however, becomes highly questionable within an environment that diffuses the norm of entrepreneurial governance and demands respective behaviours.

At the same time, the involvement of the private sector in the provision of public services blurs the line of responsibility. The private sector has, by definition, different objectives from those of the public sector.[100] For instance, the private sector focuses on practices that are profitable and please the economic interests of their shareholders.[101] Corporations do so by taking risks, setting priorities and looking for lucrative parts of the market. In contrast, the government's primary target is to ensure equity in the provision of public services, protection of the public interest and satisfaction of the electorate and taxpayers. Yet by bringing the private sector into the practices of the public, objectives and practices might become blurred.

Also, the development of public–private partnerships increases the number of the parts that are involved in E-Government projects and influences accountability. Typically, the greater the number of groups that are implicated in public service provision, the more differentiated their interests and objectives become. This, in turn, conditions conflicts over ownership and personal prevalence.[102] Consequently, we anticipate that the greater the number of units that operate in E-Government initiatives, the more blurred the line of responsibility will become.[103]

We have so far accounted for the rationale and intended and unintended consequences of the managerial and technological means that accompany E-Government. We argue that these means bring about a series of changes to officials' role, practices and knowledge. They both enable and limit officials' autonomy and discretion, thereby influencing their accountability. Specifically, E-Government imposes on officials a series of changes by standardising their practices, simplifying their knowledge, transforming their role as sellers of public services, expecting customer-oriented forms of behaviour from them and finally imposing constant job instability and output orientation through contracts. E-Government initiatives are orchestrated by the assumption that rendering officials manageable similarly renders them accountable. However, the means that accompany E-Government open up a field of multiple possibilities for officials to act, often in irresponsible, political and illegitimate ways. The way in which officials will act is not definite. They can adopt, adapt and negate the norms and roles that accompany E-Government. Their actual practices are contingent upon their personal values and priorities. One can anticipate, therefore, that within this context, accountability cannot be institutionalised as it is, at least ideally, in the bureaucratic public sector. Rather, accountability in the context of E-Government is individualistic, political and contingent; it is always in the process of being broken down.

Conclusions

E-Government has changed the way in which we conceptualise accountability in the public sector. In the bureaucratic public sector, accountability was ensured by law and hierarchy. Accountability was embedded in the behavioural norms and the rules of the bureaucracy and was part and parcel of officials. Consequently, accountability was unquestioned. By contrast, in the E-Government context accountability is a technicality to be achieved through the establishment of various managerial, IT and organisational technologies. Nevertheless, as I have argued, the means that accompany E-Government – namely contractualisation, re-engineering of administrative procedures, joining up and the imperative for customer orientation – condition entrepreneurial forms of conduct and open up to officials a field of multiple possibilities for legitimate and illegitimate action. Under these circumstances, I argue that accountability cannot be taken for granted. Rather, accountability becomes contingent upon officials' personal values and priorities.

Key points

- This is a conceptual chapter which draws on Weber's work on bureaucracy, studies on E-Government and critical studies on the reformation of the public sector.
- The aim of this chapter is to understand what accountability is and how it is supposed to be ensured in typical E-Government initiatives.
- Critical analysis of means is supposed to engender accountability.
- Those means' potential consequences for officials' behaviour and accountability are discussed.
- In the E-Government context, accountability is supposed to be engendered through adopting ICTs, re-engineering of administrative procedures, joining up, contracting private agents and establishing the imperative for customer orientation. How? By standardising officials' behaviours and eliminating discretion.
- The deployment of officials also opens up the possibility for autonomous action and free thinking.
- Within this context, accountability cannot be established as it is in the ideal public sector. Rather, accountability becomes dependent upon officials' priorities and personal values.

Notes

1 Yildiz, M. (2007) 'E-Government Research: Reviewing the Literature, Limitations, and Ways Forward', *Government Information Quarterly* 24: 646–665.
2 Basu, S. (2004) 'E-Government and Developing Countries: An Overview', *International Review of Law Computers* 18/1: 109–132.
3 Yildiz, M. (2007) 'E-Government Research: Reviewing the Literature, Limitations, and Ways Forward'; Zhang, J. (2002) "Will the Government Serve the People"? The Development of Chinese E-Government', *New Media & Society* 4/2: 163–184.
4 Bekkers, V. (2003) 'E-Government and the Emergence of Virtual Organisations in the Public Sector', *Information Polity* 8: 89–101; Huang, Z. and Bwoma, P. (2003) 'An Overview of Critical Issues of E-Government', *Issues of Information Systems* 4/1: 164–170; Moon, J. (2002) 'The Evolution of E-Government among Municipalities: Rhetoric or Reality?', *Public Administration Review* 62/4: 424–433; Silcock, R. (2001) 'What is E-Government?', *Parliamentary Affairs*, 54/1: 88–101; Vintar, M., Kunstelj, M., Decman, M. and Bercic B. (2003) 'Development of E-Government in Slovenia', *Information Polity* 8/3–4: 133–149; Von Haldenwang, C. (2004) 'Electronic Government (E-Government) and Development', *European Journal of Development Research* 16/20: 417–432.
5 Bellamy, C. and Taylor, J. (1998) *Governing in the Information Age*, Maidenhead: Open University Press; Fountain, J. (2001) *Building the Virtual State: Information Technology and Institutional Change*, Washington, DC: The Brookings Institution; Hazlett, S. and Hill, F. (2003) 'E-Government: The Realities of Using IT to Transform the Public Sector', *Managing Service Quality* 13/6: 445–452.
6 Ho, T. A. (2002) 'Reinventing Local Governments and the E-Government Initiative', *Public Administration Review* 62/4: 434–444.
7 Hazlett, S. and Hill, F. (2003) 'E-Government: The Realities of Using IT to Transform the Public Sector'.

8 Basu, S. (2004) 'E-Government and Developing Countries: An Overview'; Curthoys, N. *et al.* (2003) 'E-Government', in P. Jackson (ed.) *E-Business Fundamentals*. Abingdon: Routledge; Gil-Garcia, R. *et al.* (2007) 'Collaborative E-Government: Impediments and Benefits of Information-Sharing Projects in the Public Sector', *European Journal of Information Systems* 16: 121–133; Kumar, R. and Best, M. (2006) 'Impact and Sustainability of E-Government Services in Developing Countries: Lessons Learned from Tamil Nadu, India', *The Information Society* 22/1: 1–12; Lenk, K. (2002) 'Electronic Service Delivery – A Driver of Public Sector Modernisation', *Information Polity* 7: 87–96; Moon, J. (2002) 'The Evolution of E-Government among Municipalities: Rhetoric or Reality?'; Vintar, M., Kunstelj, M., Decman, M. and Bercic, B. (2003) 'Development of E-Government in Slovenia'; Von Haldenwang, C. (2004) 'Electronic Government (E-Government) and Development'; Zhang, J. (2002) 'Will the Government "Serve the People"? The Development of Chinese E-Government'.
9 Weber, M. (1948) 'Bureaucracy', in H.H. Gerth and W. Mills (eds) *From Max Weber: Essays in Sociology*, Padstow: T.J. Press (Padstow) Ltd.
10 Blau, P. (1970) 'Weber's Theory of Bureaucracy', in D. Wrong (ed.) *Max Weber*. Englewood Cliffs, NJ: Prentice Hall.
11 Weber, M. (1948) 'Bureaucracy'.
12 Blau, P. (1970) 'Weber's Theory of Bureaucracy'.
13 Weber, M. (1948) 'Bureaucracy'.
14 Ibid.
15 Blau, P. (1970) 'Weber's Theory of Bureaucracy'; Clarke, J. and Newman, J. (1997) *The Managerial State: Power, Politics and Ideology in the Remaking of Social Welfare*. London: SAGE Publications.
16 Ibid.
17 Weber, M. (1948) 'Bureaucracy'.
18 Ibid.
19 Ibid.
20 Hoggett, P. (2005) 'A Service to the Public: The Containment of Ethical and Moral Conflicts by Public Bureaucracies', in P. Du Gay (ed.) *The Values of Bureaucracy*. Oxford: Oxford University Press.
21 Weber, M. (1948) 'Bureaucracy'.
22 Du Gay, P. (2000) *In Praise of Bureaucracy: Weber, Organisation, Ethics*. London: SAGE Publications.
23 Heinrich, C. (2002) 'Outcomes-Based Performance Management in the Public Sector: Implications for Government Accountability and Effectiveness', *Public Administration Review*, 62/6: 712–725.
24 Du Gay, P. (2000) *In Praise of Bureaucracy: Weber, Organisation, Ethics*.
25 Weber, M. (1948) 'Bureaucracy'.
26 Du Gay, P. (2005) 'Bureaucracy and Liberty: State, Authority and Freedom', in P. Du Gay (ed.) *The Values of Bureaucracy*. Oxford: Oxford University Press; Felts, A. and Jos, P. (2000) 'Time and Space: The Origins and Implications of the New Public Management', *Administrative Theory & Praxis* 22/3: 519–533.
27 Weber, M. (1948) 'Bureaucracy'.
28 Kallinikos, J. (2004) 'The Social Foundations of the Bureaucratic Order', *Organisation* 111: 13–36.
29 Blau, P. (1970) 'Weber's Theory of Bureaucracy'; Clarke, J. and Newman, J. (1997) *The Managerial State: Power, Politics and Ideology in the Remaking of Social Welfare*; Du Gay, P. (2000) *In Praise of Bureaucracy: Weber, Organisation, Ethics*; Stokes, J. and Clegg, S. (2002) 'Once upon a Time in the Bureaucracy: Power and Public Sector Management', *Organisation* 9/2: 225–247.
30 Clarke, J. and Newman, J. (1997) *The Managerial State: Power, Politics and Ideology in the Remaking of Social Welfare*; Kallinikos, J. (2004) 'The Social Foundations of the Bureaucratic Order'; Stokes, J. and Clegg, S. (2002) 'Once upon a Time in the Bureaucracy: Power and Public Sector Management'.

31 Du Gay, P. (2005) 'Bureaucracy and Liberty: State, Authority and Freedom'.

32 Weber, M. (1948) 'Bureaucracy'.

33 Clarke, J. and Newman, J. (1997) *The Managerial State: Power, Politics and Ideology in the Remaking of Social Welfare*; Farrell, C. and Morris, J. (2003) 'The "Neo-Bureaucratic" State: Professionals, Managers and Professional Managers in Schools, General Practices and Social Work', *Organisation* 10/1: 129–156.

34 Blau, P. (1970) 'Weber's Theory of Bureaucracy'; Clarke, J. and Newman, J. (1997) *The Managerial State: Power, Politics and Ideology in the Remaking of Social Welfare*; Dean, M (1999) *Governmentality: Power and Rule in Modern Society*. London: SAGE Publications; Flynn, R. (1999) 'Managerialism, Professionalism and Quasi-Markets', in M. Exworthy and S. Halford (eds) *Professionals and the New Managerialism in the Public Sector*, Buckingham: Open University Press; Rose, N. (1993) 'Government, Authority and Expertise in Advanced Liberalism', *Economy and Society* 22/3: 283–299.

35 Moon, J. (2002) 'The Evolution of E-Government among Municipalities: Rhetoric or Reality?'.

36 Basu, S. (2004) 'E-Government and Developing Countries: an Overview'; Curthoys, N. *et al.* (2003) 'E-Government'; Huang, Z. and Bwoma, P. (2003) 'An Overview of Critical Issues of E-Government'; Moon, J. (2002) 'The Evolution of E-Government among Municipalities: Rhetoric or Reality?'; Schelin, H. (2002) 'E-Government: An Overview', in D. Garson (ed.) *Public Information Technology: Policy and Management Issues*. US: Idea Group; Silcock, R. (2001) 'What is E-Government?'.

37 Holden, S. and Millet, L. (2005) 'Authentication, Privacy and the Federal E-Government', *The Information Society* 21: 367–377; Moon, J. (2002) 'The Evolution of E-Government among Municipalities: Rhetoric or Reality?'.

38 Basu, S. (2004) 'E-Government and Developing Countries: An Overview'; Holden, S. and Millet, L. (2005) 'Authentication, Privacy and the Federal E-Government'; Schelin, H. (2002) 'E-Government: An Overview'; Silcock, R. (2001) 'What Is E-Government?'.

39 Schelin, H. (2002) 'E-Government: An Overview'.

40 Moon, J. (2002) 'The Evolution of E-Government among Municipalities: Rhetoric or Reality?', Silcock, R. (2001) 'What Is E-Government?'.

41 Avgerou, C. and Cornford, T. (1998) *Developing Information Systems: Concepts, Issues and Practice*, 2nd edition. London: Macmillan; Bellamy, C. and Taylor, J. (1998) *Governing in the Information Age*.

42 Garson, B. (1988) *The Electronic Sweatshop: How Computers are Turning the Office of the Future into the Factory of the Past*. New York: Simon & Schuster.

43 Bloomfield, B. and Hayes, N. (2004) 'Modernisation and the Joining-Up of Local Government Services in the UK: Boundaries, Knowledge and Technology', Paper presented at the workshop on Information, Knowledge and Management: Reassessing the Role of ICTs in Private and Public Organisations, Superior School of Public Administration, Bologna; Curthoys, N. *et al.* (2003) 'E-Government'.

44 Wilkins, P. (2002) 'Accountability and Joined-Up Government', *Australian Journal of Public Administration* 61/1: 114–119.

45 Silcock, R. (2001) 'What is E-Government?'

46 Cowell, R. and Martin, S. (2003) 'The Joy of Joining-Up: Modes of Integrating the Local Government Modernisation Agenda', *Environment and Planning C: Government and Policy* 21/2: 159–179.

47 Newman, J. (2000) 'Beyond the New Public Management? Modernizing Public Services', in J. Clarke, S. Gewirtz and E. McLaughlin (eds) *New Managerialism, New Welfare?* London: SAGE Publications.

48 Pollitt, C. (2003) 'Joined-Up Government: A Survey', *Political Studies Review* 1: 34–49.

49 Ibid.

50 Martin, S. (2002) 'The Modernisation of UK Local Government', *Public Administration Review* 4/3: 291–307; Wilkins, P. (2002) 'Accountability and Joined-Up Government'.

51 Cole, M. and Fenwick, J. (2003) 'UK Local Government: The Impact of Modernisation on Departmentalism', *International Review of Administrative Sciences* 69/2: 259–270; Illsley, B., Lloyd, G. and Lynch, B. (2000) 'From Pillar to Post? A One-Stop Shop Approach to Planning Delivery', *Planning Theory & Practice* 1/1: 111–122.

52 Curthoys, N. *et al.* (2003) 'E-Government'.

53 Bellamy, C. and Taylor, J. (1998) *Governing in the Information Age*; Knights, D. and Willmott, H. (2000) 'The Reengineering Revolution? An Introduction', in D. Knights and H. Willmott (eds) *The Reengineering Revolution: Critical Studies of Corporate Change*. London: SAGE Publications.

54 Gunge, S. (2000) 'Business Process Reengineering and the "New Organisation"', in D. Knights and H. Willmott (eds) *The Reengineering Revolution: Critical Studies of Corporate Change*. London: SAGE Publications; Heeks, R. and Davies, A. (1999) 'Different Approaches to Information Age Reform', in R. Heeks (ed.) *Reinventing Government in the Information Age: International Practice in IT-Enabled Public Sector Reform*. London: Routledge.

55 Cibbora, C. (2003) 'Unveiling E-Government and Development: Governing at a Distance in the New War', *London School of Economics Working Paper No. 126*. Available online, http://is2.lse.ac.uk/wp/pdf/WP126.PDF (accessed 15 March 2008).

56 McGabe, D. and Knights, D. (2000) 'BPR against the Wall of Functionalism', in D. Knights and H. Willmott (eds) *The Reengineering Revolution: Critical Studies of Corporate Change*. London: SAGE Publications.

57 Kumar, R. and Best, M. (2006) 'Impact and Sustainability of E-Government Services in Developing Countries: Lessons Learned from Tamil Nadu, India'; Von Haldenwang, C. (2004) 'Electronic Government (E-Government) and Development'.

58 McGabe, D. and Knights, D. (2000) 'BPR against the Wall of Functionalism'.

59 Ibid.

60 Henriksen, H. Z. and Damsgaard, J. (2007) 'Dawn of E-Government – An Institutional Analysis of Seven Initiatives and Their Impact', *Journal of Information Technology* 22: 13–23.

61 Tan, C. and Pan, S. (2003) 'Managing E-Transformation in the Public Sector: An E-Government Study of the Inland Revenue Authority of Singapore', *European Journal of Information Systems* 12/4: 269–281.

62 Andersen, K. (1999) 'Reengineering Public Sector Organisations using Information Technology', in R. Heeks (ed.) *Reinventing Government in the Information Age: International Practice in IT-Enabled Public Sector Reform*. London: Routledge

63 Cibbora, C. (2003) 'Unveiling E-Government and Development: Governing at a Distance in the New War'.

64 Lenk, K. (2002) 'Electronic Service Delivery – A Driver of Public Sector Modernisation'.

65 Fountain, J. (2001) Building the Virtual State: Information Technology and Institutional Change'.

66 Kellough, E. (1998) 'The Reinventing Government Movement: A Review and Critique', *Public Administration Quarterly*, Spring: 6–20.

67 Hood, C. (1991) 'A Public Management for All Seasons?', *Public Administration*, 69/1: 3–19, Flynn, R. (1999) 'Managerialism, Professionalism and Quasi-Markets'.

68 Stewart, J. and Walsh, K. (1992) 'Change in the Management of Public Services', *Public Administration* 70: 499–518.

69 Du Gay, P. (2000) *In Praise of Bureaucracy: Weber, Organisation, Ethics*.

70 Chadwick, A. and May, C. (2003) 'Interaction between States and Citizens in the Age of the Internet: E-Government in the United States, Britain and the European Union', *Governance: An International Journal of Policy, Administration and Institutions* 16/2: 271–300; Felts, A. and Jos, P. (2000) 'Time and Space: The Origins and Implications of the New Public Management'.

71 Stewart, J. and Walsh, K. (1992) 'Change in the Management of Public Services'; Du Gay, P. (2000) *In Praise of Bureaucracy: Weber, Organisation, Ethics*; Ferlie, E., Pettigrew, A., Ashburner, L. and Fitzgerald, L. (1996) *The New Public Management in Action*. Oxford: Oxford University Press.

72 Du Gay, P. (2000) *In Praise of Bureaucracy: Weber, Organisation, Ethics.*

73 Illsley, B. *et al.* (2000) 'From Pillar to Post? A One-Stop Shop approach to Planning Delivery'.

74 Lenk, K. (2002) 'Electronic Service Delivery – A Driver of Public Sector Modernisation'.

75 Bloomfield, B. and Hayes, N. (2004) 'Modernisation and the Joining-Up of Local Government Services in the UK: Boundaries, Knowledge and Technology'.

76 Du Gay, P. (1996) 'Organizing Identity: Entrepreneurial Governance and Public Management', in S. Hall and P. Du Gay (eds) *Questions of Cultural Identity.* London: SAGE publications.

77 Bloomfield, B. and Hayes, N. (2004) 'Modernisation and the Joining-Up of Local Government Services in the UK: Boundaries, Knowledge and Technology'.

78 Yeatman, A. (1998) 'Interpreting Contemporary Contractualism', in M. Dean and B. Hindess (eds) *Governing Australia: Studies in Contemporary Rationalities of Government.* Cambridge: Cambridge University Press.

79 Rose, N. (1993) 'Government, Authority and Expertise in Advanced Liberalism', *Economy and Society* 22/3: 283–299.

80 Alford, J. and Baird, J. (1997) 'Performance Monitoring in the Australian Public Service: a Government-Wide Analysis', *Public Money & Management* 17/2: 49–58; Heinrich, C. (2002) 'Outcomes-Based Performance Management in the Public Sector: Implications for Government Accountability and Effectiveness'.

81 Alford, J. and Baird, J. (1997) 'Performance Monitoring in the Australian Public Service: A Government-Wide Analysis'.

82 Hall, C. and Rimmer, S. (1994) 'Performance Monitoring and Public Sector Contracting', *Australian Journal of Public Administration* 53/4: 453–461.

83 Hall, C. and Rimmer, S. (1994) 'Performance Monitoring and Public Sector Contracting'; Boland, T. and Fowler, A. (2000) 'A Systems Perspective of Performance Management in Public Sector Organisations', *International Journal of Public Sector Management* 13/5: 417–446.

84 Yeatman, A. (1998) 'Interpreting Contemporary Contractualism'.

85 Bovens, M. and Zouroudis, S. (2002) 'From Street-Level to System-Level Bureaucracies: How Information and Communication Technology is Transforming Administrative Discretion and Constitutional Control', *Public Administration Review* 622: 174–184.

86 Weber, M. (1948) 'Bureaucracy'.

87 Suchman, L. (1987) *Plans and Situated Actions: The Problem of Human–Machine Communication,* Cambridge: Cambridge University Press; Gunge, S. (2000) 'Business Process Reengineering and the "New Organisation"'.

88 Fountain, J. (2001) *Building the Virtual State: Information Technology and Institutional Change.*

89 Garson, B. (1988) *The Electronic Sweatshop: How Computers are Turning the Office of the Future into the Factory of the Past.*

90 Goodsell, C. (2005) 'The Bureau as Unit of Governance', in P. Du Gay (ed.) *The Values of Bureaucracy.* Oxford: Oxford University Press; Lipsky, M. (1980) *Street-Level Bureaucracy: Dilemmas of the Individual in Public Services.* New York: Russell Sage Foundation.

91 Bellamy, C. and Taylor, J. (1998) *Governing in the Information Age*; Bloomfield, B. and Hayes, N. (2004) 'Modernisation and the Joining-Up of Local Government Services in the UK: Boundaries, Knowledge and Technology'; Cibbora, C. (2003) 'Unveiling E-Government and Development: Governing at a Distance in the New War'.

92 Du Gay, P. (1996) 'Organizing Identity: Entrepreneurial Governance and Public Management'.

93 Bardouille, N. (2000) 'The Transformation of Governance Paradigms and Modalities', *The Round Table* 353: 81–106; Campbell, C. (1993) 'Public Service and Democratic Accountability', in R. E. Chapman (ed.) *Ethics in Public Service.* Edinburgh: Edinburgh University Press.

94 Weber, M. (1948) 'Bureaucracy'.

95 Du Gay, P. (2007) *Organizing Identity: Persons and Organizations after 'Theory'.* London: SAGE Publications.

96 Clarke, J. and Newman, J. (1997) *The Managerial State: Power, Politics and Ideology in the Remaking of Social Welfare*; Ferlie, E. *et al.* (1996) *The New Public Management in Action*; Flynn, R. (1999) 'Managerialism, Professionalism and Quasi-Markets'; Lipsky, M. (1980) *Street-level bureaucracy: dilemmas of the individual in public services*.

97 Cibbora, C. (2005) 'Interpreting E-Government and Development: Efficiency, Transparency or Governance at a Distance?' *Information Technology and People* 18/3: 260–279.

98 Du Gay, P. (2000) *In Praise of Bureaucracy: Weber, Organisation, Ethics*.

99 Bloomfield, B. and Hayes, N. (2004) 'Modernisation and the Joining-Up of Local Government Services in the UK: Boundaries, Knowledge and Technology'.

100 Ibid.

101 Cibbora, C. (2005) 'Interpreting E-Government and Development: Efficiency, Transparency or Governance at a Distance?'.

102 Clarke, J. and Newman, J. (1997) *The Managerial State: Power, Politics and Ideology in the Remaking of Social Welfare*.

103 Pollitt, C. (2003) 'Joined-Up Government: A Survey'.

Further reading

Andersen, K. (1999) 'Reengineering Public Sector Organisations using Information Technology', in R. Heeks (ed.) *Reinventing Government in the Information Age: International Practice in IT-Enabled Public Sector Reform*. London: Routledge

Bekkers, V. (2003) 'E-Government and the Emergence of Virtual Organisations in the Public Sector', *Information Polity* 8: 89–101

Chadwick, A. and May, C. (2003) 'Interaction between States and Citizens in the Age of the Internet: E-Government in the United States, Britain and the European Union', *Governance: An International Journal of Policy, Administration and Institutions* 16/2: 271–300.

Henriksen, H. Z. and Damsgaard J. (2007) 'Dawn of E-Government: An Institutional Analysis of Seven Initiatives and Their Impact', *Journal of Information Technology* 22: 13–23.

Pollitt, C. (2003) 'Joined-Up Government: A Survey', *Political Studies Review* 1: 34–49.

7 Addressing the real world of public consultation

Whither E-Consultation?*

*David O'Donnell, Paul McCusker, G. Honor Fagan,
Simon Stephens, D. R. Newman, John Morison
and Michael Murray*

Summary

One of the key elements often mooted in the ongoing debates on E-Government is the possibility of using ICT to widen and deepen public consultation processes in decision making, hence improving policy outcomes. This chapter draws on the findings of eight focus group discussions on 'real world' consultation processes in both Northern Ireland and the Republic of Ireland to map out how the early history of ICT-engendered participation may not illustrate such a smooth and uncontested road. As the history and present cultural, social and political identities of the people on the island of Ireland amply demonstrate, democracy is a fragile process that first has to be established and institutionalised and then continuously re-generated from local lifeworlds. We find that there exists a massive culture of cynicism and frustration among activist citizens with respect to state- and administration-initiated consultation processes. This begs the key question: If such levels of cynicism exist – regardless of the sophistication of the ICT technology employed – whither the effectiveness of future E-Consultation processes? We present no simplistic, naive or premature conclusions here, but we tease out some implications of these findings where we grant precedence to deliberative democracy, following Habermas, over technology. Following the critical theory agenda, we challenge the potential reproduction, via electronic means, of a dominant mode of social ordering that, from the evidence presented, appears to actually constrain human possibilities. In conclusion, the problems related to extant public consultation processes identified here are essentially problems of democracy – and not problems that can be solved by technology alone. All those involved in E-Democracy and E-Government research and practice dare not lose sight of this insight. '[T]he *discursive level* of public debates constitutes the most important variable.'[1]

* The research presented here is funded by the European Union's Peace and Reconciliation Fund and administered through the Irish Higher Education Authorities. We especially thank all focus group participants and acknowledge the input of our research colleagues Anne-Marie Logue, Michele Smyth, Ashish Italiya and Yan Chen. A much earlier version of this paper was presented at ECEG Conference, Antwerp in June 2005.

Introduction

Citizens simultaneously occupy two positions in democratic society: they are both members of society and bearers of the political public sphere.[2] As members of society (e.g. employees, consumers, taxpayers, patients, clients of administrative state bureaucracies, etc.), they are exposed to the requirements, benevolence and failures of the corresponding service systems – such systems or subsystems being viewed here as the primary responsibility of government. Private spheres and local community lifeworlds, in turn, link to the public spheres of deliberative democracy. Not forgetting that in the final instance 'only the state can act', the threshold separating these spheres is marked not 'by a fixed set of issues or relationships but by *different conditions of communication*' that channel the flow of communication from one to the other.[3]

We begin an exploration in this chapter on such flows of communication in the context of a discussion on real-world public consultation processes. It follows that our main focus fits more within an E-Democracy – as distinct from an E-Government – discourse, but our findings are relevant to both. We emphasise that the empirical findings presented here represent a preliminary – but key – element in our ongoing research on E-Consultation on the island of Ireland. Currently, a strong consultation culture exists on the island of Ireland. In many cases, this is due to legislative requirements, even if participation rates are extremely low. Northern Ireland, in particular, prefigures one of the most extreme expressions of a consultation culture, with its Civic Forum and the duty in Section 75 of the Northern Ireland Act, which requires all public bodies to develop an equality strategy through widespread consultations.[4]

We present a simple argument here and we pose a fundamental question. Based on focus group research, we claim that there exists a massive culture of cynicism and frustration among participating citizens and community activists with respect to extant consultation processes. This brings us to our key question: If such levels of cynicism exist – regardless of the sophistication of the ICT technology or software systems employed – whither the effectiveness of future E-Consultation processes? We present no simplistic, naive or premature conclusions here; we do, however, grant normative precedence to deliberative democracy over technology. Where possible, we allow the voices of these activist citizens to narrate their stories themselves.

The structure of the remainder of the chapter is as follows. Some background to the debate on consultation and E-Consultation in the context of E-Government and E-Democracy is very briefly introduced; we then tease out some specific insights from the focus group transcripts; finally, we argue that these findings point to enormous challenges in successfully moving from traditional consultation towards E-Consultation and that the process of deliberative democracy itself, as distinct from the attributes of ICT technology, is *the* fundamentally pragmatist point of departure for any future discussions on E-Consultation on the island of Ireland or elsewhere within democratic societies.

Background

Internationally, many governments – not all democratic – have already developed some of the potential of ICT in facilitating the emergence of the 'ambient intelligent' environment,[5] including E-Consultation.[6] Moreover, the literature on both public policy analysis and deliberative democracy advocates an increase in public engagement in decision-making processes that directly affect them.[7] The European Union, for example, is driven by the need for greater access and service enhancement. Examples include the general modernising government agenda in the UK, the modernising policies for service delivery in Finland, strategies on the information society in Ireland and the drives to upgrade infrastructure in Northern Ireland and Sweden through their targets of broadband everywhere. Just as some have unrealistic expectations of the efficiency gains and cost savings resulting from E-Government initiatives, there is also a belief in some quarters that the Internet is an open and inherently democratic medium. It follows, from this line of reasoning, that when governments go online they will immediately and automatically become more open, which, in turn, will improve the quality of E-Democracy. This mode of one-sided discourse and argument is both naive and overly simplistic.

Adopting a more critical modernist stance in this chapter, we claim that such ICT-mediated improvements are in no way inevitable. E-Government does not necessarily correlate with E-Democracy. As this chapter is intended to demonstrate, the scope for mere replication of current problems means that future systems may need not only to change the media through which consultation processes are conducted, but also to move deeper into the processes and practices of deliberative democracy itself. The problems of democracy cannot be solved by technology alone. Broadly in line with the Frankfurt School critical modernist tradition, we assume here

> that effective social critique for democratic policy making requires a discriminating appropriation of science in the service of social analysis and critique. In short, the critic must not only target science but must also use the findings of science.[8]

Detailed discussion of the particular complexities of present-day politics on the island of Ireland is beyond the scope of the present chapter.[9] Notwithstanding this complexity – following Habermas[10] here – a dual perspective is required in that the communicative action of citizens in local lifeworlds injects its own citizen-centric rationality, somehow, into its relations with the functional sub-systems of government, hence influencing these systems as distinct from the extant top-down (and usually overly directive) consultation processes, of which the vast majority of citizens remain totally oblivious or simply ignore. In the information systems, field application of Habermasian ideas is not new and is now well developed.[11] A synergy between this literature and E-Governance is now emerging.[12]

Today's 'civil society', in contrast to its original meaning in the Marxist tradition,

> no longer includes the economy as constituted by private law and steered through markets in labour, capital and commodities. Rather, its institutional core comprises those non-governmental and non-economic connections and voluntary associations that anchor the communicative structures of the public sphere in the society component of the lifeworld. Civil society is composed of those more or less spontaneously emergent associations, organisations and movements that,

attuned to how societal problems resonate in the private life spheres, distil and transmit such reactions in amplified form to the public sphere. The core of civil society comprises a network of associations that institutionalise problem-solving discourses on questions of general interest inside the framework of organised public spheres. These 'discursive designs' have an egalitarian, open form of organisation that mirrors essential features of the kind of communication around which they crystallise and to which they lend continuity and permanence.[13]

More recently, the Carnegie Trust's *Inquiry into the Future of Civil Society in the UK and Ireland* defines civil society as 'a goal to aim for (a "good" society), a means to achieve it (associational life), and a framework for engaging with each other about ends and means (arenas for deliberation)'.[14] This *Inquiry* asks the key question: 'How does civil society influence the development of technology so it supports the development of a "good society" rather than undermines it?'[15] Central to our argument here is the notion that technology is a subordinate player, and one that needs civil society-proofing in the production of the good society. The *Inquiry* further asks how civil society is to connect to representative politics at all levels, indicates that a good civil society is dependent on the outcomes of and relationships between government, statutory agencies, the business sector and the media, and concludes with the idea of civil society as arenas or spaces for public deliberation.[16] It follows that consultation processes, according to our definition, are incidences of civil society, and activist citizens engage in such deliberative arenas. Reporting on, understanding and critiquing activist citizens' perceptions of consultation processes is, therefore, a central objective of this chapter.

Governmental broadband initiatives, however, are initially driven by the imperative of providing services to areas with the necessary critical economic mass. In Habermasian terms, the *Systems* of *Money* and *Power* take precedence over the *Lifeworlds* of ordinary citizens and of the public sphere. This results in an ever-widening gap between those citizens who are online and those who are left on the outside. A major obstacle to both E-Government provision and to the practice of E-Democracy, including E-Consultation, is that many marginalised groups and geographical areas have neither the technological skills nor the local infrastructures to access ICT-based systems – whether these be E-Consultation or other. Some supporting evidence is presented below. The most recent comprehensive study of ICT in the Republic of Ireland, for example, finds that

> the main digital divide among private individuals relates to divergences between groups defined in terms of education, social class, age and economic status. Age and education are possibly the most important structural dimensions of potential e-exclusion.[17]

Beyond system influences, there are issues related to motivation and participation that are 'inherently human in character and there is a limit to what technical solutions can do'.[18] Most citizens remain totally unaware or gloriously oblivious of the existence of consultation processes; others totally ignore such processes and do not participate. As a leading article in the *Irish Examiner*[19] succinctly, if somewhat colourfully, puts it:

> Newspaper notices from government departments and state agencies announcing public consultation periods are usually as dull as Lent in Siberia and are rarely a match for the full-colour price war advertisement or lingerie feature leaping out from the opposite page.

In the following sections we provide some insights from our discussions with activist citizens from the institutional core of civil society on the island of Ireland – both Northern and Southern – on how they perceive extant real-world public consultation processes. We elicit their views on the future potential of E-Consultation.

Methodology

In total, eight one-hour focus group discussions on the theme of consultation were conducted between November 2004 and January 2005 – six in the Republic of Ireland and two in Northern Ireland. Focus group methodologies have a good track record in conducting research on and with community groups in Ireland.[20] The main focus was on 'consultation' as distinct from 'E-Consultation'; the research group believed that this was a key first step in grasping relevant insights to direct further, more specific research and development on E-Consultation and would perhaps lead to useful theoretical insights emerging.[21] The ongoing results of this research were forwarded to key policymakers on the island of Ireland.

One focus group was female only, with the others reasonably balanced between male and female participants. Forty-four citizens participated in total: 21 male and 23 female. These sessions were taped and transcribed, generating in excess of 100,000 words. These were then read and discussed by the research group members, and emergent themes identified. Participants were generally activist citizens from the institutional core within their communities. They were community activists, members of voluntary organisations, youth group members, training group members, peace group members, elderly needs activists, disability action activists and rural development activists. Our findings, therefore, relate to the perceptions and experiences of such activist citizens; the citizenry as a whole generally does not participate in such consultation processes.

Findings and discussion

The main finding, across all groups, is the striking and unequivocal levels of cynicism and frustration which emanate from these activist citizens towards state- or administration-initiated consultation processes. In Habermasian terms (*Between Facts and Norms*, 1996), the relationship between *System* and *Lifeworld* is perceived as largely, if not totally, negative. Some view such consultation processes as public relations exercises or an expression of political correctness. Others, as our focus group transcripts amply demonstrate, participate because they believe they have to in order to ensure that certain resources – usually material or financial – will flow in their direction from the administrative sub-systems of government. In other words, they play the game, doff the cap and kow-tow to the perceived power of the *System* within the consultation process to protect the interests of their local *Lifeworlds*. However, they do not really believe that their views are heard, or that such views will have as much as an iota of effect on policy. Addressing *Power*, these citizens exude power-*less*-ness. Such is definitely not consultation, which, by definition, would imply a two-way flow, however unbalanced, of communication and influence.

Not all is negative, however. Many, if not all, of the participants acknowledged that current difficulties with time, cost and long-distance travel would be greatly reduced if ICT were both accessible and usable by the majority of citizens. This is a useful finding in terms of dynamics, procedures and processes, whatever about content and actual influence of future E-Consultation processes, as most of these citizens live in geographical areas that are distant from the administrative centres of power in Belfast, Dublin and London. Other positive themes that emerged were that consultation processes, when conducted properly, have the potential to generate community spirit, provide a voice for under-represented groups, provide a forum for discussion, allow all interested parties to move forward together and balance the policy process through its feedback mechanisms.

These citizens, despite the levels of cynicism and frustration expressed, believe in consultation as a valuable exercise that can generate more detailed and relevant information than other methods of information gathering. Consultation allows participants the opportunity to voice their opinions and concerns on issues and, when conducted properly, can foster a spirit of partnership, resulting in enhanced decision making, better policy-making and more socially acceptable outcomes. This is all very much in line with the arguments presented by Carnegie on the good society.[22] Throughout, face-to-face consultation was viewed as the optimal medium.

> [T]he underlying important thing about any consultation . . . if it's properly structured and you have the, shall we say, correct range of people there . . . it's not just an opportunity to have everything on the table and move your project forward, it's also an opportunity to dig your heels in and say 'hang on are we going the right way here, do we need to step back' and I think . . . sort of . . . the important thing there is how you set up the consultation.

In theory, any consultation process between state and citizen or citizen and state should be a mutually beneficial and worthwhile exercise. However, participants note that consultation has become a legislative requirement of the administrative decision-making process as distinct from the idea-generating or real fact-finding exercise that it could, or indeed should, be. Participants want consultation to be a meaningful exercise – not simply a meaningless rubber-stamping legislative and procedural requirement – but they perceive changes in current practices and processes as far more important than the mere introduction of new consultation media. This signals to us that the lifeworld process of deliberative democracy may be a better point of departure for thinking about future E-Consultation processes than instrumental system dictates, whether these be E-Government or E-Administration. Participants generally said that conducting consultations via electronic means is a good idea in theory. However, this is qualified by their belief that E-Consultation would also create new problems in practice and, more critically if implicitly, that extant fundamental problems would simply be replicated in electronic mode, which would do absolutely nothing to enhance either the quality of extant consultation processes or, indeed, the democratic process itself.

Citizens enter consultations for a number of reasons: they wish to make changes in something or other; they want to have some input into decision-making processes and policy formation; or they want to highlight issues that state or system representatives have not previously considered or of which they may simply be unaware. Focus group participants indicated that in some cases they were receiving as many as five invitations a week to attend various consultations. (Note once again that these are activist citizens; such invitations are rarely received by the public at large other than implicitly in bleak newspaper communications, as noted above.) These invitations are often met with either cynicism or annoyance. This cynicism results in some participants wishing that they could withdraw completely from such processes. In many cases, however, activist citizens are unable to do so as their financing is controlled by those administrative or system agents who are orchestrating or directing such consultation processes. As responsible representatives of their local communities or associations, it follows that they have little choice but to play the game or else their association, community or lifeworld will suffer the consequences. Some expressed an interest in the idea of E-Consultation, but some of these were alienated within their groups by favouring technology. This split within some, if not all, of these focus groups, if representative of society at large, is also indicative of future difficulties in designing and implementing successful E-Consultation processes. Once again, technology alone is not perceived to be the solution to extant problems within consultation processes.

In theory, democratic society allows the citizen to have input into the laws, regulations and institutions that govern it. In practice, however, participants indicated that this was very, very far from the norm. Important decisions are made on a regular basis without any significant citizen input. This increases the overall sense of frustration that these citizens direct towards many consultation events. Participants noted that administrative system agents regarded consultation as a regulatory requirement, simply a box that has to be ticked off in some politically correct fashion before they get their own way or do what they were already going to do anyway. Systems, and their administrative agents, are perceived to totally dominate their lifeworlds. Promises were broken on numerous occasions, leading the participants to pose an apt question: What's the point? It is difficult to accurately envisage how ICT-mediated E-Consultation will ameliorate, let alone solve, any of the current problems. Such problems were noted as citizens being unaware that consultations are taking place; system or administrative agents viewing the process as a mere legislative or regulatory requirement; citizens' views not being really heard; decisions being made before the consultation actually takes place; consultations being too time-consuming and frequently taking place at times and locations that are unsuitable to participants; and so on.

Citizens are expected to participate, voice their concerns and draw on their local knowledge[23] for the betterment of their associations, communities or local lifeworlds.

These are the vanguard, the full hall, the committees, the volunteers and so on who enter into the process with some hope of having significant input into the consultation process by influencing policy-making and decision making. Significantly, sometimes it does work:

> [T]he volunteer groups are out there you know . . . the Care of the Aged group in Donegal is one of the best in the country because Donegal is divided in five regions, and say Inishowen is a region and the regional committees . . . there are eight committees now in Inishowen, and we go to a regional meeting and we sent representatives to a county coordinated meeting where the five regions meet, and we meet . . . at that particular meeting with health people . . . health people and Donegal county councillors and other people [who] want to come and give talks . . . we bring that back to the regional and the regional fans it out to the local committees and that is a brilliant network that's sitting there to be used by anyone [who] wants to throw in some money for us to do things for the local people anywhere . . . you know . . . and we can do it . . . [consultation] should be a useful exercise.

However, they often go unheeded. Input is collected but all too often diluted, reworked or ignored. In general, these citizens are willing to participate in consultation processes when conducted properly as consultation is perceived to be the best way of eliciting information that is relevant to their lifeworlds:

> [T]he underlying important thing about any consultation . . . if it's properly structured and you have the . . . shall we say . . . correct range of people there . . . it's an opportunity to have everything on the table and move your project forward.

But they become very disheartened when the end product does not incorporate their viewpoints and needs. Worse, the end product often does not arrive at all and these citizens are left suspended in a silent non-communicative no-man's land, wondering what, if anything, is ever going to happen. Too often they do not even expect a response from '*them*': 'I wouldn't expect to hear anything back from *them* and I think that's people's general perception.' We do not, of course, identify the particular 'them' in this instance – we merely note the probable general applicability of the term. As Habermas puts it:

> The structures of a power-ridden, oppressed public sphere exclude fruitful and clarifying discussions. The 'quality' of public opinion, insofar as it is measured by the procedural properties of its process of generation, is an empirical variable. From a normative perspective, this provides a basis for measuring the legitimacy of the influence that public opinion has on the political system. Of course, actual influence coincides with legitimate influence just as little as the belief in legitimacy coincides with legitimacy. But conceiving things this way at least opens a perspective from which the relation between actual influence and the procedurally grounded quality of public opinion can be empirically investigated.[24]

An understanding of power dynamics must be central to future work on E-Consultation. Ainsworth *et al.*[25] analysed postings to two online forums to explore the Internet's capacity to foster democracy and to investigate how power and resistance are exercised through this medium. Rather than equate resistance with participation, as some models of democracy do, they argue, based on their findings, that the dynamics of power and resistance are more complex, and that resistance and power can take both participative and non-participative forms.

The nature of community activism on the island of Ireland suggests that citizen activists participate in such consultations for the following reasons. First, it is due to a desire to shape public policy 'to actually support the local community . . . For the enhancement of the local area or projects' and the need to use the process to highlight the 'needs' of particular groups – both of which admirably fit the dictates of what a functioning deliberative democracy can be by streaming the flows of communication from their lifeworlds, or through the public sphere, to the administrative, legislative or political systems – hence, exerting some influence on these systems. Alternatively, it is due to a basic dictated need to please, appease, satisfy or massage their funding administrative body or system or their agents – a much more instrumental and latently strategic purpose that is a million miles from anything that could remotely be termed 'deliberative democracy' and far closer to a Nietzschean or Foucauldian type slave–master relation. Sadly, our empirical findings suggest that the latter is presently the more dominant driver for activist-citizen participation in many real-world consultation processes on the island of Ireland. Foucault[26] notes the methodological distinction between 'archaeology', appropriate for an analysis of 'local discursivities', and 'genealogy', which provides the 'tactics whereby, on the basis of the descriptions of these local discursivities, the subjected knowledges which were thus released would be brought into play'. The evidence presented here suggests that much local knowledge fails to find its way from the consultation process into the play of the policy-making process.

Whereas consultations are widespread across the island of Ireland, we must now seriously question the structure, efficiency and effectiveness of such consultation processes. From the perspectives of the lifeworld and deliberative democracy, we appear to be witnessing a culture of democratic failure with little evidence that these citizens distil and transmit their viewpoints in amplified form to the public sphere or somehow influence the will-formation of administrative, legal, political or governmental systems or their agents. There are serious structural problems with the nature of the communicative flows of local knowledge, information and influence evident here. As three focus-group participants astutely put it:

'It's loaded . . . a lot of the questions are even asked in such a way that you can only give one answer, you know . . .'

'. . . maybe the way to deal with this isn't to ask people what their responses or answers are to a particular set of questions but maybe what they should be doing is asking people what the questions are . . .'

'. . . Yeah . . . and I suppose the other thing is sometimes it's the questions that people never had the chance to answer . . . that nobody asked before, which can get a good response . . . you know . . . if somebody says – What are the difficulties you face because you live in a rural area? – and you want to tell them because nobody has asked before . . .'

Such failure is manifest in many forms. Citizens can be left out of the discussion, resulting in apathy or disquiet when the final service or product is delivered. The structure of the consultation and the questions posed quite often do not allow participants to voice their real concerns. When they do not attend, they have no voice at all. The initial consultation is often both the beginning and the end of their participation. It is a token gesture, an effort to appease. Such tokenism is detrimental to real consultation processes, resulting in such citizens becoming alienated from the process as a whole: 'oh jeepers not another . . . now there's more bother . . .'.

Participants in improperly run consultations felt used, as if their input had only been accommodated to adhere to system or legislative guidelines or requirements. Consultation is all too often mere rubber-stamping or a 'for the sake of doing it' approach to evidence-based policy-making or decision making. In some cases, 'the powers that be had no idea' of the situations faced by the participants in their everyday lifeworlds. They believe that administrative or governmental agencies, systems or agents regularly make incorrect or generalised assumptions about their circumstances. This belief increases feelings of anomie and alienation and sometimes even generates hostility among the participants themselves ('you have no right to judge that . . .'), leading to withdrawal, disillusionment, frustration and/or cynicism. This malaise filters through to other consultation processes which are often genuine and conducted in a more professional manner. Feedback on the views gathered is often not forthcoming and participants are regularly confused about the nature of the ongoing process:

'. . . like the only way I ever find . . . getting any results is talking . . . by talking to the person . . . people face-to-face . . .'

'But since . . . there was almost a statutory requirement to send out information and to have consultations carried out almost at a functionary level. We don't see any return in terms of old people's strategy, youth strategy . . . you don't see . . . you can't actually even find within their documents your information that was provided, and there is no formal way of providing it back.'

Such processes result in outcomes that do not reflect the views of the participants accurately:

'. . . and unfortunately [in] the majority . . . [of] consultation processes that community groups are involved in . . . the decision has already been made . . .'

'We're being consulted and frequently we find con . . . I find consultation takes place and it's an area where the decision has actually been made . . . there is a sense of going through the motions and being seen to listen . . . and being seen to take things on board when actually . . . when it comes to the final decision maker, whether it's to do with charges for personal health care or whether it's to do with water charges or whether it's to do with rating policy, at the end of the day . . . whenever the final decision is made . . . that's made and in many cases that decision has been made before you've been invited in . . .'

These perceived instances of decision making actually preceding their associated consultation processes are not unique to the island of Ireland. Flyvbjerg,[27] to take just one example, describes in minute Foucauldian detail how the decision to locate a bus terminal in the city of Aalborg in Denmark was actually taken before the official investigation, consultation and decision-making processes were even begun. Policymakers and the public widely subscribe to the view that policy-making should be well informed. The normative ideal of evidence-based policy-making, however, is often unmatched by the provision of resources to collect such evidence. Our participants spoke of consensus-building policy shaping actual decision making. These citizens exhibited huge levels of frustration when they could not have any real input into policy that directly affected their lifeworlds or associations. They noted that it was not enough to simply consult with people; they had to be listened to, and their ideas had to be somehow incorporated in shaping public policies:

'It's important to have consumers involved from the start of any consultation and not dragged in at the end to . . . kind of fulfil a criterion.'

'At the end of the day the powers that be go back to their offices in Dublin and say "well we're still going to do it our way despite what the people in the North West say".'

'Maybe the people's expectations of outcomes were not realistic.'

Participants spoke about access difficulties that were perhaps system-generated in latently strategic fashion in order to preclude or exclude extreme or unwanted views. For example, consultations were held at times or in locations that were unsuitable to a section of the potential audience: 'It's about finding the best fit for the individual.' Or consultation processes are perceived as being unrealistic in their expectations because they are more about 'the boys slapping themselves on the back' than dealing with the real issues that are of concern to citizens. Consultations are shows put on so that the powers that be can be seen to be doing something. However, these day-long consultations are often nothing but a real inconvenience to such activist-citizens, who have to take (often uncompensated) leave from their regular work in order to attend. These types of consultations leave such citizens feeling even more frustrated:

'. . . what you find as well . . . you see all the bigwigs there . . . and they are all there to be seen. Yet, you know, when you ring them on a day-to-day basis looking for help with funding or maybe you've got a problem [with] something, you can never get in contact with them, and they are there in front of you . . . and you have the perfect opportunity to talk to them, yet you've some guy from

> . . . there [was] a guy up from South Africa yesterday doing a talk, yet why weren't they up? . . . you know . . . it didn't take somebody from South Africa to come up and tell us what peace is about . . . and I know . . . I understand where they are coming from and it's great to get that diversity and so on . . . but . . . [*mild profanity excluded here*] the real issues are obviously with the training bodies and with the European funding and we . . . we never get . . . a direct contact with them . . . . like they were all there yet we couldn't get talking to them, we weren't actually allowed to talk to them.'

Such findings indicate strong levels of frustration with current consultation processes. The possible future role of ICT in E-Consultation, albeit broadly if not over-enthusiastically welcomed, is not seen as the solution here to many of the major concerns put forward during the focus group discussions:

> 'There are an awful lot of families who have a list of priorities and a PC is way down the bottom of the line . . .'

> 'It's not even as simple as that though because . . . technology is just so bad here [that] if you start a[n online] questionnaire . . . I know for me at home . . . I get kicked out and then I've lost everything and I have to go back in again.'

One participant summed up the situation very succinctly: 'I wouldn't see it as the be all and end all of everything, to be honest with you. I would think that it could be just one additional mechanism in relation to a range of options that could be used.'

What those options are remains very much an open question.

Conclusion

Whither E-Consultation? Theoretically, in a fully ICT-mediated ambient environment within the context of deliberative E-Democracy, citizen access and input to local processes of opinion and will formation, E-Consultation processes, the public sphere and the administrative, legislative, political or E-Governmental systems is unlimited *if* – and this is one particularly large *if* – citizens can make use of their collective ICT base to contact, participate in and perhaps influence such discourses and systems. The communicative rationality of local lifeworlds may, theoretically, be communicated by citizens via E-Consultation processes with the purpose of influencing decision-making processes and public policy that directly affects them.

If Habermas[28] is anywhere near accurate, however, in claiming that 'the "quality" of public opinion, insofar as it is measured by the procedural properties of its process of generation, is an empirical variable', then the empirical findings presented here on the quality of extant consultation processes on the island of Ireland are, to put it mildly, startlingly troublesome. Presently, participation in consultation processes is decidedly the pursuit of a tiny minority of activist citizens and representatives of interest groups on the island of Ireland. We found that consultation was rarely executed in a way that was conducive to positively moving a process forward. The major theme to emerge was that consultations were conducted for consultation's sake; they are an exercise of form filling and/or tokenism for the state or administrative bodies and their agents. Participants believed that decisions were often already made and that consultation was a cosmetic attempt to meet statutory or regulatory requirements prior to policy implementation. This sentiment is supported in the key themes that emerged: cynicism, scepticism and frustration are based on previous negative experiences; there is a failure to reach all layers of the community; and consultation is often perceived to be merely an exercise in system- or administrative-driven tokenism.

Returning to Habermas:[29]

> Deliberative politics acquires its legitimating force from the discursive structure of an opinion and will-formation that can fulfil its socially integrative function only because citizens expect its results to have a reasonable *quality*. Hence the *discursive level* of public debates constitutes the most important variable. It must not be hidden away in the black box of an operationalisation satisfied with crude indicators. [emphasis in original]

Flyvbjerg[30] notes the 'tension between the normative and the real, between what should be done and what is actually done' and argues that developing an 'understanding [of] this tension is crucial to understanding modern democracy, what it is and what it could be'. The pragmatist conclusion that we reach here in addressing this tension is that the problems to be initially understood in terms of E-Consultation are essentially problems of democracy and not solely problems of technology. Addressing consultation, as a prelude to thinking about the future of E-Consultation, the point of departure for future work, demands that the foundations be solidly built on an understanding of the democratic process itself – particularly local democratic processes. This demands that participation, legitimacy and mutual influence, as distinct from one-way system-driven tokenism, take precedence over the dictates of technology. Technology, however sophisticated, is merely a tool, a means to an end. The danger, in terms of E-Consultation, is that the technology itself becomes viewed as the end. Were this to happen, it is probable that extant problems with consultation processes would merely be replicated via electronic means and large segments of the citizenry would simply be further marginalised.

As the history and present cultural, social and political identities of the people on the island of Ireland amply demonstrate, democracy is a fragile process that has first to be established and institutionalised, and then continuously re-generated from local lifeworlds. The citizens who conversed with us in the focus groups indicated that they want better and more mutually beneficial legitimate and influential consultations – that is, they want better democracy. Following Dewey,[31] 'the essential need [. . .] is the improvement of the methods and conditions of debate, discussion and persuasion'. Following the critical theory agenda we have 'stirred things up'[32] by challenging the potential reproduction, via electronic means, of a dominant mode of social ordering that, from the evidence presented here, appears to actually constrain human possibilities. In conclusion, the problems related to extant consultation processes identified here are essentially problems of democracy, not problems that can be solved by technology alone. This is the insight of which that all those involved in the vanguard of E-Consultation should not lose sight.

Key points

- Flows of communication are examined in the context of a discussion on real-world public consultation processes.
- Internationally, many governments – not all democratic – have already developed some of the potential of ICT towards an ambient intelligent environment, including E-Consultation.
- Key argument: There exists a massive culture of cynicism and frustration among participating citizens and community activists with respect to extant consultation processes.
- Key question: If such levels of cynicism exist – regardless of the sophistication of the ICT technology or software systems employed – whither the effectiveness of future E-Consultation processes?
- From a critical modernist viewpoint, ICT-mediated improvements are in no way inevitable.
- The communicative rationality of local lifeworlds may, theoretically, be communicated by citizens via E-Consultation processes with the purpose of influencing decision-making processes and public policy that directly affect them.
- However, empirical findings from focus groups in Ireland suggest that cynicism, scepticism and frustration are based on previous negative experiences; there is a failure to reach all layers of the community; and consultation is often perceived to be merely an exercise in system- or administrative-driven tokenism.
- Technology is a subordinate player. It needs civil society-proofing in the production of the 'good society'.
- Problems related to extant consultation processes are essentially problems of democracy, not problems that can be solved by technology alone.

Notes

1 Habermas, J. (1996) *Between Facts and Norms*. Cambridge: Polity, p. 304.
2 Ibid. p. 365.
3 Ibid. p. 366. Original emphasis.
4 Morison, J. (2004) 'Models of Democracy: From Representation to Participation?', in D. Oliver and J. Owell (eds), *Changing Constitution*, pp. 144–170, Oxford: Oxford University Press. See also http://www.equalityni.org/index.cfm; http://www.nicva.org; http://www.caj.org.uk.
5 Davis, S. (2002) *Click on Democracy: The Internet's Power to Change Political Apathy into Civic Action*. Boulder, CO: Westview Press; OECD (2003) *Promise and Problems of E-Democracy: Challenges of Online Citizen Engagement*. Paris: OECD.
6 Coleman, S., Hall, N. and Howell, M. (2002) *Hearing Voices: The Experience of Online Public Consultation and Discussions in UK Governance*. London: Hansard Society; Morison, J. and Newman, D. R. (2001) 'On-Line Citizenship: Consultation and Participation in New

Labour's Britain and Beyond', *International Review of Law Computers & Technology* 15/2: 171–194.

7   Flyvbjerg, B. (1998) 'Habermas and Foucault: Thinkers for Civil Society?', *British Journal of Sociology* 49/2: 210–233; Habermas, J. (1996) op. cit.; Hamlett, P. W. (2003) 'Technology Theory and Deliberative Democracy', *Science, Technology, & Human Values* 28/1: 112–140; Macintosh, A. (2004) 'Using Information and Communication Technologies to Enhance Citizen Engagement in the Policy Process', in *Promises and problems of E-Democracy: Challenges of online citizen engagement.* Paris: OECD; Macintosh, A., Coleman, S. and Lalljee, M. (2005) *e-Methods for public engagement: Helping local authorities communicate with citizens.* Bristol City Council for the Local eDemocracy National Project; http://itc.napier.ac.uk/ITC/documents/eMethods_guide2005.pdf; O'Donnell, D. and Henriksen, L. B. (2002) 'Philosophical Foundations for a Critical Evaluation of the Social Impact of ICT', *Journal of Information Technology* 17/2: 89–99.

8   Rehg, W. (2000) 'Critical Science Studies as Argumentation Theory: Who's Afraid of SSK?', *Philosophy of the Social Sciences* 30/1: 33–48.

9   For a review see Bew, P. (2001) 'The *Belfast Agreement* of 1998: From Ethnic Democracy to a Multicultural, Consociational Settlement?', in M. Cox, A. Guelke and F. Stephen (eds), *A Farewell to Arms? From 'Long War' to Long Peace in Northern Ireland*, pp. 40–48, Manchester: Manchester University Press; Laver, M. (1994) 'Are Irish Parties Peculiar?', in J. H. Goldthorpe and C. T. Whelan (eds), *The Development of Industrial Society in Ireland*, pp. 359–381, Oxford: published for the British Academy by Oxford University Press; Wilford, R. and Wilson, R. (2006) *The Trouble with Northern Ireland: The Belfast Agreement and Democratic Governance*, Dublin: TASC/New Island Publishing.

10 Habermas, J. (1996) op. cit.

11 See Hirschheim, R. and Klein, H. K. (1989) 'Four Paradigms of Information Systems Development', *Communications of the ACM* 32/10: 1199–1216; Hirschheim, R. and Klein, H. K. (1994) 'Realizing Emancipatory Principles in Information Systems Development: The Case for ETHICS', *MIS Quarterly* 18/1: 83–109; Hirschheim, R., Klein, H. K. and Lyytinen, K. (1996) 'Exploring the Intellectual Structures of Information Systems Development: A Social Action Theoretic Analysis', *Accounting, Management and Information Technologies* 6/1–2: 1–64; Klein, H. K. and Myers, M. D. (1999) 'A Set of Principles for Conducting and Evaluating Interpretive Field Studies in Information Systems', *MIS Quarterly* 23/1: 67–93; Ngwenyama, O. K. and Lee, A. S. (1997) 'Communication Richness in Electronic Mail: Critical Social Theory and the Contextuality of Meaning', *MIS Quarterly* 21: 145–167; O'Donnell, D. and Henriksen, L. B. (2002) op. cit.

12 See Heng, M. S. H. and de Moor, A. (2003) 'From Habermas's Communicative Theory to Practice on the Internet', *Information Systems Journal* 13: 331–352; Coleman, S. (2004) 'Whose Conversation? Engaging the Public in Authentic Polylogue', *The Political Quarterly* 75/2: 112–120; Ainsworth, S., Hardy, C. and Harley, B. (2005) 'Online Consultation: e-Democracy and e-Resistance in the Case of the Development Gateway', *Management Communication Quarterly* 19/2: 120–145.

13 Habermas, J. (1996) op. cit. p. 367.

14 Carnegie UK Trust (2007) *Futures for Civil Society: Summary.* Available: www.carnegieuktrust.org.uk, p. 9.

15 Ibid. p. 7.

16 Ibid. p. 9.

17 Williams, J., Blackwell, S. and Whelan, B. J. (2004) *Survey Assessments of the Information Society in Ireland*, p. 87, Dublin: Economic and Social Research Institute.

18 Heng, M. S. H. and de Moor, A. (2003) op. cit. p. 349.

19 6 August 2004, p. 14.

20 McCusker, P., McDaid, P. and O'Dubhchair, K. (1998) 'Using Focus Groups in the Community', Discussion paper, University of Ulster.

21 See Fagan, G. H., Newman, D. R., McCusker, P. and Murray, M. (2006) *E-Consultation: Evaluating Appropriate Technologies and Processes for Citizens' Participation in Public Policy.* Final Report for the HEA. http://www.nuim.ie/nirsa/econsult/.

22 Carnegie UK Trust (2007) op. cit.

23 Geertz, C. (1983) *Local Knowledge: Further Essays in Interpretive Anthropology*. New York: Basic Books.
24 Habermas, J. (1996) op. cit. pp. 62–63.
25 Ainsworth, S., Hardy, C. and Harley, B. (2005) op. cit.
26 Foucault, M. (1980) 'Two Lectures', in C. Gordon (ed.), *Power/Knowledge: Selected Interviews and Other Writings 1972–1977 by Michel Foucault*, pp. 78–108, New York: Pantheon Books.
27 Flyvbjerg, B. (1991) *Rationalitet og Magt, Bind II: Et Case-baseret Studie af Planlægning, Politik og Modernitet* (Rationality and Power, Volume II: A case-based study of planning, politics and modernity). Aalborg: Akademisk Forlag.
28 Habermas, J. (1996) op. cit. pp. 362–363.
29 Ibid. p. 304.
30 Flyvbjerg, B. (1991) op. cit. p. 210.
31 Dewey, J. (1954 [1927]) *The Public and Its Problems*, p. 207 Athens, OH: Swallow Press cited in Habermas (1996) op. cit.
32 Alvesson, M. and Deetz, S. (2000) *Doing Critical Management Research*. London: Sage.

Further reading

Guy B. Peters (2001) *The Politics of Bureaucracy*, 5th edition. Routledge: New York.
Cohen, Jean L. and Arato, A. (1992) *Civil society and political theory*. Cambridge, MA: The MIT Press.
Coleman, Stephen (2005) *Direct representation: Towards a conversational democracy*. London: Institute for Public Policy Research (IPPR).
Lukensmeyer, Carolyn, J. and Torres, Lars Hasselblad (2006) *Public deliberation: A manager's guide to citizen engagement*. Washington, DC: IMB Center for The Business of Government.

Part III

E-Government in practice

8 Online dispute resolution, E-Justice and Web 2.0

Joseph Savirimuthu

Summary

This chapter explores the implications of the convergence of communication technologies for the resolution of civil disputes. Enabling parties to make informed decisions, the use of third parties and technology help identify key issues and present disputants with realistic solutions. This can only serve to enhance the quality of the administration of justice. The convergence between information communication technologies (ICTs) and mechanisms for the resolution of civil disputes provides us with an invaluable opportunity to re-think orthodox conceptualisations of access to justice, particularly in the light of Article 6 of the European Convention on Human Rights. This chapter describes and explains the transformative capabilities of new technologies for traditional methods of dispute resolution and identifies the key policy priorities for E-Justice.

Introduction

Online communication technologies have become an integral part of social, economic and political activity. As the Bangemann Report observed in its opening statements:[1]

> Throughout the world, information and communications technologies are generating a new industrial revolution already as significant and far-reaching as those of the past. It is a revolution based on information, itself the expression of human knowledge. Technological progress now enables us to process, store, retrieve and communicate information in whatever form it may take – oral, written or visual – unconstrained by distance, time and volume. This revolution adds huge new capacities to human intelligence and constitutes a resource which changes the way we work together and the way we live together.

More than two decades later, computers have become ubiquitous. Internet penetration continues to increase. An estimated 1.4 billion people had access to the Internet in 2008. With increasing connectivity and decreasing cost of broadband, there is likely to be further growth. From a regulatory perspective, we are still coming to terms with the information society phenomena – from intellectual property, social networking and online child safety to concerns about identity, security and territorial sovereignty – and the constraints imposed by new technologies to governance strategies and institutional infrastructures.[2] The disruptive tendencies of technologies should not, however, distract us from the current emphasis on harnessing technology to better deliver public services and information. One of the goals of the information society project is to leverage the exponential resources of communication technologies to educate, empower and engage citizens.[3] The aim of this chapter is to better understand how communication technologies are transforming the role of citizens in the management and resolution of civil disputes. Improving a citizen's access to appropriate and effective mechanisms for dispute resolution, or E-Justice, is not a convenient political rhetoric; if the political vision of empowering individuals to assume greater responsibility in settling disputes materialises, there are undoubted cultural, administrative and regulatory consequences for the traditional role of courts and administrative tribunals.[4] For our purposes, E-Justice will be taken to mean[5] 'the use of ICTs and related management practices to enhance process efficiency in undertaking the work of the justice sector and in delivering services to the public as well as other government users'.

In this chapter I demonstrate that the convergence between information communication technologies and mechanisms for resolution of civil disputes provides us with an invaluable opportunity to re-think orthodox conceptualisations of 'access to justice', particularly in the light of Article 6 of the European Convention on Human Rights.[6] The chapter begins with an examination of the significance of the increasing trend towards embedding alternative dispute resolution norms in the civil justice system. This will help us better understand the relevance of online dispute resolution services and products for enhancing the processes through which disputing parties assume greater responsibility for the management of their disputes.[7] The chapter concludes that policymakers, judges and online service providers continue to have important roles in encouraging disputing parties to adopt effective and consensual approaches to the settlement of disputes.

E-Justice and alternative dispute resolution procedures

A ten-day trial can result in costs of over £250,000 being incurred. Increasing workloads, opportunistic behaviour, time involved in processing disputes and costs continue to place strains on the judicial and administrative machinery. Online dispute resolution is not the 'silver bullet' that will alleviate the long-standing pathologies of the civil legal system.[8] While policies that aim to deliver greater economic efficiencies in existing mechanisms for dispute resolution are legitimate priorities, any attempt to transpose the formalised judicial procedures for dispute resolution onto online processes should be approached with some circumspection. Before we turn to the central issue regarding the values that can properly be embedded in online dispute resolution (ODR) platforms, it is useful to understand the background against which current debates on the role of ODR take place.

Overview

Dispute resolution mechanisms, broadly speaking, are concerned with bringing conflicts between parties to a speedy and effective conclusion. These can involve, on the one hand, single-issue monetary claims and disputes between two individuals or, on the other hand, complex multi-party trans-border commercial disputes. Mechanisms for dispute resolution can be broadly divided into formal processes, as is the case for court proceedings and informal processes, where parties enter into direct communications with the aim of reaching a settlement.[9] Within both sets of processes, parties with disputes have a number of options available to them.[10] These are negotiation, mediation,[11] conciliation,[12] early neutral evaluation,[13] adjudication,[14] arbitration[15] and litigation. In the case of litigation, the judge hears the evidence and provides a ruling based on the applicable law. The proceedings are adversarial and formal. Alternative dispute resolution (ADR), however, is an umbrella term used to describe processes and options which facilitate settlements without recourse to litigation.[16] Arbitration, mediation, conciliation and negotiation are frequently regarded as mechanisms through which disputes can be resolved without formal court proceedings.[17] The settings are informal and the proceedings are not intended to be adversarial. This is not to suggest that there is no adjudicative component in ADR. Arbitration, for example, is an adjudicative process in the sense that a neutral third party (called an 'arbitrator') hears the evidence from the parties and presents them with a decision that is intended to be binding. Mediation, conciliation and negotiation are non-adjudicative. Neutral third parties appointed under these processes aim to facilitate communications between the disputing parties. Unlike arbitration or litigation, the object of processes like mediation, negotiation and conciliation is to enable parties to reach a mutually acceptable settlement.

ODR involves the use of ADR processes and mechanisms to resolve disputes between parties. ODR retains many of the attributes associated with processes like mediation and negotiation. ODR involves, but not exclusively, the use of information and communication technologies to enable parties to reach settlements.[18] The growing popularity of ODR not only reflects the transformative role of technology, but can also be regarded as meeting a cultural need for mobile, interactive, less formal, speedy and inexpensive approaches to dispute resolution. Insurance companies now use expert software platforms to resolve monetary claims made by policyholders. Businesses now host portals where consumers can communicate their grievances and have matters resolved speedily. It is not uncommon to find law firms integrating ODR platforms into their business models. ODR is not limited to the private sector. The convergence of communication technologies and dispute resolution mechanisms is now regarded as an integral part of facilitating greater accountability and responsiveness of local authorities to its constituents.[19] A number of government organisations now have websites and online information services aiming to process and handle complaints from constituents.[20]

There are undoubted efficiency benefits in leveraging communication technologies for the settlement of disputes. Technologies increase the flow of information and facilitate opportunities for reflection and deliberation without the parties having to turn up in court or the solicitor's office.[21] With increased use of ODR platforms, consumers and individuals now have a range of mechanisms for resolving disputes at their disposal. For example, monetary claims involving minor penalties like parking fines can be expedited without all the parties having to exchange correspondence of a repetitive nature or be physically present at the local authority's premises.[22] An email exchange can often help identify relevant issues, define the obligations of the parties and arrest any misunderstandings that may have led to the grievance arising in the first place. Communication technologies are particularly invaluable where there are cross-border issues involved. Asynchronous exchanges not only introduce greater flexibility, but also create opportunities for deliberation in any decision-making process.[23] These are welcome trends and they are indicative of the impact of communication technologies on the processes for settlement of disputes. In the light of the foregoing discussion, one question remains to be addressed: How should we conceptualise 'access to justice' (in particular, the relationship between E-Justice, ODR and Article 6 of the European Convention on Human Rights)? The remainder of this section will be devoted to considering the issues raised by this question.

Access to justice and alternative dispute resolution

The policy of focusing on educating, engaging and empowering citizens in managing their disputes legitimately and effectively adheres to the principles of equality and fairness that underpin the administration of justice. Access to justice has a procedural dimension. Article 6 of the European Convention on Human Rights provides that[24] 'In the determination of his civil rights and obligations . . . everyone is entitled to a fair and public hearing within a reasonable time by an independent and impartial tribunal established by law. Judgments shall be pronounced publicly.'

One reading of this provision is that disputes should be brought before judicial and administrative proceedings within a reasonable timeframe. Reducing barriers to dispute settlement proceedings is one aspect of fulfilling an individual's expectations of speedy and timely hearing of disputes. There is a wider sense in which the term 'access' can be understood, and this is to do with providing individuals with greater support in terms of services and processes for managing disputes. As the Ministry of Justice seems to recognise, there is a role for the State in making it easier for individuals to have issues relating to their civil rights and obligations addressed through alternative mechanisms for dispute resolution:[25]

> [W]hen people do need help, there are effective solutions that are proportionate to the issues at stake. In some circumstances, this will involve going to court; but in others, that will not be necessary. Someone charged with a criminal offence should have access to proper legal advice and representation, when the interests of justice require it. But in civil matters, for most people, most of the time, going to court is, and should be, the last resort. It is in no-one's interest to create a litigious society. People must make responsible choices about whether a case is worth pursuing; whether to proceed by negotiation, court action, or in some other way; and how far to take a relatively minor issue.

Access to justice, in this context, is about transforming the way individuals can assume greater responsibility in processing and resolving disputes. Of course, there are qualifications. Whether the State continues to assert its monopoly over the issues that can be left for private determination will depend on whether the matters involve criminal or civil liability. In criminal proceedings, public interest considerations may justify vesting the State with the ultimate responsibility for providing a centralised forum for dispute resolution. Additionally, since the sanctions imposed by the criminal law potentially curb an individual's liberty and freedom, the ends of justice require speedy and inexpensive access to legal services and representation. There is unlikely to be any disagreement, however, concerning the creating of supportive infra-structures in relation to civil disputes. Indeed, the civil legal system is already meeting this need. The idea that courts should only be seen as a matter of last resort is not a new one and we should not overlook the long-standing role of the judiciary in encouraging legal advisers and disputing parties to seek alternatives to court proceedings.[26] For example, following the recommendations of Lord Woolf, the UK courts have been instrumental in encouraging parties to settle their disputes without resorting to litigation. The focus on reducing barriers to the resolution of disputes has for example, transformed the way disputes are processed and managed. The Civil Procedure Rules create new opportunities for disputes to be settled out of court. Courts now have an obligation to manage those disputes either where parties have been unable to agree or where alternative mechanisms for dispute resolution are not appropriate.[27] Under Rule 1.1, a court is encouraged to undertake an 'active case management' role.[28] This entails the court assuming a proactive role, which includes:

(e) encouraging the parties to use an alternative dispute resolution procedure if the court considers that appropriate and facilitating the use of such procedure;
(f) helping the parties to settle the whole or part of the case;
(g) fixing timetables or otherwise controlling the progress of the case;
(h) considering whether the likely benefits of taking a particular step justify the cost of taking it;
(i) dealing with as many aspects of the case as it can on the same occasion;
(j) dealing with the case without the parties needing to attend at court;
(k) making use of technology; and
(l) giving directions to ensure that the trial of a case proceeds quickly and efficiently.

The case management process can be regarded as an attempt to provide parties with incentives to broker a settlement. Financial incentives also figure in the case management process. For example, the court is now required to have regard to the conduct of all the parties, including, in particular, the conduct before, as well as during, the proceedings and the efforts made, if any, before and during the proceedings in order to try to resolve the dispute.[29] There is also a growing trend towards encouraging courts and legal service providers to adopt best practice dispute settlement methods. The *Court Mediation Service Toolkit*, published by Her Majesty's Court Service, can be regarded as one attempt to promote greater understanding of the benefits of reaching efficient and fair settlements.[30] The *Toolkit* provides courts, judges and mediation providers with guidance on handing and processing disputes. Access to legal services and ADR have now entered into the mainstream of public discourse. Media campaigns and online services have been launched by the government to promote greater awareness of the advantages of resolving disputes out of court.[31] Increasingly, the value of sustaining good relations is used to encourage parties to adopt ADR. This message is now getting through to a range of legal services providers. The Tribunals Service launched a pilot scheme for the use of mediation in employment tribunals in England and Wales.[32] Courts in the small claims system have assumed a pivotal role in using mediation rather than litigation in resolving conflicts.[33] There is an expectation that the legal profession now deliver services which are readily accessible and of good quality.[34] Members of the legal profession are encouraged to develop ADR techniques and skills. The legal profession is also audited on how complaints made by the general public in respect of its members are handled. The Office of the Legal Services Complaints Commissioner now provides an important oversight over the Law Society's management of complaints. Finally, it is also recognised that increasing parties' access to relevant information can enhance the quality of the deliberative and decision-making process. Pre-action Protocols have been developed to enable information sharing between disputing parties with a view to producing speedy outcomes to conflicts.[35] The rationale for the protocols should be readily apparent: parties are seen as less likely to rely on litigation when the information presented identifies realistic options, outcomes and consequences of non-settlement. Legal advisers now regard counselling, where appropriate, on the benefits of reaching settlement out of court as central to discharging the professional duties to their clients. The evolving regulatory culture of empowering disputing parties, as evidenced by measures like Pre-action Protocols and case management, is very much in keeping with some of the core values of Article 6. The values of deliberation, informed decision making, choice and party autonomy underpin the principles of equality and fairness. To be sure, these values also correspond with the policy informing the European Commission, as illustrated by its green paper on alternative dispute resolution in civil and commercial law.[36] According to the Commission:[37]

> ADRs are an integral part of the policies aimed at improving access to justice. In effect, they complement judicial procedures, insofar as the methods used in the context of ADRs are often better suited to the nature of the disputes involved. ADR can help the parties to enter into dialogue where this was not possible before, and to come to their own assessment of the value of going to court.
>
> It is worth highlighting the role of ADRs as a means of achieving social harmony. In the forms of ADR in which the third parties do not take a decision, the parties do not engage in confrontation but rather in a process of rapprochement, and they themselves choose the means of resolving the dispute and play a more active role in this process in such a way that they themselves endeavour to find the solution best suited to them. This consensual approach increases the likelihood that, once the dispute is settled, the parties will be able to maintain their commercial or other relations.

The idea of promoting parties' access to appropriate and economical mechanisms for solving problems is not inconsistent with the broad goal of promoting access to justice. It should not be forgotten, however, that ADR does not override an individual's Article 6 rights to have access to judicial or administrative proceedings. It is important to acknowledge this as there has been some debate on whether mandatory arbitration or mediation clauses should be introduced into ADR. Some clarification regarding the issues raised in this debate has been forthcoming in the form of the approval by the European Parliament of the Council's Mediation Directive.[38] One of the aims of this Directive is the promotion of consensual approaches towards the resolution of disputes. Even though the focus is on mediation, the observations are particularly relevant to the matters discussed in this chapter:[39]

> Mediation should not be regarded as a poorer alternative to judicial proceedings in the sense that compliance with agreements resulting from mediation would depend on the good will of the parties. Member States should therefore ensure that the parties to a written agreement resulting from mediation can have the content of their agreement made enforceable. It should only be possible for a Member State to refuse to make an agreement enforceable if the content is contrary to its law, including its private international law, or if its law does not provide for the enforceability of the content of the specific agreement. This could be the case if the obligation specified in the agreement was by its nature unenforceable.

It is worth observing that the Directive acknowledges the instrumental role of extra-judicial dispute resolution mechanisms. The Directive, however, sees the importance of adopting a coherent approach towards the role of ADR within the general framework of dispute resolution processes. Accordingly, its acceptance that curbs could be placed on the freedom of parties to override the outcome of mediation is not without qualification. National sovereignty and public interest considerations will of course take precedence over any agreements governing a party's right to seek judicial determination. The Directive also goes on to state that two conditions must be fulfilled if a decision reached in mediation is to be binding on the parties. First, the decision to seek an alternative to court proceedings has to be grounded on a party's access to all relevant information:[40]

> (15) The fairness of the procedures should be safeguarded by allowing the parties to provide any necessary and relevant information. Depending on the organisation of the procedure, information provided by the parties should be treated as confidential unless they expressly agree otherwise, or, if an adversarial approach is used at any stage appropriate measures should ensure its fairness. Measures should be envisaged to encourage and monitor the parties' cooperation with the procedure, in particular by requiring information that may be necessary for the fair resolution of the dispute.

> (16) Before the parties agree to a suggested solution on how to settle the dispute they should be allowed a reasonable amount of time to consider the details and any possible conditions or terms.

> (17) In order to ensure that procedures are fair and flexible and that consumers have the opportunity to make a fully informed choice, they must be given clear and understandable information in order that they can reflect on whether to

agree to a suggested solution, obtain advice if they wish or to consider other options.

Second,[41]

they should aim to overcome the associated problems of cost, delay, complexity and representation. Measures guaranteeing proportionate or no costs, easier access, efficiency, the monitoring of the progression of the dispute and keeping the parties informed are necessary to ensure its effectiveness.

One observation that could be made is that these two conditions are necessary safeguards against potential abuse and/or opportunistic behaviour. They are also clear reminders to parties of the need to assume responsibility for the choices they make when using ADR. Providing parties have a clear sense of their roles at the outset, solutions and consequences of the outcome to the proceedings is very much consistent with the spirit of ADR.

Conclusion

The civil legal system does not have a monopoly over the mechanisms for dispute resolution. To be sure, the proactive role of the judiciary in case management and the evolving cultural attitude towards the settlement of disputes is consistent with general understandings of access to justice in the information society. I identify three key ideas about the evolving attitude towards dispute resolution in this environment. First, it is in the public interest that individuals have access to the mechanisms for dispute resolution provided by the civil legal system. Second, lawyers have an important role in counselling their clients to seek more efficient mechanisms for settling their differences. Third, deliberation, autonomy and choice may now provide a set of values through which we can construct legitimate and workable processes for conflict resolution.

E-Justice, online dispute resolution and Web 2.0: case studies

In this section I aim to describe and explain how ODR systems are transforming the way parties deliberate and make choices about how and when disputes are settled. The discussion of these ideas in the context of ODR is relevant to providing us with an answer to the following question: Can convergence between legal and business processes increase the likelihood of parties accessing appropriate and effective mechanisms for dispute resolution?

Overview

The Internet is redefining the way individuals in society now define their expectations, activities and relationships.[42] Digitalisation of information and interconnectivity has, for example, been seen as having disruptive tendencies, re-defining the relational dynamics between the State and civil society and creating multiple public spheres of communication. Increased availability of communication technologies has important implications for the way policymakers, judges, the legal profession and individuals perceive the processes for managing disputes.[43] New communication technologies now make available a number of advantages, which can only enhance the processes through which individuals assume greater responsibility over the management of civil disputes: facilitating decentralised decision making, embedding flexible structures for dispute resolution, encouraging deliberative approaches to problem solving and promoting norms that sustain relationships.[44]

ODR embodies three features that are critical to the trend towards engaging, educating and empowering individuals in this environment. First, the transaction costs for information production, capture and transmission can be kept to a minimum. Second, the distributed nature of communication platforms enables the traditional barriers of time and distance to be overcome. Third, parties now have ready access to the various platforms and media for resolving disputes.[45] One outcome of the convergence between dispute resolution services and communication technologies is that individuals are increasingly regarded as having a legitimate expectation in assuming direct responsibility for the way disputes are managed and resolved. The expansion of the market for ODRs mirrors consumers' choices and expectations.[46] There is some evidence that the ODR industry is responding to individuals' desire to have a co-ordinated framework for choice, information sharing, interactivity and deliberation. Many commercial ODR service providers now integrate a wide array of technologies into the processes for consensual problem solving. These include email exchanges, instant messaging, online synchronous/ asynchronous discussions/negotiations, mobile telephones, texting, teleconferencing and audio/video streaming.

These developments are not restricted to the private sector. Organisations in the public sector have begun to integrate these technologies into their mechanisms for dispute resolution. A practical illustration of how values like autonomy, deliberation and choice are configured into the design of dispute resolution platforms can be seen in the way monetary claims are processed online. Money Claim Online (MCOL) is Her Majesty's Courts Service Internet-based service for claimants and defendants.[47] This facility is only available for sums of less than £100,000 (excluding any interest or costs claimed). Parties using this online dispute facility are required to comply with Part 7 of the Civil Procedure Rules and the claimant cannot be (a) a child or protected party; or (b) funded by the Legal Services Commission.[48]

In the next section I highlight some of the ways the design values embedded in ODR mechanisms go a long way towards promoting norms that maximise values like fairness, equality and efficiency.

ODR and embedding E-Justice norms

Judges and practitioners recognise that settlements concluded with the assent of parties and perceived as fair generally reduce costs associated with litigation and ameliorate the problems of enforcement. ODR relies on a culture of enabling parties to take responsibility for managing disputes in a fair and efficient manner.[49] A review of the ODR literature suggests that decisions to use ADR have invariably depended on perceptions of fairness, value of harmonious relations, welfare-enhancing role of consensus, problems of enforcement and opportunity costs in pursuing litigation.[50]

The eDispute© system

The eDispute application system[51] has been developed to address some of the logistical challenges frequently encountered in traditional dispute resolution mechanisms: burdensome structures for accessing and disseminating documentation, opportunistic behaviour and delays in the resolution of disputes. Since the relevant documentation will be stored in one portal and readily accessible to all parties, quick referencing and identification of key issues can be undertaken speedily and without the parties having to leave their computer terminals.

Virtual Courthouse

Virtual Courthouse[52] is another example of ODR service providers leveraging the potential of new communication technologies. The Virtual Courthouse model utilises business processes and multimedia technologies to replicate real world-type dispute resolution mechanisms. This dispute resolution service provider not only makes available a range of settlement options, but also gives parties a greater role in the way the settlement proceeds. Parties using Virtual Courthouse assume responsibility for submitting their claims, responses and evidence online. The website has a readily accessible information facility guiding claimants and respondents to a dispute. The disputing parties have a choice of ADR services, including arbitration, mediation, neutral case evaluation and a settlement conference chaired by members of a panel of neutrals. The service provider's role is to structure the ADR process. Parties can rely on the service provider to ensure that meetings are properly organised and not duplicated, communications between parties take place in a secure environment and communications between parties are readily accessible at all times. Another advantage of hosting settlement conferences online is that evidentiary materials and documents can be uploaded without delays in transmission or distribution.

Electronic Consumer Dispute Resolution

The Electronic Consumer Dispute Resolution (ECODIR)[53] is another example of a free dispute resolution service provided to consumers and businesses. The online dispute resolution facility is, however, only available for disputes that originate from an online transaction. Additionally, one party to the dispute must be a consumer. Disputes involving illicit content, corporal damages, family, taxation and intellectual property issues are not covered by ECODIR.

eBay

Third party facilitators can now create structured processes that reflect many of the pre-litigation protocols and Civil Procedure Rules (CPR) rules advocating voluntary settlements. Innovative and effective use of ICTs in mediation process is envisaged by implication. eBay[54] uses communication technologies to enhance an individual's access to dispute resolution mechanisms that are effective, flexible and preserve party autonomy. eBay oversees complaints relating to unpaid items, non-selling sellers, disputes about feedback and items not being received or not described correctly. eBay's ODR model relies on evolving community norms to the resolution of dispute between members. Let us take an example of a seller who lodges a complaint on eBay's dispute console in respect of an unpaid item by a buyer. eBay encourages users to attempt to seek a mutually acceptable resolution to their dispute. The process for resolving dispute is both structured and transparent. The Dispute Console enables the seller to track, discuss and resolve the dispute. Sellers wishing to lodge complaints about unpaid items are given 45 days to make a report. eBay facilitates the communication exchange between the parties by sending the buyer an email reminder that payment on an item is outstanding. eBay imposes strict time limits for the resolution of dispute. Payment by the buyer brings the dispute to a close. If the matter is not resolved after 60 days, the dispute is deemed to be closed. Should a buyer not respond to the email or pop-up message within seven days, the seller may request a final value fee credit. The seller also becomes eligible for an automatic free re-list credit for the insertion fee.

Smartsettle

As the online dispute resolution industry evolves, we are likely to see the utilisation of technologies that attempt to capture hidden values in negotiation and settlement proceedings. A good example of such a development is the expert system platform provided by Smartsettle.[55] Blind bidding is a well-known practice in auction sites. Offers and demands are hidden and are not disclosed to the other party. Smartsettle's system is unique: the proposals are visible and known to the other party. Acceptances made by each party are, however, hidden. The secure neutral site server ensures confidentiality of communications and enables suggestions for resolution to be generated. A typical dispute settlement process is as follows. The first session of a bid proposal is designed to achieve two immediate objectives. First, the facility of making the bid proposals visible is intended to identify the scope for negotiations. Second, following the initial bid proposals, the computer program generates a sequence of suggestions, which either party can accept.

Smartsettle generates a sequence of suggestions that are visible to both parties, just as proposals are visible. What is hidden (or unknown) in the Smartsettle process is each party's acceptance of a value or package, as Figures 8.3 and 8.4 illustrate.

When one or more mutually accepted values or packages are detected at the end of a session, the system declares one of the accepted values or packages as the agreement.

The goals are clear. The identification of possible zones of agreement not only keeps the settlement process moving, but the transparency engendered encourages parties to reach a settlement based on what they deem as being fair. The design values of the Smartsettle system very much correspond with ideas we associate with legitimate and effective settlement processes: autonomy, choice and deliberation. Let

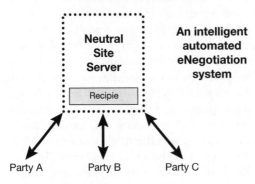

Figure 8.1 Smartsettle

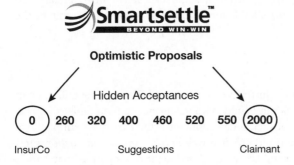

Figure 8.2 Smartsettle

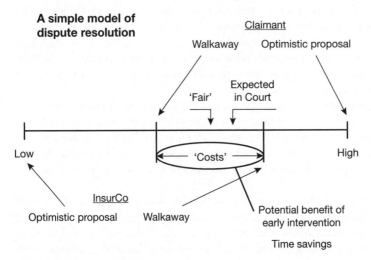

Figure 8.3 Dispute resolution

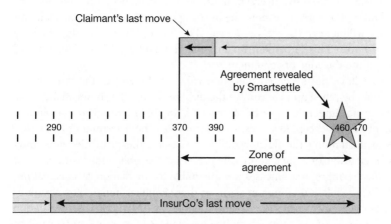

Figure 8.4 Last move

us consider how this form of E-Justice translates into a hypothetical dispute involving an insurance claim relating to a damaged household. A claimant wishes to be paid £2,000. The insurer will, of course, want to pay the lowest possible amount. Traditionally, money claims involve lengthy negotiations and frequent communications in the forms of telephone exchanges, written correspondences, bids and counter-bids.

Smartsettle's server-based technology assists the parties by ensuring that the settlement process keeps moving. The negotiation process is clearly structured and parties are provided with a sequence of suggestions on which each party can place hidden acceptances. As noted previously, these suggestions are not accessible to the other party. One common difficulty encountered in insurance claims negotiations is that each party has its own view of the best alternative to a negotiated agreement.

The value-added input of the Smartsettle technology lies in the way Smartsettle rewards the party that moves soonest to the zone of agreement. The formula for determining the agreement value is:

$$\text{Reference} = (Tc * Ac + Ti * Ai) / (Tc + Ti)$$

where

Ac = the least preferred accepted value of Claimant at the end of the previous session

Ai = the least preferred accepted value of InsurCo at the end of the previous session

Tc = the size of Claimant's move

Ti = the size of InsurCo's move

The agreement becomes the accepted value that is closest to the reference. For example, during the penultimate blind bidding session, the claimant and insurer proposed £390 and £290 respectively. Both proposed acceptances were hidden from the parties. During the current session, the insurer proposed £470 and the claimant expressed his willingness to accept £370. The final settlement identified by Smartsettle is £460. This settlement favours the claimant since the claimant had moved soonest into the zone of agreement.

If the parties have not accepted the same value at the end of the last session, arbitration could be relied upon to resolve the dispute. Figure 8.5 shows an alternate scenario where no agreement has been reached. In this situation, the arbitrator chooses one of the last accepted values, whichever one s/he determines to be closer to 'fair'. Notwithstanding the flexible online processes, the principles governing arbitration, mediation or conciliation still prescribe the obligations and roles of each party. Furthermore, not all cases are amenable for mediation or conciliation. Disputes involving violation of human rights or those conflicts initiated by vexatious litigants are not generally regarded as being suitable for ADR. Likewise, mediation would not be appropriate in cases which involve matters of morality and/or public interest.

Old wine, new bottles

The above discussion aptly demonstrates the way new approaches to managing and settling disputes are advancing the notion of E-Justice. Software systems are embedding opportunities for deliberation, party autonomy, choice and solutions. There is a need to go beyond questions of whether or not parties should be compelled to arbitrate or whether or not sanctions should be imposed for those who do not utilise alternative mechanisms for dispute resolution. Some have suggested that the quality of justice can be enhanced if agreements reached are enforceable and presumably preclude Article 6. Two observations can be made as to why we should overemphasise such issues. First, it is necessary that parties utilising ADR are made aware of their respective obligations, the options available to them and the consequences for not reaching a settlement. ODR encourages parties to approach disputes voluntarily and

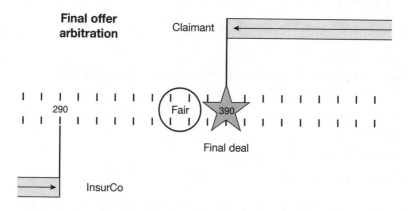

Figure 8.5 Final offer

in the spirit of reaching mutually acceptable settlements. Technologies like those identified above demonstrate the benefits of exploring new approaches to dispute resolution. Second, prescribing sanctions and compelling parties to arbitrate or mediate introduces an additional set of problems. Ultimately, the role we ascribe to ODR involves a trade-off between the consensual nature of the process and the binding nature of ODR. Should we reduce the autonomy of individuals in shaping the outcome? At first sight this would appear to be a relatively straightforward issue. Surely, ODR mechanisms should not be subjected to less stringent requirements than, for example, a contract dispute in the civil courts? The answer is, however, a little more complex. For example, disputes involving consumers are seen as being amenable to mediation or arbitration. That said, in the EU there are additional procedural safeguards for consumers. These safeguards are not generally available in other jurisdictions. In the EU, arbitration clauses are presumptively regarded as being 'unfair', and are accordingly treated as lacking binding force against consumers.[56] The Unfair Terms in Consumer Contracts Regulations state that terms which have the object or effect of excluding or hindering a consumer's right to take legal action or exercise any other legal remedy, particularly by requiring the consumer to take disputes exclusively to arbitration not covered by legal provisions, unduly restricting the evidence available to him or imposing on him a burden of proof which, according to the applicable law, should lie with another party to the contract, are deemed to be unfair.[57] Furthermore, Section 91 of the Arbitration Act 1996 regards mandatory arbitration provisions which attempt to bind a consumer as unfair in relation to claims of £5,000 or less.[58] A better approach to the issues posed by the question would be to begin by demarcating the disputes that would be suitable for ODR, identify the obligations of the parties and thereafter proceed to create processes that correspond with the intentions and expectations of the parties. In the relatively short history of ODR, the strategies for reaching settlement are inextricably bound up with norms like good faith. It is true that allowing parties to enter into settlement proceedings based on trust and good faith may consequently produce some regulatory uncertainty. We may have to accept this consequence if we are to advance the goals of the next generation of innovative ODR services and products.

Conclusion: the future is here

This chapter has explored the implications of the convergence of communication technologies for the resolution of civil disputes. Innovative use of communication technologies should not obscure policy priorities for E-Justice. Policymakers and legal services providers have important roles in articulating the role of ODR and the best ways of achieving its objectives. How do we nurture and sustain ODR mechanisms? Should we permit parties to shape the processes and outcomes to their disputes? How do we integrate the principles of access to justice and party autonomy into trans-border disputes? These are formidable and complex questions. Inevitably, we are faced with having to engage in trade-offs. Notwithstanding the complexity of the challenges facing policymakers and the legal services industry, three critical areas in the provision of ODR need to be regularly monitored: the quality and range of expert system platforms and services; the embedding of ODR within the culture of the legal profession; and the mapping of future directions for ODR. The considerable gains to be made from increasing an individual's access to appropriate mechanisms can be undermined if regulatory infrastructures are poorly co-ordinated, the practices of ODR services providers lack coherence, or inter-operability and technical standards for ODR products and services create invisible barriers to access. ODR provides us with a fresh opportunity to re-think the traditional methods for dispute resolution. Lord Phillips has recently stressed the benefits of treating litigation as a measure of last resort by pointing to the importance of preserving harmonious relations between the disputing parties, the illusory nature of viewing dispute resolution purely through the structured framework of the judicial process, and, more generally, the costs borne by the parties and society when opportunities for reaching settlement are forgone.[59] The policy priorities for E-Justice bring us back to an a-priori question that is often overlooked: How should we conceptualise consensus in dispute resolution?

Key points

- Increasingly, policymakers and judges are encouraging parties to utilise alternative mechanisms for resolving their disputes.
- Information and communication technologies (ICTs) now make available new opportunities through which individuals can assume greater roles in managing and resolving disputes.
- Online dispute resolution (ODR) service providers are embedding values like deliberation, autonomy and choice into expert software systems.
- E-Justice need not be understood in terms of increasing an individual's access to judicial and administrative tribunals. Communication technologies make a range of alternative dispute resolution (ADR) mechanisms and solutions available to individuals.
- Policymakers, judges and online service providers have important roles in encouraging disputing parties to adopt effective and consensual approaches to the settlement of disputes.

Notes

1 M. Bangemann, *Europe and the Global Information Society: Recommendations to the European Council* ('Bangemann Report') (Brussels: European Commission). Available at http://europa.eu.int/ISPO/docs/basics/docs/bangemann.pdf.
2 http://www.europarl.europa.eu/summits/tam_en.htm.
3 See Recommendation Rec(2003)14 of the Committee of Ministers of the Council of Europe to member states on the interoperability of information systems in the justice sector, https://wcd.coe.int/ViewDoc.jsp?id=65459&BackColorInternet=9999CC&BackColorIntranet=FFBB55&BackColorLogged=FFAC75. See also: Recommendation Rec (2002)10 of the Committee of Ministers to member states on mediation in civil matters (Adopted by the Committee of Ministers on 18 September 2002 at the 808th meeting of the Ministers' Deputies).

4   See eEurope (2005): *An Information Society for All*, COM(2002)263 final. Available at:
    ec.europa.eu/information_society/eeurope/2002/news_library/documents/eeurope
    2005/eeurope2005_en.pdf. See now Communication from the Commission to the
    European Parliament, the Council, the European Economic and Social Committee and
    the Committee of the Regions – i2010 – Annual Information Society Report 2007:
    http://ec.europa.eu/information_society/eeurope/i2010/key_documents/index_en.
    htm; OECD, 'Guidelines for Consumer Protection in the Context of Electronic
    Commerce' (OECD, 1999). Available at http://www.oecd.org/dsti/sti/it/ec/index.htm.
    European 'Directive on electronic commerce' (98/0325 (COD)) and Trustmark services:
    http://www.trustmark.org.uk/.

5   http://sdnhq.undp.org/wiki/Ejustice.

6   Recommendation Rec(2001)9 of the Committee of Ministers to member states on
    alternatives to litigation between administrative authorities and private parties (Adopted
    by the Committee of Ministers on 5 September 2001 at the 762nd meeting of the
    Ministers' Deputies): https://wcd.coe.int/ViewDoc.jsp?Ref=Rec(2001)9&Language=lan
    English&Site=CM&BackColorInternet=9999CC&BackColorIntranet=FFBB55&Back
    ColorLogged=FFAC75 (last accessed 8 August 2008).

7   eEurope (2005): *An Information Society for All*, COM(2002)263. Also see i2010 e-government
    Action Plan – *Accelerating E-Government in Europe for the Benefit of All* – COM(2006)173
    final.

8   See Department of Constitutional Affairs, 'Delivering Simple, Speedy, Summary Justice:
    An Evaluation of the Magistrates' Courts Tests' (2007). Available at: http://www.dca.
    gov.uk/majrepfr.htm#dss. Also Lord Woolf (1996) 'Access to Justice: Final Report', July.
    Available at http://www.dca.gov.uk/civil/final/intro.htm.

9   See Office of Government Commerce Dispute Resolution Guidance: http://www.ogc.
    gov.uk/supplier_relations_b7_dispute_resolution_guidance_.asp.

10 http://www.e-mediator.co.uk/.

11 'Mediation is a process based on the intervention of a neutral third party (the mediator).
    The solution remains in the hands of the disputing parties, but the mediator helps them to
    communicate, diffuse emotions, identify key issues and find solutions that could satisfy
    both parties. The mediator helps each party to understand the other's perspective and
    interests and to agree to compromise and find a mutually acceptable solution' (http://
    www.ecodir.org/odrp/faq.htm).

12 Conciliation is a process where a conciliator attempts to get two parties to resolve their
    differences. It is commonly used in employment and housing disputes.

13 'Early neutral evaluation (ENE) is a preliminary assessment of facts, evidence or legal
    merits. This process is designed to serve as a basis for further and fuller negotiations, or, at
    the very least, help parties avoid further unnecessary stages in litigation. The parties
    appoint an independent person who expresses an opinion on the merits of the issues
    specified by them. It is a non-binding opinion but provides an unbiased evaluation on
    relative positions and guidance as to the likely outcome should the case be heard in court'
    (http://www.cedr.com/CEDR_Solve/services/ene.php).

14 'Adjudication is intended as an interim dispute resolution process with the adjudicator
    giving a decision on disputes as they arise during the course of a construction contract.
    The decision is binding unless or until the dispute is finally determined by court
    proceedings, arbitration or agreement of the parties (http://www.cedr.com/CEDR_
    Solve/services/adjudication.php).

15 'Arbitration is a private process in which an independent third party is appointed to decide
    the outcome of a dispute between two or more parties. The process may be conducted by
    a sole arbitrator or a panel, according to party requirements. The decision is final and
    binding (http://www.cedr.com/CEDR_Solve/services/arbitration.php).

16 See Lord Woolf, op. cit., Chapter 4.7.

17 See Office of Government Commerce Dispute Resolution Guidance, http://www.ogc.
    gov.uk/supplier_relations_b7_dispute_resolution_guidance_.asp.

18 Yuan, Yufei, Head, Milena and Du, Mei (2003) 'The Effects of Multimedia Communication on Web-Based Negotiation', *Group Decision and Negotiation* 12/2: 89–109.

19 See National Audit Office, Citizen Redress: What citizens can do if things go wrong with public services, HC, 21 Session 2004–2005, 9 March 2005, http://www.adrnow.org.uk/go/SubSection_21.html; *Parr* v *Wyre* BC [1982] HLR 71 and http://www.publiclaw project.org.uk/index.html.

20 See for example http://www.direct.gov.uk/en/Diol1/DoItOnline/DG_4018266 and http://www.cedr.co.uk/CEDR_Solve/.

21 See for example the various dispute resolution platforms in www.themediationroom.com.

22 See as an example: http://www.direct.gov.uk/en/HomeAndCommunity/Where YouLive/StreetsParkingCleaningAndLighting/DG_10024872. Also Larson, D. (2004) 'Online Dispute Resolution: Technology Takes a Place at the Table', *Negotiation Journal* 20/1: 129–135; Nadler, J. (2001) 'Electronically-Mediated Dispute Resolution and E-Commerce', *Negotiation Journal* 17/4: 333–347.

23 Examples include Arbitration a Commercial Initiative for dispute resolution (www.aci-adr.com), ADR Group (www.adrgroup.co.uk), The Mediation Room, Centre for Effective Dispute Resolution (www.cedr-solve.com).

24 http://www.hri.org/docs/ECHR50.html.

25 HMCS (1998) *Modernising Justice: The Government's Plans for Reforming Legal Services and the Courts*, Cm 4155, para 1.10.

26 Speech by Lord Phillips, CJ, 'Alternative Dispute Resolution: An English Viewpoint', 29 March 2008 at para. 14. Available at www.judiciary.gov.uk/docs/speeches/lcj_adr_india_290308.pdf. Also see Civil Procedure Rule 1.1(2)(e), 1.31.4(2)(e) and 3.1(2)(m).

27 Civil Procedure Rule 1.4(1) obliges the court to further the overriding objective of enabling the court to deal with cases justly by actively managing cases.

28 Civil Procedure Rule 1.1. See also approaches in 'Pre-action Protocol' taken in *Orange Personal Communications Services Limited* v *Hoare Lea* (A firm) [2008] EWHC 223 (TCC) and *Cundall Johnson & Partners* v *Whipps Cross University Hospital NHS Trust* [2007] EWHC 2178 (TCC).

29 Civil Procedure Rule 44.5(3)(a)(ii) requires the court, in deciding the amount of costs to be awarded, to have regard to the conduct of the parties, including in particular 'the efforts made, if any, before and during the proceedings in order to try to resolve the dispute'. See also *R (Cowl)* v *Plymouth City Council* [2001] EWCA Civ 1935, [2002] 1 WLR 803; *Dunnett* v *Railtrack plc* [2002] EWCA Civ 303, [2002] 1 WLR 2434 and *Hurst* v *Leeming* [2001] EWHC 1051 (Ch), [2003] 1 Lloyds Rep 379. Cf. *Halsey* v *Milton Keynes General NHS Trust* [2004] 1 WLR 3002. The interpretation of Article 6 within the context of the court's role in encouraging alternative dispute resolution must now be doubted. The CPR anticipates an active role of the courts in the case management process: *Hurst* v *Leeming* [2001] EWHC 1051, *Dunnett* v *Railtrack* [2002] 2 All ER 850, *Royal Bank of Canada* v *Ministry of Defence* [2003] EWHC 1479.

30 http://www.dca.gov.uk/civil/adr/court-mediation-service-toolkit.pdf.

31 See Department of Constitutional Affairs, Departmental Report 2006–2007 (Cm 7097) (HMSO, 2007) para. 6.3 http://www.dca.gov.uk/dept/report2007/dp2007-full-report. pdf. Also see Government-supported initiatives at https://www.nationalmediation helpline.com/index.php, http://www.disputeresolutionservice.co.uk/, and http://www. adrnow.org.uk/.

32 Ibid. paras 6.5–6.8.

33 Small claims mediation pilot scheme in Manchester County Court, http://www.dca.gov. uk/civil/adr/small-claims-manchester.pdf.

34 Department for Constitutional Affairs (National), (2007) 'Make Legal Services More Accessible to Consumers', 26 March 2007. See also Civil Mediation Council website for complaint procedures: http://www.civilmediation.org/index.php.

35 For details of the 'Pre-action Protocol' see http://www.dca.gov.uk/consult/preaction/ preaction.htm#annb.

36 Green paper on alternative dispute resolution in civil law and commercial law, COM(2002)196 final, para 1.2. See also Proposal for a Directive of the European Parliament and of the Council on certain aspects of mediation in civil and commercial matters, COM(2004)718 final.

37 Green paper on alternative dispute resolution, op. cit.

38 Commission Recommendation of 4 April 2001 on the principles for out-of-court bodies involved in the consensual resolution of consumer disputes (notified under document number C(2001) 1016) (2001/310/EC) OJ L 109/56.

39 Ibid.

40 Ibid.

41 Ibid para. 11.

42 Castells, M. (2001) *The Internet Galaxy*. Oxford: OUP, p. 2.

43 Clark, E. and Hoyle, A. (2000) 'Online Dispute Resolution: Present Realities and Future Prospects', 17 Bileta Conference, Amsterdam, http://www.bileta.ac.uk/02papers/hoyle.html.

44 Katsh, E. and Rifkin, J. (2001) *Online Dispute Resolution: Resolving Conflicts in Cyberspace*. San Francisco, CA: Jossey-Bass.

45 Reidenberg, Joel R. (1996) 'Governing Networks and Rule-Making in Cyberspace', *Emory Law Journal* 911: 917–919, 929; Froomkin, Michael (1997) 'The Internet as a Source of Regulatory Arbitrage', in Kahin, B. and Nesson, C. (eds) (1997) *Borders in Cyberspace*. Cambridge, MA: The MIT Press; Reidenberg, Joel R. (1998), 'Lex Informatica: The Formulation of Information Policy Rules through Technology', *Texas Law Review* 76/3: 553–584; Lessig, Lawrence (2000) 'Foreword: Conference on Internet Privacy' 52 *Stanford Law Review* 987, Lessig, Lawrence (2000) 'Code Is Law: On Liberty in Cyberspace', *Harvard Magazine*, January–February and Spulber, D. and Yoo, S., 'On the Regulation of Networks as Complex Systems', American Law & Economics Association Meetings Paper 38, http://law.bepress.com/cgi/viewcontent.cgi?article=1107&context=alea.

46 Benkler, Y. (2006) *The Wealth of Networks*. New Haven, CT: Yale University Press, p. 212; Johnson, David R. and Post, David (1996) 'Law and Borders: The Rise of Law in Cyberspace', *Stanford Law Review* 48/5: 1367–1402.

47 See https://www.moneyclaim.gov.uk/.

48 For more details see Civil Procedure Practice Direction, http://www.justice.gov.uk/civil/procrules_fin/contents/practice_directions/pd_part07e.htm.

49 Raines, S. (2005) 'Can Online Mediation be Transformative? Tales from the Front', *Conflict Resolution Quarterly*, 22/4: 437–451.

50 Selected literature: Katsh, E. (1996) 'Online Dispute Resolution: Building Institutions in Cyberspace', *University of Connecticut Law Review*, 28: 953–980; Perritt, H. H. (2000) 'Dispute Resolution in Cyberspace: Demand for New Forms of ADR', *Ohio State Journal of Dispute Resolution* 15: 675–702; Rabinovich-Einy, O. (2006) 'Lessons of ODR: Rethinking Traditional Approaches'. Presentation to Fourth UN Forum on Online Dispute Resolution, 22–23 March, 2006, Cairo, Egypt; Gaitenby, A. (2006) 'The Fourth Party Rises: Evolution Environments of Online Dispute Resolution', in *Symposium on Enhancing Worldwide Understanding through Online Dispute Resolution, University of Toledo Law Review* 38/1: 371–388; Schultz, T., Kaufmann-Kohler, G., Langer, D., and Bonnet, V. (2001). 'Online Dispute Resolution: State of the Art, Issues, and Perspectives.' Report of the E-Com Research Project of the University of Geneva, p. 78, Geneva. http://www.online-adr.org/reports/TheBlueBook-2001.pdf; Consumers International, 'Disputes in Cyberspace: Online Dispute Resolution for Consumers in Cross-border Disputes – an International Survey', http://www.consumersinternational.org/Shared_ASP_Files/UploadedFiles/87454723-59BB-48B6-B1EF-9551CCA391B4_Doc29.pdf.

51 http://www.tiga-technologies.com/eDispute/.

52 http://www.virtualcourthouse.com/.

53 http://www.ecodir.org/.

54 http://pages.ebay.com/services/buyandsell/disputeres.html.

55 www.smartsettle.com. I am grateful to Mike Chalmers, Project Systems Coordinator, for helpful comments on the Smartsettle blind bidding process and permission to use slides from a presentation at 7th Annual Forum on Online Dispute Resolution, 18–19 June 2008, Victoria, BC, Canada. See in particular E. Thiessen and P. Miniato, 'Rewarding Good Negotiating Behavior with Smartsettle', http://www.smartsettle.com/download/papers/SmartsettleRewards.pdf.

56 Unfair Terms in Consumer Contracts Regulations 1999; Bright, S. (2000) 'Winning the Battle against Unfair Contract Terms', *Legal Studies*, 20/3: 331–352; MacDonald, E. (2002) 'Scope and Fairness of the Unfair Terms in Consumer Contracts Regulations: *Director General of Fair Trading* v *First National Bank*' *Modern Law Review* 65/5: 763–773; Dean, M. (2002) 'Defining Unfair Terms in Consumer Contracts – Crystal Ball Gazing? *Director General of Fair Trading* v *First National Bank plc*', *Modern Law Review* 65/5: 773–781; Brandner, H. and Ulmer, P. (1991) 'The Community Directive on Unfair Terms in Consumer Contracts: Some Critical Remarks on the Proposal Submitted by the EC Commission', *Common Market Law Reports* 28: 647–662.

57 Unfair Terms in Consumer Contracts Regulations 1999 Section 8 and Sch 2, para. 1(q).

58 See Office of Fair Trading Guidance: http://www.oft.gov.uk/advice_and_resources/resource_base/legal/unfair-terms/guidance.

59 Speech by Lord Phillips, CJ, supra, note 26. See also *Nigel Witham Ltd* v *(1) Robert Leslie Smith (2) Jacqueline Isaacs* [2008] EWHC 12 (TCC); *Darren Egan* v *Motor Services (Bath) Limited* [2007] EWCA Civ 1002.

Further reading

Katsh, E. and Rifkin, J. (2001) *Online Dispute Resolution: Resolving Conflicts in Cyberspace*. San Francisco, CA: Jossey-Bass.

Benkler, Y. (2006) *The Wealth of Networks*. New Haven, CT: Yale University Press.

Perritt, H. H. (2000) 'Dispute Resolution in Cyberspace: Demand for New Forms of ADR', *Ohio State Journal of Dispute Resolution* 15: 675–702.

Schultz, T., Kaufmann-Kohler, G., Langer, D. and Bonnet, V. (2001) 'Online Dispute Resolution: State of the Art, Issues, and Perspectives.' Report of the E-Com Research Project of the University of Geneva, p. 78, Geneva, http://www.online-adr.org/reports/TheBlueBook-2001.pdf.

Consumers International, 'Disputes in Cyberspace: Online Dispute Resolution for Consumers in Cross-Border Disputes – An International Survey', http://www.consumersinternational.org/Shared_ASP_Files/UploadedFiles/87454723-59BB-48B6-B1EF-9551CCA391B4_Doc29.pdf.

9 Identity management in E-Government service provision

Towards new modes of government and citizenship

Miriam Lips, John Taylor and Joe Organ

Summary

Identity management (IDM) has come to be at the heart of E-Government policy agendas throughout the world. As E-Government is evolving to transactional service applications, government needs new digitised personal identification and authentication to solve the emerging identity questions online: How can we 'know' the individual wanting to access online transactional public services? How can we make sure that that individual is indeed entitled or authorised to access these services? New IDM systems in E-Government service provision not only appear to enhance government's service-providing capabilities to the citizen, but also are supposed to offer enhanced customer convenience, trust, efficiency and effectiveness of public service provision and public safety, including law enforcement, for instance. It may not be surprising, therefore, that many governments perceive these newly available IDM means as the *sine qua non* for modernising or even transforming E-Government and for promoting the uptake of E-Government services.[1]

Consequently, it appears to be important to empirically investigate the implementation and use of IDM systems in citizen–government service relationships and to analyse what is happening both within and to these relationships. In this chapter we present case-study findings for three of eight case studies of a research project aiming at exploring how IDM in varying E-Government service relationships can be understood.

Introduction

Compared to traditional, paper-based citizen identification (e.g. passport, birth certificate or driver's licence) as proof of identity in public service provision, it seems likely that the introduction, management and use of digitised identity management (IDM) in citizen–government relationships will influence the design and operational level of public service provision to the citizen. With that, we anticipate that changes in information relationships between citizens and governments may be fundamental. Scholars have pointed towards substantial informational imbalances in citizen–government relationships that are a likely outcome of the introduction of new IDM systems.[2] Some perceive these new IDM systems as 'surveillance systems', which, as a result of embedded codes and values, will bring about the 'social sorting' of citizens; rationalised, automated administrative decision-making processes will lead to social classifications.[3] Perceptions such as these suggest that new ICT-facilitated information relationships between government and citizens require not only re-organisation of the E-Government service domain, but also, simultaneously, a deep reconsideration of citizens' rights and responsibilities.[4]

It is clear that the introduction of new IDM systems in emerging E-Government service relationships raises important questions as to how and to what extent these new forms of IDM have effects upon information relationships between citizens and government, particularly when compared to the use of traditional forms of IDM in paper-based public service environments, for instance. What are their implications for government and the citizen? To be able to answer these questions we seek in the sections below to conceptualise 'identity management' and its potential effects on information relationships between citizens and government as a result of the transformation from a paper-based public service environment to an ICT-based public service environment. On this point, however, little empirical evidence has been available about how emerging transactional E-Government service relationships are developing. We therefore report from empirical, case study-based research in the UK on the application and use of new digitised forms of IDM in a variety of E-Government service relationships. Finally, we consider their implications for government and citizens.

Identity management in public service relationships

Governments throughout the world are introducing new digitised IDM systems into their E-Government service relationships with individuals. These new forms of IDM are being managed and used in addition to, and increasingly in place of, traditional forms of personal identification and authentication. Current examples of these new technical solutions for identification and authentication processes are many and varied: electronic identity cards, biometric applications, smart cards and Web-based E-Authentication solutions. Digital IDM is being introduced and managed in public service environments in which traditional, paper-based proofs of citizen identity (e.g. passport, birth certificate or driver's licence) have become commonly used.[5] Increased international mobility of individuals has led to the establishment of a globally acknowledged, universal 'Trusted Identifier' in citizen–government relationships: the passport.[6]

Although on this point little empirical evidence has been available about how these new E-Government relationships are developing when compared to personal identification and authentication in the paper-based public service era, prima facie it seems that the introduction of new IDM means in public service provision will lead to a marked disjuncture from that earlier period. Traditionally, citizen identification has involved more or less standardised procedures: in face-to-face public service relationships, individuals are scrutinised on the basis of personal recognition and trust; in the case of paper-based identification, they submit their personal identification documents to the inspecting public official. Authentication in public service arrangements too has been largely constant over time; for instance, the passport holder continues to show his/her passport to the official (who is aided in some instances by a photograph) to check and verify that the document carrier is the person referred to in the document.

Normally in paper-based public service arrangements, each individual who can represent himself/herself as a legally acknowledged citizen as a result of the authentication of his/her Trusted Identifier(s) is entitled to access a specific public service. Over time, systems have been created to store and retrieve information about an individual's eligibility, leading to the emergence of generic categories of identity information on the individual, including familiar personal details such as name, address and date of birth. These generic categories of identity information have been acknowledged by government agencies as authoritative sources of identity information on the citizen. They are usually collected from, or supported with, official identification documents. Moreover, legally acknowledged citizenship identity endowed a citizen with equal status in the paper-based public service world through the general administrative principle of 'equality under the law'. This general principle has been further translated into different forms of administrative equivalence of citizens in public service relationships as set out in Table 9.1.

In general, human assessment was the decisive IDM factor in paper-based public service provision; a public official would assess and decide upon an individual's paper-based request for access to a public service on the basis of a single set of administrative norms and values which was derived from the law and therefore valid within the governmental jurisdiction concerned. In cases where administrative norms left room for discretion, a civil servant would seek to apply existing administrative values based upon the notion of administrative equivalence as far as possible (i.e. through considering case law on the matter).[7] Within this administrative system, a final assessment of a citizen's request for access to a public service could take considerable time. The various documents concerned were normally stored by the service-providing organisation in a personal file as proof of entitlement to the specific public service. In many cases citizens needed to queue until an official was able to bring one citizen's case to a close and start a new one. Usually, these personal files were kept for a certain legally acknowledged time period, again securing an element of admini-

Table 9.1 Traditional principles of administrative equivalence in public service provision to citizens

Administrative equivalence principle	Details
Access rights to services	Equal service access for all citizens within any particular governmental jurisdiction (e.g. national, regional, local, functional)
Procedure	Equal and fair treatment during the service process
Legal entitlement to a specific standard of service	Equal service outcome for similarly assessed cases, in accordance with legally embedded norms

Source: Lips *et al.* (2006); see note 4.

strative equivalence. Such information management was undertaken separately within each public service-providing organisation.

However, although identification and authentication – face to face, paper-based or otherwise – have traditionally been a central part of public service arrangements between government and citizens, the term 'identity managment' is relatively new and its meaning not entirely settled.[8] Looking at working definitions available for IDM, such as 'the set of business processes and a supporting infrastructure for the creation, maintenance, and use of digital identities'[9] and 'a set of data management systems and practices to increase confidence in the identity of individuals where appropriate',[10] it becomes clear that the IDM concept is limited in use and applies only to identification and authentication activities in emerging digital environments.

With that, key IDM concepts like 'identification' and 'authentication' are being re-defined for, and applied to, emerging digital public service environments. For instance, digital identification in E-Government service provision can be defined as the association of information with a particular human being.[11] Digital authentication, then, is the process of checking a claim or assertion made by the person about their identity, ensuring the person is the individual he or she claims to be.[12] Digital identification occurs when a person or entity compares the information items, or 'identifiers', of another person or entity with a set of identifiers that the person or entity has previously recorded, and finds a match between the two.[13] Generally in new digitised forms of IDM, the following categories of identifiers can be distinguished:[14]

- something that you are – a characteristic that is inherent in a person or attached to an individual's physical body (e.g. DNA, fingerprints, voice signatures, etc.);
- something you do – a characteristic that relates to the behaviour of an individual (e.g. click behaviour in a digital environment, attitudes in a specific social context, etc.);
- something you know – the characteristic of having some distinct knowledge, usually knowledge that few others have (e.g. passwords, mother's maiden name, etc.);
- something you have – the characteristic of possessing some distinct item; these identifiers are often called 'tokens' (e.g. smart cards, software tokens like digital certificates, keys, etc.);
- something you are assigned to – an identifier that is socially defined for, and associated with, the person, but is not inherent or attached (e.g. name, address, title, social security number, etc.)

Moreover, digital identification can happen explicitly or implicitly from an individual's point of view.[15] Explicit identification involves processes in which the person is aware of, and even participates in, identification. Implicit identification relates to processes in which an individual's identity information is captured and analysed without the person's awareness.

Compared to IDM in the paper-based public service era, where many of the identifiers mentioned above would not be applicable, it becomes clear that digital IDM takes place on a different footing than we have been used to in the past; digital IDM is about the informational representation of an individual in a public service relationship, rather than the physical or paper-based representation.[16] IDM in E-Government is information-based; transactional E-Government relationships with individuals are therefore information-dependent.[17] An important question, then, is if (and if so, how) this new information-base of public service relationships with the citizen will lead to any fundamental changes in public service arrangements (as compared to traditional public service provision).

Enabling information-age public service arrangements through IDM

Several scholars have pointed to changes which may happen to information relationships between individuals and government as a result of the introduction of new digital IDM means. Some of these scholars perceive these changes as being fundamental, bringing about substantial information imbalances in citizen–government relationships;[18] others perceive these changes as being more diverse, sometimes even contradictory, and context-dependent, with the introduction of similar IDM systems leading to multiple outcomes.[19] In general, the following informational trends are being observed as a result of introducing IDM systems in transactional public service relationships:[20]

- Information can flow freely, compared to information in face-to-face and paper-based transactions within the confines of a physical locale and relatively closed networks.
- Information can be copied and stored at almost no expense.
- Transactions become information-dependent.
- Transactional histories become more detailed and easily available to many.
- Trust depends on transactional history reports rather than on personal recognition.

Generally, these informational trends pose new questions and dilemmas for governments about the design of new E-Government service arrangements with citizens. For instance, as a result of these informational trends, an individual's ability to remain unnoticed and, after being noticed, to remain unidentified, has declined significantly in emerging digital environments. At the same time, however, we may observe an increased freedom of choice for individuals to represent themselves with the use of different types of pseudonyms (e.g. email address, phone number, credit card details, etc.) in their interactions with others. Consequently, the introduction and use of new forms of IDM in public service provision not only requires government to explore newly available digital IDM systems and reconsider IDM approaches available in the physical world, but also to more generally reassess benefits and costs related to the use of IDM in these public service relationships. Such considerations include the protection of human rights (e.g. privacy protection, freedom of speech, etc.), the enforcement of responsibility (e.g. liability and responsibility of actions) and the enhancement of user and societal capabilities (e.g. reduction of co-ordination and transaction costs).[21]

Thus far, scholars point towards the development of two opposing digital IDM strategies at the management level of organisations.[22] First, there is the business strategy of increased identification of the individual. In this case, digital IDM is utilised to maximise the collection and use of identity information related to individuals (e.g. customers). Second, and more recently, a digital IDM strategy of minimising the collection and use of an individual's identity information is emerging. We briefly explain the two IDM strategies below and for each of these strategies provide an example of digital IDM in government.

Digital IDM as maximising identity information

According to scholars, the IDM strategy of maximising the collection and use of identity information is used in both the private sector, where data mining systems and practices are increasingly being utilised as a surveillance technique to facilitate the identification and classification of customers into distinct groups or segments,[23] and in the public sector, where the increasing practice of identification is facilitated by IDM systems such as CCTV cameras, biometrics and ID cards, for example.[24] Most scholars conducting research in this area perceive the increasing amount of identification and especially the ability to gather an individual's identity information secretly and involuntarily as a major societal concern.[25]

Some perceive these new IDM systems as surveillance systems. Surveillance systems capture personal and group data in order to classify people and populations according to varying criteria and determine who should be targeted for special treatment, suspicion, eligibility, inclusion, access, etc.[26] Consequently, surveillance systems can be perceived as discriminatory technologies as they sieve and sort for the purpose of assessment, thus affecting people's life chances.[27] Discriminatory 'social sorting' of citizens would occur depending on the values embedded in computer codes used to process, assess and classify citizens' personal data.[28] As an example, Lyon argues that biometric ID cards, such as those promoted by the UK government, will permit sorting, profiling and discrimination in terms of ethnicity.[29]

With the introduction of these new IDM or surveillance systems come expectations that these new systems increasingly define public decision-making premises, which used to be determined by public officials.[30] With public decision algorithms coded into these new systems, public decision-making powers within a public service-providing organisation do not completely disappear, however. Rather, they are transferred to the designers of systems, whose task is to transfer existing administrative rules, norms and values into system algorithms, codes and modules. Therefore, according to Bovens and Zouridis,[31] it is these so-called 'system-level bureaucrats' who crucially interpret the will of lawmakers and create a formal set of decision rules through which categories of individuals will receive a certain service.

A practical example of this digital management strategy in government[32] can be found in Hong Kong, where the so-called 'Smart Identity Card System' (SMARTICS) was introduced in 2001. This multi-functional ID card is obligatory for all Hong Kong citizens who are 11 years of age and older. It is widely used for a variety of services, including public safety, online government services, library services, banking services, cross-border management and employment, as well as being used as a driver's licence. Similar to the previous ID card system in Hong Kong, the smart ID card displays the holder's photograph and several personal details, such as name, date of birth and the Hong Kong Identity Card number (ICNO). However, the new smart ID card also holds digitised data in its embedded chip. This data includes biometric templates for facial recognition and two thumbprint images as well as several personal details, such as the individual's name in English, the individual's name in Chinese, the individual's name in Chinese Commercial Code, a name change indicator, gender, date of birth, a gender change indicator, the ICNO, date of issue, date of first registration, place of birth code and resident status.[33] Moreover, digital certificates have been stored on the SMARTICS chip to enable Public Key Infrastructure two-way authentication, fingerprint and card PIN verifications and encryption of the biometric templates stored on the chip.[34]

Digital IDM as minimising the collection and use of identity information

In attempts to counterbalance the societal trend of increased identification of individuals, a digital IDM strategy based on anonymity and pseudonymity is increasingly considered as a realistic alternative for organisations.[35] Scholars perceive a particular need for the enablement of anonymity following the development of new capabilities for automated systems to collect, store and disseminate personal information, thus creating serious implications for safeguarding an individual's information privacy.[36] An alternative digital IDM strategy can be achieved through incorporating anonymity and pseudonymity into IDM systems and providing individual users with complete control over transaction requests and the transmission of their identity information.[37] An example of such privacy-enhanced IDM systems would be the use of so-called 'partial identities' in online transactions.

A practical example of this digital management strategy in government can be found in Austria,[38] where the Austrian federal government started to employ smart card technology for improving citizens' access to public services in 2003. The Austrian Citizen Card concept has been extended to other types of cards, such as ATM cards, public servant ID documents, student service cards and the Austrian health insurance E-Card, as well as to other devices, such as mobile phones, PCs and USB tokens. Individuals can use their Citizen Card for a wide range of E-Government and E-Commerce services and tasks, including online tax declaration, child allowance application, student allowance application, a digitally signed criminal record, electronic public service newsletters, authentication of documents, logon to Web services and electronic signatures on contracts.[39]

The two most important requirements for the Austrian Citizen Card are the provision of identification and a secure electronic signature in accordance with Austrian Signature Law requirements. The Citizen Card involves a signature creation device containing cryptographic keys and electronic signature. Personal data stored on the Citizen Card are the individual's name, date of birth and the 'Source PIN', which is a unique identifier for electronic transactions.[40] A Certificate Service Provider (CSP) is responsible for verifying the citizen's identity as part of the Citizen Card registration procedure, as well as requesting the identity link from the Source PIN Registration Authority (i.e. the Austrian Data Protection Commission).

The Source PIN is a unique identification number derived from the Austrian Central Register of Residence (CRR) number. All individuals registered in the CRR, which holds authoritative personal and residence data repositories, have been assigned a unique 12-digit decimal number. However, for privacy reasons, these CRR numbers are never used for any other purpose than being a primary key for records held in the CRR. The Source PIN Registration Authority is the only central governmental department with the ability to create Source PINs, at the request of a CSP. The Source PIN Registration Authority does not maintain a copy of generated Source PINs, as these Source PINs are kept solely by the individual. However, in order to protect the individual's privacy, the Source PIN itself cannot be used for identification purposes. Derivatives of the Source PIN, named 'Sector-Specific PINs' (ssPINs), are made through encryption to support an individual's online transactions with different government agencies. The application of one-way encryption also makes it possible neither to reverse-engineer the ssPIN to obtain the underlying Source PIN, nor to generate an ssPIN for another sector.[41]

New forms of IDM in UK E-Government

It is clear that the introduction of these new IDM systems may have profound informational effects on public service relationships between citizens and governments. On this point, however, little empirical evidence is available about how emerging E-Government service relationships are developing. Moreover, the narrow focus on the technical, informative capabilities of newly available digital IDM systems does not tell us about how the information collected, managed and processed through these IDM systems is actually used. Furthermore, current digital IDM conceptions do not reflect, or relate to, the unique role government has in society and, with that, the specific nature of E-Government service relationships between government and citizens.[42] IDM seems to be mainly understood as a technical means which serves many and varied purposes, issues and organisations.[43] The narrow focus on digital IDM systems also seems to ignore that individuals continue to have a relationship with government in the physical public service world, in which IDM already has an important role.[44] With public service arrangements between government and citizens existing in both online and offline worlds, it is likely that convergence between online identity and offline identity will take place.[45]

Consequently, it appears to be important to empirically investigate the implementation and use of IDM systems in citizen–government service relationships and to analyse what is happening both within and to these relationships. In a research project sponsored by the UK Economic and Social Research Council's e-Society Programme, we chose to explore, from a social science perspective, the application and utilisation of a variety of emerging IDM systems in different E-Government service domains and relationships with citizens. In order to explore what is happening to new information capture, management, flow and assessments in government, we specifically focused on the policy and managerial dimensions of the application and use of IDM systems in E-Government service relationships. Moreover, as this research project had no direct empirical antecedents, we were particularly interested in enabling deeper, broader and empirically informed understandings of the relationship between IDM systems and the nature of citizenship.

We used case study research methodology in order to bring a depth of historical and contemporary understanding to our work that would enhance reliability, enrich our subsequent analysis and theoretical development, and enhance the generalisation and transferability to policy and practice of the research findings.[46] For each of the case studies, we undertook an academic and policy document literature review to further inform us about the strategic and policy context. We also carried out 15 semi-structured interviews with key individuals at the operational, strategic and policy levels of managing identity in E-Government service relationships. Between February 2005 and March 2007, we conducted eight rich case studies across UK government, each of which had a different primary 'technological access point' for the citizen to E-Government application areas, where design and implementation choices about IDM have already been made (e.g. Internet portal, smart card, CCTV, etc.). Other variables designed into the study include different policy and service domains, differentiated institutional settings and the sensitivity level to be attached to the capture and use of personal information sensitivity.

In this chapter we present case study findings for three of our eight case studies to explore how IDM in varying E-Government service relationships can be understood. For each of the case studies, after presenting a short introduction, we present empirical findings which demonstrate ways in which IDM systems are being used in citizen–government relationships.

Case study 1: online provisional driver's licence application

Since April 2006 citizens have been able to apply for a provisional driver's licence via the UK central government's Direct.gov web portal and Government Gateway infrastructure. Applicants who wish to hold a licence to allow them to learn to drive and take a driving test can complete an online form with basic demographic details, including recent address history. First, this information is electronically matched with the UK Central Government Department's own database to retrieve any existing details for the applicant, including previous applications and driving disqualification information. Second, the demographic information is automatically transferred via a data link to an external information solutions company that employs search technology to match applicant data with a variety of public and private databases. This process assesses the applicant's digital footprint to seek assurance that the submitted name and address are bona fide and provides the UK Central Government Department with a software-generated score, which determines whether the application can be completed online. If the applicant fails the footprint assessment, he/she will be provided with an on-screen message instructing them to finish the process in the conventional paper-based and face-to-face format, for instance by sending identity documents and other information to the UK Central Government Department by post.

If the applicant progresses through the footprint assessment, he/she will be asked to submit their passport number online. Using this number, the UK Identity and

Passport Service will electronically transfer the applicant's passport photograph and signature from digital passport records to the UK Central Government Department for use on the provisional driving licence. Applicants are permitted to use alternative paper-based identity documentation, such as their birth certificate, and can choose to use an alternative photograph. For each of these cases, however, the application has to be completed offline.

Case study 2: UK local government E-Benefits system

Since 2004 a local unitary council has been using an E-Benefits system to assist citizens with housing and council tax benefits services. Previously, the claim would have been processed using a paper form submitted by the citizen (with potential support from front-office staff for filling in the form), which back-office staff would have analysed later to provide a benefits calculation.

At present, a claimant is visited at home by a council officer, who conducts an interview so as to be able to calculate and determine, on the spot, the levels of benefit that can be claimed. The officer uses a tablet PC loaded with specialized software to take personal demographic details and information regarding the claimant's living arrangements, income, bank account details, savings, assets and other benefits claimed. By inputting this information into an on-screen form, the software is able to calculate the benefits that will be received. The claimant also has to show the officer several paper identity documents, such as passport, driver's licence and payslips, in order to get access to benefits services. Both the claimant and the officer sign the form using an electronic pen; a claimant's signature is legally required to officially acknowledge the claim form. The officer's signature is acknowledged at the central ministry as enhancing the legal circumstances of a claim. The approved form is then sent via a wireless network as an email attachment to the council head-quarters, where it is stored in a central database on the council's server, which contains all approved local benefit claims.

The local council also exchanges benefits data of local benefit claimants with the UK Central Government Department of Work and Pensions (DWP). The council electronically transfers claimant information to the DWP, then the DWP matches personal details of claimants with a variety of datasets held within its own information systems and those of the UK taxation agency. The matching process helps to provide indications that the claimant may be erroneously or fraudulently claiming benefits. This information is passed to the local council to act upon at its discretion. The DWP also runs ICT-supported intricate risk analysis, which places claimants into a risk category based on their individual profile. The DWP attributes a risk score, which indicates the likelihood of error or fraud being associated with each category of claimant. This risk data is sent to the local council to follow up in its case review schedules. Council interventions based on high risk scores can lead to the discovery of both underpayments and overpayments to claimants, which are the consequences of either error or fraud.

Case study 3: smart card application in UK local government service provision

In 2001 a UK local authority introduced a multi-functional smart card. It is available free of charge to those who live in, work in or visit the borough. The smart card can be used, for instance, to borrow library books, access leisure facilities, pay for goods and services, provide proof of age and prove entitlement to concessionary bus travel.

One of the public service uses of the smart card is a cashless catering system in four secondary schools across the borough. Here, pupils periodically load money onto an E-Purse section of the card, either using wall-mounted coin machines or having their parents submit a cheque to the school's administration office for staff to update accounts. Pupils present their cards at the check-out in the canteen, where catering staff physically assess and match the photograph on the front of the smart card with the pupil and insert the card into a reader device that automatically debits the correct amount from the E-Purse. Pupils entitled to free school meals do not need to load money onto the E-Purse, but they present their card at the checkout in the same way.

Moreover, under a separate pilot project for extended smart card use, pupils swipe smart cards through a smart card reader at the beginning of each class. 'Loyalty' points are automatically accrued for every class attended. These points can then be supplemented with extra points, which are assigned at the discretion of teachers, for good or positive behaviour. The points are stored in a central database and pupils are able to exchange them for goods and services with local retailers and organisations participating in this loyalty scheme. Options for pupils include a free swim, cinema ticket or fast food meal. More recently, the authority has been investigating the possibility of using the smart card to reward healthy eating by awarding points to pupils who buy approved food items for lunch. Healthy eating points could be automatically accrued via the smart card and smart card readers at the till and stored in a central database. This may fit into an authority-wide motivational scheme whereby positive behaviour, such as recycling, voluntary work and healthy lifestyles, is rewarded via smart card point accumulation.

Analysis

What, then, happens when new forms of IDM are deployed in E-Government service relationships with citizens? What effects do they have upon information relationships between citizens and government as compared to the use of traditional forms of IDM in paper-based public service environments, for instance? What are their implications for government and the citizen? In the next two sub-sections we further analyse our case study findings.

New composite citizen identities in public service relationships

Within these emerging E-Government service relationships we observe a shift towards the collection, management and use of new citizen identifiers. Compared to the paper-based public service world where traditional personal data such as name, address and date of birth are key personal identifiers for citizens, these empirical findings point to new composite citizen identities. In composite citizen identities, traditional identifiers and new identifiers, such as a digital footprint based on a citizen's presence in various databases, a risk score derived from matching a citizen's personal data with statistical demographic data on benefit fraud, and a citizen's profile of good behaviour, are important.

As a result of new combinations of human and computer assessments (e.g. claims assessments in the E-Benefits system, the use of an E-Purse in the smart card case study, etc.) being compared, for instance, to personal data gathering in the paper-based public service world, generic categories of citizens' personal information have become more fluid categories. In the abstract, these new types of personal data can be perceived in concentric circles at varying distances from the individual's core identity.[47] Moreover, identification happens explicitly and implicitly from an individual's point of view. For example, in the online driver's licence application case study, an individual is aware of submitting personal details but unaware of the digital footprint assessment. Similarly, in the E-Benefits system case study, an individual participates in the supply of personal details and identification documents but does not know about a personal risk score being constructed.

New forms of assessment in public service relationships

New combinations of human and computer assessments also lead to the emergence of new forms of assessment as compared to assessments in traditional paper-based service provision, for instance. The smart card application in local government, where, for instance, loyalty points for class attendance are allocated automatically to pupils, the online provisional driver's licence application in which citizen information is matched electronically with both government and private sector databases and the E-Benefits system, where claimants are served at their homes, are all examples of different assessment activities arising from the use of varying digitised IDM systems.

Interestingly, in contrast to scholarly assertions,[48] our research findings indicate that human judgement-based assessments remain of substantial importance. In most of our case studies, such as in all three presented above, final assessments on public service access and forms of public service provision continue to be made by civil servants. In some of the case studies this final assessment is being restricted by determining the bandwidth within which the system is allowed to serve the citizen automatically, as we have seen in those case study findings on the loyalty scheme attached to using a local smart card and the digital footprint assessment during the online driver's licence application.

We also observe that newly available IDM supports civil servants in their assessments and further decision making in public service provision. First, civil servants are being guided by digitised systems through the public service provision process (e.g. utilising pre-filled digital forms or standardised questionnaires in their service relationships with citizens). The E-Benefits system mentioned above is a good example, where a digitised system, based on various forms and pieces of personal information collected at the home of the benefits claimant, is able to calculate and determine, on the spot, the levels of benefit that can be claimed, bringing about changes in assessment and decision-making processes. Second, support happens through the availability of improved knowledge to the civil servants in situations of assessment during public service provision. So-called 'evidence-based' public service provision can be observed, for instance, in the E-Benefits case study mentioned above, where high risk scores can lead to local council interventions.

In those cases, however, where assessments are made without the intervention of human beings (e.g. the ICT-supported risk analyses in the E-Benefits system case and the digital footprint assessment in the online driver's licence application), Lyon's arguments of social sorting come more strongly to the fore.[49]

IDM strategies in public service relationships

Customer Relationship Management (CRM), for many of our interviewees, has become an important strategy for using IDM in E-Government service arrangements to develop tailor-made service relationships with established customers. Newly available management information derived from ICT-supported interactions in the front office (e.g. smart card application) or even back office of E-Government service provision (e.g. online driver's licence application) opens up active and pro-active opportunities for enhanced service provision to the citizen. Taking data protection legislation into account and utilising available digital means only for the purpose of quality enhancement of a specific public service towards customers (i.e. not trying to profile customers by extending systems so as to include other databases or networks) were considered to be important conditions for service value compliance. Although in some cases newly available means of IDM were used across public services or public service organisations (e.g. as in the smart card case and the application of a provisional driver's licence through the UK government's Direct.gov Web portal and Government Gateway infrastructure), information flows between citizens and governments usually remained within a single public service domain, as in the traditional paper-based public service world.

New public–private partnerships for citizen identification and authentication

Another important indicator for change in public service relationships as a result of the use of new IDM systems is that government is no longer the sole responsible party for citizen identification and authentication. Instead, we observe the introduction of what we call 'third-party authentication' in E-Government service relationships with the citizen.[50] With restricted or even no knowledge of the citizen, private organisations, such as the ones trusted by the UK government (e.g. the information solutions company in the online driver's licence application case), are involved in verifying and authenticating citizen's identity. These organisations then are assessing and constructing citizens' digital footprints, which then constitute the basis for setting an individual's trust profile. This trust profile determines whether or not an individual will be granted online access to public services.

A further example of new public–private partnerships in the area of citizen identification and authentication can be found in the smart card application case. In this case, the production and issue of smart cards, as well as the management and maintenance of personal information collected through citizens using the smart card for a variety of public services, are responsibilities of a private sector company.

Implications for government, the citizen and citizenship

Empirical research findings, such as those presented above, demonstrate that new forms of IDM and informational representations of citizen identity in E-Government service provision are effecting substantial changes in citizen–government relationships when compared to those in traditional paper-based service environments. For example, the arrival of new IDM in E-Government service provision may be shifting, from a citizen's point of view, to a system wherein paper-based public service characteristics, such as form filling, queuing and waiting, become increasingly superfluous. Simultaneously, to the civil servant, the collection, management and use of large collections of paper-based documents stored in a personal file that is related to a particular public service may increasingly belong to the past. Furthermore, there seems to be a development towards digitised joint spaces where service providers meet and assess their customers on the basis of newly available information (e.g. as in the smart card application case and the online driver's licence application case).

More fundamentally, and consequent to the implementation and use of digitised IDM, citizen–government relationships appear to be changing in new directions, moving away from traditional conceptions of, and principles for, citizenship. Looking at different forms of administrative equivalence of citizens served in paper-based public service environments (Table 9.1), we may observe that new forms of public service assessments and public decision making in E-Government service relationships, such as those presented above, are moving away from the application of these principles. From general principles of administrative equity, we are moving towards differentiation in the information-based selection and assessment of citizens. In more general terms, we may recognise a gradual shift from 'universalism' to what may be called 'particularism' as an underlying conception of citizenship in an E-Government service environment. This development particularly manifests itself when the citizen is being more and more administratively sifted and sorted in a vertical way – as a unique customer of government, rather than a citizen with rights and duties equal to other citizens. An individual citizen who, due to good behaviour in using public services, receives loyalty points on his smart card for spending on local retail products provides a good example of an increasingly particularistic understanding of citizenship.

Differentiation as a result of using digital IDM systems takes place not only vertically, however, but also horizontally. For instance, new information-based public service assessments, such as establishing conditional online access for trusted citizens only (as in the online driver's licence application case), lead to new forms of citizen segmentation: those who can be trusted according to their digital footprint and those who cannot. With that, a new conception of citizenship is implied in our view: the use of new digital IDM systems in E-Government service relationships brings about public decision making on customers versus non-customers for E-Government service provision, based on different trust profiles of citizens. Thus, 'layered citizenship' is being established through 'horizontal', segmented administrative sorting of citizens.[51]

With this gradual shift from universalistic to particularistic public service provision, we are moving away, in some instances at least, from universal access rights or equal procedures, towards more individually based public service arrangements between a citizen and government. Public service arrangements increasingly based on varying types and combinations of personal identifiers, which are collected remotely or in face-to-face encounters and implicitly and explicitly, are tailor-made and used at the level of an individual citizen. Consequently, this newly emerging conception of 'citizenship' based on individual citizen identity and facilitated by new electronic modes of IDM, which is taking place more and more in combined public and private sector realms, suggests the need for fundamental re-thinking of the government's use of IDM in its service relationships with citizens. With that, important societal questions emerge about the governance of IDM and IDM policy development in information-age government, both now and in the future.

Key points

- Introducing new IDM systems in emerging E-Government service relationships questions how, and to what extent, these systems affect citizen–government information relationships as compared to traditional IDM forms.
- Paper-based and face-to-face identification and authentication are a traditional, central part of public service arrangements between government and citizens.
- Digital identification equals *informational* representation of individuals: a person/entity compares information items or 'identifiers' of another, with those previously recorded, and matches the two.
- Identifiers include things you do, are, know, have and are assigned to.
- Introducing IDM systems results in freer information flows, reduced costs for copying and storing and information-dependent transactions which are more detailed and have accessible transactional histories and which, in turn, lead to more trust.
- Introducing IDM also poses questions and dilemmas regarding the protection of human rights, enforcement of responsibility and enhancement of user and societal capabilities.
- There are two opposing digital IDM strategies at the management level of organisations: increasing identification of the individual, thereby maximising data collection and minimising info collection and use of an individual's identity.
- Three UK case studies explore how IDM in varying E-Government service relationships can be understood: online provisional drivers' licence application; a local government E-Benefits system; and smart card application in UK local government service provision.
- There are new composite citizen identities in public service relationships.

- There are new forms of assessment in public service relationships.
- There is a shift from 'universalism' to what may be called 'particularism'.
- Differentiation as a result of using digital IDM systems takes place vertically and horizontally.
- There is a need for fundamental rethinking of government's use of IDM in its service relationships with citizens.

Notes

1 e.g. Varney, D. (2006) *Service Transformation: A Better Service for Citizens and Businesses, a Better Deal for the Taxpayer*, HSMO, available at: http://www.hm-treasury.gov.uk/media/4/F/pbr06_varney_review.pdf; EU Ministerial Declaration on E-Government, presented at Ministerial E-Government Conference 2005, Transforming Public Services, Manchester, 24 November 2005.

2 Murakami-Wood, D., Ball, K., Lyon, D., Norris, C. and Raab, C. (2006) 'A Report on the Surveillance Society', available at: http://www.ico.gov.uk/upload/documents/library/data_protection/practical_application/surveillance_society_full_report_2006.pdf; The LSE (2005) *The Identity Project. An Assessment of the UK Identity Cards Bill and Its Implications*, The LSE Identity Project Interim Report, March 2005.

3 Lyon, D. (2001) *Surveillance Society. Monitoring everyday life*, Buckingham: Open University Press; Lyon, D. (2003) 'Surveillance as Social Sorting. Computer Codes and Mobile Bodies', in D. Lyon (ed.) *Surveillance and Social Sorting: Privacy, Risk and Digital Discrimination*. London: Routledge, pp. 13–30.

4 Lips, A. M. B., J. A. Taylor and J. Organ (2006) 'Identity Management, Administrative Sorting and Citizenship in New Modes of Government', Paper presented at the Journal of Information, Communication and Society 10th Anniversary International Symposium, University of York, 20–22 September 2006.

5 Camp, L. J. (2003) *Identity in Digital Government*. A Research Report of the Digital Government Civic ScenarioWorkshop, Kennedy School of Government, Harvard University, Cambridge, available at: http://www.ljean.com/files/identity.pdf.

6 Torpey, J. (2000) *The Invention of the Passport: Surveillance, Citizenship and the State*. Cambridge: Cambridge University Press.

7 Snellen, I. Th. M. (1998) 'Street Level Bureaucracy in an Information Age', in I. Th. M. Snellen and W. B. H. J. van de Donk (eds) *Public Administration in an Information Age. A Handbook*. Amsterdam: IOS Press.

8 Bamford, J. (2007) 'Identity Management: Achieving Data Protection Compliance and Inspiring Public Confidence', Position Paper for the forum on e-Infrastructures for Identity Management and Data Sharing, Oxford Internet Institute; Crompton, M. (2004) 'Proof of ID Required? Getting Identity Management Right', Paper presented at the Australian IT Security Forum, 30 March 2004.

9 e.g. The Burton Group, p. 43 in Scorer, A. (2007) 'Identity Directories and Databases', in D. G. W. Birch (ed.) *Digital Identity Management. Technological, Business and Social Implications*, 2007, Aldershot: Gower, pp. 41–49.

10 Crompton, M. (2004) op. cit. p. 1.

11 Clarke, R. (1994) 'Human Identification in Information Systems: Management Challenges and Public Policy Issues' *Information Technology and People* 7/4: 6–37.

12 Crompton, M. (2004) op. cit. p. 1; Greenwood, D. (2007) 'The Context for Identity Management Architectures and Trust Models', Paper presented at the OECD Workshop on Digital Identity Management, Trondheim.

13 Harper, J. (2006) *Identity Crisis – How Identification Is Overused and Misunderstood*. Washington, DC: The Cato Institute.

14 e.g. Harper, J. (2006); FIDIS (Future of IDentity in the Information Society) (2005) WP2, D2.1. *Inventory of Topics and Clusters*, 21 September 2005, available at http://www.fidis.net/resources/deliverables/identity-of-identity/#c1755; Anrig, B., Benoist, E. and Jaquet-Chiffellet, D. O. (2004) *Virtual? Identity*, paper delivered within the scope of the European project Future of Identity in the Information Society (FIDIS), available at http://www.vip.ch/papers/virtual_identity.pdf.

15 FIDIS (Future of IDentity in the Information Society) (2005) op. cit. pp. 38–39.

16 Lips, A. M. B., J. A. Taylor and J. Organ (2006) op. cit.; Lips, A. M. B. (2007) 'Separating the Informational from the Electronic: Challenges and Opportunities for New Zealand Government in an Information Age', Inaugural Lecture, Victoria University of Wellington, 20 November 2007, in: *Policy Quarterly*, forthcoming.

17 Lips, A. M. B. (2008) 'Identity Management in Information Age Government. Exploring Concepts, Definitions, Approaches and Solutions', Working paper, June 2008, pp. 56, available at http://www.e.govt.nz/services/authentication/library/docs/idm-govt-08.pdf.

18 Murakami-Wood, D., Ball, K., Lyon, D., Norris, C. and Raab, C. (2006) op. cit.

19 Marx, G. T. (2006) 'Varieties of Personal Information as Influences on Attitudes toward Surveillance', in Haggerty, K. and Ericson, R. (eds) *The New Politics of Surveillance and Visibility*, University of Toronto Press, available at http://web.mit.edu/gtmarx/www/vancouver.html.

20 Camp, L. J. (2003) op. cit. pp. 7–8.

21 FIDIS (Future of IDentity in the Information Society) (2005) op. cit.

22 Lips, A. M. B. (2008) op. cit.

23 Gandy, O. (1989) 'The Surveillance Society: Information Technology and Bureaucratic Social Control', *Journal of Communication*, 39/3: 61–76.

24 Murakami-Wood, D., Ball, K., Lyon, D., Norris, C. and Raab, C. (2006) op. cit.

25 Danna, A., and Gandy O. (2002) 'All That Glitters Is Not Gold: Digging beneath the Surface of Data Mining', *Journal of Business Ethics*, 40/4: 373–386; Marx, G. T. (1998) 'An Ethics for the New Surveillance', *The Information Society* 14/3: 171–186; Marx, G. T. (2004) 'What's New about the "New Surveillance"? Classifying for Change and Continuity', *Knowledge, Technology, and Policy* 17/1: 18–37; Lyon, D. (2003) op. cit.; Gandy, O. (1989) op. cit.

26 Lyon, D. (2003) op. cit. p. 20.

27 Ibid.

28 Lyon, D. (2001) op. cit.; Lyon, D. (2003) op. cit.

29 Ibid.

30 Lyon, D. (2003) op. cit.; Bovens, M. and Zouridis, S. (2002) 'From Street-Level to System-Level Bureaucracies: How Information and Communication Technology Is Transforming Administrative Discretion and Constitutional Control', *Public Administration Review* 62: 174–184.

31 Ibid.

32 Lips, A. M. B. (2008) op. cit.

33 Hong Kong Immigration Department (2002) *FS on AVC for IMMD – Appendix C Relevant Areas of SMARTICS*. Retrieved 20 April 2008, from http://www.immd.gov.hk/pdf/apvc/avc/appendixc.pdf.

34 Hong Kong Trade Development Council (2005) 'Hong Kong Immigration Department's smart thinking gets APICTA', available at http://ict.hktdc.com/suc-e335.htm.

35 Lips, A. M. B. (2008) op. cit.; PRIME-project, www.prime.project.eu; FIDIS-project, www.fidis.net; Clarke, R. (1997) 'Introduction to Dataveillance and Information Privacy, and Definitions of Terms', paper available at http://www.anu.edu.au/people/Roger.Clarke/DV/Intro.html; Gilbert, D., Kerr, I. R. and McGill, J. (2006) 'The Medium and the Message: Personal Privacy and the Forced Marriage of Police and Telecommunications Providers', *Criminal Law Quarterly* 51/4: 469–507.

36 Gilbert, D., Kerr, I. R. and McGill, J. (2006) op. cit.

37 e.g. Crompton, M. (2005) 'Trust, Identity and Connected Government', 24 June 2005, paper presented at the Forum for the Research, Development and Evaluation Commission 'The Evolution of E-Government – From Policy to Practice', Taipei; Crompton, M. (2006) 'The Revolution of RFID – Challenges and Options for Action: A Consumer Perspective', paper presented at the CeBIT 2006; Hansen, M., Berlich, P., Camenisch, J., Clauß, S., Pfitzmann, A. and Waidner M. (2004) 'Privacy-Enhancing Identity Management', *Information Security Technical Report* 9/1: 35–44; Rössler, T., Posch, R. and Hayat, A. (2005) 'Giving an Interoperable Solution for Incorporating Foreign e-IDs in Austrian E-Government', paper presented at the IDABC Conference, 2005.
38 Lips, A. M. B. (2008) op. cit.
39 http://alt.buergerkarte.at/en/was_ist_die_buergerkarte/konzept_buergerkarte.html.
40 Rössler, T., Posch, R. and Hayat, A. (2005) op. cit.
41 Ibid.
42 Lips, A. M. B. (2008) op. cit.
43 Ibid.
44 Ibid.
45 Greenwood, D. (2007) op. cit.
46 Seale, C. (1999) 'Quality in Qualitative Research', *Qualitative Inquiry* 4: 465–478.
47 Marx, G. T. (2006) op. cit.
48 Lyon, D. (2003) op. cit.; Bovens, M. and Zouridis, S. (2002) op. cit.
49 Lyon, D. (2001) op. cit.; Lyon, D. (2003) op. cit.
50 Taylor, J. A., Lips, A. M. B. and Organ, J. (2007) 'Information-Intensive Government and the Layering and Sorting of Citizenship', *Public Money and Management* 27/ 2: 161–164.
51 Ibid.

Further reading

Otjacques, B., Hitzelberger, P. and Feltz, F. (2007) 'Interoperability of E-Government Information Systems: Issues of Identification and Data Sharing', *Journal of Management Information Systems* 23/4, Spring: 29–51.
McKenzie, R., Crompton, M. and Wallis, C. (2008) 'Use Cases for Identity Management in E-Government', *Security and Privacy*, IEEE 6/2: 51–57.

10 Biometrics

From biometricised borders to securitising non-territorial space

Juliet Lodge

Summary

This chapter argues that in the context of E-Government, biometrics are not a problem per se, but the different ways of defining them and the use made of them are a problem. Why is securitising borders using biometric tools stored by ICTs a problem? Three reasons for this are explored: (1) the definition and use of biometrics; (2) the practices of E-Government information sharing and interoperability; and (3) the nature of political controls. Making accountable and securitising access to space within and beyond territorially defined borders highlights the intangibility and elusiveness of the frontiers of new digi-spaces.

Introduction

Why is securitising borders using biometric tools stored by ICTs a problem? Three reasons for this are explored: (1) the definition of biometrics; (2) the practices of interoperability; and (3) the nature of political controls. Securitising access to space within and beyond territorially defined borders highlights the intangibility and elusiveness of the frontiers of visible political accountability in new digi-spaces. The chapter argues that the use of new technologies designed to cut risks by enhancing our capacity for reducing uncertainty (i.e. biometrics and automatic information exchange) is not free of risk. The chapter begins by defining biometrics and outlining the underlying premises governing the non-territorial use of biometrics to secure territorial borders. It goes on to argue that EU information exchange and the state of play of inter-operability confront the EU with a triple deficit. This renders 'security' susceptible to being captured by hostile or complacent interests that could potentially challenge and erode EU practices of democracy and liberty.

Theoretical concerns

The examination of biometrics is often located within frameworks of the tech-nologisation of the political and surveillance and security on the one hand, and identity on the other hand. In the first instance, theoretical propositions relate to the notion of the pan-opticon and the all-seeing state, to policing and tracking at macro and micro levels. In the second instance, identity is located in the discourse on the philosophical traditions and norms of identity, linked to psychological conceptions and diachronic and synchronic reconfigurations of the self and the self in relation to the state. Political scientists emphasise power and order, global civil society and the relationship between the state and the individual – the exchange of fealty in return for protection within defined 'state' borders. The link between the two instances is illustrated in the discourse on exceptions[1] to the rule of transparency and openness in government; exceptionalism validates secrecy and opacity, often for operational reasons, in respect of those items that can be labelled 'defence' and 'security-sensitive'. Yet knowledge is the key to liberty. The new technologies for gaining and commodifying information, as the basis of 'knowledge', challenge liberty.[2] How this happens is explained by creeping exceptionalism and the erosion of the freedom to not be surveilled.

Surveillance and security theoretical propositions have led to a focus on political violence and terrorism, and the extent, nature and consequences of surveillance for security. Socio-legal studies focus on their implications for social control,[3] data protection and privacy,[4] and intellectual property rights.[5] Politico-legal studies home in on the implications for constitutional and institutional practices of democracy,[6] the tension between norm diffusion and confusion[7] and the impact on society.[8] Political economists explore competition policy, public procurement and the mutual dependencies of ICT industries on governments in their quest to garner shares of the global market for their new security goods. Political theorists and philosophers explore the relationship between freedom, liberty and data protection. Vagueness over what liberty, security, transparency and accountability would resemble in practical terms where E-Governance is practised means that the packaging of liberty and security in facile claims about securitising liberty by applying technology to tracking identity go unchallenged, at worst; at best, they are submerged by unwarranted inferences about assumed homogeneous cultural values.

In the context of security and surveillance, identity is determined by reference to nationality, ethnic grouping, behaviour (particularly that deemed subversive, criminal, suspect or radical) and associated profiling. This differs from identity that is self-conceived and derived from kinship, family, community, culture and nationality, although it may overlap with the latter to a degree. More specifically, in the context of internal and external security, biometric identity is defined by algorithms, where a mathematical profile or 'solution' maps a biometric identifier (e.g. a fingerprint). This, in turn, is embedded in a document that can be automatically read by a machine. The test in this case may be whether the biometric presented (e.g. a fingerprint) matches that stored in the biometric identifying document.

Biometric identity challenges conceptions of identity and de-territorialises both borders and security. The structural relationship between the citizen and the state is tested and mediated by public–private partnerships and inadequate technical security architectures, which undermine data protection law. Together, they challenge the balance between liberty and security. From a scientific viewpoint, the question ceases to be one of 'identity', as framed by traditional social theories. Instead, it is: What does a biometric identifier tell us about identity and processes of authenticating identity? What does the deployment of such technologies tell us about the balance between liberty and security in Western liberal democratic societies, where E-Government is the means by which public services are increasingly dispensed and access to which is increasingly mediated by the provision and exchange of information about individuals, including digitised biometric data?

This chapter is informed by such propositions, but is not a test of them. Rather, it explores the question of how the application of inter-operable technologies to the realisation of a common security goal shared by EU governments has a transformative impact on both our understanding of the democratic bargain and E-Government public–private partnerships, especially in a supranational, cross-border setting. It explores this through an examination of the introduction of biometric identity documents that governments claim will enhance individual and collective cross-border security.

Defining biometrics

At the level of policy-making, 'biometrics' is a term that is employed loosely but instrumentally by state authorities concerned with securitising borders against illegal crossing of those borders into defined territorial spaces. Biometric characteristics are also seen as tools to establish the unique identity of an individual. Possession of, and the ability to verify, that uniqueness then becomes the key by which the owner accesses a range of private services (e.g. commercial transactions), public services (e.g. online registration of civil matters like births, car tax and E-Administration of socio-economic welfare entitlement information and application forms) and mixed private–public services and provisions (e.g. health insurance, medical records and, increasingly, passports and other civil state documents administered on the state's behalf by outsourced agents). The territorial location of the point at which a biometric is presented has particular relevance in relation to the use of biometrics for the crossing of state borders. However, a biometric identity may also be used for transactions in non-territorial, digitised space where presentation, verification, authentication and exchange may occur in one or several different jurisdictions.

For our purposes, a biometric is a measure of a physical attribute of an individual, such as his iris, his face or his fingerprint. As such, the biometric identifier is a tool, a short-cut to establishing and verifying a person's claim that they are who they claim to be. The question is then whether or not a given fingerprint, for example, matches one previously given by the person offering it. Checking and verifying the match can be done by a human, as it has been traditionally done at passport border checking posts. Increasingly in prospect, this could now be done automatically by scanners, ambient intelligence or by automated methods when presented with machine-readable documents in which biometric data are embedded.

Whereas the EU use of the term 'biometrics' is precise – a measurement – the US definition is ambiguous and connotes profiling, intelligence gathering and creating new data. This makes the deployment and exchange of biometric information and documents for security purposes far more controversial since the assumptions underlying the differential definition raise different aspirations and expectations as to their legitimate use and re-use. The former is associated primarily with verifying identity; the latter is associated with profiling (and the assumptions inferred from specific profiles and different distinctions made between information and intelligence) and hence with justifying a range of (sometimes) vague policy goals framed as essential for maintaining security.[9]

EU biometric discourse centres on migration, the detection and prevention of the abuse of the right to asylum and visa fraud. Biometric discourse in the US is mired in the 'war on terror'. This is reflected in measures to expand pan-opticon technologies (e.g. ECHELON and the Spy in the Sky scenarios) to track individuals and to store information in, and allow the FBI *inter alia* remote access to, large databases or use new through-the-wall surveillance techniques.[10] This reflects very different conceptions of the purpose, purpose limitation, proportionality and functions of usage and strong biometric data. In the EU, this translates into verification of identity and concerns with ownership, privacy and data protection. In the US, this relates to data mining, profiling and associated means of using intelligence data to detect people suspected of criminal behaviour. In both, the nature of the ICTs used for both purposes lends itself to function creep and to data mining and data coupling techniques which potentially compromise individual liberty. Belated concerns with privacy impact assessment, privacy compliance and peer-reviewed audit trails do not disguise a growing accountability deficit.

To boost border management, both the EU and the USA intend to extend the use of biometric identifiers to permit entry to defined territorial spaces and to exit from them regardless of whether or not entry visas are already required from third states. In November 2007 the EU Commission proposed a scheme obliging airlines to compile and transfer passenger details to national security agencies. In February 2008 this was extended to measures requiring anyone – citizens and third-country nationals – to gain permission to enter and exit the EU by air, land or sea. Digital fingerprints and facial photos are the chosen biometrics for automatically verifying identity in these cases. This mirrors the measure introduced in March 2008 in the USA for US citizens entering and leaving the US by air or sea. The EU system, EUROSUR, will apply initially to third-country nationals. The aim is to use the Australian model, eventually requiring people leaving the EU to gain prior authorisation. It combines biometric checks, border patrols using RABIT and Frontex with surveillance using high-resolution satellite and unmanned aircraft to monitor areas for border movements. Frontex's role is set to increase in terms of surveillance, tracking and information exchange management. The Commission suggests it be a central exchange point on illegal immigration, do joint risk analyses with Europol, develop pre-frontier intelligence and examine merging semi-permanent Frontex operations with the European Patrol Network.[11] From 2011, biometrics will be required from all third-country nationals entering Schengenland (including Norway and Iceland but not all EU states).

Using biometrics to check people in and out of borders: background to the rationale

Using biometric identifiers to verify the identity of a claimant to that identity is not new. Biometric measures have featured in passports and travel documents for a long time. The digitisation of such identifiers, the embedding of them in chips and especially automatic recognition and verification, transfer and storage, however, is newer and poses new challenges to public policymakers and the advocates (both global commercial traders in the related technologies) of deploying biometrics in administrative functions moderated by information and communication technological applications. Moreover, these processes require co-operation among different departments of government as well as with offices of data protection, privacy, transparency and technology within and across state boundaries, whether on a bi- or multi-lateral basis. The EU and US, for example, aim to develop a comprehensive framework for automatic transfer of law enforcement and public security information 'without ad hoc negotiations of data protection laws in connection with each such transfer'.[12]

The rising demand for short weekend foreign travel breaks, tourism and migration compound pressure on border posts to increase their efficiency in managing entry and exit. This demand likewise significantly increases the demands on consular posts in states responsible for the processing of visas. Onerous burdens arise from the differences between Schengenland and EU non-Schengenland, and from the rising number of third-country spouses of UK citizens presenting themselves at Schengenland posts seeking visas and entry via, say, Paris to the UK as an ultimate destination. The new EU Blue Card system will not necessarily lessen this pressure.[13]

The new security-led requirements for additional biometric identifiers – facial image plus at least two fingerprints – place additional demands on the administrative staff responsible for processing visas. This is heightened by the goals of EU legislation prescribing swifter processing with the unintended consequences of more visa-(s)hopping as people apply at the posts with the swiftest processing times, rising numbers of people trying to get into the EU without the necessary documents,[14] and an administrative response informed by chalk-face pressures of the logistics of managing people trying to cross borders. On the surface, biometrics seems to supply a solution to tracking the movement of individuals and overcome the problem of fraudulent documents and impersonators using genuine documents to enter the EU.

However, the requirement to enrol fingerprint biometrics at the administrative level of those responsible for processing fingerprints and visas has led to unanticipated longer times in processing each application. This holds true even if personal interviews, appointments for interviews and personal appearances to collect visas are ignored. The resulting loss in efficiency cannot be met by governments with finite resources to pay for more staff in buildings of finite capacity. Instead, steps are being advanced among consular staff to pool, exchange and outsource some of the information collection process (e.g. the enrolment of fingerprints). This in turn creates a new form of public–private partnership between government departments and the biometrics industry. It also qualifies the nature of accountability and responsibility of the state towards its citizens.

The biometric business and the lure of inter-operability: from visas to multi-purpose IDs

Biometrics is big business. Biometric deployment in machine-readable travel documents and other identity documents is being rolled out apace by governments around the world, creating exaggerated expectations of infallibility. (Fake identity detection, matches and error rates are higher than commercial interests suggest.) Outsourcing the checking and sending of passports is also big business. In the UK, the Post Office has a contract to do this. Private companies charging premium call rates to enquirers exploit a new commercial opportunity; the Identity and Passport Service (IPS, set up in 2006) could do no more than complain to the regulator of premium phone lines, PhonepayPlus.[15]

A few examples illustrate the transformative impact outsourcing has on the conduct and accountability of public policy for outcomes resulting not simply from the traditional deliberations of state government, but more so from the complex, mutual dependencies of public–private partnerships in securitising borders developing and using, where possible, inter-operable systems. Inter-operability allows two or more networks or systems to exchange and use information between them. Inter-operability and standardisation are big business in a diverse and fragmented global market.

The logic of advancing inter-operable systems for the purpose of accessing and exchanging information among services, such as visa processing posts, seems compelling. Biometric data have been recorded, checked and stored for many years in the EU. The Eurodac database of migrants is one example. Checking ten fingerprints of each visa applicant led to the identification of individuals who were making multiple applications by using different names and claiming different identities. Examining such information, alongside penalising employers for employing illegal immigrants, put a premium on procedures that readily check identity and entitlement claims. A small illustration shows how this is rationalised and rolled out by member states.

The UK government saw biometric immigration documents for foreign nationals as a solution to the problem of over 60 different documents circulating among foreign nationals who were seeking to prove their identity and claim a right to work. By 2009, the UK was already in the process of constructing a central database against which travellers' details from some 50 per cent of countries around the world can be checked prior to travel. The e-Borders pilot, known as Project Semaphore, held, by March 2007, data on 21 million passengers and led to 9,000 alerts to border agencies. Airline liaison officers outside the UK prevent people without proper documents from boarding aircraft to the UK. Controls in France and Belgium, such as those at Eurostar terminals, led to a 70 per cent fall in unfounded asylum applications to the UK. Belgium started using biometric passports in November 2004, followed by Sweden and Norway in October 2005 and Germany in November 2005. Alongside the existing ID card, Sweden simultaneously issued a voluntary biometric ID card which complied with ICAO standards and could be used both as proof of identity and citizenship and as a travel document within the Schengen area.

Germany was the first EU state to use fingerprint biometrics in the new E-Passport. (Left and right index fingerprints are stored on an RFID chip, beside face and personal data.) Germany had installed 18,000 fingerprint scanners across Germany in time for the November 2007 roll-out of the second generation of E-Passports containing fingerprint biometrics.[16] Its supplier, Dermalog, having traditionally supplied automated fingerprint recognition technology (AFIS) for the public sector (including bio-payment systems), had developed multi-finger biometric applications in spring 2006 that could read one flat fingerprint, four flat prints or two flat thumbprints. Its systems read, identify and verify ICAO standard passports, visas, ID cards, RFID chips with biometrics and 2D PDF417 barcodes containing biometric or other data, as well as arrival and departure cards and tickets.

In Norway, 21 BioEnrol biometric-capture kiosks were developed by Motorola with the Norwegian Ministry of Foreign Affairs and National Police Computing and Material Service. The kiosks hold two-dimensional facial images, ten fingerprints for visas and two fingerprints for passports and the signature of visa and passport applicants. Eleven kiosks which can capture three biometrics will be tested in Norway, and ten others will be tested in embassies in Cairo, Kiev, London, Nairobi and Stockholm.[17] The process is designed to be fast and intuitive, linking biometric data and demographic information. In short, this enrolment process has potential for profiling.

The idea of requiring nationals to supply fingerprints in order to access public services, including the issuing of passports, proved to be far more controversial in some countries where fingerprinting was associated with forensic detection of crime.[18] Biometric ID cards were to be introduced in Britain in 2009, the hitherto largely hostile public having been softened up by the government's statistics and tools relating to a migration, crime and fraud agenda. In practice their introduction was scaled back to a voluntary basis, with compulsory ID cards for foreign workers only as a first step at least. During the preceding five years, steps were taken to introduce mandatory biometric identity documents. The controversy over this was eclipsed by scandals over the big system failures of the National Health Service and the loss of personal data by Ministry of Defence and social security officials (as well as through the theft of laptops). As a result, government rhetoric was exposed as deeply flawed. The government struggled to persuade the public of the rationale – and technological facilitator – for linking, sharing and making inter-operable databases containing biometric and related information. However, it persisted in using the discourse of 'security threats' from 'the other' (i.e. migrants) to roll out biometrics for identification and tracking purposes. The government justified their application to migrants with reference to the need to combat fraud, trafficking and undue economic pressure on socio-economic and welfare services and access. It did so by linking and publicising statistics on crime with an agenda of immigration and biometric ID.[19] Biometric IDs were presented as a means to combat this. Also, the government exploited the technical capacity for function creep of the systems being introduced before the 2020 census. How?

On 2 October 2007 it was announced that the Criminal Records Bureau (CRB) had been part of a joint trial of passports and ID cards with the Identity and Passport Service to accelerate and deepen background checks on people seeking work with vulnerable adults and with children.[20] The government claimed that biometric identity documents could be used by the CRB to check an applicant's Identity Registration Number (IRN) against criminal records, and that the IRN would expedite such searches significantly. The National Identity Scheme (NIS) is to be managed by the IPS, incorporating the former UK Passport Service, and capitalising on its expertise in confirming nationality and identity. The IPS also works closely with the Home Office Border and Immigration Agency (BIA) and UK VISAS. An identification verification service is built in to verify that a record matches an ID.

The IPS is involved in joint ventures on procurement and delivery of the NIS scheme with other organisations. The General Register Office (GRO) in England and

Wales has become part of the UK's identity and passport service from 1 April 2008, when the Office of National Statistics (of which it is part) became independent. The IPS has already had E-Access to GRO data. The aim is to integrate passport, identity card and life event registration processes. Other joint ventures are proceeding with the retail sector (on proof of age checks for items like alcohol, knives and solvents), the DWP and the Government Gateway. The potential for data linkage, mining and creation of new data is evident here and in relation to associated databases of vehicle registration and motor insurance records, electoral rolls and local government use of fraud checkers and identity trawlers such as Experian.

A pilot scheme, BioDevII, to develop biometric registration solutions for eight EU states, designed to enable them to integrate them into existing national visa processing systems to test their inter-operability, ended in April 2008 in Austria, Belgium, France, Germany, Luxembourg, Portugal, Spain and the UK. Consular posts and seaports are involved. Country-customised hardware and software (including fingerprint capture and ICAO compliant pictures) for consulates, border control and central AFIS systems, and secure communication between them, is being developed. Motorola supplies the requisite technology for most states, with Sagem supplying France, and Zetes responsible for German trials and an operational installation at the Belgian embassy in Kinshasa.

In the UK, the trial builds on the Border and Immigration Agency's goal to check the biometrics of all non-EEA non-visa nationals at UK arrivals control points by 2011. UK VISAS has been collecting fingerprints from visa applicants as part of an overhaul of the UK's border security systems. This, in turn, is part of an inter-locking circle approach to enhancing security by taking and checking biometric data at three points: processing identity in a biometric visa at the point of application before an individual travels to the UK; checking the biometric visa at the physical border; and introducing ID cards for foreign nationals in the UK. Fingerprints are compulsorily taken for visa applications in over 100 countries and checked against a UK database. The aim is to prevent visa shopping and fraud, cut unfounded asylum claims and enhance the efficiency of the visa service. The logic for fingerprints on second-generation E-Passports and ID cards unfolds in the discourse on unique identity verification.

All this implies a database storing information against which presented documents and data can be checked and identities authenticated. Multiple biometrics can be fused onto smart cards and E-Passports. Countries like the UK prefer centralising databases and exchanging information (e.g. passports, driving licences, tax, medical records, etc.) among them, whereas other countries have advocated match-on-card solutions that verify the person's claim to identity but do not track and store his information. For purposes of border control and policing, however, the lure of inter-operable and automatic recognition systems is becoming stronger. Since August 2007 at Faro, airport passengers with biometric E-Passports look into a camera and place their document on a reader which checks their physical identity against the biometrics stored in their E-Passport.[21] By mid-2007, the UK IPS had issued some 8 million E-Passports. The EU Commission remains attached to the notion of the fingerprint as a unique identifier, divorcing the concept of uniqueness from that of falsifiability. Even the recent duplication and publication of the fingerprint of the German Minister of the

Interior, and firm advocate of fingerprint identifiers, Walter Schauble – the fingerprint was taken from a glass at a public event, and printed on plastic foil that replicates it when placed on a biometric reader[22] – has not shaken governments' commitment to fingerprint use and exchange of data on which identification of suspects is based.

Newer developments that capture and match three-dimensional images against two-dimensional images held in databases expedite checkpoint processes and create three-dimensional image databases.[23] The prospect of the simultaneous creation of new databases raises further questions about control and data ownership. This problem is perhaps overcome to some extent by other multi-purpose ID card systems with contactless chips and those in which RFID tags containing biometric information are embedded, allowing identification either at a distance or in close vicinities.

Secure information exchange v. inter-operability: a problem of accountability

Security and law enforcement interests (including efficiency gains) have driven the quest for accelerating cross-border information transfer. States' technical capabilities to do so securely vary within and across administrations. There has been criticism of the failure of IT systems to ensure data quality and integrity, ensure privacy and comply with principles on use limitation, purpose specification, minimisation, data protection, audit trails and accountability rules. But far more basic breaches in the handling and management of data reveal astonishing laxness and disregard for privacy among government agencies.

It was the issue of data handling as much as the ill-understood matter of data exchange and inter-operability (which is far harder technically to facilitate) that forced the British Government to retract its plans for ID cards. Many departments failed to prevent fraud by migrants and traffickers, and maladministration and disregard for data protection in the processing and handling of personal data were endemic. Months after the Council of Europe proclaimed 28 January as Data Protection Day,[24] the Chancellor of the Exchequer told Parliament on 20 November 2007 that HM Revenue and Customs (HMRC) had lost two CDs containing personal and banking information of some 25 million child benefit claimants. As the government belatedly owned up to even more data losses,[25] pressure grew on it to abandon its ICT programmes.

In January 2008, the House of Commons Justice Committee heavily criticised government ID card policy following disclosures over sloppy administrative practices in the storage, transmission, exchange and use of personal data.[26] The government stated that it would postpone the unpopular introduction of identity cards for British citizens until 2010 (after the next general election, the Euro elections and the parliamentary ratification of the Lisbon Treaty) at earliest. Simultaneously, it announced a stealth measure derived from IPS to bring in mandatory identity cards by requiring 18-year-olds opening bank accounts to enrol for ID cards, as well as a system of unique numbers for all schoolchildren. The latter consist of a new database, Managing Information Across Partners (MIAP), which the government had suggested, in 2003, could be linked to ID cards, and which, in 2008, it claimed was supported by over 40 stakeholder bodies, including local authorities. Under the new

Education and Skills bill raising the school leaving age from 16 to 18, they have extensive powers to track and exchange information with other agencies. Opposition peers in the House of Lords criticised the government for allowing more schools to take children's fingerprints for registration, library borrowing and payment purposes.

The UK is not alone in having a poor record on data protection and function creep. The airline KLM eventually revealed that under the common code-share practice (in its case with Northwest Airlines), passenger data ceased to be its property, so Dutch and EU data protection rules could not be invoked by its passengers. Finland does not offer Finnish E-Voters the same levels of security protection as their US counterparts while using largely identical IT systems.[27] The UK and Finland are now classified as endemic surveillance societies by Privacy International. Concern grows that privacy might be sacrificed by outsourcing practices (even in countries generally believed to have the highest levels of data protection and IT security, like Sweden and Austria) and by government agreements to exchange personal data without recourse to parliaments.

Accountability – agenda setters and irrelevant parliaments?

Agenda setting by third-state governments and technology companies pervades the EU's experience of the introduction of biometrics. It is important to realise that it is not the biometric itself, but how it is used and reflected in security discourse and practice that is the problem. Anxiety over systems to exchange information arises from both the different traditions of monitoring mobility between the US and EU and the US request to suppress access to documents about the exchange of passenger name data agreements until at least 2017.[28] The recourse to new-generation biometric travel documents was a response to a demand from a third state: the United States. The US has different traditions and notions of data protection, data commodification and privacy[29] which sit uneasily with those of the EU.[30] The US is also more sanguine than many EU members about the role of private organisations in security.

In the EU there is concern that the biometrics agenda has been heavily influenced by another set of external actors: corporate non-governmental agenda-setters who set the technological parameters in line with technical functionality possibilities, rather than in response to priorities determined by accountable politicians. As a result, data protection and privacy concerns become a *post hoc* consideration. 'Security' against fraud, insider and outsider intrusion is not built in as the sine qua non of any ID or ICT system. Consequently, legislation to protect privacy and to provide the individual with easy redress against data misuse, unauthorised access or theft lags behind the capabilities of ICT tools sold to public and private sector agencies. The cost of higher, new security features may deter their adoption before they become obsolete. Moreover, outsourcing abroad makes it hard for data protection officers to enforce compliance with home data protection, especially where there is no equivalent data protection.

Plausible political claims as to cuts in risk and enhanced new security tools that are alleged to provide for individual and collective security seem increasingly phoney. A dual-pronged trust deficit ensues, with governments and parliamentarians taking the rap for something over which they seem to have inadequate technical knowledge or control. The credibility of claims is met with public incredulity and incomprehension: can the citizen trust either the public policymaker or the technological design of tools and systems which are at best opaque and at worst misleading? The new tools and systems to confirm identity and prevent its fraudulent capture become part of a techno-babble discourse about biometric encryption, privacy-enhancing technologies (PETs) and extended access controls (EAC).

When, in July 2007, the EU requested the inclusion of additional biometric fingerprints for E-Passports by mid-2009, EAC was supported for new-generation passports in order to protect access to sensitive data. Different agencies may be subject to different rules and practices regarding data access and protection, making already complex politico-bureaucratic and technological systems even more impenetrable. The prospect of new centralised databases (e.g. a DNA index) seems more attractive than inter-operable or linked ones subject to different access regimes and rules on whether, say, local police do or do not have direct access. The risk of failure by default is aggravated by the lack of an overall shared concept of what is meant politically and technically when implementing measures based on opaque E-Government public–private partnerships that public authorities claim are just and will sustain liberty and security.

In October 2007 further initiatives under the rubric of 'E-Justice' were announced as stand-alone measures. However, one is modelled on Schengen exchange practices and others presume a high degree of cross-border and domestic intra-agency co-operation and information exchange. A central register of missing children and an EU-wide child abduction alert (akin to the 'kidnap' system in France) is expected to operate like Schengen in sending an alert to all police stations in Europe. To be effective, inter-operability is desirable. Technically, this is far harder to achieve than is commonly supposed. Politically acceptable, fuzzy language is used to disguise local distrust and concerns about corruption, outsourcing, weak control or weak implementation of data protection and ambiguous and imprecise terms.

The newer concern with a 'common judicial culture' masks deep distrust and lack of frankness and transparency. Consequently, devising appropriate technical as well as publicly visible political control and accountability standards becomes ever more complicated and elusive. Worse still, where MEPs and MPs might be able to recoup some control and insist on transparency and accountability under the Lisbon Treaty, in advance of its ratification and entry into force, procedures have been introduced to normalise non-transparent practices. Under a trialogue agreement between the European Parliament and the Council in December 2007 designed to enhance efficient decision making by expediting first readings, open accountability, notably in the case of border controls, is compromised. Function creep typifies the roll-out of border control proposals combining different sets of information, such as pre-registration before flying, digital biometrics for tracking people in and out of the EU and the proposed (November 2007) PNR system for the EU requiring airlines to transfer passenger name lists to security agencies.

Nature of control and accountability

The idea of executive accountability to elected parliaments is intrinsic to democratic polities. This institutional, politically visible accountability and transparency of process implies a different kind of responsibility for and control over government policy actions and implementation than that commonly inferred from E-Government and E-Administration. This poses serious questions for the nature and practice of government and responsibility towards citizens in a digitised setting. Why?

ICT system developers interpret accountability in a way that dissociates digital accountability from formal, open, politically visible accountability to a politically visible institutional master. Accountability is construed as a means of tracking the evidence to show that a specific task has been completed. The emphasis is therefore on management or organisational codes of practice – compliance with which may be ad hoc, voluntary, industry-specific, peer-determined and peer-reviewed rather than judiciable and politically regulated. Moreover, without secure and trusted architectures and infrastructures, there is no good reason for citizens, administrations or private organisations to have confidence in the protection of any information transmitted, let alone in any data stored or new data files created. A system is as secure as its weakest link.[31] Unless public authorities that contribute to this E-Space with robust and secure infrastructures and services demand, as a pre-condition of doing so, that uniform enforceable security conditions apply, data protection and accountability are inevitably and irrevocably undermined. Since governments select private companies to create and maintain their E-Government infrastructures and all the associated data handling procedures, whether in digi-space or by traditional means of transport, they have a duty to ensure that the highest levels of data protection and security architectures are in place and sustained. This is not happening – yet. Both at the administrative level, where data sharing and exchange is justified on grounds of implied efficient gains, and at the justice and law enforcement levels, where operational requirements for secrecy are often legitimate, there are many steps where the need to share data fundamentally conflicts with the notion of data privacy. Public–private partnerships, outsourcing, careless disregard for principles of data minimisation, purpose limitation, poor staffing, vetting and training, slack management, weak and inadequate security architectures, ignorance of the duty of care and sloppiness in information handling corrode not just trust in E-Government, but trust in the values and practices of democratic accountability and legitimacy. There is no obvious benefit to citizens from complying with E-Government requirements in many countries. Rumours arising from the Big Brother surveillance society pan-opticon surround disincentives and calls for civil disobedience. Therefore, some governments resort to financial penalties for non-provision of digitised identifiers whose use generates distrust and suspicion in the public mind.

Data protection and privacy bodies have criticised the risks to individuals' privacy of intrusions into and malfunctioning of ICT systems holding their biometric identity details, as well as the cumbersome and costly process of seeking redress. Neither the industry nor governments appear overly concerned. Slippery arguments, as in the British case, have been advanced, suggesting that accountability is satisfied by dint of the involvement of public agencies, like the IPS. This misses the point that at the crux of the relationship between executives and parliaments is the presumption that a key role of parliaments is to hold the former accountable and act as the grand forum for the people of matters of concern to them. National security and exceptions to the rules of transparency invoked in the name of security erode parliaments' capacity to be seen as effective in the performance of either function in the end, at the cost of democracy and liberty. A loss of public trust in political and technological processes is inevitable.

Conclusion: fuzzy accountability

The disingenuous claims made by the British government over the equation between public bodies and parliamentary accountability have been exposed by sloppy administrative practices of outsourcing data handling and storage, slack procedures that allow individual officials to transport large data sets on laptops to private venues, and creeping legislation with inadequate safeguards against function and purpose creep. While it may be possible to legislate on data outsourcing, it is not possible to do so effectively while maintaining genuine parliamentary scrutiny and accountability if the outsourcer re-outsources, if fuzzy private–public relationships develop, if governments elude accountability and penalties that private agencies would face for data loss or misuse, or if or the principle of implied consent is abused by non-compliance with data protection rules and quality data handling standards. At issue here are the relative powers of parliaments and executives, trust and the relationship between governments and citizens.

Public information belongs to the public, not to private companies and not to the government. Private companies and the government may be involved in conducting activities for the public, but governments are, in EU democracies, supposedly acting on behalf of their people and are answerable to them subject to parliamentary accountability. Just because technology makes it possible to ignore these ideals, it does not legitimise them or give government authority to disregard its responsibilities towards citizens. In Britain, years of critical reports from the Information Commissioner failed to persuade the government to concede awareness of malpractice.[32] At the EU level, the growing reliance on trialogues to expedite decision making weakens democratic accountability and the authority of the European Parliament, especially under the Lisbon Treaty's type of provisions on justice and home affairs.

The weakened ability of parliaments to control executives and the growing tendency for governments to outsource the design of technological architectures for public policy data handling purposes in poorly defined public–private partnerships undermine democratic legitimacy and exacerbate democratic deficits. In the information society, with ubiquitous tracking, surveillance, data mining and digital forensics and the loss by the citizen of the ability to control (to a large extent) who has access to his personal information, the new type of public–private partnerships lead governments to overlook traditional modes of parliamentary accountability in favour of codes of practice for the industry – which themselves potentially undermine the norms and values that underpin liberty and security. Codes of practice prescribe minimum and ideal processing times and costs. These may be unrealisable in many places, and so induce 'backhanders' and corruption – rife in some EU states.

Alternatively, they can allow the wealthier to be fast-tracked (e.g. via annual iris recognition enrolment (Schiphol), the collective unintended result being social division. Its impact is unprobed and unheeded. The resulting implications for data handled and transmitted by unvetted or outsourced agents are brushed aside with increasingly disingenuous claims that digitised identity systems boost data security, personal security and collective security. Practices to reinforce privacy and data protection are added on to technology, not built in from the start. Anonymisation, pseudonymisation and biometric encryption are possible, but are not made requirements.

The need to share data conflicts with the notion of data privacy; data protection is like closing the stable door after the horse has bolted. Data protection, effectiveness and efficiency are not in balance with democracy. ICT advances and the incoherent government approach to data storage and management, as well as to breaches in good practice, fast outstrip the ability of legitimate political and judicial authorities to hold to account those who handle our data in ways inimical to personal security and, ultimately, collective security. So far, the focus has been on the perils and opportunities of achieving technical and data inter-operability between agencies' systems. This underplays perhaps the human dimension and the need to refine the way in which we view the contribution that developing the capabilities of networks of convergent and new technologies may make to enhancing human security.

In the interim, if the state is no longer able to be the guardian of the citizen and, worse still, if the state colludes with private agencies (because it has not thought out the consequences) in privatising and commercialising personal data, what is the impact on citizen security and on trust in elected, authoritative political masters? What are the legitimate expectations that privately digitised citizens might have of the state and the elusive private agency partners? How do private–public contracts transform the relationship between the state and the citizen both within states and in digi-space? If the authoritative locus of authority and accountability is invisible, and if our digitised identity is inaccessible to us, what becomes of our identity? How is it relevant to our security and liberty? Ultimately, what becomes of our collective identities? Are we who we say we are?

Until governments openly discuss strategies, policies and operational implications of public–private partnerships for E-Governance and security purposes in ways that are clear and make the outcomes subject to visible political parliamentary controls, they risk aggravating the triple democratic deficit: that of weak and non-transparent accountability to parliaments, sub-optimal ICT security architectures and growing public distrust in the technology and its masters. The result challenges the assumptions about transparency and accountability; to be held accountable, government actions need to be relatively transparent. The practices of exceptionalism and creeping surveillance and information-exchanging technologies make them ever more opaque at a time when the lives of those to whom they should be accountable are rendered ever more open to scrutiny by unknown and unknowable automatic or human agents. This makes it harder for citizens to recognise surreptitious erosions of liberty and the ultimate locus of authority and responsibility, as well as to challenge those upon whom the security of their individual and collective E-Identities and physical selves rely.

Key points

- Securitising borders using biometric tools stored by ICTs is a problem because of the definition and use of biometrics, the practices of E-Government sharing and inter-operability, and the nature of political controls.

- Governments, in EU democracies, supposedly act on behalf of their people and are answerable to them subject to parliamentary accountability.

- One may legislate on data outsourcing. However, it is not possible to do so effectively while maintaining genuine parliamentary scrutiny and accountability, if the outsourcer re-outsources (negating UK government claims).

- At the EU level, the growing reliance on trialogues to expedite decision making weakens democratic accountability and the authority of the European Parliament.

- The need to share data conflicts with the notion of data privacy. To be held accountable, government actions need to be relatively transparent.

- Exceptionalism, creeping surveillance and information-exchanging technologies make transactions ever more opaque while citizens are rendered ever more open to scrutiny by unknown and unknowable automatic or human agents.

- This makes it harder for citizens to recognise surreptitious erosions of liberty and the ultimate locus of authority and responsibility, as well as to challenge these.

Notes

1 Epstein, C. (2007) 'Guilty Bodies, Productive Bodies, Destructive Bodies: Crossing the Biometric Borders', *International Political Sociology* 1/2: 149–164; Agamben, G. (2004) *The State of Exception*. Chicago: University of Chicago Press; Lyon, D. (2004) 'Globalising Surveillance: Comparative and Sociological Perspectives', *International Sociology* 19/2: 135–149; Helmig, J. and Kessler, O. (2007) 'Space, Boundaries, and the Problem of Order: A View from Systems Theory', *International Political Sociology* 1/3: 240–256.

2 Liberatore, A. (2007) 'Challenging Liberty', in J. Lodge (ed.), *Are you who you say you are? The EU and biometric borders*. Nijmegen: Wolf Legal Publishers; Huysmans, J. (2006) *The Politics of Insecurity*. London: Routledge; Daase, C. and Kessler, O. (2007) 'Knowns and Unknowns in the "War on Terror": Uncertainty and the Political Construction of Danger', *Security Dialogue* 38/4: 411–434.

3 Foucault, M. (1991) 'Governmentality', in P. Miller (ed.) *The Foucault Effect: Studies in Governmentality*. Chicago: University of Chicago Press, pp. 87–104.

4 Brouwer, E. (2007) *Digital Borders and Real Rights*. Nijmegen: Wolf Legal Publishers.

5 Guild, E. and E. Brouwer (2006) *The Political Life of Data: The ECJ Decision on the PNR Agreement between the EU and the US*. CEPS Policy Briefs, no. 109.

6 Statewatch (1998) 'An Appraisal of Technologies of Political Control' (for the EP STOA Committee); available at http://www.statewatch.org/news/2005/may/steve-wright-stoa-rep.pdf.

7 Merlingen, M. (2007) 'Everything Is Dangerous: A Critique of "Normative Power Europe"', *Security Dialogue* 38/4, 435–453.

8 Cannataci, J. A. and Mifsud Bonnici, J. P. (2005) 'Data Protection Comes of Age: The Data Protection Clauses in the European Constitutional Treaty', *Information and Communications Technology Law* 14/1: 5–15.

9 The US-VISIT programme prioritises 'the security of our citizens and visitors' over the facilitation of travel and trade, integrity of the immigration system and the privacy of visitors, VIS prioritises 'implementation of the common visa policy' in first place (Art. 2 top and paras (a) to (f) VIS-Reg.), over the 'prevention of threats to internal security' (Art. 2 (g). VIS-Reg.). See Hobbing, P. (2007) 'A Comparison of the Now Agreed VIS Package and the US-VISIT System'. See http://www.libertysecurity.org/IMG/pdf_EST17239.pdf.

10 The Server in the Sky project to collect and exchange personal biometrics and data comprises the USA, UK, Australia, Canada and New Zealand. They set up Cold War and later the ECHELON surveillance system in the 1980s. See http://www.statewatch. org/news/2001/sep/echelon.pdf.

11 European Commission (2008) 'The FRONTEX Agency: Evaluation and Future Development', Press Release, Memo/08/84, 13 February: http://europa.eu/rapid/press ReleasesAction.do?reference=MEMO/08/84andformat=HTMLandaged=0andlangua ge=ENandguiLanguage=en.

12 US Department of Homeland Security (2007) 'Privacy Office Annual Report to Congress, July 2006–July 2007'. Washington, DC.

13 Guild, E. (2007) *EU Policy on Labour Migration: A First Look at the Commission's Blue Card Initiative*, CEPS Policy Briefs, no. 145.

14 Bundestag (2008) *Leistungsbilanz des Bundesgrenzschutzes bzw. der Bundespolizei für die Jahre 2003 bis 2006*; available at http://www.libertysecurity.org/article1876.html.

15 In January 2008 three were fined because they implied an official link with the Government Identity and Passport Service. http://www.ips.gov.uk/identity/press-2008-01-30.asp.

16 Dermalog was reported to be pleased to have penetrated the German market given that 95 per cent of customers had so far been overseas. www.securityworld.com, 12 April 2007; www.dermalog.de/seiten/3/16/25/eBorder_Kiosk.html.

17 Details are set out in www.securitydocumentworld.com, 25 October 2007.

18 Lodge, J. (2007) op. cit.

19 The IPS statistics indicated annual costs of £20 million and £50 million in identity-related benefit fraud; £1.7 billion in ID theft; and conservatively 430,000 illegal migrants, and over 10,000 bogus passport applications. Details at http://www.ips.gov.uk/identity/ benefits-facts.asp.

20 CRB–IPS trials 25 May and 26 June 2007 in Birmingham, Bristol, Cardiff, Manchester, Liverpool and London. www.securityworld.com/public/news.cfm?m1=c_11andm2=e0 andm3=e. . .25 Oct 2007.

21 SEF (2007) Ministerio da Administração Interna, 'Electronic Border the Key for the Free Circulation of Citizens'. Available at www.rapid.sef.pt .

22 The fingerprint is discussed at http://www.ccc.de/updates/2008/schaubles-finger, 28 March 2008, and reproduced at http://www.ccc.de/images/misc/schaeuble-at trappe.png.

23 A4Vision 3D face recognition clients include the US government working with Unisys. See www.a4vision.com.

24 A 2003 Eurobarometer on privacy showed that 70 per cent of citizens felt uninformed about data protection.

25 Documents with confidential data including benefit claims, passport photocopies and mortgage payments were found on 17 January 2008 on a roundabout near Exeter Airport in Devon, UK. The carrier TNT denied the loss, saying it was not the only carrier transporting government documents. On the second Data Protection Day on 28 January 2008 see http://www.coe.int/t/e/legal_affairs/legal_cooperation/data_protection/ Data_Protection_Day_default.asp. An information campaign to be started by the Europol Joint Supervisory Body was invisible on the Europol site although Europol and Eurojust had reinforced ICT-led information exchange between them (extending Eurojust's

internal secure network to Europol's premises) and endorsed a co-operation agreement on a secure communication link subject to each respective confidentiality and security standards in June 2007.

26 House of Commons Justice Committee Protection of Private Data First Report of Session 2007–08, 17 December 2007, HC 154. Published on 3 January 2008, London: The Stationery Office.

27 The system to be piloted in the municipal elections in October 2008 is based on a Direct Recording Electronic type e-voting system from TietoEnator Finland, and a Spanish back-end provider, Scytl. Ministry of Justice response on 23 January 2008 to a member of Electronic Frontier Finland (Effi), http://www.effi. See Statewatchonline/news/Feb2008.

28 Risse, T. (2001) 'A European Identity? Europeanisation and the Evolution of Nation-State Identities', in M. Cowles, J. Caporaso and T. Risse (eds) *Transforming Europe: Europeanisation and Domestic Change*. Ithaca, NY and London: Cornell University Press: 198–216.

29 Concern that Google was becoming an information monopolist resulted in calls for the EU to establish strong privacy safeguards to combat the failure of the US Federal Trade Commission to do so during the US merger review.

30 Charlesworth, A. (2000) 'Clash of the Data Titans? US and EU Data Privacy Regulation', *European Public Law* 6(2): 253–274; Andenas, M. and Zleptnig, S. (2003) 'Surveillance and Data Protection: Regulatory Approaches in the EU and Member States', *European Business Law Review* 14/6: 765–813.

31 Rabinovich, L., Robinson, N., van Oranje, C. and Botterman, M. (2007) 'Mapping Research into the Security of E-Government', DG INFOSOC, Brussels, November.

32 IOC, Annual Report 2006–07, Foreword by Mr Richard Thomas; Kelly, P. (2006) 'The Social Theory of Anti-Liberalism', *Critical Review of International Social and Political Philosophy* 9/2: 137–154.

Further reading

Charlesworth, A. (2000) 'Clash of the Data Titans? US and EU Data Privacy Regulation', *European Public Law* 6/2: 253–274.

Downey, J. and Koenig, T. (2006) 'Is There a European Public Sphere?' *European Journal of Communication* 21: 165–187.

Huysmans, J. (2006) *The Politics of Insecurity*. London: Routledge.

11 The merger of health and technology for Europe's future

Identifying obstacles and achieving a successful E-Health implementation

Savvas Savvides and Vassiliki N. Koutrakou

Summary

The European Commission (EC) has set high-calibre aims for the adoption of E-Health in the near future. The benefits promised, including patients' taking advantage of online processes, health portals and physician web pages and becoming partners in their own health management and redefining the physician–patient relationship, are already realised by medical professionals and citizens. There are relationship, still many barriers posed on their part that limit its rapid adoption. The most prominent ones are fears about spending on technology over health, reach and privacy and, more importantly, trust. This chapter explores existing literature and builds on Fountain's Technology Enactment Framework in an attempt to suggest ways in which E-Health can be implemented so that the finalised applications both fulfil user requirements and answer medical professionals' concerns. Thus the reality of E-Health's many useful applications can override concerns and promote trust in its use.

Introduction

E-Health is certainly not a new term and there are a number of definitions.[1] Expanding on the Information Society and Media Directorate General (INFSO)'s aim-based generalised definition, the EC assigns E-Health 'to:

- facilitate the mobility of Europeans between the member states
- provide equal care to all citizens no matter how remote their location
- reduce errors
- expedite patient examinations and transactions
- allow for remote patient monitoring
- enable medical professionals from the various member states to collaborate
- improve the transfer network of patients to countries that specialise in medical areas
- tackle duplication of records in the health sector
- advance the European health-sector market (industry)
- cut costs.'

The EU Seventh Framework Programme for Research and Technological Development (FP7), which runs from 2007 to 2013, grants Health and ICTs the highest proportion of funding, with €6 billion and €9.1 billion respectively.[2] This gives a clear message that the European Union (EU) places a high priority on its citizens' fundamental well-being and the crucial effects of technological innovation upon it. E-Health has been receiving increasing attention since 1989.[3] i2010, the EU strategy for ICT development, pays particular attention to E-Health as it combines all three of the strategy's aims: innovation, inter-operability and quality of life. E-Health is justifiably promoted as an effective way of ensuring that all Europeans receive the best possible medical advice and treatment throughout the continent regardless of their socio-economic status, mobility and ethnicity.

However, as this is a matter directly concerning citizens (as patients and taxpayers), doctors, medical staff and industry, a range of issues in relation to E-Health have arisen. These have led to a crucial and complex debate. Health is a sensitive matter not just because of the enormous responsibility borne by medical professionals, but also due to the fact that it concerns private aspects of people's lives. With technology evolving and facilitating fundamental changes to the way this ancient science operates, political, legal, technological, economic and ethical issues are brought to the surface.

In addition, with computers having permeated Europeans' everyday life, it seems logical that citizens would expect ICTs to support the health sector and make it more efficient.[4] However, the EU is not yet harmonised as far as computer literacy is concerned. Especially after the Union's expansion in May 2004 and January 2007, there exists a considerable digital divide between its Eastern and Western regions, as well as between Northern and Southern regions.[5] Furthermore, Europe's multi-lingualism, generation gap and cultural diversity only make matters worse.

As with any type of information system, user acceptance is critical to the adoption of E-Health. This chapter examines existing approaches towards obstacles in E-Health deployment and, with Fountain's Technology Enactment Framework as a starting point, endeavours to examine how successful implementation can be accomplished so that E-Health's many positive characteristics can be enjoyed by all EU citizens.

The reality of E-Health in Europe

The status quo and the European Commission pitch

The European Commission's commitment to promoting E-Governance, as shown through FP7, demonstrates the significance it sees in using ICTs throughout the region. i2010, a strategy launched in 2005 to promote 'an open and competitive digital economy' while emphasising 'ICT as a driver of inclusion and quality of life',[6] essentially runs parallel to FP7 since it is what guides initiatives in the area of electronic innovation in the EU. The theme 'quality of life' indicates E-Health's priority position as an E-Government project within the broader framework of E-Governance in Europe. The EC High Level conference in Malaga[7] provides a striking example of why electronic systems are required in healthcare by reporting 34,000 deaths resulting from manual health record errors in the UK alone; Electronic Patient

Records (EPRs) provide the potential for health records to be more effectively managed, and a large number of such deaths to hopefully be avoided in future.

A look at the situation on the ground supports the strategic prioritisation of E-Health. The evidence shows that implementation of ICTs in E-Health has been lagging behind the implementation of ICTs in other sectors across European Union countries, with regard to, for example, implementation of electronic medical records, use by primary care physicians in their routine practices, clinical decision support and so on. The implementation of ICTs in EU countries amounts to approximately to one in three cases, although it is ahead of the equivalent performance in the United States, which amounts to approximately one in four cases.[8]

In a study of seven European countries conducted by Andreassen *et al.* into health-related Internet use by citizens and its consequences and citizens' expectations about E-Health services provision, it appears that for the most part, E-Health thus far supplements rather than replaces standard health provision. Citizens use the Internet to acquire information, decide whether or not to see a doctor and prepare for, follow up on or supplement doctors' appointments and advice.[9]

The Information Society and Media Directorate-General (DG INFSO), responsible for the adoption of ICTs in the EU, promotes E-Health under the tag 'Information Can Save Your Life'.[10] It proclaims that through ICT usage, administration costs are expected to significantly decrease, and it should thus be possible to shift funding towards actual healthcare. In addition, electronic means can also enable the personalisation of health, whether this means remote treatment, patient care or prevention – with prevention receiving more of the focus rather than, as is traditional, treatment. Furthermore, the (anonymous) information received from patient records via data mining techniques could potentially advance medical innovation, providing a holistic picture for more effective intervention, without compromising privacy.

i2010 falls under the jurisdiction of INFSO while European health issues are the responsibility of the Health and Consumer Protection DG (SANCO). E-Health is therefore distinct from any other initiative since it necessitates the seamless alliance of two DGs, both of which need the guidance of each other's expertise – unlike other areas that may require a mere collaboration between European bodies. Health issues will affect every single European at some point of his/her life, and they should thus be dealt with, with implicit vigilance.

The fact that the new Commissioner of the Directorate General for Health and Consumer Affairs SANCO, Androulla Vassiliou, has included cross-border co-operation as one of her priorities[11] shows her fundamental support for the targets for E-Health of the INFSO Commissioner, Viviane Reding, based on a dynamic information exchange for efficiency on both disease prevention and treatment.

Barriers to optimal adoption

Alongside the promises of E-Health to deliver a better quality of life and effective treatment, barriers challenge its adoption and limit public trust. Even though their detailed analysis lies outside the scope of this chapter, some of the most critical ones are listed below for later reference:

- The medical profession fears a shift of funding from actual healthcare provision towards ICT and industry.
- Citizens fear loss of privacy due to the electronic sharing of information, especially across borders.
- Both medical practitioners and citizens are concerned about an economically driven ICT agenda that bypasses fair healthcare service provision.
- Doctors worry that a change of current bureaucratic mechanisms could result in erroneous treatments.
- Medical practitioners are reluctant to provide online services for which they are not paid.
- The digital divide and Web-literacy can cause a biased service provision, excluding population segments.
- European diversity can be both beneficial and harmful to harmonious E-Health development.
- There are dissimilarities in healthcare practices between member states.
- E-Health finds itself in differing stages of development in different member countries.

Academic literature approaches to E-Health

Due to its many facets, E-Health has attracted global academic attention over the past few years. Various approaches can be observed in the relevant literature and this section describes some of the most commonly encountered approaches when examining ICT in health. The magnitude of complexity in introducing new technology in government-regulated structures, and therefore in the health sector too, is encountered in assessments ranging from technological determinism to social structuration. These assessments appear in discussions on New Public Management (NPM), in press coverage of stakeholders' concerns and among scholars, exemplifying how privacy might be put at stake and evoke legal issues.

Technological determinist literature focuses mainly on the research that is under way for the development of medical informatics, through which it anticipates the advancement of healthcare. Haux[12] sets three major aims – all of which are based on the development of more 'high' technology – that need to be met in order to achieve quality healthcare: the need for patient-centred systems (defined as the ability of users to assess and record data themselves alongside medical professionals); electronic decision support; and the use of patient data for research and reporting. The citizen-centric perspective is also found in Jones,[13] where E-Health initiatives are illustrated and technology focuses on what it will provide citizens with – but not necessarily how usable it can actually become. Ambient Intelligence (AmI) comes to fulfil technological determinism as it is a field that receives much research on how citizens will be surrounded by intuitive interfaces that will provide health-related services.[14] Though this chapter generally promotes the need for a more socio-technical approach to designing ICT for health, the fact that technological determinist literature sets the technical visions and standards arguably needs to be regarded as an imperative part of researching E-Health.

Technology alone has proved insufficient to aid complex applications,[15] and this is why socio-technical approaches are fundamental. As with any properly developed information system whose users need to be consulted, E-Government projects require the same handling[16] in order for their needs and expectations to be reflected in the system delivered. Of course, government-led projects, such as E-Health, are not simple; with such a large number of users, it is practically impossible for developers to receive feedback from all, or even the majority of, users. However, in a positive move, the EC has issued the 2007 Draft of Informal Public Consultation.[17]

Citizens already consult the Internet for information regarding their health – for both preventive and treatment purposes, and even psychological support[18] – but the inherent unregulated environment of the World Wide Web can pose more risk than aid to healthcare. Hence, with specialist bodies becoming involved in the dissemination and regulation of health-related information, the Internet can be used positively and, in the meantime, attract more trust from sceptical Web-users. Private sector initiatives are already taking place with organisations, setting seals of quality to be displayed in healthcare websites that meet their requirements, but they are still considered to be quite limited.[19] The principal health provider, government, is expected to certify that citizens obtain correct and quality information and support.[20] This is especially important for the health sector, which is the most regulated of all sectors.[21] Fried *et al.* explore the proper role of government regulation; whether existing health regulations are sufficient or whether the use of ICTs necessitates re-thinking the entire regulation framework; how the industry can act responsibly and apply self-regulation; and, ultimately, the role of the end-users, who are the citizens themselves.[22]

A central barrier, from which many more obstacles stem, is trust. An issue that has been concerning information systems (IS) research since the very early deployment of technology in the workplace is trust. Trust poses a threat to the successful development of E-Government projects, including E-Health. Mistrust has the power to directly affect the success or failure of an IS regardless of how good or bad the process designing was.[23] Thus, in E-Government and, particularly importantly, E-Health, citizens and medical professionals should also be presented with proven results from which they can benefit. The French philosopher Michel Serres recently stated that 'we need to create a democracy of science' for the organisational changes required by E-Health to be widely accepted and successful.[24] In effect, acceptance and trust can be further increased through educating medical professionals from an early stage about the positive aspects of ICT that can transform their profession into a more effective one; this education would thus attain their support.[25]

E-Health is influenced by NPM, like many other E-Government ventures. Applying market economics to public sector structures, NPM turns citizens into customers,[26] thus focusing on efficiency and only implying an (expected) effectiveness to result from productivity. The transformation of citizens into customers poses significant risks of discriminating between receivers of services, preferring, if only accidentally, certain groups. It is thus no wonder that CISCO believes doctors can be persuaded to use E-Health through marketing to them how E-Health can prove to be more profitable than today's healthcare system.

Cordella[27] asserts that existing bureaucratic structures assure that all citizens are treated equally, regardless of their economic and social status. Therefore, bureaucratic structures should not be replaced by market-like ones, but become embedded within

ICT. Extended into E-Health, such an approach should be considered imperative since health is one of the most basic service provisions of any state to its citizens' well-being; it is of increased importance in the EU because of its ageing population. Furthermore, similarly to Cordella,[28] Berg and Toussaint[29] state that current healthcare structures result from much experience and have mechanisms in place for the proper practice of medicine. Thus, special attention needs to be paid to modelling the knowledge – and not just the organisational structure – that drives the health sector.

Press coverage of E-Health is prominent at present, with medical professionals raising concerns that their requirements will not be sufficiently met.[30] Physicians are expressing fears that E-Health schemes will favour cutting costs rather than making healthcare more effective. Additionally, the mainstream issue of privacy and security receives much focus as doctors assert that they need to make sure that their patients are sufficiently protected. Conklin has warned about such reactions, highlighting that stakeholders often oppose new technologies due to the threat they pose to their power bases and interests or because they fear that ICT might replace them.[31]

The vision for E-Health ultimately includes the sharing of EPR contents between medical professionals, both within the patients' country of residence and, potentially, among other EU member states. This sharing will require data that, albeit anonymous, will challenge security measures, which are an ever-worrying issue in IT. Security requires constant monitoring mechanisms,[32] in addition to solving the quagmire of complex legal issues that arise when attempting to streamline the various European legal systems. (Germany, for example, does not allow the sharing of EPRs even between doctors.) With increasing incidents occurring where sensitive data have been lost or misplaced, the reassurance of medical professionals and citizens that EPRs will be sufficiently safeguarded is not an easy barrier to overcome. But with technology, and the Internet in particular, penetrating citizens' lifestyles, law and policy are what is needed to safeguard users, and thus attract their trust.[33]

In order to fully grasp the complexity of E-Health projects, Sauer and Willcocks[34] provide an insightful investigation into the UK's National Health Service (NHS) National Programme for IT, from which we can learn. They assert that 'the sheer scale almost necessarily implies that progress will not be to plan, and outcomes will not be those originally agreed', increasing the 'probability of problems' and highlighting the high degree of complexity and inherent risk in such 'mega-programmes', which have an extremely large number of users and stakeholders. With the bureaucratic governmental structure, a way needs to be found in order for the various actors involved to communicate their perspectives; as Sauer and Willcocks conclude, 'it is time for the multiple parties ... to recognise that all the other parties are intelligent and knowledgeable' and should work with 'mutual respect and a willingness to talk openly and sensibly'.

Avgerou[35] sets three principles for dealing with the innovation of technology: ICTs support social activities; innovation in any organisational structure is rarely the result of 'free choice' but is determined by the surrounding environment and possibly restricted by the international or regional arena; and IS innovation should be considered a combination of technical/rational and institutional action. The association proposed between technological innovation and the context in which it is implemented guides us to better understand the complex governmental structures.

Fountain's Technology Enactment framework

Jane Fountain's paper describes E-Health as a complex politico-economico-socio-techno-legislative venture that hence requires a holistic approach in order to comprehend the interactions between the users and the system, as well as among users themselves.[36] The Technology Enactment Framework is interested in the various actor perspectives towards the old and new system and can guide developers towards establishing a system founded on the proper organisational changes and structures.

The Framework's usefulness lies in the method by which it investigates the various actor perceptions regarding a proposed system from a subjective perspective. This results in their consequent definition of its use, which, in turn, may vary significantly from what designers and some stakeholders intended (and expected). Fountain contextualises this in the 'duality of structure', where 'individual action is constrained by structure but action maintains and modifies structure'. Moreover, she raises caution around the differences between the private and public sectors, which demonstrates the Framework's ability to elaborate on the inclusion of NPM in E-Governance and is thus directly relevant when examining the transition of paper-based healthcare mechanisms to electronic ones.

Technology Enactment serves as a representation of the bureaucratic policies that exist within a network and how they are put into effect, thus assisting decision makers, designers and stakeholders in gaining a better understanding of the scenario at hand. As a result, resources can be more efficiently and effectively allocated, thus providing for user acceptance and increasing the prospects of a successful application deployment.

Fountain's framework encompasses the need to take into consideration the existing system structures during the design of the new electronic system. This involves an examination of how individuals tend to enact a system's functions in order to meet their job requirements; actors will presumably, according to the framework, 'reproduce existing rules, routines, norms and power relations', altering the tasks initially incorporated in the technology and even omitting a number of its core features. This element of Technology Enactment can prove beneficial in lessening medical professionals' worries that, since designers will learn from them instead of simply inflicting new technologies, ICT may have negative side effects on their work. In other words, development will not only rely on how technologists comprehend user information received during the analysis, but also allow medical staff to further influence design.

Examining the communication channels that exist in the current system (communication between physician and patient, doctor and pharmacist, etc.) is another integral part of the Framework. It serves as a means of including the necessary flexibility for the communication channels to be maintained and thus enacted in the new IS, as actors seek to maintain their established links. Heeks[37] agrees with this assertion and calls for 'plasticity' in IS development. The stability of organisational structure is further highlighted in Fountain's guidelines (which run parallel to Cordella) with his proposal for the E-Bureaucratic Form to provide for standard treatment of citizens.[38] This is also highly desired by both doctors and nurses, who insist on the necessity of organisational change to focus on minimising their administrative tasks while acknowledging, and preserving, their profession's existing mechanisms.[39]

Fountain's Technology Enactment Framework is criticised by some scholars, as is summed up by Yildiz.[40] The first criticisms come from Bretschneider[41] and Norris,[42] who find it too generalised and abstract, lacking testable hypotheses and sufficient evidence that the Framework lives up to what it proclaims and not being well connected to previous public administration and IT literature. Norris goes even further by suggesting that the Framework is not about IT and institutional change, but about organisational politics; this chapter argues, though, that even if this is true, organisational politics are part of institutional change brought about by IT and can play a significant role in the acceptance or rejection of a new technology-based IS. Yang challenges Fountain's book by stating that it does not sufficiently explain how barriers are to be overcome.[43] Danziger, however, is in favour of the Framework since the very fact that it separates objective and embedded technology and the thorough examination of social networks is useful for the development of E-Government projects.[44]

Another, and quite significant, criticism comes once again from Bretschneider and Norris. They assert that the Framework is limited to examples from the United States and is thus not sufficiently transferable for use by other governments. In contrast, Grafton[45] believes that this is not important since the Framework is applicable to state and local levels and Jaeger[46] highlights that there is much to be learnt from US cases, which can often be applied to other countries.

Though advising that embeddedness needs consideration in order to avoid simplified and erroneous views of the system, this chapter finds significance in the seven propositions set out by Fountain for directing enactment, regarding:

- 'resistance that stems from fear of loss in resources
- cross-agency activities that are currently limited
- lack of resources for IT education
- intergovernmental and public–private networks overshadowing cross-agency networks
- bias in serving public interest
- [the fact that] how change is applied affects the probability of success
- whether and how an agency currently uses the Internet and technology.'[47]

Empirical insights

The European Union unites different cultures and societies under one regulatory environment. Diversity may be regarded as beneficial to its advancement through the combination of different streams of research between member states. On the citizen level, though, things seem to be different, with diversity posing serious barriers to the adoption of E-Health and technology in general. Studies show disparities in perceptions towards the Internet, technology in health and privacy fears and concerns.

A Eurobarometer survey conducted in 2003 found one in four Europeans using the Internet to find health-related information.[48] As an average, this seems positive since it is a sign of early acceptance and it potentially promises subsequent increases; the problem is that the EU is a large and still quite disparate market, and the survey found over half the Danish sought information online while fewer than a quarter of Greeks showed a similar interest. This finding explicitly demonstrates the significance of looking at EU trends at the micro level since harmonisation between member states is required in order for cross-border E-Health co-operation to succeed. The same study found that 41.5 per cent of Europeans see the Internet as a good source of health-related information, of which more than 90 per cent find the information adequate for their needs.

Five case countries have been selected to showcase penetration and acceptance of E-Health: Finland, Germany, Spain, Portugal and Greece.

Finland utilised EPR at a staggering rate of 95.6 per cent in 2005, with an 89 per cent usage by medical staff and electronic referral also being above 85 per cent.[49] Finland thus demonstrates both medical staff acceptance (through usage) and proper infrastructure.

Germany is relatively in the middle of the acceptance debate. A study conducted by the German Fraunhofer Institute for Systems and Innovation Research[50] found that even though the infrastructure existed and citizens were showing positive Internet usage, 64 per cent of the sample showed reluctance towards the innovative side of E-Health. Electronic implants and electronic privacy issues were high on the list of things they would most certainly reject.[51] Sixty-four per cent of the sample also rejected the idea of EPRs, a result that would halt the process of implementing E-Health in the country.

Katz *et al.* quote a survey in Spain which found that only 13.5 per cent of citizens used the Internet to find health-related information. Portugal was about the same with just 14 per cent. The majority of Portuguese users belonging to that percentage (8.2 per cent in all) also said that they searched for such information less than once a month.[52]

Chronaki *et al.*[53] provide samples received from Eurostat that find 22.9 per cent of Greeks actually search online regarding health issues. In addition, 53 per cent of the sample have never used the Internet alone/without guidance. An age gap is also demonstrated, with non-users' average age being 51.8 and users' average age being 33.1. Also, the facts that 66 per cent would much prefer face-to-face communication with physicians and around 60 per cent find the Internet to be 'not important' for finding health information raise concern when it comes to E-Health penetration among the population.

The digital divide in Europe is alarming and only adds to privacy concerns. Katz *et al.* also found that there is a serious digital divide between north and south, east and west Europe, in addition to an internal north and south divide within countries. With age divides making matters worse and long-term Internet users more interested in learning about E-Health, the European Commission (EC) has to find ways to overcome the barriers posed by the citizens for whom it directly purports to care.

Towards achieving a successful E-Health implementation

E-Health success factors

'E-government is simpler to describe than to realize',[54] and the same certainly applies to E-Health as many parameters affect its successful implementation, and user acceptance is vital. Medical professionals will need to embrace the new technology and subsequently refer it to their patients for them to trust it too. The European Commission is strategically tackling barriers concerning technology adoption through activities and policies 'promoting wider use'.[55] This chapter does not attempt to delve deeply into how the barriers will be surpassed. Rather, it shows how a successful deployment of E-Health can be accomplished through understanding its users, who currently experience not rejection of technology, but technology concerns, inequality and needs. In addition, a path of winning over doctors first is followed. Fountain's Technology Enactment Framework will guide this discussion by enabling medical staff and citizens to actively demonstrate their expectations and thus enable designers to provide a globally-leading E-Health example.

Fountain's propositions

There are seven propositions to consider. First, there is possible fear by stakeholders that resources will be placed somewhere other than in healthcare itself. Even though the EC explains that E-Health will provide more resources towards healthcare by savings from administrative tasks, there is already the fear that too much emphasis is placed on ICT. Indeed, with ICT funding on top of the agenda of FP7, it is only logical for the medical profession across Europe to worry about part of the health funding also going in that direction. Thus, before any push to deploy E-Health, there need to be dedicated channels for answering and explaining how E-Health will be beneficial (as Michel Serres, mentioned earlier, also advises). 'Answering' does not only include websites, leaflets and conferences, which medical professionals often do not have the time to read or attend; a more effective suggestion would be pilot schemes used as 'prologues' or 'introductions' to the intended application. Such demonstrations can practically answer any concerns on whether time is gained. Funds still remain in health registers for traditional uses, while designers can receive invaluable feedback for final versions. It should be noted that the European Commission does run pilots but with a shortcoming: they are not deployed in every member state, thus risking a patchwork of failure and success stories by not acknowledging diversity.

Second, Fountain's proposition regarding limitations in cross-agency activities needs to be considered. This is expected to go smoothly when it comes to health due to the ad hoc networks of co-operation between specialists and pharmacists; in fact, a strengthening of these relationships may be expected. Nonetheless, the fact that E-Health seems industry-driven in the eyes of medical professionals – with the EC stressing that EPRs can be beneficial for the industry to develop better equipment and medicine – can strain, and even reduce, the existing co-operation between the industry and the profession. Once again, the EC needs to understand the medical profession's worries and put in place the boundaries of how much the industry can intervene in E-Health, thus safeguarding the power balance between physicians and technologies. (It is the former that patients trust the most.[56])

Third, educating doctors and nurses can be a challenge because they have very tight schedules and are constantly on call. Hence, a lack of time resources needs to be considered. But IT education is vital in promoting acceptance and the suggestion here is of a bottom-up approach; designers should focus on user interface (UI) designs that, under the justified hypothesis that doctors are of above-average education, can be easily comprehended and rapidly put to use. As learning from users is a widely used IS technique, E-Health demonstrations could request simple, closed-ended questions for feedback. Therefore, in conjunction with INFSO's promotion of wider use, this barrier may be overcome while used for learning through enactment.

Fourth, Fountain makes a proposition that is closely linked to the second proposition. Assurance that the EC acknowledges the importance of doctors and nurses in the field (as it has traditionally done) and does not trade this commitment for economic ties with the private sector will most definitely need to be provided. NPM inherently brings an association between the public and private sectors that medical professionals do not seem to favour.

Fifth, citizens' rights will also need to be catered for through for policies so that the digital divide does not bring a 'health divide'.[57] People who live in remote areas, have no or limited Internet access or have a disability which limits their IT usage need to be considered so that everyone benefits equally. Expanding on this, Cordella's Bureaucratic Form proposition is also highlighted so that health mechanisms maintain their unbiased provision of services to all citizens, regardless of their status. Besides, doctors take the Hippocratic oath before legally practising medicine, unlike IT developers, industry economists and policymakers.

Sixth is the proposition of organisational change. As previously discussed, European doctors and nurses highlight the need for organisational change, but raise concern over which areas it affects. E-Health promises to aid the tackling of administrative tasks, but the health sector has some ageing mechanisms. Technology being utilised to attempt to change these structures can be both tricky and trivial since any mistakes will potentially cost not just time, money and effort, but something much more important: lives. Technology enactment is thus critical when it comes to organisational change. Business analysts and strategists may be qualified to optimise management techniques and supply chains in the private sector, but it is medical professionals who have the experience and know-how of hectic, multi-disciplinary and equitable health service provision. In other words, consulting needs to be drawn from the demonstrations acting as E-Health's prologue applications, as proposed by this chapter.

Seventh, but not least, is the proposition of taking into account current IT usage. Medicine has received invaluable aid from technology thus far, and E-Health aims at providing even more support. Accordingly, even if the medical profession is to some degree accustomed to IT, the proper plasticity needs to be embedded in systems so that technology is formed, through a time plan, around the needs and practices of staff. Reality-oriented systems can gradually be delivered through enacting and monitoring how professionals use some aspects of the technology to maximise their work effectiveness while leaving some other aspects unused.

Further considerations

Effective use of the Technology Enactment Framework can result in considerable gains for E-Health and the health sector in general. Through a realisation of Europe's diversity and retrieving constructive feedback directly from users and enactment monitoring, E-Health applications can fulfil their promise towards Europeans' quality of life. For inclusion to be successful, designers will have to bridge communication and cultural differences between member states. According to the Framework, communication channels will need to be enabled and any restriction avoided so that users can keep their much-needed networks active. Standardisation is a contemporary approach to such a task;[58] the challenge posed by the European reality, though, is that internal communication channels in the various countries might extend beyond things that can be standardised. Social relations can be key to current systems and maintaining them might be tricky – even body language and tone of voice on making requests can differ, especially between north and south regions. By utilising enactment, users can show designers how bridging can take place when the means of cross-border communication and collaboration are provided in a dynamic environment without imposing restrictions on how tasks are to be carried out.

Finally, attention is drawn to the fact that users often omit powerful capabilities of IT applications and enact them according to their everyday needs. i2010 has set objectives that require significant advances in the way Europe-wide health mechanisms operate. In addition, INFSO aspires to attract as much ICT innovation as possible in order to make Europe a powerful player in the global arena.[59] However, rushing technology adoption might backfire with high rates of rejection and failure. Enacting technology, especially in a multi-cultural environment like the EU, can require long-term planning to be successful. Since negotiation is required for all stakeholders to be satisfied, ICTs also need to be implemented soon, thus keeping political and economic players interested. This chapter argues that the industry, policymakers, politicians and medical professionals can be assured of positive results through a technology enactment that deploys fully usable applications with the necessary plasticity to be modified as required. Citizens are of course not left out of the equation; when the requirements of all specialists from all fields have been fulfilled, the result can only be expected to benefit the recipients of the work done. After all, the whole debate revolves around what is best for Europe and its citizens.

The last barrier that might remain is about privacy, but the fact that the decision will be left up to the patient to permit the use of an EPR can cover that issue,[60] at least in the short term. Goldman and Hudson pose the rhetorical question of whether manual records are safer locked in cabinets and assert wider EPR adoption without the need for consent.[61] On the one hand, they are right. On the other hand, at least unlawful access is limited to those who are willing to physically break into health centres, whereas EPRs are susceptible to security breaches from hackers sitting in the comfort of their couch. This chapter does not seek to provide a final answer to the privacy issue since an additional lengthy analysis would be required, but a variety of models have been proposed to address this issue, including Riedl *et al.*'s PIPE (Pseudonymisation of Information for Privacy in E-Health) model.[62] Besides, Etzioni[63] has dedicated a whole book to the issue. Nonetheless, citizens should have the right to choose how their data is used, and the current trend satisfies this democratic need.

Conclusion

E-Health is undeniably a promising field for advancing the quality of life of Europeans. Many barriers exist, however, that make its successful adoption challenging and result in distrust towards it. Alongside the European Commission's efforts to lessen the digital divide among Europeans, there are measures that can be employed in order for E-Health applications to fulfil potential users' expectations and needs. This chapter presented an overview of the issues and analysed and proposed how, with the Technology Enactment Framework, users can be enabled to mould systems developed for them into ones that are optimal for their needs. In addition, it proposed that, due to the sensitivity and importance of providing an unbiased healthcare service that seeks to minimise errors, current practices in health provision are kept and efficiency alterations focus on administrative tasks in order for medical staff to have more time for patients.

The European Union has the enormous responsibility of tackling a variety of issues directly and indirectly affecting its citizens. Without underestimating its efforts hitherto, the discussion focused, nevertheless, on suggestions that could make the work of INFSO and SANCO as effective and beneficial as possible for all Europeans throughout the Continent.

Key points

- E-Health is at the top of the EU's Seventh Framework Programme for Technological Development (FP7) priorities.
- E-Health concerns citizens (as patients and taxpayers), doctors and medical staff, as well as industry. E-Health also involves a paramount public good: health.
- Barriers to E-Health adoption include fears of a shift of funding from healthcare to ICT; loss of privacy due to electronic information sharing; worries that mechanism change can result in erroneous treatments; the digital divide and Web-literacy; European diversity, which also means dissimilarities in healthcare practices; and trust.
- Fountain's Technology Enactment Framework looks at various actor perspectives towards old and new systems. It can guide developers towards establishing a system that is founded on the proper organisational changes and structures.
- Suggestions for a successful E-Health implementation: use pilot scheme prologues of the intended application in order to answer stakeholders' worries; strengthen cross-agency communication to improve understanding between the industry and the medical profession; educate medical professionals as a channel for embracing innovation; observe citizens' rights and ensure that the digital divide does not translate into a health divide; and create organisational change.

Notes

1 E-Health and Health Policies: Synergies for Better Health in a Europe of Regions High Level Conferences and Exhibitions, Malaga, Spain. European Commission Papers 2006.
2 FP7 (2006); ICT Work Programme (2007).
3 E-Health (2006) op. cit.
4 Chiarugi, F., Antolin, P., Camara Melgosa J., Hansen, K. M., Zacharioudakis, G., Thestrup, J., Tsiknakis, M., Rosengren, P. and Meadows, J. (2006) 'Ambient Intelligence Support for Tomorrow's Health Care: Scenario Based Requirements and Architectural Specifications of the eu-DOMAIN Platform', *Proceedings of ITAB*; see also: Cabrera, M., Boden, M., Burgelman, J.-C., da Costa, O. and Rodríguez, C. (2004) *E-Health in 2010: Realising a Knowledge-based Approach to Healthcare in the EU, Challenges for the Ambient Care System*, Report on E-Health-related activities by IPTS – European Commission, Directorate General, Joint research centre, 11–107.
5 Katz, J. E., Acord, K. S. and Rice, R. E. (2005) 'Uses of Internet and Mobile Technology in Health Systems: Organisational and Sociocultural Issues in a Comparative Context', Paper prepared for The Network Society and the Knowledge Economy: Portugal in the Global Context, Lisbon; http://ec.europa.eu/information_society/activities/ict_psp/about/index_en.htm.
6 ec.europa.eu, http://www.E-Healthconference2006.org/images/stories//rising_p.pdf, p. 17.
7 E-Health (2006) op. cit.
8 Anderson, James G. (2007) 'Social, Ethical and Legal Barriers to E-Health', *International Journal of Medical Informatics* 76: 480–483.
9 Andreassen, Hege K., Bujnowska-Fedak, Maria M., Chronaki, Catherine E., Dumitru, Roxana C., Pudule, Iveta, Santana, Silvina, Voss, Henning and Wynn, Rolf (2007) 'European Citizens' Use of E-Health Services: A Study of Seven Countries', *BMC Public Health*, 7: 53; http://ec.europa.eu/information_society/tl/qualif/health/index_en.htm.
10 ec.europa.eu, op. cit., http://www.E-Healthconference2006.org/images/stories//rising_p.pdf, p. 17.
11 ec.europa.eu, op. cit., http://ec.europa.eu/commission_barroso/vassiliou/index_en.htm.
12 Haux, R. (2002) Health Care in the Information Society: What Should Be the Role of Medical Informatics? *Methods of Information in Medicine* 41/1: 1: 31–35.
13 Jones, T. M. (2004) 'National Infrastructure for E-Health: Considerations for Decision Support', in I. Iakovidis, P. Wilson and J. C. Healy (eds), *E-Health: Current Situation and Examples of Implemented and Beneficial E-Health Applications*, 100.
14 Chiarugi *et al.* (2006) op. cit.
15 Willcocks, L., Petherbridge, P. and Olson, N. (2002) *Making IT Count: Strategy, Delivery, Infrastructure*. Oxford: Butterworth.
16 Katz *et al.* (2005) op. cit.
17 ec.europa.eu, http://ec.europa.eu/information_society/newsroom/cf/itemdetail.cfm?item_id=3540.
18 Cabrera *et al.* (2004) op. cit.; Katz *et al.* (2005) op. cit.; Fried, B.M., Weinreich, G., Cavalier, G.M. and Lester K.J. (2000) 'E-Health: Technologic Revolution Meets Regulatory Constraint', *Health Affairs* 19 (6): 124–131.
19 Fried *et al.*, op. cit.
20 Paskaleva-Shapira, K. (2006) 'Transitioning from E-Government to E-Governance in the Knowledge Society: The Role of theLegal Framework for Enabling the Process in the European Union's Countries' *ACM International Conference*, 151: 181–196; see also: Kassirer, J. P. (2000) 'Patients, Physicians, and the Internet', *Health Affairs*, 19/6: 115–122.
21 Katz *et al.* (2005) op. cit.
22 Fried *et al.* (2000) op. cit.
23 West, D. M. (2004) 'E-Government and the Transformation of Service Delivery and Citizens Attitudes', *Public Administration Review* 64/1: 15–27. See also: Conklin, Wm. A. (2007) 'Barriers to Adoption of E-Government', *Proceedings of the 40th HICSS*, 1–8.

24 http://www.euractiv.com:80/en/health/doctors-unconvinced-E-Health-policy/article-170213, accessed 11/07/2008.
25 Chiarugi *et al.* (2006) op. cit; Levy, J.A. and Strombeck, R. (2002) 'Health Benefits and Risks of the Internet', *Journal of Medical Systems* 26/6: 495–505.
26 Cordella, A. (2007) 'E-Government: Towards the E-Bureaucratic Form?', *Journal of Information Technology* 22: 265–274. See also: Heeks, R. (1999) *Reinventing Government in the Information Age*. New York: Routledge.
27 Cordella (2007) op. cit.
28 Ibid.
29 Berg, M. and Toussaint, P. (2003) 'The Mantra of Modelling and the Forgotten Powers of Paper: A Sociotechnical View on the Development of Process-Oriented ICT in Health Care', *International Journal of Medical Information* 69 (2/3): 223–234.
30 www.euractiv.com, op. cit.
31 Conklin (2007) op. cit.
32 Cabrera *et al.* (2004) op. cit. See also: Etzioni, A. (1999) *The Limits of Privacy*. New York: Basic Books.
33 Terry, P.N. (2000) 'Structural and Legal Implications of E-Health', *Journal of Health Law* 33/4: 1–4.
34 Sauer, C. and Willcocks, L. (2007) 'Unreasonable Expectations – NHS IT, Greek Choruses and the Games Institutions Play around Mega-programmes', *Journal of Information Technology* 22: 195–201.
35 Avgerou, C. (2001) 'The Significance of Context in Information Systems and Organisational Change', *Information Systems Journal* 11: 43–63.
36 Fountain, J. E. (2001) *Building the Virtual State: Information Technology and Institutional Change*. Washington, DC: Brookings Institution Press.
37 Heeks, R. (2005) 'E-Government as a Carrier of Context', *Journal of Public Policy* 25/1: 51–74.
38 Fountain (2001) op. cit.; Cordella (2007), op. cit.
39 www.euractiv.com, op. cit.
40 Yildiz, M. (2007) 'E-Government Research: Reviewing the Literature, Limitations, and Ways Forward', *Government Information Quarterly* 24: 646–665.
41 Bretschneider, S. (2003) 'Information Technology, E-Government and Institutional Change', *Public Administration Review* 63/6: 738–741.
42 Norris, D.F., (2003) 'Building the virtual state . . . or not: A critical appraisal', *Social Science Computer Review* 27/4: 417–424.
43 Yang, K. (2003) 'Neoinstitutionalism and E-Government: Beyond Jane Fountain', *Social Science Computer Review* 21/4: 432–442.
44 Danziger, J. N. (2004) 'Innovation in innovation: The Technology Enactment Framework', *Social Science Computer Review* 22/1: 100–110.
45 Grafton, C. (2003) 'Shadow Theories in Fountain's Theory of Technology Enactment', *Social Science Computer Review* 21/4: 411–416.
46 Jaeger, P.T. (2003) 'The Endless Wire: E-Government as a Global Phenomenon', *Government Information Quarterly* 20/4: 323–331.
47 Fountain (2001) op. cit. p. 103, Proposition 7.
48 Eurobarometer Special Report (2003) 58.0, 'European Union Citizens and Sources of Information about Health', March.
49 Hamalainen, P., Reponen, J. and Winblad, I. (2007) 'E-Health of Finland: Checkpoint 2006', *Stakes Report*, 6–52.
50 Cuhls, K., von Oertzen, J. and Kimpeler, S. (2007) *Future Information Technology for the Health Sector*. Karlsruhe: Fraunhofer-Institut für System- und Innovationsforchung, 10–187.
51 Zarcadoolas, C., Blanco, M., Boyer, J.F. and Pleasant A. (2002) 'Unweaving the Web: An Exploratory Study of Low-Literate Adults' Navigation Skills on the World Wide Web', *Journal of Health Communication* 7/4: 309–324(16).
52 Katz *et al.* (2005) op. cit.

53 Chronaki, C. E., Esterle, L., Kouroubali, A., Orphanoudaki, E., Roumeliotaki, T., Stathopoulou, A. and Tsiknakis, M. (2005) 'E-Health Consumer Trends Survey in Greece: Results of the 1st phase', 1–55; see also: epp.eurostat.ec.europa.eu.
54 Heeks (2005) op. cit.
55 ec.europa.eu/dgs/information_society.
56 Chiarugi *et al.* (2006) op. cit.
57 Eng. R. Thomas (2002) 'E-Health Research and Evaluation: Challenges and Opportunities', *Journal of Health Communication* 7/4: 267–272.
58 Ball, M. J. and Lillis, J. (2000) 'Review: E-Health: Transforming the Physician/Patient Relationship', *International Journal of Medical Informatics* 61/1: 1–10.
59 ec.europa.eu/dgs/information_society.
60 Cabrera *et al.* (2004) op. cit.
61 Goldman, J. and Hudson, Z. (2000) 'Virtually Exposed: Privacy and E-Health: Privacy Concerns Are Keeping Consumers from Reaping the Full Benefit of Online Health Information', *Health Affairs* 19/6: 145–146.
62 Riedl, Bernard, Drascher, Veronika, Fenz, Stefan and Neubauer, Thomas [Secure Business Austria] (2008) 'Pseudonymisation for improving the Privacy in E-Health Applications', Proceedings of the 41st Hawaii International Conference on System Sciences.
63 Etzioni (1999) op. cit.

Further reading

Ball, Marion J. and Lillis, Jennifer (2001) 'E-Health: Transforming the Physician/Patient Relationship', *International Journal of Medical Informatics* 61/1: 1–10.
The Silicon Trust (2008) 'A Picture of Maturity', *Card Technology Today*, April.
Layne, K. and Lee, J. (2001) 'Developing Fully Functional E-Government: A Four Stage Model', *Government Information Quarterly* 18/2: 122–136.

12 Overcoming barriers to innovation in E-Government

The Swiss way

Gianluca Misuraca, Pierre Rossel and Olivier Glassey

Summary

This chapter sets out to give an overview of the developments of E-Government in Switzerland. It attempts to outline how the particular nature of Swiss democracy and governmental structure has facilitated the growth of a particularly Swiss form of E-Government. The chapter demonstrates that the development of E-Government is not homogeneous and that the prior formation of existing state structures, together with societal norms, has contributed towards a shaping effect upon the development of E-Government systems and upon their implementation. The chapter looks at Switzerland's performance in various rankings of E-Government performance and seeks to explain those rankings, at least in part, by examining the innovative solutions that have been undertaken in the various institutions and agencies. The Swiss experience can, the authors conclude, offer a potential blueprint for application within the European Union.

Introduction: Switzerland's controversial data require an explanation

As we have already seen in earlier chapters, steps towards the creation of information societies have led to a situation where e-Gov is pushing public administrations towards new levels of efficiency, being less of a burden and servicing the citizen more closely, and all that thanks to the informatisation/digitisation of traditional administrative forms and transactional procedures. A second expectation concerned the facilitation of enterprise activity and in particular of its relationships with the administration. Finally, the third facet of the concept was to help the citizen in participating in a more meaningful, more substantial and also more transparent and responsible democratic life, as well as surmounting various forms of social and digital divides.

In spite of the attractiveness of this scenario and the money invested in operationalising it, the achievement looks today (2009) rather modest. That is not to say that nothing has happened, that no innovative services have been created along the way or that leveraging of tasks and cuts in administrative costs cannot be identified here and there. However, we can say that the overall output is still very modest and not great. Cost/benefit ratios, and even the way to measure whether any E-Government investment has been productive at all, are still in their infancy. We can all identify a number of quite interesting transitions and new perspectives on more effective-looking E-Government services, particularly in the second category of objectives. However, the most controversial issue in the E-Government design is the model itself. The model primarily stresses the seminal role of government – or rather an electronically supported administration – for the economy and society in general, and secondarily stresses the accessibility of the step-by-step construction scheme of the so-called 'e-government maturity model'.[1] This model itself proceeds from an earlier KPGM proposal that was launched at the end of the 1990s for the Information Society in general; it is now a sort of rule of E-Government that is stated in main OECD, UN and EU official strategies and analysis. Let us also emphasise that the model suggests a natural evolution from the information delivery to the transaction capability level, and, almost at the same time – but how, exactly, remains a mystery – from a passive to a participatory attitude of users and citizens, magnifying the democratic possibilities of our society. At this stage, we can ask ourselves whether the model is simply not too far from reality.

This is precisely what we examine in the case of Switzerland. Beyond that particular situation, however, our opinion is that there is a need to re-conceptualize E-Government's roles and modes of deployment. First, in this chapter, we use Switzerland as a case study to revise traditional models of E-Government and substantiate the various dataset and rankings that have marked the battle for situating, stimulating and evaluating Swiss progress in E-Government. Second, we point out a series of real measures, programmes and innovative evolutions hiding behind those datasets and rankings. Third, we reconsider the notion of barriers, re-thought in the Swiss context. Fourth, we draw some lessons for general use in the area of E-Government at large, to finally suggest some new – and hopefully more meaningful – avenues for future e-Gov developments.

The ranking question mark: how to explain Switzerland's move upward?

According to the Capgemini Ernst & Young (CGE&Y) benchmarking analysis, focusing on the online availability of 20 key public services and the number of public services fully available online,[2] Switzerland is lagging behind in the 'E-Government race'. Switzerland was ranked only fifteenth out of 18 countries for availability and sophistication of E-Government services in 2002, and twentieth out of 28 countries in 2004. This poor performance was blamed (by someone) on its federalist structure.[3] In 2005, a survey published by IT services company Unisys and the Bern University of Applied Sciences revealed that despite 'a strong demand for E-Government in Switzerland the offer of public E-Services was below the expectations of the population'.[4] In 2006, Capgemini[5] conducted their sixth and last benchmarking survey. Switzerland was classified twenty-second out of 28. The evolution of Switzerland in comparison with the EU 15 and EU 28 according to the Capgemini benchmarking is shown in Figure 12.1.

Yet at the same time, either in terms of investments, Internet connections, broadband access or other issues such as coverage or number of PCs per inhabitants, enterprise, school, etc., ICTs' standing in Switzerland is quite high. The gap between the two sets of data, to say the least, demonstrates that there is no mechanical

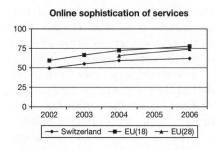 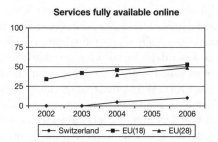

Figure 12.1 Switzerland's online availability of public services and comparison with the EU

Source: EU, CapGemini "Online Availability of Public Services: How Is Europe Progressing? 2006.

correlation between ICT equipment and the level of E-Government effectiveness, and beyond that, suggests that the reality is probably more complex and needs to be better understood and explained.

According to the latest World Economic Forum 'Global Information Technology Report' 2007–2008,[6] Switzerland, which is classified second out of 131 countries in the 2007–2008 Global Competitiveness Index, is classified third out of 127 in the Networked Readiness Index, climbing from the fifth position (out of 122 countries) in 2006–2007 and the ninth (out of 115 countries) in 2005–2006.[7]

More importantly, the Networked Readiness Index is based on a measurement framework that intends to untangle the underlying complexity behind the role of ICTs in a nation's development. The frameworks and its components not only provide a model for computing the relative development and use of ICTs in countries, but also allow for a better understanding of a nation's strengths and weaknesses with respect to ICTs. The overall score of Switzerland – 5.53 out of 7.00 – includes ratings on environment component (i.e. infrastructure, market, policy and regulatory framework), readiness component (i.e. individual, business and government readiness) and usage component (i.e. individual, business and government). As a matter of comparison, out of 127 countries, the UK is twelfth (score of 5.3), Germany is sixteenth (score of 5.19), France is twenty-first (score of 5.11) and Italy is forty-second (score of 4.21).

Our hypothesis here is that there is a double explanation accounting for the gap evoked earlier.

First, there may be some methodological twist (e.g. the fact that the evidence behind the appraisal of all the European national situations was in reality very light). On the one hand, the number and nature of services taken into account supports the idea that the survey is seriously done, but on the other hand, it is quite hard to appraise the actual level of performance that lies behind the claims. Offering the possibility of a service online does not explain how (much) it is used, how (much) it actually delivers, what the drawbacks are or what the contrary learning stepping stones to be reported upon are. Also part of the methodological twist is the fact that in Switzerland, the central state is not the only reality through which the Swiss ICT or E-Government state of play should be evaluated; most domains are, in reality, under the control and authority of the cantons and the cities.

Measurement frameworks are designed for a specific goal. Once the goal or target changes, the same measurement framework cannot be applied. If the delivery model itself is then revised, the measurement model must be reconsidered.

Second, there may well be a key explanation that has to be found in the Swiss reality itself. In this respect, we have identified four main clues:

1   Switzerland is not a state, but a confederation of states, each one having a strong level of sovereignty and initiative capacity in many key domains.
2   The Swiss administrations function well, and the perceived need for change is not acute. On the contrary, a faster course towards E-Government would even appear to many Swiss citizens as risky or uncertain.
3   Switzerland still has a village culture in which proximity and social contacts are more important than absolute productivity perspectives. For example, there has been a huge fight to maintain some post offices which are not so clearly productive or useful; the debate emphasised the importance of other, more qualitative and citizen-oriented factors, such as leaving a space for contact of elderly people in almost any small village of the country.
4   E-Government has often been announced as a means to decentralise the administration and to empower the citizen, but in Switzerland, there has never been any centralisation. Altogether, between federal, cantonal and municipal voting occasions, Swiss citizens have some 15 to 20 opportunities to express their opinion each year – far more than citizens in most other countries on the planet.

However, these four clues may well not be enough. As we have seen, Switzerland, through diverse WEF and OECD indicators, stands very high in innovation, research, research and development (R&D) and industrial and service productivity rankings. So why are the administration and the way government functions not showing better uptakes in that capacity? This requires a specific explanation. On the one hand, it is quite clear that in the Swiss culture, the State and its apparatus are not the objects of any veneration. There is a strong tradition of decentralisation and laissez-faire which makes innovation a process that develops rather outside the realm of the central State (which has its role, along with many other factors, but no more than that). The high level of productivity and competitiveness emphasised by the rankings is more due to systemically effective relationships of the economy and the social cohesion of the country and regions than to the drive and future-oriented strategy of the central state.

In Switzerland, innovation in the administration is most often based upon involving the initiative of local communities and citizens, rather than being linked to central dictates. When there is a question on whether change could take place in the administration or in the government, the referee is the subsidiarity principle, where by problems have to be solved and resources managed at the lowest appropriate level.

More recently, however, Switzerland, in addition to being ranked high in the competitiveness and the Information Technology indexes, is also quickly climbing some of the various E-Readiness indexes, as surveyed by various organisations. For example, The Economist Intelligence Unit awarded Switzerland a score of 8.61, which included differential rating on connectivity and technology infrastructure,

business environment, social and cultural environment, legal environment, government policy and vision, and consumer and business adoption, placing it fourth out of
69 countries. The UK is seventh (score of 8.59), Germany is nineteenth (score of 8.00),
France is twenty-second (score of 7.77) and Italy is twenty-fifth (score of 7.45).[8] In the
Brown University survey, Switzerland secured the twelfth position out of 198
countries.[9]

Finally, in the latest report (2008) by the United Nations Department of Economic
and Social Affairs (UNDESA), Switzerland was in twelfth position out of 182
countries. The report included indices on Web Measurement, Infrastructure, Human
Capital and E-Government Readiness.[10] Table 12.1 shows a specific comparison
with other Western European countries and with the position held in the 2005
ranking.

The more recent rankings, in particular WEF's and UNDESA's, are based on more
composite factors than the Capgemini approach. They show an impressive progression of Swiss E-Government performance – to the point that we can even ask
whether Switzerland is really lagging behind in the area of E-Government or whether
it is in fact in advance. We substantiate this argument in the remainder of this chapter.

Perhaps one can argue that the newer rankings are based upon a better understanding of what E-Government is really about, and therefore show aspects of the
Swiss situation that are closer to the reality; and Switzerland developed a more
gradual and more priority-oriented and integrated set of achievements, which is now
starting to show some effectiveness. In this sense, E-Government in Switzerland is not
a digitised and substitute form of a traditional administration and government, but
most likely a series of proportioned and, hopefully, useful and diversified attempts at
exploring how new forms of informatised support, in servicing citizens, inhabitants
and users (including other administrations and enterprises), could complete and
improve the existing forms of government. New forms could do this either in complement to, in parallel with or, in a few specific cases, as substitutes for rather satisfying
forms of government.

Table 12.1 UN E-Government readiness in Western Europe

Country	2008 Index	2005 Index	2008 Ranking	2005 Ranking
Netherlands	0.8631	0.8021	5	12
France	0.8038	0.9925	9	23
Switzerland	0.7626	0.7548	12	17
Luxembourg	0.7612	0.6513	14	28
Austria	0.7428	0.7802	16	16
Germany	0.7138	0.8050	22	11
Belgium	0.6779	0.7381	24	18
Liechtenstein	0.5486	0.1789	29	168
Monaco	—	0.2404	—	148
Region	0.7329	0.6248		
World	0.4514	0.4267		

Source: UN E-Government Survey, 2008.

What kind of measure, programmes, initiatives and innovative evolution can really be identified?

Our goal in this section is not to compare Switzerland with external standards, but to understand how, at different levels, Switzerland's governments and administrations are developing E-Government as an integrated component of Swiss society while coping with such difficult and diverse challenges as security, mobile communication, social inclusion and knowledge economy principles.

The federal level: a series of guidelines and framework encouragement and facilitating references

Switzerland has been one of the front-runners in implementing ICTs in its work environment at different levels and in several areas, with a special effort – and excellent results – from the private sector. However, despite the National Strategy on Information Society set out in 1998 and updated in 2006,[11] the implementation of E-Government was only officially approved by the Federal Council on 24 January 2007. The strategy delineated a joint effort by the federal administration, cantons and municipalities setting out the objectives, principles and guidelines and cataloguing priority projects. It also stressed the cross-organisational collaboration for exchange of information which helps in using the same software solutions in multiple administrative and para-state organisations.

After having confirmed the basic principles underpinning the building of an information society, such as universal service, access and empowerment for all, respect for federalism, but also co-operation and international exchanges, the federal council set priorities on the programmes and measures to be taken, like E-Government, E-Health and the concept for internal government use of electronic data and documents, drafting specific strategy documents in each of these priority areas. We should not forget, after all, that the World Summit on Information Society took place in Switzerland in 2003, and this not only because of the physical location of UN agencies in Geneva, but also because of the key role played by the Swiss government in defining and driving that process.[12]

With specific regard to E-Government, the objective of the Swiss strategy is to use information and communication technologies (ICTs) to make administrative activities as efficient, economical and close to the people as possible throughout all Switzerland. So far, this objective seems rather standard. However, less typical, the implementation of the activities is co-ordinated in a decentralised manner and under the supervision of a steering committee and a programme office and is defined by an outline agreement on E-Government co-operation between the Confederation and the cantons.[13]

The E-Government strategy is then deployed and implemented though concrete projects. It is to be drawn upon the *Catalogue of Priority Measures*, an important road-mapping tool that is regularly updated and contains a selection of identified E-Government services. A distinction is made here: whether cross-organisational co-ordination is absolutely necessary or whether comprehensive implementation can be achieved in a decentralised way with mutual exchange of experiences.[14]

The initial strategy outline comprised the following programmes:

- *eCH*: an association aimed at promoting and adopting standards (in both technical and operational domains) in E-Government to facilitate and enhance the co-operation among government bodies and between government bodies, citizens, private businesses, organisations and the scientific community;
- *eVanti.ch*: an initiative managed by the Federal Strategy Unit for Information Technology (FSUIT) in close co-operation with cantons and municipalities to intensify the knowledge transfer and collaboration between the various E-Government players in Switzerland;
- *ePower*: an initiative aimed at engaging politicians in the promotion of ICTs through raising public awareness of its importance, and operated through collaboration of leading representatives from parliaments, the private sector, public administration and the scientific community;
- *eProcurement*: a project driven by the Federal Department of Finance and the Federal Procurement Commission to grasp the benefits of ICTs for conducting internal and external procurement transactions efficiently and at a low cost;
- *eGovCH*: an activity that intends to establish a Switzerland-wide networked system, as well as developing standards and architectures to promote electronic co-operation across administrations between Confederation, cantons, munici-palities and the private sector, with the final objective of decreasing the efforts and costs of the State and the process execution times;
- *eHealth*: a specific strategy has been adopted by the Federal Council to improve the efficiency, quality and security of electronic services in the health sector, with a short-term objective of establishing an electronic patient database and an overall aim to expand the online health services in a broad manner throughout the country.

Some of these programmes did not go too well. eCH, for instance, lacked leadership and was scattered in too many actions and loci of the administration; besides, the redundancy with other programmes, like eGovCH, for instance, remained problematic. Other programmes developed well, but partially, like the Hermes method part of eVanti.

The basic concept underlying the Swiss strategy for E-Government is that specific technical and organisational solutions are to be developed by an early adopter scheme, and then adopted by others on the basis of the 'find once, apply many times' principle. In this way, federalism aims to deploy a creative pool, rather than to represent an obstacle to top–down progresses.

To facilitate E-Government in Switzerland, legal foundations have been revised. These revisions face the new challenges posed by the construction of an effective Information Society. For example, on 21 November 2007 the Federal Council decided, as part of the implementation of the E-Government strategy, that the Harmonisation of Registers Act and the corresponding ordinance should enter into force on 1 January 2008. On the one hand, the Act's provisions describe the minimum content of the cantonal and municipal registers of residents and of the Confederation's register of persons. On the other hand, it lays down the formal aspects related to the management of public information. In addition, common standards and regulations for the exchange and use of the corresponding data have been defined.[15] In the same line, it was approved that the completely revised Federal Census Act should enter into force on 1 January 2008. This means that, in the future, the census will no longer take place as a large-scale full survey of the entire population every ten years, but will take the form of an integrated statistical system which combines the use of data from existing registers of persons and random sample surveys. The new system will be operational from 2010.

There have also been revisions of the Federal Data Protection Law (DPL), which entered into force on 1 January 2008. The revisions ensure that persons whose data is collected or processed are better informed about these activities. The partial revision of the Copyright and Associated Property Rights Act, adopted in March 2006 in order to ratify two World Intellectual Property Organisation (WIPO) agreements and, in terms of security and trust, the legal regulations on the electronic signature (ZertES, VzertED and the corresponding amendments to the OR), entered into force on 1 January 2005. This means that the ZertES-compliant electronic signature is legally equivalent to a handwritten signature and anchors in law the accountability of the owner of the signing key with regard to careful handling of the key. The electronic signature is already in use for documents transmitted electronically between lawyers' practices and the courts, as well as between courts of different instances. It is also being used to ensure secure electronic voting. In future, the electronic signature is expected to be used for the signature of medical data generated by health professionals, data from official registers transmitted electronically and enforcement documents transmitted between creditors and the competent enforcement authority.[16] In order to fight cybercrime and manage risks linked to information and ICTs, the Swiss Coordination Unit for Cybercrime Control (CYCOS) has been established as the central Swiss contact point for people who would like to report suspicious Internet content. After an initial check and back-up, the reports are forwarded to the competent prosecution authorities at home and abroad.[17]

Infrastructure development has been facilitated by the Federal Communications Commission (ComCom) decision to designate Swisscom as the universal service licensee from 1 January 2008 onwards.[18] In accordance with the Federal Council's decision in September 2006, the content of the universal service was extended to include a broadband connection from 1 January 2008.[19] The universal service guarantees that a periodically updated basic telecommunications services is made available to all categories of the population and in all the regions of the country. These services must be affordable and reliable. Moreover, a revision of the Radio and Television Act (RTVA) and the corresponding ordinance (ORTV) entered into force on 1 April 2007. It strengthens the public service and relaxes market access regulations for private companies in order to guarantee control of media policy and broadcasting which reflect the plurality and cultural diversity that is a specific characteristic of Switzerland.[20]

Finally, in terms of visibility and electronic channelling of the information to citizens and users, the Swiss portal, ch.ch, after an initial and rather controversial phase of development (with quite low efficiency and level of use in the first period), is currently being successfully established and becoming a reference point for E-Government in

Switzerland.[21] Administrative procedures and the relevant information can be seen at a glance: the new section on 'Elections and Voting' facilitates the forming of opinions; 'Web tips' and 'Special' refer the user to special items such as the 'Canton window', where the individual cantons present themselves, or the '3D photo gallery'. In addition, the directory of authorities throughout Switzerland now features location maps. In addition to the main portal, a specific Swiss employment portal, www.ch.ch/publicjobs, was established in 2007. The Confederation, cantons, municipalities and public agencies can now publish their employment and apprenticeship opportunities here, on a single website. Job-seekers can find information about vacancies without having to be aware of the relevant websites of the individual authorities.[22]

A particular effort has also been deployed in order to guarantee accessibility of electronic content of public service websites promoting the use of technology by the disabled, through the Swiss Access for All foundation, a mediator between disabled users, equipment suppliers and information providers in the public and private sectors.[23] In 2004 the eCH association, a body working towards the setting of E-Government standards in Switzerland, adopted version 1.1 of SAGA.ch as the norm for Swiss E-Government, which we could also translate as the will to establish a framework for ensuring that new systems are designed with interoperability as a top priority.[24]

However, only recently, with the establishment of the Reference e-Gov CH project, are results becoming visible and the co-operation in the E-Government domain has been operationalised among the several actors involved. This key initiative is intended to promote the harmonisation of the overall national E-Government system, developing standards and architectures that facilitate electronic co-operation across administrations between the Confederation, cantons, municipalities, and private parties. It has an overall objective of deploying a Switzerland-wide networked system that is respectful of local peculiarities and adheres to subsidiarity principles.

At cantonal and city level: a plurality of innovative initiatives

While the E-Government initiatives elaborated above are being managed at the federal level, there have been many E-Government projects implemented at canton and municipal levels, such as e-Voting, online transport ticketing and other transport ICT-supported systems, health patient record issues, e-Education initiatives of various kinds[25] and tourism promotion for villages, cities and regions. Instead of offering E-Services centrally, Swiss public authorities are to participate in a number of local E-Government pilot projects.

A well-known example, and perhaps to some extent overemphasised, is the case of electronic voting. The electronic voting systems which have been developed in Switzerland as innovative experiments in several cantons – first Geneva, but then also Neuchâtel and Zurich – are now available to all other Swiss cantons. It is up to the cantons to examine which system best meets their needs. In the legislative period from 2008 to 2011 the electronic voting trials will be extended. The Federal Council, in fact, enacted the 23 March 2007 amendment to the federal legislation concerning political rights on 1 January 2008, and at the same time amended some provisions of the ordinance on political rights. In future, Swiss voters living abroad will also be able to vote electronically.[26]

Considering the complex structure of the governance system in Switzerland, with 26 Cantons, 175 Districts and 2,800 municipalities, there is a plethora of divergent intitiatives taking place. As an example let us examine the E-Government strategy of Lausanne, a city of approximately 100,000 people.

Lausanne is in the process of deploying its E-Government solutions, enabling citizens, businesses and public sector organisations to interact directly with its information system rather than visiting the office. The deployment strategy is based on a three-phase approach, the first two of which last one year each. The first phase, completed in 2007, has revamped the existing websites (intranet and Internet) to provide easier access to all forms required for all services provided by the administration, along with guidelines for all categories of users. The second phase, currently in progress, is invisible to the users; it focuses on back-office applications and databases re-engineering through the implementation of comprehensive Enterprise Architecture based on Service Oriented Architecture (SOA). The third phase, which started in 2009, includes selected online and mobile services available for users to access securely through an authentication mechanism. Additional features allowing electronic collaboration, such as E-Participation, both internal and external to the administration, are also planned in the third phase (and are currently under experimentation). The city works very closely with the Canton of Vaud and the Swiss Confederation to make sure users will have a seamless experience while interacting with the different levels of E-Government.

Of course many other examples could have been taken, from government experiments in Geneva to original electronic health patient records and E-Tourism initiatives in diverse places, just to mention a few. The case and the various programmes evoked in this section emphasise how in Switzerland, the local level (i.e. cantonal and municipal levels) is important and the kind of margin its authorities have to launch programmes of their own shape the context of E-Government in the country.

Private initiatives and innovations: Web 2.0, E-Participation and more

Besides projects initiated by public authorities which deal directly with experimentation in E-Voting through cantonal and federal initiatives, one can also point to the growing importance of other ideas that are emerging from the private sphere. The Swiss context of holding numerous elections and democratic votes provided an opportunity for the development of a wide range of new Web services which offer new tools to help citizens come to an opinion and, eventually, make political choices. The most recent federal elections (October–November 2007) demonstrated the growing importance of new communications platforms (e.g. blogs, forums, etc.), which re-mixed geographic, administrative and public sphere boundaries of political participation through the use of Web 2.0 technologies.[27] The Smartvote Web portal,[28] a private Web platform launched in 2003, is a good example of the impact of such new trends. Citizens answer an online survey of 70 questions, and the system suggests the political group or the individuals who have the closest opinion to them. In 2007, some 84 per cent of the 3,239 candidates at both the national and state council filled out their questionnaire within the website.[29] The system delivered over 963,000 vote recommendations, which is quite significant if one considers the population of 2,300,000 active voters in Switzerland. The real influence of such devices and platforms remains to be established.[30] However, some of these services have become quite popular among citizens and could have a lasting impact on their behaviour in e-Participation terms in the future.

Barriers or paradoxes

Switzerland is a decentralised country where most democratic and administrative initiatives take place close to the people, empowering them, in the course of this process, with quite a number of capabilities. Yet at the same time, this has led to a fragmentation. There are a lot of heterogeneous and rather uncoordinated states – hardly enough to reach any critical mass – making it difficult to promote harmonisation and the standardisation of anything. No large project can emerge – the national culture is somehow averse to that – and no heroic figure can be associated with it. It therefore seems that the qualities of the system convey some inhibitory features. Legacy is another issue, as all the states have the habit of launching their own programmes, styles and ways of doing things; even in the world of ICT-enabled activities and procedures, past decisions and commitments have an impact.

The fragmentation and legacy problem is also made more acute by the language diversity prevailing in the country; there are four official languages, in addition to important foreign national communities, such as those of the Albanians, Spanish and Portuguese. States are small, language outreach is small – the biggest one, the Swiss German community, accounts for 4.5 million people and is scattered in numerous sub-territories and dialects – and the political will to overcome this multiplicity is often lacking. In this situation, with so many legislative frameworks and stakeholders, it appears quite difficult to mutualize solutions and resources.[31]

Guidelines rather than a master plan, leaders rather than masterminds

There is a national strategy, indeed, but it is more of an alignment process with what exists elsewhere, which certainly slows down the E-Government implementation rhythm. The strategy may also create a schizophrenic situation where one looks at what the EU is doing, while at the same time trying to be loyal to the special way the country's leaders and experts have to deploy their ICT strategy. It can, on occasion, produce rather bizarre problems (e.g. telecoms).

As Switzerland does not have a great centralised master plan, the private sector often sets the way Swiss people engage in the information society (through banks, insurances, tourism and leisure platforms in particular). Public administration is more often a follower, with some exceptions here and there (as seen in the previous section).

The telecom fortress

One of the major limiting factors of E-Government development and of most ICT expansion in Switzerland is probably due to the particular legacy of the telecom monopoly of Swisscom. Swisscom is ex-PTT and still controls between 65 and 80 per cent of the main telecom market segments after 11 years (since 1998) of liberalisation.[32] After many byzantine battles, broadband retentions, roaming overprices and mobile tariffs higher than anywhere else are the most immediate consequences of not having been able to (politically) solve the typical issues linked with a post-liberalisation phase.[33] This constrains innovation and makes it difficult for new actors to enter the game. A lot more local initiatives could take place in a more open and stimulating environment.

Some barriers can be positive

If we take a key domain such as security, we see that there are several approaches (not to mention philosophies) and solutions or tools to promote it across ICT networks in Europe. Switzerland has to align its positions with the EU, but not always with the same advantages as member states, yet on some issues, the degree of freedom that is left to cantons has nearly no equivalent in the EU. Switzerland's rather slow and old-fashioned approach to continuing education (in the larger sense) and to bridging the digital divide fits within the same problem: almost nothing systematic is done, but in the end, a lot of diverse initiatives of various scales and aims tend to constitute a field of action with some level of systemic effectiveness, precisely due to the large mix of options more or less intertwining with each other.[34]

In fact, due to the high level of equipment and also knowledge among many sectors, actors and users of the Swiss ICTs scene, what seems at first to be a handicap is gradually turning out to be an advantage, leaving room for informal, diversified and multi-purpose forms of re-mediation. This pattern of development, which we have been able to observe in the case of digital divide issues, is in fact a general deployment perspective. First came the banks, then insurance, tourism, tele-education, transport and leisure followed, then government and administration. These sectors all benefited from the other sectors' advances and cross-domain experience.

Conclusion

A recent report analysed the status of E-Government in Switzerland in terms of the quality level of the offer, needs and expectations of the citizens and online service satisfaction.[35] The report suggested that citizens are more and more oriented to use advanced online services that go beyond the browsing of information – today well covered by cantonal and municipal websites – and give the opportunity to carry out full administrative tasks completely online – today scarcely or only partially covered by public administration websites. Citizens see in that opportunity the possibility to complete their duties with the authorities in a much more flexible and comfortable fashion. This is good news if one considers that citizens consider the usability and accessibility of the information on the cantonal website as poor and being an obstacle, and that, in spite of this shortcoming, the overall satisfaction with the cantonal websites is more than sufficient.

When it comes to the perception of the authorities, it is also worth stressing that the public administrations surveyed (at cantonal level) know nothing or very little about how the citizens use the E-Government services and content on their websites.[36] Therefore, E-Government still has some potential to grow in order to better meet the needs of the citizens. However, with the increasingly ageing population, it is reasonable to foresee that the electronic channel will remain an additional means of communication for the interaction with government services.

The comparison between what is on offer and the satisfaction of the citizens (and companies) shows encouraging results for the cantonal administrations. In particular, the organisations surveyed indicate the cantonal website to be the primary source for retrieving useful information and services. However, ample opportunities for improvements (in terms of service innovation and usability) are definitively visible.

This study is only one indication of what takes place. Users of the administration are more than just citizens. Users are also enterprises and other administrations, as we have emphasised. However, there is no strong defiance, at cultural level, against the deployment of E-Government. This leaves open the promising idea that in the middle, between no E-Government and a gradual and integrative series of E-Government solution to be implemented, there is a true and deep learning pattern to be acknowledged. This, of course, advocates considering E-Government not as a panacea or as an obvious process, but as a means to achieve something which other, more classical means cannot achieve. This opens the way for other lessons to be learnt from the Swiss case.

The first lesson, which builds upon an observation made in our introductory section, is that the offering on the administration websites and the reality of actually using online services do not necessarily match and that, to a large extent, only the latter dimension ultimately matters. A similar observation also leads us to acknowledge that level of equipment and E-Government usages are not mechanically connected. However, due to the existence of high-level equipment all across the sectors and territories of the Swiss context (with differences of course), usages are being deployed in a quite gradual manner. This hints at a second lesson.

The second lesson is that E-Government should not be envisaged as a driver, superior or automatically triggering other capabilities in the whole of society, but more as one of the components of a global cultural and operational capability that has to evolve in a socially consistent way. In this sense, the multi-dimensionality of the Information Society should be the goal, and within that composite perspective, E-Government can emerge with its role and specificities.

The third lesson is probably that in a decentralised state, there is no central way to E-Enforce decentralisation. Developments in this area need to converge with the dominant cultural flow, in particular here with a deep attachment to the subsidiarity principle. Could Swiss federalism be conceived as a barrier? It seems in reality to be a strength, capable of simultaneously ensuring the homogeneity and diversity of how various facets of E-Government can be integrated.

The fourth lesson is that E-Government can best develop when supported by a wide array of measures and programmes, addressing the multiple and complex issues, domains, and needs for services that the State, its representatives and agencies have to cope with regarding citizens and other administration users, including enterprises and, also, administrations themselves.

Finally, the fifth lesson is that social divides are taken care of smoothly.

In reality, but probably as the result of a local model of innovation and the building of the Information Society, the E-Government Strategy of Switzerland, targeting a period of four years (2007–2011), is nevertheless very much in line with the i2010 strategy of the European Union, which aims to remodel the EU into the most competitive, knowledge-based economic region. The EU plans to do this through the use of ICT while promoting social integration within the community.

The largely decentralised approach chosen for implementation of E-Government in Switzerland, reflecting the federal political organisation and recognising the need for a common strategic framework for action in close collaboration with the cantons and with a broad consultation of municipalities and other stakeholders, may actually represent an innovative model for E-Government that should be considered by other countries and, especially, the European Union; one can consider Switzerland a miniature version of Europe, where each canton represents a nation, and each city represents a region of Europe. Perhaps solving the Swiss paradoxes may open new worlds for E-Government in Europe.

Key points

- The fast track of easy wins may hide false positives and negatives; statistics and rankings in the E-Government domain need to become deeper and more robust (against straightforward and superficial have/have not counts). Switzerland represents an interesting case.
- The Swiss tradition of territorial diversity and decentralisation gradually shows the benefits of a rather bottom-up and pragmatic approach to E-Government development that will lead to a further successful take-up of E-Services and demonstrate the requirement of a solid base for ICT-enabled innovation in governance to be fully beneficial to society.
- National policy and administration strategy on E-Government tend to be geared towards integration objectives and useful guidelines for the harmonisation of multiple local initiative forms, procedures and practices, aiming at effective social cohesion and inclusion.
- Progressive and increasingly comprehensive forms of learning take place, pushing effectiveness indicators upward as they stem not just from a few E-Government experts and civil servants, but from a large variety of stakeholders and users who take up the services emerging in the information society framework at large. This concerns the services of the public administration, the workplace, the private sphere and the civil society organisations.
- Cantons, but also cities, are clearly the actors and innovators at the forefront in experimenting with steps towards next-generation technologies and services. They are often supported, or even pressured, by citizens and formal and informal groups of stakeholders.

Notes

1 e.g. Baum, Christopher and Di Maio, Andrea (2000) *Gartner's Four Phases of E-Government Model*, Stamford, CT: Gartner; Baum, Christopher (2000) *The Four Phases of E-Government: Phase 2 – Interaction*, Stamford, CT: Gartner; Keller, Bill (2000) *Four Phases of E-Government: Phase 4 – Transformation*, Stamford, CT: Gartner; Kreizman, Gregg (2000) *The Four Phases of E-Government: Phase 3 – Transaction*, Stamford, CT: Gartner.

2 These indicators were defined in 2000, when the objective of E-Government for the EU was that 'Member States should ensure generalized electronic access to main public services' (EC Communication, e-Europe 2002).

3 'Swiss lag behind in E-Government'. Swissinfo, 9 March 2005.

4 *E-Government News*, 22 March 2005.

5 In 2005, for administrative reasons the measurement was not carried out. It was executed in April 2006.

6 'The Global Information Technology Report' 2007–2008, World Economic Forum, 2008.

7 Among the key figures, we can mention the Internet bandwidth (Mbit/s) per 10,000 inhabitants, which in 2005 reached 97.9, or the Internet penetration (number of users per 100 inhabitants), equal to 60 per cent in 2006.

8 *2007 E-Readiness Rankings: Raising the Bar.* A white paper from the Economist Intelligence Unit, in collaboration with IBM, 2007.

9 Global E-Government 2007, Brown University.

10 UN E-Government Survey 2008: *From E-Government to Connected Governance*, UNDESA NY 2008. www.unpan.org.

11 http://www.bakom.ch/org.

12 On the World Summit on Information Society 2003 and 2005, and its follow-up, see: http://www.itu.int.

13 The institutional architecture for the implementation of ICT in Switzerland basically comprises three levels, viz., federal level, canton level and municipal level. However, the implementation of E-Government has seen the formation of committees and conferences which have a mix of the three levels, serving as an excellent communication and coordination bridge.

14 The Catalogue also contains the preconditions indispensable for several of the services and for which nationwide coordination is necessary. A first version of the Catalogue is already available and will be continuously updated by the Secretariat, in collaboration with experts from all federal levels, and adopted by the Steering Committee.

15 The legally regulated exchange of data between registers is to be simplified by the systematic introduction of the new social insurance number (AHV) in registers of persons. The amendment to the federal Old-Age and Survivor's Insurance Act (AHV), which defines the new social insurance number, entered into force on 1 December 2007. The cantons therefore have at their disposal all the information relating to federal law, which enables them to draw up the subsidiary legislation to introduce harmonisation of registers in their field.

16 In addition to Swisscom Solutions, QuoVadis, Trustlink Schweiz AG and SwissSign AG, the Federal Office of Information Technology, Systems and Telecommunication (FOITT) was recognised in 2007 for the delivery of certification services in accordance with the provisions of the federal act on certification services in the area of the electronic signature (CSES).

17 As CYCOS reported in 2007, the number of reports relating to suspicious activities on the Internet in Switzerland did fall slightly; however, this fall was offset by improved quality of the reports. This means that Internet users are increasingly better able to judge when they are dealing with illegal activities on the Internet.

18 It is the responsibility of ComCom to award the universal service licence. The universal service includes telephony, telefax, data transmission, broadband Internet connections, access to the emergency call services, public payphones and the provision of special services for the disabled. Swisscom was the only company to submit an application during

the public invitation to tender launched in October 2006. Swisscom will therefore be obliged to provide the services forming part of the universal service in the telecommunications sector for the next ten years.

19 From January 2008, the universal service licensees have to guarantee the provision of a broadband connection enabling Internet access at a minimum transmission speed of 600/100 kbit/s. A ceiling price of CHF 69, excluding VAT, has been fixed for this service, which includes not only the broadband access connection but also the provision of a voice channel, allocation of a telephone number and an entry in the public telephone directory. It should be noted that in exceptional cases, the speed may be lower. In addition, the universal service licensee is not obliged to provide broadband access when a comparable alternative offering is offered on the market by another operator.

20 At the centre of the new RTVA there is the intention to maintain an independent Swiss offering of programme services which cover all linguistic regions to the same standard and which can compete with programming from financially stronger broadcasters from neighbouring states.

21 http://www.ch.ch.

22 www.ch.ch/publicjobs was created in cooperation with the Federal Chancellery (FC), the Federal Office of Personnel (FOPER) and various administrative authorities of the canton of Zurich. Zurich's cantonal printed matter and materials centre (KDMZ) operates the portal.

23 In November 2007, the eCH association for the establishment and dissemination of standards in E-Government and e-Health adopted standards on the accessibility of public service websites (eCH standard 0059) and aids to implementing these accessibility standards in web projects (eCH standard 0060). eCH standard 0059 is based on the Confederation's directives for the design of barrier-free websites, which in turn refers to the internationally recognised Web Content Accessibility Guidelines WCAG 1.0 of the World Wide Web Consortium. Implementation of these regulations is intended to ensure that all Internet users, regardless of their limitations, can access Internet offerings.

24 'E-Government Standards Approved in Switzerland', *E-Government News*, 15 June 2004.

25 With regard to the specific area of ICTs and education, even though education is a cantonal and municipal competence there have also been some important federal programmes, such as the 'The Public Private Partnership – Schools on the Net', the Swiss Virtual campus (SVC), Switch, or more recently the Swiss Coordination Conference on ICT and Education (SKIB). On this see http://www.isb.admin.ch.

26 This will require harmonisation of the corresponding electoral roll. Before mid-2009, the cantons will have time to amend their legislation accordingly, thereby meeting the preconditions for electronic voting by Swiss citizens living abroad. Generally speaking, until 2011 the electronic voting trials will continue to be limited to a maximum of 10 per cent of those entitled to vote. The Federal Council reserves the right to continue to restrict trials geographically, substantively and chronologically in order to ensure that the risk remains calculable.

27 As an example of Web 2.0 mash-ups in the context of local elections, see http://www.blogandbreakfast.ch/.

28 http://www.smartvote.ch/.

29 Source: NCCR Democracy 21, *Newsletter* no. 4, November 2007.

30 A survey related to a former use of Smartvote in election showed that 74 per cent of people questioned thought that the recommendation provided by the system had an influence on their own vote. Fivaz, J. and Schwarz, D. 'Nailing the Pudding to the Wall: E-Democracy as Catalyst for Transparency and Accountability', paper presented at the conference 'Direct Democracy in Latin America', Buenos Aires, 13–15 March. Available at http://www.dd-la.ch/download/Fivaz_Schwarz.pdf.

31 Let us observe here that '*mutualiser*', so fashionable in French and in France, in particular to hint at a key E-Government objective, made possible thanks to lower collective transaction costs, has no strict equivalent in English. '*Mutualiser*' is more than sharing; it means creating commons mediated by ICTs.

32 Just to give a comparative point of view: in a supposedly conservative and closed country like Japan, DoCoMo has now less than 50 per cent of the market.
33 It is not necessarily the fault of Swisscom; Swiss politicians have done little to clarify options for Swiss citizens, recalled M. Price (the surveillance of price authority), stressing that consumers still have too much loyalty to the incumbent in spite of high prices (the habit of changing, comparing and lobbying being still in its infancy).
34 See Vodoz, Luc, Rossel, Pierre, Pfister, Giauque Barbara, Glassey, Olivier and Steiner, Yves (2005) *Ordinateur et précarité au quotidien: les logiques d'intégration provisoire de la formation continue.* Lausanne: C.E.A.T. [Rapport final PNR 51, Fonds national suisse de la recherche scientifique; http://ceat.epfl.ch; see also Rossel, P. and Glassey, O. (2005) 'Bridging over the Dynamic Divide: When E-Activities are E-Learning Reinforcement Contexts', Proceedings of the 4th WSEAS International Conference on E-ACTIVITIES (E-Learning, E-Communities, E-Commerce, E-Management, E-Marketing, E-Governance, E-Health, Tele-Working), Miami, 17–19 November 2005.
35 'The Quality of E-Government in Switzerland', TEC-Lab, University of Lugano, February 2008, a report produced on behalf of the inter-cantonal working group 'Studien und Rankings'. The report crystallizes the key findings of four studies carried out from 2005 to 2007. It does not present all the results of the studies that have been carried out (for which the published studies can be read), but it does offer a synthetic perspective and an operative vision on them.
36 In this regard, a very interesting analysis is conducted by the Institute for Applied Argumentation Research (IFAAR) in Bern, which, since 1994, has been developing special systems for computer-based content analysis. The IFAAR delivers studies and analyses on digital content (e-content), which allow conclusions on usability and efficiency of E-Government, E-Health and other websites. http://www.ifaar.ch.

Further reading

University of Lugano, TEC-Lab (2008) *The Quality of E-Government in Switzerland*, Lugano: University of Lugano, TEC-Lab.
Yammine, Anne (2002) *A New Approach to the Phenomenon of E-Government: Analysis of the Public Discourse on E-Government in Switzerland.* Berlin and Heidelberg: Springer.
Glassey, O. (2004) 'A Global View on E-Governance and E-Government in Switzerland', in: International Conference on Knowledge Society Governance, Law University of Lithuania, Vilnius, 23–24 January 2004. *Public Policy and Administration*, No. 10. Publishing Center of the Mykolas Romeris University.
Wilde, Erik and Müller, Willy (2005) *Organizing Federal E-Government Schemas*, Computer Engineering and Networks Laboratory, ETH Zürich, Zürich, Switzerland, TIK Report 212.
Curtin, Gregory G., Sommer, Michael H. and Vis-Sommer, Veronika (2003) *The World of E-Government.* New York: The Haworth Press.
Lake, Alison Review of (2006) *Innovations in E-Government: The Thoughts of Governors and Mayors,* ed. Erwin A. Blackstone, Michael L. Bognanno and Simon Hakim. New York: Rowman & Littlefield.

13 Elected politicians and their tastes for E-Democracy

Experiences from the Netherlands, the United Kingdom and Norway

Arthur Edwards

Summary

This chapter investigates the key role of elected politicians in the evolution of E-Democracy. It presents a theoretical framework for explaining politicians' use of online tools for communication with citizens. This framework includes such factors as politicians' role perceptions, their views on democracy and citizenship, personal dispositions and competences in using online tools and political system factors. In their daily work, politicians face various challenges and dilemmas. In addition to ambiguities and signs of reluctance and resistance, experiences also show potentially important positive changes.

Introduction

Politicians seem to have ambiguous attitudes towards the use of ICTs in democratic practices. Discussing a comparative research project among members of parliament in seven European countries, Hoff[1] concludes that MPs generally have very positive attitudes towards the democratic potential of ICT. They expect ICT to encourage more citizens to participate in politics, increase the number of topics on the political agenda and improve interactive dialogue within the political system, particularly between elected representatives and citizens/voters.[2] On the other hand, studies by Mahrer[3] and by Mahrer and Krimmer[4] consider politicians as an 'inhibiting factor' in the further evolution of E-Democracy. Their research findings show that 'the more citizen participation specific concepts of e-democracy that were suggested, the less support for these concepts would be provided by politicians'.[5] They suggest that reasons for the politicians' approach stem from a strong belief in the concept of representative democracy combined with a widespread distinctive scepticism concerning all forms of direct political participation by the 'common citizen'.

In this chapter, we discuss the role of politicians as a key factor for the successful use of ICTs in democratic practices. We make a distinction between ICT uses in representative democracy and in participatory democracy. We see participatory arrangements not as a substitute for representation, but as a way of opening new channels connecting citizens to agenda setting and policy-making. We assume that

ICTs have the potential to strengthen democratic practices, especially in terms of more responsive agenda setting and policy-making, although empirical studies indicate that these benefits are modest, incremental and dependent on numerous contextual factors. Politicians' attitudes are one of these factors.

Clearly, attitudes of politicians are only to be considered as a problem in so far as the development of E-Democracy depends on politicians. Many projects of E-Participation are civil society and bottom-up initiatives in which politicians are not involved, apart from their role as decision makers on the issues that are promoted in these initiatives. In the government-led initiatives, politicians are involved in two basic roles. First, they are involved in the decision-making process on public (e-)participation projects, on such matters as the goals, scope and weight of public participation. Second, they are involved (or, at least, expected to be involved) as participants and users. In this chapter, we look at how politicians actually participated in online communication practices with citizens. The above-mentioned research project discussed by Hoff was based on a survey, which may have resulted in a rosier picture than is the case in actual practice.[6] Especially when it comes to actual behaviour of politicians in democratic innovations, the literature testifies to mixed experiences. In their report on online public participation, Coleman and Gøtze, for instance, observe that '[i]n most policy engagement or consultation initiatives, elected politicians are conspicuous by their absence'.[7] In a similar vein, Klijn and Koppenjan[8] observe that elected politicians find it hard to play a constructive role in 'interactive' policy processes, because they fear that these new forms of participation threaten their 'political primacy'. These authors emphasise that the engagement of politicians with the public *during* the participatory process is crucial for public participation to become more than a ritual.

An enquiry into the factors affecting the behaviour of politicians in forms of E-Democracy covers a broad and complex range of issues. The aim of this chapter is to conduct an exploration and to present a theoretical framework. On this basis, we chart the challenges and difficulties of a more political nature faced by E-Government, in particular E-Democracy. We discuss a number of experiences with online communication between citizens and politicians, both within representative democracy and in participatory democracy, in particular deliberative democracy.

We understand democracy as a political system in which the members have equal, effective input into the making of binding collective decisions.[9] Democracy can be institutionalised in different ways. One can refer to several 'models of democracy'.[10] Representative democracy involves the delegation of political decision making to a small number of professional politicians elected by the people. The competition between political parties and their candidates is the core mechanism by which the interests and wishes of the people are taken into account.[11] Deliberative democracy relies on the integrative mechanism of discussion. Citizens' preferences are critically examined and weighed against each other by the exchange of information and arguments. According to Coleman and Gøtze,[12] public deliberation at its best is characterised by access to balanced information; an open agenda; time to consider issues expansively; freedom from manipulation or coercion; a rule-based framework for discussion; participation by an inclusive sample of citizens; scope for free interaction between participants; and recognition of differences between participants (but rejection of status-based prejudice). The deliberative model is one of the most influential models of democracy in the current literatures, and it inspires various experiments in democratic practices, such as citizen juries, round-table conferences and online policy exercises.[13]

The structure of this chapter is as follows. In the second section I present a theoretical framework. In the third and fourth sections I use this framework for a discussion of research on how politicians use online tools in democratic practices. I use our own research on Dutch experiences and research done by others in the United Kingdom and Norway. The third section focuses on representative democracy. I discuss politicians' uses of online forums and blogs. The fourth section looks at democratic innovations in the domain of participatory democracy. In the fifth section I draw some conclusions.

Theoretical framework

Figure 13.1 represents our theoretical framework. It includes three groups of factors. The first group, which constitutes the dependent variable, refers to the nature of the politicians' uses of online tools. Focusing on an online discussion forum, we can distinguish (a) observing the communication, (b) participating in the communication and (c) using results of the communication in their work as representatives.

The second group refers to how politicians define the objectives and functions of the online tool, and the criteria they employ regarding their usage or non-usage of it.

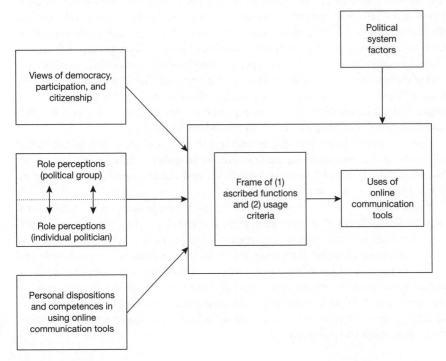

Figure 13.1 Theoretical framework

Objectives can range from information provision on citizens' wishes and concerns to consultation or political campaigning. The usage criteria are normative considerations of a secondary nature and relate to the following:

- medium: politicians' assessments of the effectiveness of online communication relative to communication through other media or face to face;
- participants and their self-representation, including the perceived representativeness of online participants, and issues concerning anonymity and tone of postings;
- content of the participants' messages (e.g. their political relevance).

The third group of factors consists of four independent variables: (a) general views on democracy, participation and citizenship; (b) role perceptions; (c) personal dispositions and competences regarding online tools; and (d) political system factors. To start with the second variable, a basic idea underlying the theoretical framework is that politicians' uses and frames are related to their role perceptions. From the literature we derive various sets of possible roles for elected representatives, both within the domain of representative democracy and in participatory arrangements. In his analysis of MPs' use of blogs, for instance, Jackson[14] follows Rush's framework, which identifies three MPs' roles.[15] The partisan mainly supports the party's political views: the scrutiny role is geared towards acting as a parliamentary watchdog on behalf of all citizens; the constituency role looks after the individual and collective interests of the electors. The constituency role is divided into two different approaches: the 'welfare role' and the 'local promoter'. For the welfare role, any communication between an MP and a constituent remains private and should not be used by the MP for political purposes. As local promoters, however, MPs are more likely to promote their activities as part of their public constituency work. Role perceptions can be viewed as an individual attribute – a personal 'style of representation' – but also as a sort of culture at the level of political groups, in terms of shared role perceptions and values. 'Views on democracy, participation and citizenship' captures the politicians' general ideals about democracy, the importance attributed to citizen participation and politicians' own ideas of what it means to be a 'good citizen'.

Our research indicates that affinity with online communication tools and skills that allow effective communication with citizens on an online forum are still important. We added the factor of 'personal dispositions and competences' to the theoretical framework to account for this.

Political system factors are also included in the explanation. One institutional political system factor is the electoral system. The Dutch system of proportional representation does not particularly encourage a strong personal style of representation among the ordinary political representatives. Instead, it induces party discipline and enhances the role of the party group leader. Another political system factor is the competition between party groups, especially between party groups in support of the executive and those in the opposition. Because of the 'observed by many' character of online communication, one can expect politicians to be reluctant to make postings that they consider as politically risky.

Deliberation within representation: politicians' use of online communication tools in representative democracy

In this section, we first discuss an online forum that was established by the council of the Dutch city of Dordrecht and functioned for more than two years (2004–2006). This analysis covers all the elements of the theoretical framework (whereas the other cases in this chapter highlight only specific parts of it).

As I indicated above, a central element in the theoretical framework is the idea that politicians' use of online communication tools reflects their role perceptions. I mentioned Rush's distinction between the partisan role, the scrutiny role and the constituency role. Tops and Zouridis[16] add the idea that councillors have basic orientations to their work as representatives. The authors identify various dilemmas with which councillors are confronted in their daily work. These dilemmas include the choice between emphasising administration or representation, between adopting a party-political profile or a focus on social interests, between promoting a political vision or interactive governance and between relying on bureaucratic information or information from citizens. How individual councillors deal with these dilemmas depends on their 'styles of representation': the distinctive pattern of values, attitudes and actions through which councillors involve themselves in their council work. Tops and Zouridis[17] distinguish five styles of representation, which resemble Rush's MPs' roles: (1) the party-politician, (2) the administrator, (3) the ombudsman, (4) the coach and (5) the follower. Party politicians pursue strategies based on the election programme of their party, thereby seeking to accommodate the concerns of specific, politically relevant constituencies. Administrators emphasise their internal role with regard to the executive. Ombudsmen invest most of their time in the local community; their primary concern is to ensure that policy proposals fulfil the concerns and needs of the people and that they have broad support among the citizenry. Coaches are prototypical networkers; they address local problems by emphasising stakeholder collaboration, providing concrete support to citizens in this process. Followers do not make explicit choices; they are loyal members of their political groups, and they follow the dominant procedures and routines.

The online forum 'Tell-it-the-council' (the Netherlands)

The Dutch city of Dordrecht has about 120,000 inhabitants. It is one of the more innovative Dutch cities with regard to public service delivery and E-Government. In May 2004 the online discussion forum 'Tell-it-the-council' was initiated by the Council Registrar. The goal of the project was to provide a forum in which citizens could express their opinions and feelings about issues in the city. The forum consisted of a thematic part in which the council could place specific propositions for consultation, and a general forum. The forum was established primarily as a channel for one-way communication from citizens to the council. The text on the website implied the 'possibility' that councillors might enter into discussions with citizens. This design allowed the councillors considerable freedom regarding how to use the forum.

The forum was established as an open online facility. Visitors were not required to register in order to participate in the discussion. In May 2006, however, the forum was transformed into a half-open forum, for which participants were required to register using their name and email address. A general rule was formulated regarding the content of the postings: the moderator reserved the right to delete postings that could be regarded as 'very hurtful'.

Out of 2,751 total postings, 352 (12.8 per cent) were made by councillors. The average number of citizen participants was 46 per month, and the average number of postings by citizens was 71. After the forum was launched in May 2004, the average numbers of citizen participants and their postings rose rapidly to 78 participants and 107 postings per month in the period between June 2004 and January 2005. The numbers subsequently declined somewhat, with a short increase in the period between February and April 2006, probably due to the municipal election on 7 March 2006. Following the introduction of registration in May 2006, forum usage decreased sharply, particularly in terms of the number of participants, and it continued to do so until the council decided to terminate the forum in January 2007.

Councillors' use of the online forum

Councillor participation varied widely across parties and individual councillors. Table 13.1 presents the distribution of postings over the parties represented in the council. The parties are ordered according to their number of seats. Two parties accounted for the greatest proportion of postings by councillors: the local party Eco-Dordt and the Christian Democrats (CDA).

Almost all of the councillors interviewed indicated that they had welcomed the forum when it was established. At the same time, the general view among the councillors was that the forum had the potential to be more accessible than other media in allowing citizens to express their opinions and concerns.

All of the councillors reported that they had initially visited the forum regularly. Some political groups soon made specific arrangements, which probably affected the frequency of visits among the councillors over the course of time. The Labour Party (PvdA) assigned one party member, who was not a member of the political group, to follow the discussion and report to the group about relevant issues. CDA assigned the political group leader and one other member the task of following the discussion and posting reactions.

The initial positive feelings towards the forum gradually decreased, and some of the councillors indicated that they had abandoned the forum altogether. Councillors gave several reasons for their decreasing interest in the forum. The most frequently

Table 13.1 Postings by political party

	PvdA	VVD	BVD	CDA	Green Left	CU/ SGP	Party of the Elderly	ECO- Dordt	D66	Total
Absolute number of postings	12	5	27	108	25	0	12	155	8	352
Percentage	3.4	1.4	7.7	30.7	7.1	0	3.4	44.0	2.3	100.0

mentioned reasons involved a gradually narrowing circle of participants on the forum, a coarsening of tone and an increasing number of anonymous postings.

Despite their mixed feelings, most of the councillors acknowledged that the forum had indeed performed a useful signalling function, especially regarding themes that elicited a relatively large number of postings. They mentioned the discussion on speed ramps as an example. One councillor indicated that this discussion had contributed to a change in the party group's standpoint on this issue. On several occasions, councillors referred to the forum in formal questions to the executive.

Frames of ascribed functions and usage criteria

The dominant view among the councillors concerning the forum's function was that it could serve as an outlet through which citizens could express their concerns and suggestions. This implies that the primary function of the forum would be a signalling function. One councillor (the leader of the social democrats) pointed out that he had refrained from posting reactions because of the purely signalling function he ascribed to the forum. Other councillors also mentioned this outlet function as a secondary consideration, indicating the absence of a need to react. One CDA councillor indicated that, in addition to its signalling function, the forum served as a means of profiling his political group. This rather obvious consideration was not mentioned by any other councillor. We may conclude from this that the parties did not consider the online forum important as an outlet for publicity.

In addition to the functions that they ascribed to the forum, the councillors indicated some other viewpoints and criteria regarding their uses of the forum. In the theoretical framework we distinguish between criteria regarding (a) the medium, (b) the participants and (c) the substance of their postings.

VIEWPOINTS REGARDING THE MEDIUM

In the context of citizen–councillor communication, several councillors indicated a preference for personal contact, whether by phone, letter or face to face. A number of councillors indicated a preference for continuing online communication initiated by citizens exclusively in one-to-one settings. This preference for one-to-one communication might be partly related to a reluctance among politicians to enter into more probing communication with citizens on a medium with such a public scope as the Internet. The 'observed by many' communication that occurs on an online forum places politicians under scrutiny from their political opponents and the wider public – a 'political system factor' in our theoretical framework.

VIEWPOINTS REGARDING THE PARTICIPANTS

With the exception of the two most active councillors and the youngest councillor in the sample, all of the councillors expressed strong feelings against anonymity. The main objection against anonymity was based on the value of accountability. Several councillors pointed out that they are prepared to communicate only with people who take responsibility for their opinions by revealing their names (i.e. full name). In a similar vein, councillors wondered how seriously they should take opinions that are expressed in a discussion by people who remain anonymous. Several councillors reinforced this argument by referring to the idea of civic dialogue. 'Revealing your own name shows respect for your fellow citizens; it is as a norm of citizenship'; 'A relationship between two citizens, one of whom is anonymous, is not equal'. An empirical argument against anonymity was expressed by associating anonymity with 'hooligan' behaviour. Objections against anonymity were thus accompanied with considerations regarding the tone of the discussions. The interactional consequences attached to anonymity are straightforward: people who are anonymous have no right to a reaction. One councillor reasoned by making an analogy to written communication: 'We do not answer anonymous letters either.'

VIEWPOINTS REGARDING THE SUBSTANCE

Considerations with regard to the substance of the postings did not figure prominently in the councillors' assessments. Some councillors pointed out that the forum was not the appropriate channel for very specific, 'clientelistic' questions and complaints, which they perceived to be advanced relatively frequently.

Independent variables

Our analysis of postings, in combination with the interview data, suggests that style of representation influenced the action of the councillors who used the forum most actively (i.e. by making postings). The political group leader of the CDA exhibited his political-administrative style of representation in his postings; his colleague of the local party ECO-Dordt exhibited an ombudsman-coach-like style of representation in her communication with citizens.[18] It is necessary to consider other factors, however, when attempting to explain why some councillors became active and did not content themselves with using the forum as a signalling instrument, as other councillors did. An obvious political system factor may have played a role in the discussion on speed ramps. The alderman responsible for this politically sensitive issue was a social democrat.

Personal dispositions and competences regarding online communication also provide a partial explanation. Two of the councillors expressed general reservations towards online communication, considering it 'superficial' and 'impersonal'. Such attitudes towards online communication together with a personal sense of competence, as positively exhibited by the active councillors, came out as relatively important factors in this investigation.

In the normative accounts of their resistance against anonymity and 'rude' behaviour, councillors drew upon specific ideas on what it means to be a 'good citizen'. For a theoretical reconstruction of these normative ideas on citizenship, we can refer to Van Gunsteren's conception of neo-republican citizenship.[19] In this conception, citizenship is conceived of as an 'office' in the public realm. Every citizen has the right to exercise this. One of the defining elements of this conception is the notion of 'virtue': 'Virtue stands not only for competence, but also for an ethic of civility, of decent behaviour.'[20] In this respect, the councillors' reasoning was apparently supported by a normatively important theory of citizenship.

Politicians' use of blogs (United Kingdom)

Over recent years, politicians have started to use blogs as a communication tool with the public. A blog is a regularly updated web page, with (textual, photographic or video) information presented in reverse chronological order. In the context of representative democracy, blogs have the potential to strengthen political communication between citizens and politicians, bypassing the mediating role of journalists.[21] However, whether blogging does in fact assist in enhancing representative relationships between politicians and their electorate is open to question.

In terms of the frame of ascribed functions box in Figure 13.1, research on blogs indicates that politicians have various motives for blogging. In their interviews, Francoli and Ward[22] established that some politicians see blogging as a means of engaging a sceptical public, especially young people. Other politicians started blogs as campaign tools for elections. In some cases, internal party campaigning has also been a reason to start a blog. Often, blogging is seen as a useful activity for reflection in the daily work: 'It forced them to sit down, think about an issue and to succinctly, and clearly summarize policy, events . . .'[23] Research on councillors' use of blogs in the UK suggests that councillors use blogs as tools of representation rather than for campaigning.[24]

In general, only a small minority of MPs and councillors use their blogs as a tool for hearing citizens' opinions and engaging in debate: 'the majority were actually akin to the traditional soapbox style of broadcast monologue'.[25] It must be acknowledged, however, that readers generally choose not to add comments to blogs.[26] Taken together, this means that the potential for engagement with citizens remains largely unfulfilled.

Wright also observes that blogs give councillors a more individualised platform to express themselves, with the potential of loosening party controls: 'some local parties are trying to restrict and control what their councillors write in their blogs through various methods. . . . Councillors admit to self-censoring themselves in an attempt to avoid such difficulties'.[27] This interesting observation highlights the importance of party discipline as one of the political system factors in our theoretical framework.

Representation within deliberation: politicians' use of online communication tools in deliberative democracy

Since the 1990s, participatory and deliberative models of democracy have inspired many new initiatives in democratic practice. These initiatives emerged from the recognition that the legitimacy of old styles of governing and representation have eroded and that new forms of political participation had to be offered to the (less deferential and more self-confident) citizens. It was also acknowledged that modern citizens possess valuable local knowledge and experience expertise, which should be mobilised to improve the quality of public policies. The experiences with public participation practices are rather mixed. Citizen participation needs due considerations regarding design, mutual confidence and trust. If government officials and politicians show a lack of interest, citizens will opt out.

The co-existence of representative and participatory devices creates tensions. Politicians must, of course, continually balance their loyalty to their party's platform and conception of the general interest with responsiveness to the concrete concerns and wishes of citizens. These tensions are intensified with the introduction of participatory projects. Klijn and Koppenjan[28] observe that although politicians often initiate 'interactive' policy processes, they do not give enough support to these processes when they are in progress. Furthermore, the outcomes of the participatory processes often remain unused in the formal political procedures that follow. Politicians seem to view public participation as a threat to their 'political primacy'. The authors argue that it is necessary to avoid situations in which participants expect politicians to adopt their proposals unaltered. At the same time, however, politicians should not make their final decisions without using the results of the participatory process. Klijn and Koppenjan[29] propose possible roles for politicians in interactive policy processes. At the start of the process, politicians have a motivating and legitimating role; during the process, they are actively involved in a monitoring and supportive role. They can also opt for an active role in the discussion, especially when an online forum is established for discussing public issues. The presence of politicians is, then, a crucial factor for the success of these online forums.[30] At the end of the process, they reconcile points of view and subsequently select and combine alternatives. In this way, the relationship between representative and participatory democracy can be seen as mutually supportive.[31]

In this section, we look at an online forum that functioned in Norway. Rose and Saebø[32] investigated the interaction between citizens and politicians in this forum. Their analysis highlights the tensions between different views on democracy.

The online forum 'Democracy Square' (Norway)

In 2003, the online forum Democracy Square was initiated by Kristiansand and other municipalities in southern Norway, with support from the Norwegian government. The project's objectives were to increase availability of information, democratic openness and contact between citizens and politicians, as well as to improve citizens' engagement in the political process.[33] The site opened a month before the local election in September 2003. In this period, 525 contributions were made. After the election, activity declined to almost nothing (68 contributions in the nine months thereafter, until the end of the data-gathering period in June 2004). The number of contributors was 102, of whom 31 were politicians.[34] Rose and Saebø conducted a form of qualitative content analysis aimed at the identification of 'genres' (i.e. 'patterns of communicative acts [. . .] sharing similarities of structure, content, style, intended audience, purpose, form and functionality').[35] The analysis was focused on the citizen–politician relation. Five genres were identified: (1) the Challenge and Riposte, (2) the Political Manifesto, (3) the Rational Debate, (4) the Respectful Question and Answer and (5) the Unanswered Question. By far the most frequent genre was the Challenge and Riposte (303 out of 540 occurrences). Rose and Saebø provide the following characterisation of this genre:

> Criticism of, or concern about political events, decisions or persons voiced by citizens who express their opinions using a challenging, sometimes aggressive tone. The expressed opinion is often followed by a more or less controversial,

sometimes rhetorical question. Politicians rebut or deny the criticism using rational argument and factual examples (emphasizing their role as elite/ specialists). In addition they often comment on the citizens' tone – suggesting that it should be more reasoned, un-emotional, concrete or factual. They often try to close the debate, offering no questions or invitations for further suggestions.[36]

The authors explain this genre in terms of a 'conflict of interest' between politicians and citizens, which can be related to conflicting models of democracy. Following Bellamy,[37] the politicians' interests are characterised as 'demo-elitist'. In this model of democracy, the citizens' main interests in life are assumed to lie outside politics, being focused on economic prosperity and services, whereas the political elite is involved in the articulation of policies and the definition of services. Citizens' primary role is confined to voting, whereas the political elite seeks to legitimise its position by displaying superior knowledge and abilities. In contrast, citizens are assumed to adopt the neo-republican model of democracy: they have the desire to engage in the political process and to contribute to the political debate as effective opinion formers. The high frequency of the Challenge and Riposte genre testifies to the estrangement between citizens and their political representatives, and highlights one of the mechanisms whereby citizens are squeezed out of the political conversation about societal problems and possible solutions. In the Respectful Question and Answer genre (48 occurrences), this conflict of interest is accommodated by an informal netiquette and certain self-control of the participants:

'The politicians who reply adopt the demo-elitist expert tone (but without displaying or showing off so much) and focus on the issue which they clearly consider important and accept responsibility for.'[38]

'Citizens generate questions about issues of concern but use a respectful tone which acknowledges the expert status of the politician.'[39]

The authors propose some design strategies to accommodate this democratic conflict of interests. The first alternative is to strengthen the position of citizens in the Challenge and Riposte genre by including web features that make it harder for politicians to neglect citizen opinion (e.g. E-Petitions and online voting). The second possibility is to facilitate the Respectful Question and Answer genre by arranging Web-meetings with politicians, focusing on specific topics, with discussion rules agreed by the participating politicians and citizens.

Conclusions

The role of elected politicians is a key factor in the use of ICTs in democratic practices. We started from the assumption that politicians tend to have ambiguous attitudes towards the use of ICTs for involving citizens in public policy-making. Some researchers consider politicians even as an inhibiting factor in the further evolution of E-Democracy. However, politicians operate in a complex environment, and the factors impinging on their actual behaviour in democratic practices deserve careful consideration. The aim of this chapter was to conduct an exploration into these factors. We presented a theoretical framework for explaining politicians' uses of online tools for communication with citizens. This framework includes such factors as politicians' role perceptions (i.e. styles and cultures of representation), their views on democracy and citizenship, personal dispositions and competences in using online tools, and political system factors. The practices discussed in this chapter show that elected politicians are facing various challenges and dilemmas in their daily work. Resistance of politicians to democratic innovations is a natural phenomenon and can, in the long run, even contribute to more robust democratic practices.

The experiences also indicate the differences in how politicians use online communication tools. The fact that some representatives used online tools effectively and in a responsive manner suggests that others may have passed over a number of opportunities to communicate with citizens. This indicates the desirability of common learning processes. One other practical implication of our study is that it highlights the importance of design, in terms of functionalities, discussion rules and moderation.[40] In addition to ambiguities, reluctance and even resistance, the experiences also show potentially important positive changes:

- The role of politicians is a key factor in the evolution of E-Democracy. Politicians are involved in two basic roles. First, they are involved in the decision making on public (e-)participation projects. Second, they are involved (or, at least, expected to be involved) as participants and users.
- A number of factors affect the politicians' use of online tools for communication with citizens. These factors include politicians' role perceptions (i.e. their styles and cultures of representation); politicians' views on democracy and citizenship; politicians' personal dispositions and competences in using online tools; and political system factors.

Key points

- The role of elected politicians in the evolution of E-Democracy is key.
- The theoretical framework presented includes as factors politicians' role perceptions, politicians' views on democracy and citizenship, politicians' personal dispositions and competences in using online tools, and political system factors.
- In everyday use of online communication tools, politicians face challenges and dilemmas.
- Examples in this chapter are taken from the Netherlands, Norway and the United Kingdom.
- There are ambiguities, reluctance and resistance, but also positive changes.

Notes

1 Hoff, J. (2004) 'Members of Parliaments' Use of ICT in a Comparative European Perspective', *Information Polity* 9: 5–16; Hoff, J. (2004a) 'The Democratic Potentials of Information Technology: Attitudes of European MPs towards New Technology', *Information Polity* 9: 55–66.

2 The study was conducted in 2001/2002 in Austria, Denmark, Germany, the Netherlands, Norway, Portugal and Scotland. Interestingly, Dutch MPs were much less positive than their colleagues in the other countries.

3 Mahrer, H. (2005) 'Politicians as Patrons for E-Democracy? Closing the Gap between Ideals and Realities', *International Journal of Electronic Government Research* 1: 51–68.

4 Mahrer, H. and Krimmer, R. (2005) 'Towards the Enhancement of E-Democracy: Identifying the Notion of the "Middleman Paradox"', *Info Systems Journal* 15: 27–42.

5 Mahrer, H. (2005) op. cit. p. 55.

6 Mahrer and Krimmer conducted semi-structured interviews with parliamentarians, providing the opportunity to probe somewhat deeper into personal views and attitudes.

7 Coleman, S. and Gøtze, J. (2001) *Bowling Together: Online Public Engagement in Policy Deliberation*. London: Hansard Society. p. 20.

8 Klijn, E. H. and Koppenjan, J. F. M. (2000) 'Politicians and Interactive Decision-making: Institutional Spoilsports or Playmakers', *Public Administration* 2: 365–387.

9 Saward, M. (1998) *The Terms of Democracy*. Cambridge: Polity Press.

10 Held, D. (2006) *Models of Democracy*. Cambridge: Polity Press.

11 Miller, D. (1983) 'The Competitive Model of Democracy', in G. Duncan (ed.) *Democratic Theory and Practice*. Cambridge: Cambridge University Press.

12 Coleman, S. and Gøtze, J. (2001) op. cit. pp. 6–7.

13 Chambers, S. (2003) 'Deliberative Democratic Theory', *Annual Review of Political Science* 6: 307–326.

14 Jackson, N. (2008) '"Scattergun" or "Rifle" Approach to Communication: MPs in the Blogosphere', *Information Polity* 13: 57–69.

15 Rush, K. (2001) *The Role of the Member of Parliament since 1968: From Gentlemen to Players*. Oxford: Oxford University Press.

16 Tops, P. and Zouridis, S. (2002) *De binnenkant van de politiek*. Amsterdam: Atlas.

17 Ibid.

18 Edwards, A. R. (2008) 'What E-Politicians Do with Words: Online Communication between Councillors and Citizens', *Information Polity* 13 (3/4).

19 Van Gunsteren, H. R. (1998) *A Theory of Citizenship: Organizing Plurality in Contemporary Democracies*. Boulder, CO: Westview Press.

20 Ibid. p .25.

21 Coleman, S. and Wright, S. (2008) 'Political Blogs and Representative Democracy', *Information Polity* 13: 1–6.

22 Francoli, M. and Ward, S. (2008) '21st Century Soapboxes? MPs and their Blogs', *Information Polity* 13: 21–29.

23 Ibid. p. 33.

24 Wright, S. (2008) 'Read My Day? Communication, Campaigning and Councillors' Blogs', *Information Polity* 13(1/2) 81–95.

25 Coleman, S. and Wright, S. op. cit. p. 3.

26 Wright, S. (2008) op. cit.

27 Ibid. p. 93.

28 Klijn, E. H. and Koppenjan, J. F. M. (2000) op. cit.

29 Ibid.

30 Coleman, S. and Gøtze, J. (2001) op. cit.; Linaa Jensen, J. (2003) 'Public Spheres on the Internet: Anarchic or Government-Sponsored – A Comparison', *Scandinavian Political Studies* 26: 349–374.

31 Saward, M. (2001) 'Making Democratic Connections: Political Equality, Deliberation and Direct Democracy', *Acta Politica* 4: 361–379.

32 Rose, J. and Saebø, Ø. (2005) 'Democracy Squared: Designing On-line Political Communities to Accommodate Conflicting Interests', *Scandinavian Journal of Information Systems* 17: 133–168.
33 Ibid.
34 Ibid.
35 Ibid. p. 145.
36 Ibid. p. 155.
37 Bellamy, C. (2000) '"Modelling Electronic Democracy": Towards Democratic Discourses for an Information Age', in J. Hoff, I. Horrocks and P. Tops (eds) *Democratic Governance and New Technology: Technologically Mediated Innovations in Political Practices in Western Europe.* London: Routledge.
38 Rose, J. and Saebø, Ø. (2005) op. cit. p. 153.
39 Ibid. p. 156.
40 Wright, S. and Street, J. (2007) 'Democracy, Deliberation and Design: The Case of Online Discussion Forums', *New Media and Society* 9: 849–869.

Further reading

Coleman, S. and Gøtze, J. (2001) *Bowling Together: Online Public Engagement in Policy Deliberation.* London: Hansard Society.
Edwards, A. R. (2008) 'What E-Politicians Do with Words: Online Communication between Councillors and Citizens', *Information Polity* 13 (3/4).

Part IV

Perceptions, subversions and new challenges to E-Government

14 Challengers to traditional E-Government (non-governmental actors)

Paul G. Nixon, Antje Grebner and Laura Sudulich

Summary

As the Internet started becoming more and more of a mass medium, its political implications emerged, and they have been debated ever since. Therefore, it is impossible to ignore both the new forms of interaction facilitated in cyberspace and the threats and opportunities that these offer to existing NGOs. This study assesses whether the availability of E-Government tools has changed interactions between governmental and non-governmental agencies. To do so, we propose an analysis based on NGOs typology, which provides us with a clear set of expected patterns for the future.

Introduction

It has been clear for some time that, particularly in Western democracies, there is a crisis of confidence in the ability of traditional political systems to be able not just to deliver desired services, but to match the changing aspirations of an increasingly articulate, media-savvy and demanding public, and thus to shape society in a modern reflexive, albeit inherently complex, form. As that public has been seen to reject, at least partially, traditional fixed political party positions, seeking instead numerous outlets to meet their wishes and aspirations, those wishes and aspirations are more fluid and fragmented, and indeed being continually re-fragmented, along changing lifestyle issues and concerns, as identified, for example, by Beck.[1]

One can witness the rise in importance of organisations that both complement and compete with governments, political parties, trade unions, social movements, etc. In this chapter, we intend to concentrate mainly upon traditionally recognised non-governmental organisations (NGOs) and to largely leave social movements and their less formally structured organisational forms, operational fluidity and consequently better potential adaptability to global developments for a subsequent publication. That said, it is of course impossible to ignore the new forms of interaction facilitated in cyberspace and the threats and opportunities that these offer to existing NGOs.

As Habermas[2] points out, the diffusion of political activity in the last few decades has rendered public spheres more complex; the same is true for concepts such as civil society and the third sector. One thing we should stress, which is sometimes overlooked due to an over-emphasis on ICTs as opposed to their effects, is that we are still really talking about human interaction. For all the talk of technological shifts, as Warkentin[3] notes, the Internet is a socially constructed medium and it is people who determine the outcomes of the activities undertaken.

The pace of the changes noted by Habermas[4] can, at times, seem to be accelerating, although there are also periods of retrenchment with power and or influence ebbing and flowing between issues, institutions, ideologies and individuals, though still remaining in the hands of the few. This continued concentration of power seems to contradict at least some of the transformational characteristics claimed by early exponents of a digital revolution of society,[5] who foresaw or perhaps hoped to wish into being a more egalitarian environment in which citizens would interact with government utilising ICTs.

NGOs have inspired politics and society in recent decades by bringing neglected or ignored issues into public debate with spectacular, media-effective campaigns, thus forcing governments, business and the general public to act and react. Campaigns such as the Brent Spar campaign by Greenpeace in 1995[6] or the continuous campaigning and lobbying for an International Criminal Court (ICC) by the international NGO network Coalition for the International Criminal Court (CICC) since 1995[7] made NGOs active and powerful political players that can no longer be left aside in modern political decision making. They have become an integral part of our societies and our political systems. They continue to claim and reclaim a voice and space in the political arena on the local, national and trans-national levels.

At the same time, NGOs are increasingly recognised by governments and supranational and international organisations, such as the European Union, as necessary and viable partners to find solutions for local, national and global issues and to manage the increasingly demanding challenges of twenty-first-century governance. Over the past decades, a continuing and upward trend has been recorded in employment and expansion of the NGO sector, as well as in its active engagement in policy-making in all areas. However, this trend also brings with it certain difficulties concerning the classification of NGOs and the clarification of where the boundaries lie between NGOs, the state, inter-governmental organisations and supranational institutions.

The impact of the Internet on non-governmental action increasingly mystifies insights into and understanding of the structures, methods and strategies of NGOs, and only exacerbates any useful attachment of meaning to the concept of NGOs. It is therefore important to look at the classification of NGOs and its usefulness in trying to explain new modes of communication and participatory action.

As the Internet started to become more and more of a mass medium by facilitating business, communication and information diffusion around the mid-1990s, its political implications emerged, and they have been debated by theorists, politicians and political science scholars ever since. Undeniably, the Internet has had a strong impact on the political sphere with regard to a number of issues. On the one hand, the possibility of cutting costs in terms of resources and time has pushed governments towards adopting so-called 'instruments of E-Government' in order to provide and deliver better services to citizens by cutting waiting times and expenses in general. On the other hand, a higher expectation for the establishment of a richer democracy, both qualitatively and quantitatively, has accompanied the Internet's mass diffusion.

The Internet has indeed acquired a political relevance as politics has acquired a relevant position on the Internet. The impact of new media has had, and still has, consequences for a number of elements and actors within the democratic system. Government, as well as private citizens, lobby groups, NGOs and political parties, have adopted new technologies as part of their everyday activities. At the same time they have all also adapted to them, and some have found that new activities, opportunities or strategies have been facilitated by the ICT usage.

The little research produced on the relation between new media and new political actors represents a clear lacuna in the literature, which emphasises the necessity of investigating the relationship between other political entrepreneurs and the rise of the World Wide Web. Previous studies[8] pointed out how the Internet had modified pre-existing models of understanding of NGOs, producing a revolution in their communication environment.

So far, academic research on the topic has concentrated on giving an account of how NGOs use the Internet by establishing their presence online through websites and portals. Thus the focus has been on the relationships between NGOs and their members, NGOs and other NGOs and, finally, NGOs and the public at large. This study aims to address whether the availability of E-Government tools has changed interactions between governmental and non-governmental agencies. Therefore, we focus on one particular perspective, acknowledging that our contribution fits a more complex puzzle.

NGOs, citizens and new forms of participation

A better-informed and more participatory society is what many theorists of strong democracy had in mind. Myths such as the 'open society' and the 'public sphere' are now illuminated by the new technological development; the Internet is rapidly becoming a platonic form of democratic advancement. Some very enthusiastic voices claim that 'the Internet offers a potential for direct democracy so profound that it may well transform not only our system of politics but also our very form of government'.[9] Other voices point out how the Internet might change inherent power structures,[10] and some scholars highlight the importance of the Internet for a transition to democracy;[11] in plain terms 'the Internet is a thing that changes things, more than a "mere" object'.[12]

We might disagree on what the potential of the Internet is and to what extent it might affect the political process, but we can probably all agree on the fact that it has a capacity for facilitating change. It has indeed changed modes of communication in terms of speed and in terms of quantity, but what probably better characterises the Internet is the change it has brought about in terms of the direction of communication. The Internet, in fact, entitles those with access to the technology to diffuse information on the Web; it provides people with spaces and visibility, almost cost-free. It is, however, important to remember that access is still an issue not just in the developing world, but also, albeit to a lesser extent, in more developed societies. However, for those with access to the technology we can see how anybody can create information – no matter what kind or what quality – and anybody can diffuse information. That is probably the most revolutionary characteristic of the Internet:

the consumer's role can be augmented with that of producer. Theoretically at least, there are no limits to information dissemination; the Web is accessible from every part of the globe, removing most, if not all, geographical constraints. Moreover, the Internet empowers people by offering them a capacity to react to the information gathered online, and to make public their reaction as well. It does represent a revolution for the information systems, but what does have it to do with politics?

Even though the vast majority of activities performed online do not concern political participation, or even political information, the political implications of the Internet are widely recognised not only by intellectuals, professional politicians and academics, but also by citizens who perform a number of political activities online.[13]

The literature on the political implications of the Internet mostly tends to focus on entrepreneurs such as political parties – under the assumption that parties embody the linkage between citizens and governments and that no modern democracy could work without parties. However, political parties do not entirely cover, on their own, the wide spectrum of interests present in complex contexts such as modern Western democracies. Moreover, political disenfranchisement and detachment from traditional form of politics, such as through party membership,[14] has dominated the European scenario in the past 15 years, opening up new forms and paradigms of political engagement. Such a phenomenon has transformed the prominence of NGOs from fringe to mainstream. However, it is also clear that different types of NGOs use new technologies differently. For instance, advocacy groups use new technologies differently from service providers, yet both can be classified as NGOs.

The changing face and space of NGOs

Classification of 'non-governmental organisations' is not easy; some would claim it is impossible. The term originates from and was first used in Article 71 of the United Nations Charter of 1945:

> The Economic and Social Council may make suitable arrangements for consultation with *non-governmental organisations* which are concerned with matters within its competence. Such arrangements may be made with international organisations and, where appropriate, with national organisations after consultation with the Member of the United Nations concerned.[15]

However, as Frantz and Mertens point out,

> despite the fact that the UN introduced the term NGO, it provided an insufficient definition. Both in article 71 of the Charter as well as in all subsequent resolutions the UN mainly restricts itself to regulating the relationship *between* NGOs and the UN.[16]

With the increasing heterogeneity of the organisations collected under the term 'non-governmental organisations' and an increasing blurring of the boundaries to distinguish between NGOs and other institutional structures, as well as changing structures due to the influence of the Internet and the process of globalisation, it has become almost impossible to define the non-governmental sector.

If NGOs are to be placed within the structures of a democratic political system, then they are depicted as one corner of a triangle, facing government on one corner and business on the other. This triangular three-sector approach is widely accepted as the model to classify different organisational structures. NGOs are thus frequently designated as third-sector organisations, the first sector being the government and public administration and the second sector being for-profit organisations and business corporations.[17]

Alternatively, NGOs are also sometimes depicted as hovering somewhere between the public and the private spheres. This slightly different model takes into account the fact that leaving out the private from political discourse excludes large parts of society. It places NGOs as a mediator between the state, the market and the private (families and society).[18] However, the boundaries between the political, economic and private are also increasingly blurred and thus make clear classifications and definitions even more difficult.

Whichever model one prefers, NGOs have become the core element of interaction between the State and its citizens, as well as between the market and the citizens. In this sense, NGOs are often viewed in terms of civil society in its structured form. This only adds to the confusion of how to define NGOs since the concept of civil society not only is contested, but also has normative functions attached to it.

Zimmer[19] distinguishes between civil society and the third sector: civil society refers to the social dimension. Civil society is governed by a normative orientation and requires the guarantee of basic democratic structures in a state in order to be able to operate. Civil society is organised and institutionalised in organisations and associations. In contrast, the third sector refers to this organised form of civil society, or what Zimmer calls the 'core of civil society' (i.e. it refers to a meso-level between private social commitment and the social dimension).[20] Thus there are two different perspectives: the third sector as organisations providing social services; and the third sector as an organised form of civil society with democratising potential.

The third sector as the core and structural dimension of civil society is referred to as non-governmental, voluntary, not-for-profit, non-profit or non-commercial and sometimes independent.[21] Referring to characteristics that all non-governmental organisations share, although they might have different legal status (e.g. legal status of a charity, non-profit association or a foundation), the European Commission[22] adopted the following definition of 'non-governmental organisation':

- NGOs are not created to generate personal profit. Although they may have paid employees and engage in revenue-generating activities they do not distribute profits or surpluses to members or management.
- NGOs are voluntary. This means that they are formed voluntarily and that there is usually an element of voluntary participation in the organisation.
- NGOs are distinguished from informal or ad hoc groups by having some degree of formal or institutional existence. Usually, NGOs have formal statutes or other governing document setting out their mission, objectives and scope. They are accountable to their members and donors.

- NGOs are independent, in particular of government and other public authorities and of political parties or commercial organisations;
- NGOs are not self-serving in aims and related values. Their aim is to act in the public arena at large, on concerns and issues related to the well-being of people, specific groups of people or society as a whole. They are not pursuing the commercial or professional interests of their members.

In this sense, NGOs can be distinguished from political parties, social movements and for-profit organisations, as well as from self-interested lobby groups. However, it also means that, apart from the claim of being independent, which is being called into question, considering the close linkages between state, market and NGOs as service providers, NGOs are largely defined by what they are not. As Lewis[23] notes, this 'is more than just a semantic problem, because labelling has important resource and policy implications in terms of "who is in and who is out"'.

Such classification is important in so far as it determines the relationship between the organisation and the other two sectors. It determines, for example, which organisations may be eligible for funding or, in a more authoritarian context, which organisations are allowed to register and thus are eligible to exist. It also determines the way these organisations operate. The problem is that any definition covers only part-aspects of the form and structure, the kind of activities or the type of membership of any NGO, and it cannot encompass all at the same time. NGOs that are predominantly engaged in advocacy, human or civic rights, justice, environment or similar causes often find themselves in opposition to the other two sectors; NGOs predominantly engaged in humanitarian aid, providing services to the public in health and social care or in the field of education frequently find themselves in co-operation with the two other sectors. In many ways, the position an NGO finds itself in also determines its self-understanding and modus operandi.

The term 'non-governmental organisation' thus encompasses a plethora of very different organisational forms of civic engagement, ideological leanings, activities, scope, scale and lifetime, self-image and image given to them by others. This is further complicated by renewal, re-invention and re-direction, in some cases a shape-shifting of traditional NGOs, partly as a consequence of ICT usage and adoption. At first glance, it seems therefore more apt to label NGOs according to their field of activity. The European Commission[24] elaborated a typology of NGOs that are operating in the field of (a) service provision, (b) advocacy and lobbying, (c) self-help and mutual aid and (d) intermediary bodies that provide a bridge between the third and the first sector. While this typology must remain as inconclusive as the above-noted classification, it becomes somewhat clearer how NGO activity determines its relations with public authorities. Yet inclusive it remains, since NGO activity is also guided by its own self-belief, motives and ideology. Thus, for example, a development NGO that is engaged in advocacy to curb the negative impact of globalisation might find itself either inside the conference rooms of G8 and UN meetings to negotiate compromises or outside the fenced-off venue to demonstrate against it, depending on its own ideology and strategy.

Naturally, the impact of globalisation and increasing inter-connectedness and inter-relations of global issues led to an increased use of ICT and network building away from focusing on national politics towards a global civil society that overcomes geographical obstacles by increasingly moving their activities into the virtual space. This fundamentally changes the structure, form and modus operandi of NGOs. Cammaerts and van Audenhove[25] identify four main types of 'virtual' organisation based upon earlier work by Bekkers:[26]

- *umbrella organisations*, which perform tasks on behalf of autonomous members;
- *portal organisations*, which bring together differing but inter-related sites and or information and performs a selection or editing function;
- *platform organisations*, which bring together differing but inter-related sites and or information but do not mediate and perform no selection or editing function;
- *Web organisations* whereby individuals utilise interactive tools such as forums and discussion groups without a clear structure, e.g Indymedia.[27]

While international governmental organisations such as the UN or the EU are rapidly moving towards incorporation of NGOs into their systems to increase their legitimacy and bridge the gap between themselves and national civil societies,[28] there is still a gap in the deploying of E-Government features on an international and trans-national level. E-Government seems to be more designed to operate on the national – in the case of the EU, possibly supranational – level, while NGO activity takes place more and more on a global level. In widening their scope, the NGO community are rapidly moving into cyberspace. NGOs increasingly find trans-national networks to give their voice more power. The Internet provides an ideal platform for trans-national and global communication and information exchange. For example, it gives smaller local NGOs the opportunity to have their plight heard internationally and gain access to larger networks and international organisations. In addition, the Internet is an ideal platform to address and activise large numbers of people that are otherwise not yet united in a global civil society.

NGOs and ICT

The ways in which NGOs are making use of ICTs are myriad but can be broadly seen to fall into one of two areas:

1   improving internal communication and administration via email, Internet and applications accessible via mobile telephony (see NGOs and E-Activism relating to Amnesty International, below);
2   improving external communications both by using the above-mentioned ICT-related applications, but also by expanding communication by operating on social networking sites and thus projecting their message to a wider audience of potential supporters or adherents.

Diani[29] produced a synthesis of how ICT could serve NGOs' goals, being: (a) inexpensive; (b) fast; (c) immediate; and (d) participatory, facilitating interactions between organisations and members/activists. Unquestionably, ICT usage is inexpensive and fast when compared to traditional forms of communication; email is faster than regular mail, buying Web space is less pricey than any other form of advertisement (e.g. TV, papers, leaflets, etc.) and information reaches targets directly and without filtering. Overall, the nature of the relationship between NGOs and ICT is multi-dimensional, allowing for a shifting of power, or what Alkalimat and Williams identify as three types of cyberpower:

- *Individual*: empowering individuals and creating new human capital.
- *Social*: collectives engaged in cyber-organising harnessing individual human capital.
- *Ideological*: ideas and policy promoted by individual and social cyber-power.[30] A prime example of this would be the flourishing anti-capitalist movement and its associated organisations, e.g. Indymedia.[31]

According to Scott and Street,[32] the Internet is ideal for social movements' utilisation as it allows 'for meso-mobilisation – co-ordination between movements networks across borders and without the need for a transcending hierarchical organisational form . . . for a high impact without needing major resources' and it allows 'organisations to retain editorial control over content and external communication; . . . organisations to bypass state control and communicate in a safe environment'.

To date, research on the relationship between the Internet and social actors as NGOs has been investigated from a single perspective,[33] the fulcrum of the research being the kind of use social actors make of the Web by developing their own websites. NGOs' interaction strategies are based on the targets they intend to focus on, which are basically other NGOs, their members, the public at large and the government. Furthermore, the types of opportunities for communication offered by ICT are not limited to uploading a website; with the diffusion of Web 2.0 instruments, there is now a broad range of new possibilities. However, the level of interaction and the building of human capital is somewhat limited to date.[34]

The evidence on how NGOs use the Internet is somewhat fragmented and contradictory, particularly as such research knowledge is at an embryonic stage. Vernis *et al.* argue that new technologies give great opportunities to NGOs in terms of 'management improvements in areas such as internal and external communications, fund-raising, volunteer work and so on, to new venues in social advocacy and activism'.[35] However, they also allege that these new opportunities bear a potential threat by which NGOs are pushed into alliances and actions in contraposition to their mission and where 'they need to find a balance between the urge to communicate and the respect for their missions and values'.[36] Another constraint for traditional NGOs is the nature of Internet communities and activists. Network sociality embodies looseness and informality. Individuals engage in networks randomly, keep their anonymity if they so wish, pick and choose the activities and sign out when they have lost interest, moving on to something else. NGOs, which are dependent on active and constant membership, find it hard to adjust their strategies to this new environment.

Interviewed by Michael Fehner, Geert Lovink points out that, in contrast to NGOs, which went through the process of institutionalisation, the net community or net sociality evades this process. Lovink reiterated that this is not necessarily a negative development:

> The absence of the social, the community, etc. is not something we should complain about. Loose ties are constitutional these days. We should stop reading them in terms of decline . . . Engagement comes in radically new ways. Networks are playgrounds; they are probes. A lot is happening – but please let's abandon all hope of recreating fixed social structures such as a party or a church. Networks are not the surrogates of nineteenth-century sociality.[37]

Lovink ascertains that NGOs had to go through a necessary process of incorporation into the system to be fully operable; however, network communities so far have escaped this incorporation.[38] So far, it thus has been difficult for NGOs to fully engage the potential of network sociality. Moreover, there is still not enough NGO activity, in terms of simply disseminating information in blogs, podcasting and social networks (e.g. Facebook) or actively participating in these communities – although this also is slowly changing, at least in terms of podcasts and online video-sharing communities (e.g. YouTube).

While having some sympathy with Lovink's arguments that NGOs have fallen behind in utilising ICTs and adopting newer communication channels,[39] we find his criticisms ignore the changing nature of NGOs, particularly in issue areas such as social entrepreneurship. He posits NGOs as being top-down in their use of ICTs and slow to embrace change, citing the corporate consultancy culture that has built up around the NGO 'business sector' as discouraging innovation and re-shaping.

Groups within civil society, particularly NGOs, partially through ICT-facilitated capability, enable new or amorphous forms of post-democratic governance to exist via networked communities, engaging in interactions that are, often, outside the purely historic concepts of democratic activity and are not necessarily designed to fit into traditional explanations of democratic legitimacy. They are adding ICT-enabled capabilities to what Tilly describes at their 'repertoires of action'.[40]

Also, we can already see that the spreading adoption of ICTs by NGOs and social movements is changing the ways in which those organisations operate.[41] As Van Der Donk *et al.*[42] note, these changing developments offer opportunities, but also pose challenges to social movements and NGOs. Moreover, we can see that the research base on which to draw in this area is limited when compared to that of more formal political and government activities. The changing nature of technologies is also creating new and innovative responses. Ten years ago Locke argued that '[w]ithin about ten years most households will have one box that will combine together our present domestic technologies of TV, telephone and computer.'[43] While Locke imagined that the technologies would be incorporated into the digital television, it is in fact the hand-held device of the most modern mobile phones that best illustrates the morphing of technologies – and certainly its portability allows interactivity previously unimagined outside the realm of science fiction.

The rise of the mobile phone is creating differing types of activity and the private sector, never slow to sense a market opportunity and re-inforce the concept of corporate social responsibility, is keen to promote such diversification by providing information and ideas to NGOs. One example of how this is achieved is through such tools as blogs and case study material placed on a website that has been created by Nokia and Vodafone[44] in response to requests from NGOs for guidance on how to maximise the potential of mobile phone use. Posting to the site is on a wiki basis, and there are a number of case studies displayed there to give ideas.

NGOs and E-Activism

One of the most prominent and famous forms of new NGO trans-national strategies is so-called 'dot causes', which are 'cause-promoting networks whose organisational realm falls largely within Internet space'.[45] An example of this would be the recent online petition[46] against EDVIGE, a database for use by French intelligence services and police. The database is seen as being highly intrusive as it collects data on an individual's health and sexual orientation. Given the propensity for governments to share information with each other, the potential for such information to be used in a discriminatory way intensifies. There are worries that proposals by President Sarkozy's government will weaken the role of existing data protection agencies such as the Commission Nationale de l'Informatique et des Libertés (CNIL) and La haute autorité de lutte contre les discriminations et pour l'égalité (HALDE). Support for the campaign has spread into the French parliament. A further example would be the recent petition designed to prevent former British Prime Minister Tony Blair from becoming the President of the European Union.[47]

Of course there are many examples where existing NGOs harness the undoubted power of the Internet to further their cause, using the new technologies to add to their repertoires of action.[48] The Association for the Taxation of Financial Transactions for the Aid of Citizens (Association pour une Taxation des Transactions Financières pour l'Aide aux Citoyens), more often known by its acronym ATTAC, is an example of the way in which organisations are utilising ICTs to further their aims and objectives, and are also, in some cases, subject to the possibility of organisational transformation. Started in France in June 1998 as a way of grouping together disparate groups around the central theme of the introduction of a Tobin tax to help regulate financial markets and discourage currency speculation, the organisation is now active in 39 countries.[49] The major concentrations are in Europe and South America. There are organisations in more widely spread Francophone nations in Africa and also in the Canadian province of Quebec. This reflects the cultural heritage and particularly non-Anglo-Saxon economic philosophy underpinning ATTAC's *raison d'être*.

ATTAC, while registered as an NGO, is also frequently referred to, and is portrayed as, a social movement, especially since it operates as an umbrella organisation for a plethora of NGO members in the policy network. On the one hand, this very much reflects the way ATTAC operated through deregulation, decentralisation and, mainly, using new technologies for dissemination and organisation of events and activities. On the other hand, it also portrays a picture that is endorsed by ATTAC in its attempt to distance itself from what it sees as an overly structured and rigid NGO sector.[50] The Internet offers an ideal platform for evading hierarchical rigidity. Vernis *et al.*[51] argue that the development of new technologies provides an array of information and communication breakthroughs – in velocity, cost reductions and so on – that bear a significant impact on organisational structures – for instance, offering a real option for decentralized work, ensuring remote coordination and so on.

While the use of ICTs has clearly helped ATTAC to broaden its aims and develop its repertoires of action,[52] as Le Grignou and Patou note, 'it is merely an addition to the movement's more traditional repertoires of action'.[53] As they go on to show, while accepting that the Internet can facilitate differing forms of information exchange and protest mechanisms (most noticeably in the collapse of the 1998 Multilateral Agreement on Investment, where a successful campaign was heavily reliant on Internet-enabled resources), they argue that ATTAC was, and still is, a space for the exchange of expertise.

One can see many other examples of the ways in which ICT use is helping NGOs develop beyond simply increasing the ease of communication flows. Amnesty International (AI) is developing specialist networks in themes (e.g. children's human rights, lesbian, gay, bisexual and transgender, trade unions and women's action) which allow people with similar skills or interests to come together.

We can also see evidence of AI adding to their repertoire of action by creating an alternative to their highly successful use of letters from individuals protesting at the incarceration and/or torture of prisoners of conscience. AI is now also using mobile telephony to spread campaigns, inviting individuals to register their support for campaigns on behalf of individuals throughout the globe via an SMS which is then relayed to the detaining authority, thereby increasing pressure upon them.[54]

NGOs and E-Government

As we have seen, non-governmental action increasingly, if at times hesitantly, makes use of cyberspace. Yet, more organised forms of public–NGO interaction in terms of E-Government seem to be neglected by NGOs. The question thus remains to what extent and how NGOs are making use of methods and means of E-Government. As suggested above, it seems the channels of E-Government have found their way more profoundly into decision making on the national level and, in the case of the European Union, a supranational level. It is logical that on the local level more direct and face-to-face interaction is more advantageous; on the national level, NGO ICT usage vis-à-vis governmental authorities still seems to be confined to information and knowledge exchange, as well as lobbying via e-mail.

Using the Speyer definition of E-Government,[55] the possibility of NGOs' engagement in E-Government can be illustrated as in Table 14.1.

Thus, in a field of all possible forms of electronic communication between the sectors, there are seven possibilities involving E-Government: government to citizen (G2C); citizen to government (C2G); government to government (G2G); business to government (B2G); NGOs to government (N2G); government to business (G2B); and government to NGOs (G2N).[56] The authors of the Speyer definition believe that G2N, G2C, C2G and N2G will develop immensely in the future, although currently the whole potential is far from being used; the main usage of ICTs currently still

Table 14.1 E-Government services and public–private actors

	Population/ citizens	First sector/ state/public administration	Second sector/ business	Third sector/NGOs
Population/citizens	C2C	C2G	C2B	C2N
First sector/state/ public administration	G2C	G2G	G2B	G2N
Second sector/business	B2C	B2G	B2B	B2N
Third sector/NGOs	N2C	N2G	N2B	N2N

Source: Von Lucke and Reinermann (2000) (see note 17).

focuses on the use of the World Wide Web in combination with e-mail and electronic data exchange.[57]

In addition, it seems that data provision and communication still remain fairly one-way in the sense of downloadable data and information provision, rather than two-way communication. The European Commission, for example, provides all the necessary information and forms to be filled in to apply for project funding on its website. Yet the forms need to be downloaded and sent by mail. There is no provision for online forms or even email responses. Similarly, in the case of N2G, communication is more often than not confined to reports being sent via email to responsible authorities.[58]

Conclusion

The ubiquity of ICTs is in every part of our lives, coupled with the shift of the average individual in modern Westernised societies from being simply an information consumer to a more multi-faceted role of information consumer, producer and critic via the developing multi-channel outlets that ICTs provide.

As well as NGOs, business and governments have recognised the influence that can be gained from exposure in media outlets such as Facebook, MySpace, Hyves, etc. They have also colonised the spaces offered by new ICTs. No self-respecting social networking site is free from business or politicians, and traditional media have not been slow to expand their activities into the digital world. Indeed, one can see a very interesting adaptation of how NGOs are re-defining themselves at www.unltdworldd. com. Here, there is an enterprise blog and one can join a virtual community of like-minded individuals, share expertise, utilise resources and build collaborative capacity and value. The research lab based on the site offers the prospect of being able to map social entrepreneurship and social and environmental issues.

In relation to NGOs and E-Government, two main scenarios can be posited:

1   NGOs make use of E-Government tools without challenging them. Communication takes place mainly by email and by browsing the Web and gathering information.

2   NGOs actually challenge traditional forms of E-Government. They promote actual interaction by challenging government to implement discussion forums, chat rooms, video conferences and bi-lateral and multi-lateral interaction.

As such, both scenarios are possible and they may happen simultaneously; indeed, our expectations do change primarily according to the type of NGO. With regard to the typology discussed above we expect the picture shown in Table 14.2.

Table 14.2 summarises what we would expect to happen in the future. Service-delivering NGOs would perform at high standards in terms of their own activity online and be extremely challenging in terms of demanding high government performances. At the opposite extreme, self-help and mutual aid NGOs would only make limited use of E-Government services and they would not challenge existing instruments. Moreover, they would be active online only under a number of circumstances (depending on geography and issue). Advocacy NGOs would be active in developing their own Web strategy and communication online, but they would probably not challenge E-Government, following a rather traditional pattern in their N2G interaction. The last type of NGOs – resource and co-ordination – are seen as going the opposite way, being extremely challenging with regard to interaction with governmental actors online and quite inactive in terms of developing their own strategy of online action and interaction.

In conclusion, while we have considered the role of NGOs in the present and we have attempted an assessment of what sort of impact they may have on government in a changing communication environment, one cannot avoid the thought that perhaps there is one piece of the jigsaw missing. While there is some evidence to suggest that despite the impressive list of commitments coming out of the World Summit on the Information Society (WSIS), when one looks at what is enshrined in its guiding principles, an examination of the ethical components (WSIS, section B10), one can only agree with Lovink when he argues that '[i]t is remarkable that there are no global NGOs like Greenpeace, Amnesty or Oxfam that critically investigate the Internet and the new media/telecom sector'.[59] Clearly, if the discourse around the transformational nature of ICTs, a networked society and the potential for misuse and bias are even to be half believed, it seems inconceivable that such a powerful societal element force lacks the scrutiny of such a counterbalancing force that a worldwide NGO could bring to bear. The problems, of course, would centre around issues of who would control such an organisation. Given the disparate conceptions of freedom of information and freedom of speech held in differing countries, whose agenda would such an organisation follow? Evidently there is a need for such a body, but it would seem, at least at present, that there is precious little public demand for it.

Table 14.2 Expectation on NGOs and computer-mediated communication

	Service-delivery NGOs	Advocacy	Self-help and mutual aid	Resource and co-ordination
E-Activism	High	High	Low/high	Low
E-Government	High	Low	Low	High

The pace of change and the reactions to such changes are proving ever more difficult to codify. The shape-shifting of NGOs as they seek to adapt to changing times and the blurring of virtual and non-virtual action make this area of study interesting and fruitful for further research.

Key points

- The Internet facilitates social and political change by empowering people.
- The political implications of the Internet are potentially crucial to a plurality of political actors, among which are NGOs.
- It is changing the ways in which political communication debate, and even direct action, is taking place.
- The complexity of defining NGOs and their role in a democratic society makes it more difficult to assess the ways in which they make use of ICTs and the purposes for which they make use of them.
- Shifting boundaries also shift the functions and roles of NGOs.
- The importance of the Internet in governance is complemented by a growth in media awareness among the general public.
- We would expect this trend to intensify as digital natives become the majority group in society.
- There is a much greater level of political discourse which is being influenced by, and in some cases taking place via, Web 2.0 tools.
- Fragmentation and the notion of 'networked individualism' are leading to less entrenched political positions and a greater willingness to embrace solutions rather than political parties or any particular organisations.
- Web 2.0 applications are changing the ways in which NGOs and wider society interact.
- There is no indication of homogeneity in their use. Different types of NGOs have differing online behaviours.
- There are nascent indications that the use of Web 2.0 tools by the participants in the public domain are shaping new forms of relationships between those who govern and the governed.

Notes

1 Beck, U. (1992) *Risk Society: Towards a New Modernity*. London: Sage.
2 Habermas, J. (English translation 1989) *The Structural Transformation of the Public Sphere: An Inquiry into a Category of Bourgeois Society*. Cambridge, MA: The MIT Press.
3 Warkentin, C. (2001) *Reshaping World Politics*. Accessed online at http://books.google.com/books?id=QJYR5_9SZJkCandprintsec=frontcoveranddq=Reshaping+World+Politics++By+Craig+Warkentin.
4 Habermas, J. (1989) op. cit.
5 For example Toffler, A. (1980) *The Third Wave*. London: Pan; Becker, T. (1981) 'Teledemocracy: Bringing Power back to the People', *Futurist*, December: 6–9; Bekkers,

V. J. J. M. (1998) *Grenzeloze overheid: over informatisering en grensveranderingen in het openbaar bestuur.* Alphen aan den Rijn: Samson.

6 Frantz, M. and Martens, K. (2006) *Nichtregierungsorganisationen* (NGOs). Wiesbaden: Verlag für Sozialwissenschaften.

7 Coalition for an International Criminal Court (CICC) (2008) 'Who Are We and What Do We Do?'. CICC, http://www.iccnow.org/?mod=about.

8 Brainard, L. and Siplon, P. (2002) 'Cyberspace Challenges to Mainstream Nonprofit Health Organisations', *Administration and Society* 34/2: 141–175; Kurtz, J. (2002) 'NGOs, the Internet and International Economic Policy Making: The Failure of the OECD Multilateral Agreement on Investment', *Melbourne Journal of International Law* 3 (October): 213–246.

9 Morris, D. (2001) 'Direct Democracy and the Internet', *Loyola of Los Angeles Law Review* 34/3: 1033–1053. p. 1033.

10 Howard, P. N. (2003) 'Digitalizing the Social Contract: Producing American Political Culture in the Age of New Media', *The Communication Review* 6: 213–245. p. 213.

11 Cherian, G. (2003) 'The Internet and the Narrow Tailoring Dilemma for "Asian" Democracies', *The Communication Review* 6: 247–268. p. 248.

12 Nafus, D. (2003) 'The Aesthetics of the Internet in St. Petersburg: Why Metaphor Matters', *The Communication Review* 6: 185–212. p. 204.

13 Van De Donk, W., Loader, B. D., Nixon, P. G. and Rucht, D. (eds) (2004) *Cyberprotest: New Media, Citizens and Social Movements.* London: Routledge.

14 Gallagher, M., Laver, M. and Mair, P. (2001) *Representative Government in Modern Europe: Institutions, Parties, and Governments,* 3rd ed. New York: McGraw-Hill, p. 273.

15 United Nations (1945) UN Charter, http://www.un.org7aboutun/charter. Original emphasis.

16 Frantz, M. and Martens, K. (2006) op. cit. p. 24.

17 For examples see Anheier, H. (2005/2007) *Nonprofit Organisations – Theory, Management, Policy.* Abingdon and New York: Routledge; Birkhölzer, K., Klein, A., Priller, E. and Zimmer, A. (eds) (2005) *Dritter Sektor/Drittes System – Theorie, Funktionswandel und zivilgesellschaftlicht Perspecktiven. Bürgergesellschat und Demokratie,* Band 20, Wiesbaden: Verlag für Sozialwissenschaften; Breit, G. and Massing, P. (eds) (2002) *Bürgergesellschaft, Zivilgesellschaft, Dritter Sektor,* Schwalbach: Wochenschau Verlag; Lewis, D. (2007) *The Management of Non-Governmental Development Organisations,* 2nd ed. London and New York: Routledge; Vernis, A., Iglesias, M., Sanz, B. and Saz-Carranza, A. (2006) *Nonprofit Oranisations – Challenges and Colloboration.* Basingstoke: Palgrave Macmillan; Von Lucke, J. and Reinermann, H. (2000) *Spyerer Definition von Electronic Government,* Ergebnisse des Forschungsprojektes Regieren und Verwalten im Informationszeitalter, Forschungsinstitut für öffentliche Verwaltung, Online Publikation, url: http://foev.dhv-speyer.de/ruvii; Zimmer, Annette (2002) 'Dritter Sektor und Sozialkapital'. Münsteraner Diskussionspapiere zum Nonprofit-Sektor – Nr. 19 (Januar), Arbeitssteller Aktive Bürgergesellschaft, Institut for Politikwissenschaft, Westfälische Wilhelms-Universität, Münster; Zimmer, Annette (2004) 'Civil Society Organisation in Central and Eastern European Countries: Introduction and Terminology', in Annette Zimmer and Eckhard Priller (eds) *Future of Civil Society – Making Central European Non-Profit Organisations Work.* Wiesbaden: VS Verlag für Sozialwissenschaften.

18 Breit, G. and Massing, P. (2002) op. cit. (2002) op. cit.; Vernis *et al.* (2006) op. cit., Zimmer (2002) and (2004) op. cit.

19 Zimmer (2002) and (2004) op. cit.

20 Zimmer (2002) pp. 41–42.

21 Deakin, N. (2001) *In Search of Civil Society.* Basingstoke: Palgrave. pp. 8–10.

22 European Commission. 'The Commission and Non-Governmental Organisations: Building a Stronger Partnership', Discussion Paper, presented by President Prodi and Vice-President Kinnock, http://www.ec.europa.eu/civil_society/ngo/docs/communication_en.pdf. Original emphasis.

23 Lewis, D. (2007) *The Management of Non-Governmental Development Organisations,* 2nd ed. London and New York: Routledge. p. 43.

24 European Commission (1997) Communication from the Commission on Promoting the Role of Voluntary Organisations and Foundations in Europe, COM/97/0241final.
25 Cammaerts, B. and van Audenhove, L. (2003) 'ICT-Usage among Transnational Social Movements in the Networked Society'. Accessed online at www.lse.ac.uk/collections/EMTEL/reports/cammaerts_2003_emtel.pdf. pp. 24–25.
26 Bekkers, V.J.J.M. (2000) Voorbij de Virtuele Organisatie? Over de bestuuskundige betekenis van virtuele variëteit, contingentie en parallel organiseren. *Oratie,* Erasmus Universiteit Rotterdam.
27 http://www.indymedia.org/nl/index.shtml. Original emphasis.
28 Frantz, M. and Martens, K. (2006) op. cit.
29 Diani, M. (2001) 'Social Movement Networks: Virtual and Real', in Frank Webster (ed.) *Culture and Politics in the Information Age.* London and New York: Routledge.
30 Alkalimat, A. and Williams, K. (2001) 'Social Capital and Cyberpower in the African-American Community', in L. Keeble and B.D. Loader (eds) *Community Informatics: Shaping Computer Mediated Social Relations.* London: Routledge, p. 203. Original emphasis.
31 http://www.indymedia.org/nl/index.shtml.
32 Scott, A. and Street, J. (2001) 'From Media Politics to E-Protest? The Use of Popular Culture and New Media in Parties and Social Movements', in F. Webster (ed.) *Culture and Politics in the Information Age, A New Politics?,* pp. 32–51. London: Routledge. p. 46.
33 For example Lusoli, W., Ward, S. J. and Gibson, R. K. (2002) 'Political Organisations and Online Mobilisation: Different Media – Same Outcomes?' *New Review of Information Networking* 8: 89–108; Pickerill, J. (2004) 'Rethinking Political Participation: Experiments in Internet Activism in Australia and Britain', in R. Gibson, A. Roemmele and S. Ward (eds) *Electronic Democracy: Mobilisation, Organisation and Participation via new ICTs.* London: Routledge.
34 Meijer, A., Burger, N. and Ebbers, W. (2009) 'Citizens4Citizens: Mapping Participatory Practices on the Internet', *Electronic Journal of E-Government* 7/1: 99–112. www.ejeg.com. p. 111.
35 Vernis *et al.* (2006) op. cit. p. 4.
36 Ibid. p. 5.
37 Feher, M., Krikorian, G. and McKee, Y. (eds) (2007) *Nongovernmental Politics.* New York: Zone Books. pp. 302–303.
38 Ibid. p. 303.
39 Lovink, G. (2008) *Zero Comments.* London: Routledge. p. 179.
40 Tilly, C. (1978) *From Mobilisation to Revolution.* Reading, MA: Addison-Wesley.
41 Hajnal, P. I. (ed.) (2002) *Civil Society in the Information Age.* Aldershot: Ashgate.
42 Van De Donk *et al.* (2004) op. cit.
43 Locke, T. (1999) 'Participation, Inclusion, Exclusion and Netactivism: How the Internet Invents New Forms of Democratic Activity', in B.N. Hague and B. D. Loader (eds) *Digital Democracy: Discourse and Decision Making in the Information Age.* London: Routledge. p. 221.
44 www.shareideas.org.
45 Clark, J. and Themudo, N. (2006) 'Linking the Web and the Street: Internet-Based "Dotcauses" and the "Anti-Globalisation" Movement', *World Development* 34/1: 50–74, downloaded from: www.elsevier.com/locate/worlddev (doi:10.1016/j.worlddev.2005.09.001), p. 50.
46 http://nonaedvige.ras.eu.org.
47 http://stopblair.eu/.
48 Tilly, C. (1978) op. cit.
49 As of 28 November 2008.
50 Franz and Maartens (2006) op. cit. p. 16.
51 Vernis *et al.* (2006) op. cit. p. 71.
52 Tilly, C. (1978) op. cit.
53 Le Grignou, B. and Patou, C. (2004) 'ATTAC(k)ing Expertise: Does the Internet Really Democratise Knowledge?' in Van De Donk *et al.* (2004) op. cit.
54 http://www.amnesty.nl/in_actie/actienetwerken.
55 Von Lucke, J. and Reinermann, H. (2000) op. cit.

56 Ibid.
57 Ibid.
58 Conversation with an NGO member of the German government–NGO human rights liaison committee *Forum Menschenrechte*.
59 Lovink, G. (2008) op. cit. p. 180.

Further reading

Anheier, H. (2005/2007) *Nonprofit Organisations: Theory, Management, Policy*. Abingdon and New York: Routledge.
Lewis, D. (2007) *The Management of Non-Governmental Development Organisations*, 2nd ed. London and New York: Routledge.
Meijer, A., Burger, N. and Ebbers, W. (2009) 'Citizens4Citizens: Mapping Participatory Practices on the Internet', *Electronic Journal of E-Government* 7/1: 99–112. www.ejeg.com.
Mosco, V. (2004) *The Digital Sublime: Myth, Power, and Cyberspace*. Cambridge, MA and London: The MIT Press.
Van De Donk, W., Loader, B. D., Nixon, P. and Rucht, D. (2004) *Cyberprotest: New Media, Citizens and Social Movements*. London: Routledge.
Vernis, A., Iglesias, M., Sanz, B. and Saz-Carranza, A. (2006) *Nonprofit Organisations: Challenges and Collaboration*. Basingstoke: Palgrave Macmillan.
Webster, F. (2001) *Culture and Politics in the Information Age: A New Politics?* London: Routledge.

15 Responding to cyberterror

A failure to firewall freedoms?

Rajash Rawal

Summary

While campaining for office of President of the United States in 2008, Barack Obama described a 'net attack' as being as serious and grave a problem as any potential nuclear or biological threat. Obama's concerns echo long-standing criticisms of the Internet and its capacity, such as its openness and the lack of a regulatory power. Governments have readily highlighted that terrorists have been quick to utilise the potential that the cyberworld has to offer them to deliver their messages, communicate with each other and retain their anonymity. As a result, efforts to curb and contain have often trampled over human rights, privacy and civil liberties. This chapter examines the developments by looking at the actual threats of cyberterrorism and what threats are posed by the use of the Internet by terrorists. This chapter analyses the trends in government measures to attempt to control hyperspace, question the nature of these measures and present how these measures threaten E-Democracy while at the same time highlighting the need for legitimate E-Identity mechanisms to be created.

Introduction

Barack Obama described a 'net attack' as being as serious and grave a problem as any potential nuclear or biological threat when running for office of President of the United States in 2008. He suggested that the 'War on Terror' had to become more diverse in its range of action in order to cope with the diverse threats being presented by the modern terrorist. Obama followed up on his words by launching a full cybersecurity review soon after being sworn into office in an attempt to shore up his nation's efforts in this area.[1]

Obama's concerns echo long-standing criticisms of the Internet and its capacity (i.e. its openness and the lack of a regulatory power).[2] Governments have readily highlighted that terrorists have been quick to utilise the potential that the cyberworld has to offer them in delivering their messages, communicating with each other and retaining their anonymity.[3] Scott and Street[4] further argue that the Internet has presented the opportunity for groups to plot in secret and 'bypass' nation-state mechanisms.

This chapter examines the developments by looking at what the actual threats of cyberterrorism are and what threats are posed by the use of the Internet by terrorists.

It analyses the trends in government measures to attempt to control hyperspace, questions the nature of these measures and presents how these measures threaten E-Democracy while at the same time highlighting the need for legitimate E-Identity mechanisms to be created. Finally, the chapter endeavours to present a conclusion as to whether (or not) cyberterrorism is a real and actual threat to modern society.

Background

As suggested above, governments and media alike have been very keen to present the threats of cyberterrorism and the use of the Internet by terrorists as being very grave and real.[5] Indeed, the lack of a regulatory power for the Internet has been a topic of much discussion for some time now.[6] Due to this lack of a regulatory power, government is on the back foot and can merely react; it is unable to act proactively.[7] The scenario of doom and gloom is only alleviated by the somewhat strange hope, given the ideas stated above, that the terrorists will be stopped. However, there are potent questions that need to be asked at this juncture such as: What evidence is there of any cyberterrorist attacks? Is it really true that little can be done to limit the terrorists who use the Internet?

These are questions which this chapter endeavours to answer in more detail. However, it is interesting to note at this point that a strange anomaly occurs when trying to look for examples of cyberterrorist attacks. Matai[8] suggests that the power outages across northeast North America, which affected cities such as New York, Detroit and Toronto in August 2003, were caused by the MSIBlast worm, which created a digital traffic jam. This, in turn, overloaded North American power stations and led to the collapse of electric power on a scale never before seen. The UK, Sweden, Denmark, Italy and Switzerland suffered power outages around this time too. The US government investigations suggested that while the outage was rare, no foul play was suspected. This is rather strange considering we are warned of the threats of a cyberterrorist attack, yet when one allegedly takes place, it is dismissed as an unfortunate accident. A reason for this is perhaps that such an attack taking place successfully would further undermine the notion of national security, which is held so dearly by governments around the world. Moreover, it would challenge the argument to move to E-Government systems as surely these large databases would be lucrative targets for the cyberterrorist. That said, we remain perfectly happy to raise the profile of potential attacks. One example is a report of a US Congressional panel which warned the outgoing Bush Administration in November 2008 that 'China was "stealing" vast amounts of sensitive information from US computer networks'.[9] A further example is Kyrgyzstan's recent suffering of a Distributed Denial of Service (DDoS) attack which paralysed the nation's Internet capabilities. The attack was officially blamed on Russia playing out Kyrgyzstan's potential as a victim, but spectators suggest there may have been domestic foul play.[10]

However, as governments seek to clamp down on the threat cyberterrorism poses, there are differences presented by the use of the Internet by terrorists which affect our basic freedoms more. It is these differences which this chapter examines.

Cyberterrorism v. terrorist 'use' of the Internet

Defining traditional terrorism is a very difficult task and cyberterrorism is no different. Cyberterrorism, a term first coined by Barry Collin[11] in the 1980s, is a wide-reaching concept which has no one, universally accepted definition. Crudely put, it is considered that cyberterrorism consist of acts of terror which take place in cyberspace; it is worth noting that it is not the same as cybercrime, as it must have strong terrorist elements. Terrorist attacks must seek to instil terror and fear; additionally they must have a political motivation, whereas cybercrime does not. Painter[12] adds the notion of 'cyberactivism' to the fray, which can be easily confused with cyberterrorism by the authorities and is one which limits our civil freedoms. The May Day riots of 2000 and the anti-globalisation protests of 2001 were all partially organised online, with websites being created to inform activists of their legal rights and give phone numbers of sympathetic lawyers.

However, Denning contests that 'Cyberterrorism exists only in theory'[13] while cybercrime and cyberactivism are real. The following definition can be posited:

> Cyberterrorism is the convergence of cyberspace and terrorism. It refers to unlawful attacks and threats of attacks against computers, networks and the information stored therein when done to intimidate or coerce a government or its people in furtherance of political or social objectives. Further, to qualify as cyberterrorism, an attack should result in violence against property or persons, or at least cause enough harm to generate fear.[14]

This definition implies a very involved element in contrast to the concept of cyberterrorism. Potential examples of cyberterror include spreading viruses, spamming (a 23-year-old was jailed in the UK for 'anarchic behaviour' after spreading abusive spam emails threatening to fire-bomb the headquarters of his county's trading standards office and petrol-bomb his local police office[15]), digital jamming and hacking (the Israelis and Palestinians were engaged in a cyberwar between 1999 and 2002, where each party attacked the other's Web resources[16]). Aggressive campaigns fought out on the Internet, or so called 'NGO-swarms',[17] have also been identified by the American military think tank RAND as potential forms of cyberterrorism. Additionally, in the aftermath of the riots that swept French cities in the autumn of 2005, French authorities jailed two bloggers for inciting violence.[18] It is questionable as to whether the latter can be considered to be an act of cyberterror or terrorist use of the Internet, as is illustrated later in this chapter. The authorities will often confuse protest and terror, allowing them to classify protest as terror to meet their own political needs.

However, it can be argued that the standard definition of cyberterrorism as quoted above is not one to which the wider public would adhere. They view cyberterrorism as the use of the Internet by terrorist groups to propagate their message. This view is further endorsed by the popular media,[19] which, as 'conduits for symbolism',[20] have become enmeshed in the symbolic war against terror, where fear becomes the main element.

'In newspapers and magazines, in film and on television, "cyberterrorism" is the zeitgeist.'[21] Moreover, Lanzone[22] adds a special new 'war on terror' element to cyberterrorism, which he phrases as 'cyberjihad'. In addition to this, Weimann[23] identifies that terrorism on the Internet is a very dynamic phenomenon. However, what exactly does this involve? What is cyberterrorism and how do terrorists use the Internet?

Why terrorists use the Internet

Considering Webster's assertion that ICTs have had a 'massive and ongoing'[24] impact on society, it is natural, as Knight and Ubayasiri suggest, that terrorist groups have 'embraced the Internet'[25] and have challenged the existing balances on information flow and news coverage. This point is further emphasised by Scott and Street,[26] who suggest that the Internet has shifted 'editorial' control to activists, allowing them to present news and opinion as they like. As a result, terrorist use of the Internet is very vibrant; websites appear, change format and disappear or simply change their addresses to avoid closure.[27] This equates to normal progression in regard to the development of protest politics, as noted by Dahlgren, as cyberspace has become a 'vital link and meeting ground for the civically engaged and politically mobilized'.[28] Weimann[29] further expounds the idea that terrorists are drawn to the web to target three main audience categories:

- *Supporters*: Terrorist websites keep supporters informed of their (recent) activities. Merchandise can be sold to help raise funds. Organisations localise their site in order to provide more detailed information; this often is done in minority languages. Al Qaeda is one such group which employs this tactic.
- *Public opinion*: Even those who are not directly involved may be affected. Most sites offer information in a number of languages in order to draw as wide an audience as possible. The Basque Separatist Group (ETA), for example, has pages in Basque, Castilian, German, French and Italian. The main premise of this is perhaps to capture international journalists' attention and hence get the organisation into the traditional media. One of the Hezbollah's websites is aimed exclusively at journalists, inviting them to email the group's press office.
- *Enemy publics*: This is one of the less obvious targets, but an equally important one. Sites will aim to promote the past activities of the terrorist group and threaten more, wider and dangerous campaigns. The idea is to try to demoralise the enemy. This is turn gathers media attention and begins debate and may weaken the governments' rule, which is the ultimate aim of most groups. An example of this is the 11 March 2003 bombings in Madrid. The ruling People's Party maintained through the state-run news agency EFE that ETA were behind the attacks; however, various wings of Al Qaeda began to spread news via the web that they were responsible. The commercial, non-state-run media began to publish this and the citizenry began to doubt the government. This contributed to the ruling party being ousted in favour of the Socialist Party in the 13 March election.

Attractions of cyberspace

Heralded as the integrator of cultures, the Internet[30] has also been the 'instrument of a political power shift'.[31] As one of the first many-to-many broadcasting systems, as opposed to the one-to-many systems, it has opened up numerous possibilities for groups of activists to freely air their views and opinions.[32] It has become a medium in which businesses, consumers and governments communicate with each other. It is, as such, unparalleled in its creation of a truly global forum which provides for the virtual existence of McLuhan's much-quoted 'global village'.[33] However, as positive a development as the Internet has been, utopian visions were quickly challenged by the proliferation of sites such as those which contain (child) pornography, violence and extremist aims.[34] That said, the Internet remains an exciting proposition as it challenges existing regimes of power and presents information and opinion in a less hierarchical way than traditional media.[35]

The attractions that the Internet holds for terrorist are manifold. It is an ideal arena for activity as it offers the advantages shown in Figure 15.1.[36]

In their approach to combat terrorist use of the Internet, governments have had to be imaginative and creative in their policy-making. An evaluation of the mechanisms introduced and their wider implications is put forward later in this chapter.

How do terrorists use the Internet?

There is a clear lack of an answer to the above question when considering modern, or rather post-September 11, terrorism, and the obvious difficulties the Internet has presented in policing terrorism. How does one identify a terrorist using a computer to further their aims, as distinct from an ordinary user? The actual identifying of a terrorist remains a perilously difficult thing to do and has been the subject of many heated debates. Consequently, a broad-brush approach is often taken by authorities, who categorise all members of particular ethnic or religious groups by the actions of a few. The dangers of 'risk-profiling' potential terrorist suspects are highlighted by Kip Viscusi and Zechauser,[37] as well as by Muhammed Abdul Bari, head of the Muslim Council of Britain, who feels the current climate of 'unease' may only 'help some people to recruit young [people] to terrorism'.[38] This is further illustrated by the shooting of Jean Charles de Menezes, who was wrongly identified as a terrorist suspect partially due to his appearance after the 7 July 2005 bombings in London.

- Easy access
- Little or no regulation/government control
- The potential for huge global audiences
- Anonymity (false identities are easy to create and use), unsecure networks open to abuse and distortion
- Speed of information flow
- Inexpensive to develop and maintain
- Multimedia possibilities (websites can combine text, graphics, films and sound, which can be downloaded by users)
- Ability to gather attention (mass media increasingly use the Internet as source for news stories)

Figure 15.1 Advantages of the Internet

Source: Amended from Weimann (2004), Knight and Ubayasiri (2002).

Terrorist websites are rife and appear in all shapes and forms. Almost all major terrorist organisations have websites; many have more than one and appear in several languages. Terrorist organisations have embraced the Internet as a vital cog in their machinery, as shown in Figure 15.2.[39]

Although the use of the Internet as a tool may be new, terrorist groups have always sought to spread propaganda by whatever means possible. The appeal of the Internet is that it goes beyond the means of traditional media and 'allow[s] for completeness of storytelling'.[40] It means that the terrorists can now bypass media controls and edit their own news agendas; one should consider the potential of social-networking sites such as Facebook and the group possibilities that exist here.

One of the earliest known postings by terrorists was back in March 1996 when the 'Terrorist's Handbook' was placed online. The handbook contained guidelines on how to make a bomb – the same type of bomb as was later used in the Oklahoma bombings.[41] With today's advances in technology, the handbook has now been supplemented by training videos which can be uploaded onto video-hosting sites. An obvious candidate here would be sites such as YouTube; however, these sites are regularly monitiored. In an interview with a web analyst[42] it was revealed to me that terrorists prefer to use 'unmonitored' porn sites such as Red Tube, where videos are hidden away in the annals of the back catalogue.

Another example of how terrorists use the Web aside from creating websites is by registering blogs. 'Blogging', as it is commonly referred to, offers terrorists the potential to air their views and present information is an unedited way, while at the same time allowing others to voice their support by joining in discussions held in the forum. It would appear that all viewpoints are available and given equal space and prominence; however, the owner of the blog can decide whose viewpoints he/she wishes to publish, hence there is a form of editorial control in the hands of the terrorist blogger. The examples of the French bloggers arrested on suspicion of inciting violence given earlier in this chapter[43] and the proposed €70 million expenditure of the British government 'to undermine extremist influences' in 'ungoverned' online spaces illustrate how seriously the authorities take this potential threat.[44]

It is further argued by Weimann[45] that terrorists seek to use the Internet to maintain their 'psychological warfare'. Their websites will not only re-enact past actions, but also present more general threats aimed at illustrating to the public the potential of their reach (i.e. disabling air traffic, destroying networks, etc.). An example of this was the airing of the murder of the American hostage Daniel Pearl in 2004, which was issued on several terrorist websites. Groups can also spread disinformation, which exaggerates the scope of their potential attacks and can generate cyberfear. Al Qaeda has been particularly successful at this, continually talking of the impending attack on

- Transmit propaganda on their aims and objectives
- Raise money by selling articles, merchandise or asking for donations
- Attract new members
- Communicate with existing activists

Figure 15.2 Why terrorists use the Internet

the United States, which has kept the nation on high alert since September 11 2001. Moreover, many terrorist organisations have created their own newsgroups to counter the power of traditional journalists.[46]

Al Qaeda has proven to be an excellent example of how a terrorist group can utilise the Internet. According to Knight and Ubaysiri,[47] the structure of this organisation is in many ways parallel to the Internet, which affords limitless possibilities for it. They are listed in Figure 15.3.

Consequently, we can say that Al Qaeda is 'simultaneously everywhere and nowhere'.[48] National governments often complain of the lack of wherewithal to control the Net due to its borderless, translucent world; the United States government has found it tough to eliminate and negate the threat Al Qaeda poses.

Mechanisms of government control

Thus far this chapter has only really examined the measures that terrorists take in using the Internet. It has also looked at the weakness that governments feel they have in their arsenal in being able to deal adequately with the potential threats. However, the picture of a meek, mild and limited executive does not really fit the mould. The somewhat considerable powers that government have are considered in this section and I challenge the notion the Internet is a wilderness beyond control.

Internet regulation and governance

One of the greatest myths of the Internet age is that there is no control over the Internet whatsoever. Sunstein argues that mechanisms exist to monitor and regulate the Internet: '[it] is hardly an anarchy or regulation free'.[49] The Internet Corporation for Assigned Names and Numbers (ICANN), based in California, has long since been the main body which has regulated how Internet domain names and addressing systems function, as well as managing how email and Net browsers direct their traffic. It was established in 1998.[50] ICANN has a direct link to the United States government.[51]

It is this very issue – the United States' relationship with ICANN – which formed the basis of heated debate during the World Summit on the Information Society (WSIS) held in Tunis in November 2005. Nations such as Brazil, China, France, Iran and South Africa wanted a more neutral body to be created under UN auspices to oversee the Net,[52] while others, such as the Internet think tank group the Internet Governance Project (IGP), wanted greater reforms of ICANN's powers and a democratisation of its structure.[53]

- Is transitional
- Lacks a geographic centre
- Consists of disparate nodes or activist cells
- Relies on software of ideas, rather than hardware of the military (e.g. aeroplanes as bombs)

Figure 15.3 Analogies between Al Qaeda and the Internet

A concept paper prepared by IGP identified the main criticisms of ICANN to be:[54]

- the unilateralism of the United States government in its control and supervision of ICANN;
- dissatisfaction with ICANN's Government Advisory Committee (GAC), where governments have only advisory powers;
- that ICANN does not reflect the needs and interests of developing countries in balance to those of developed countries;
- the general feeling that ICANN lacks legitimacy.

This concept paper was mooted during WSIS in attempt to create an agreement which would see the development of an internationally and legally recognised body to replace supervision by the US government with a more multi-lateral body similar to the International Telecommunications Union, which was founded in 1865.[55] It was further suggested that ICANN, while being central to Internet governance, does not meet all of the challenges that are faced, and indeed lacks transparency, account-aliblity and legitimacy itself. These ideas were substantiated by the Working Group on Internet Governance (WGIG), which last met in June 2005, and presented four models for Internet governance.[56]

However, despite these pressures for reform of ICANN, the outcome of WSIS resulted in little change to the current situation. ICANN remains in the hands of the United States, although an agreement was reached to set up an Internet Governance Forum (IGF) under the guidance of the United Nations Secretary General.[57] Kawamoto argues that a body that satisfactorily regulates the Internet should be created. Kawamoto points to the role of the UN as being a key international body in the past when looking to form a global consensus; these experiences should not be lost and the UN should have a major role in his opinion.[58] The IGF has a tough task ahead of it.

In addition to the ICANN provisions, however, there are other ways in which the Internet is regulated. The Security Intelligence Products and Systems (SIPS) framework has been in operation since 1995. It forms part of the British-based mi2g Intelligence unit and boasts 'the world's largest digital attack database'.[59] SIPS contains information on all major hacking groups and Internet malware attackers (sabateurs) and has relationships with virtually all global actors in order to maintain a peerless status in holding confidential information with regard to digital risk.[60]

A secondary wing of the above-mentioned intelligence unit is the Asymmetric Threats Contingency Alliance (ATCA), which was initiated post-September 11. ATCA monitors activity throughout the world, focusing on terrorist and organised crime cartels. ATCA draws up a thorough database of potential threat by compiling monthly reports on posting of information gathered through monitoring of terrorist groups, websites and intercepted communications of terrorist organisations. However, a fundamental criticism of ATCA is that it continually infringes civil liberties and confuses protest with terrorist activity.

Control of Internet users

As important as it is that cyberspace is regulated, it it is also of equal importance to monitor the users that surf the World Wide Web. A simple reason for this is highlighted by the fact that the September 11 hijackers booked at least nine of their airline tickets online a few weeks prior to the attacks.[61] It is further suggested that the hijackers set up a number of 'largely anonymous . . . temporary [email] accounts',[62] such as Hotmail accounts, and accessed the Web from public places such as libraries. Notably, these are all actions which are perfectly legal. Had the tickets been booked in the conventional way with a travel agency, would we now want to control travel agencies' services more stringently?

In order to combat this element of Web abuse, authorities are beginning to introduce a number of new measures. One such example is in Italy, where anti-terror laws affect how people can access the Internet in public places. Celeste[63] suggests that these new laws are part of the most extensive anti-terror packages introduced in Europe. While encompassing more than Internet use, these laws now require people who wish to use the Internet in public places such as libraries or Internet cafés to submit a photocopy of their passport before being allowed to log on. Moreover, Internet cafés have to obtain public communications business licences and install expensive tracking software, or so-called 'eavesdropping technology',[64] costing up to US$1,400.[65]

Additionally, the European Union introduced a directive which will allow police authories to access users 'traffic data'.[66] The directive, which was introduced in every member state of the European Union by the deadline of July 2007, compels every telephone company and Internet service provider (ISP) to save call and Internet records for up to two years. The ISP data is comprehensive and includes websites visited and header information of email correspondence detailing the sender, recipient, date, time and Internet address.[67] Whereas law enforcement agencies welcomed the new legislation, privacy advocates fear for the wider implications. The prospect Gibb presents of our communication tools forming part of the largest surveillance system ever created in the near future surely is enough reason to worry.[68]

One could ask whether these restrictions are enough when we once more analyse the use of technology by terrorists in reality. As reported by Spanish media following investigations into the 11 March 2003 train attacks by Al Qaeda in Madrid, it was found that in order to not have their messages intercepted on Hotmail, the terrorists merely amended their use of the free email service. Current legislation allows authorities to monitor inboxes and no more. The Madrid attackers simply used one email account which was accessed by all and stored messages in the 'drafts' folder of the account. Once more, legislation seems to be one step behind.

Do governments pose a threat to cyberfreedom?

Government controls and their ensuing implications for society have left spectators lamenting the abuses of privacy and freedoms that governments can now legitimately undertake under the guise of protecting their citizens. Indeed, as noted by the Geneva-based NGO International Commission of Jurists, many governments have used the anti-terror drive as an excuse to curb freedoms and limit the use of domestic opponents on the Internet – a charge levelled most acutely at the US and UK executives.[69] These initiatives, which have introduced surveillance and removed the protection of privacy, may threaten the healthy existence of democracy.[70] The benefits of E-Government in making society more open and democratic may be undone by E-Policing and E-Control.

The dynamics at play here bring together the divergent needs of government and society. On the one hand, as mentioned earlier, the Internet has enabled society to freely express its opinions at a global level. Borders have been in some cases rendered irrelevant. On the other hand, as positive an element for society as this may have been, it has also triggered a need for governments to adjust antiquated laws and regulations, which the existence of the Internet has challenged. For example, it is illegal to own a copy of Adolf Hitler's *Mein Kampf* in Germany. In the pre-Internet world this was a simple policy to implement and maintain, as the book was not available. However, in the new Amazon.com age it was easy to order a copy of the book online without the authorities ever knowing about it. A law change was needed.

Post-September 11 the world seemed to legitimise the opportunity for governments to make these changes due to the large-scale public fear that was generated by the media for potential terrorist threats, although the actual desire to adjust laws pre-dated September 11 – indeed, the British government has been interested in the idea of data retention since 1998,[71] as has the German government.[72] However, as Loundy suggested before September 11 2001, the Internet must not be made a scapegoat ahead of other methods of communications, despite concerns over its mis-use being 'legitimate'.[73] If there are concerns that terrorists communicate using email, why are there no such concerns that they may communicate using regular mail? It is this question which guardians of Internet privacy ask in retort to the clampdown and ultra-secure era that is dawning in the cyberworld. Indeed, as noted by Loader, the Internet has presented a 'paradigmatic change in the constellation of power relations'[74] between governments and individuals. This is perfectly illustrated by Williams, who argues that post-September 11, the Internet became an invaluable source for 'neutral' information as the traditional media was seen as the mouthpiece of the US government.[75]

However, the opportunities to harness the new cyberworld were only fully grasped by governments post-September 11. The fear of terrorism, in all its forms, has heightened since September 11, becoming part of our daily political diet and thus becoming the '*raison d'être* for countless examples of political excess'.[76] Cynics have argued that there has been an over-emphasis of the threats faced so that the public would accept a diminishing of rights without a public outcry – although, as Sunstein argues, free society has always known some form of regulation.[77]

Legislation passed in the United States, Britain, France, Germany, Spain, Italy and Denmark, tied in with policy from the European Union, the Council of Europe and the G8, has limited cyber freedoms in some way.[78] The danger of many of these law changes is that not only do they challenge personal freedoms, but they also risk turning ISPs and telecommunication companies into a potential arm of the police. The upshot is that governments seem to be willing to exact 'a high price in terms of liberties to the high toll of terrorism'.[79] Many well-meaning initiatives have fallen 'far short'[80] of promises made and have created new problems of limiting freedom and augmenting the unaccountability of government and corporations.

The risk is that society has accepted changes without much debate, whereas had changes been introduced to control more traditional media and methods of communication, discussion would have been rife.[81] The need for a legitimate form of developing E-Identities has never been greater. As presented by Fishenden,[82] the need for E-Identities to monitor online government services and online commerce now encompasses online security.

Can the ordinary citizen do more?

As illustrated above, governments across the world have been keen to introduce restrictions in order to protect the citizenry from the terrorist potential. However, these restrictions, though accepted without discussion at their inception, have been rounded on as curbing our natural freedoms. Nevertheless, the threat exists and something needs to be done. However, perhaps there is something that we, as ordinary citizens, can do to limit the possibilities that terrorists have of using the Internet to meet their needs.

A first and very simple step is to limit the visibility of our own digital equipment. Many of us enjoy simple, easy access to the Internet through our domestic wi-fi environment; however, we extend this courtesy to all and sundry when we do not secure our networks. As mentioned earlier, the potential terrorist thrives on anonymity and an unsecured network allows them to have access to an ISP which cannot be traced back to them – better still, it can be traced to an unsuspecting innocent citizen caught in the crossfire. This is, incidentally, also true for the Bluetooth facility on mobile devices, which, as factory default, come as 'visible to all' and should be set to 'password protected'.

We can also make sure our information is safe by making sure our access to the Internet is safe too. Increasingly, as illustrated by other chapters in this volume, we turn to the online world for our interaction with government (i.e. for taxes, health, education, etc.). By filling in an online form for a tax return, for example, we send out vital information about ourselves which can be adopted and used to criminal, and potentially terrorist, use. So-called 'bloggers' wait to prey on any lapse of security in order to gain personal information which they can sell on to the highest bidder.[83] The problem is so rife that the British Information Commissioner's Office published a 'Personal Information Tool-Kit' in January 2007. Unfortunately, two years after its publication the success of this leaflet was not as widespread as the leaking of personal information or indeed the 'cybercrime tool kits' which can be easily purchased.[84]

In short, the citizen can never safeguard everything; we will always need government protection too, but by being aware of our actions and their implications we can begin to remove some of the threat to our online security that we face. We must also apply common sense when we interact over the Internet. We would never post money in an unsealed envelope through regular post, so why transact over unsecure Internet sites? Public complacency sits oddly with public paranoia.[85]

Conclusions

We have reached an important juncture in the so-called 'zeitgeist' of cyberterrorism. Governments have acted and their policy-making counteracts the growing prospective threats of cyberterror, but terrorists continue to seek a safe haven in the dark corners of cyberspace to advance their campaigns based on creating fear and panic.

However, as Matai notes, 'physical terrorism and digital attacks go hand in hand',[86] thus the potential of cyberterror should not be overestimated and exaggerated, which has been the case with politicians 'using fear of terror'.[87] Terrorists will continue to use violence to overcome their 'invisibility'.[88] However, the use of the Internet by terrorists is a far more alarming prospect and one which is tougher to combat. It is here that a delicate balance needs to be addressed. On the one hand, restrictions need to be tough enough to serve as an adequate deterrent, but on the other hand, they need to maintain the existing freedoms and allow cyber society to develop. Mechanisms to monitor public Internet access points, as in Italy, can work. However, they should not burden the host (i.e. Internet café) to the extent that the host is impeded by the requirement for financial capital needed to meet modern regulations, as this may only lead to closure of much-needed public access points, which help address the issue of the digital divide.[89]

In our fight against modern terrorism and its role in cyberspace, a few things must be noted. The War on Terror has not been a watershed, it has been an excuse. The threat existed before September 11, and nothing since this date has heightened its potential as a threat. However, events since this date have legitimised government attempts to implement restrictive legislation which they have wanted to introduce for some time now (see the above-mentioned examples of the UK and Germany). The simple fact remains that we (both government and citizen alike) need to better monitor how the Internet is used and limit its capacity to be abused by Internet-savvy terrorists. However, heavy-handed restrictions will only hand the initiative to authoritarian governments that may violate privacy, curb the free flow of information and hamper freedom of expression – ironically, the very core values of the society we are claiming to be trying to protect. Moreover, it will enable undemocratic regimes to refer to our own counter-terror mechanisms as examples to justify their own abusive practices. As noted by Moore,[90] the relationship between democracy and cyberspace is a complex, multi-dimensional one, and we must all engage in nurturing it.

Key points

- Governments have readily highlighted that terrorists have been quick to utilise the potential that the cyberworld has to offer them to deliver their messages, communicate with each other and retain their anonymity.
- Terrorist groups have embraced the Internet and have challenged the existing balances on information flow and news coverage. The Internet has shifted editorial control to activists. This allows them to present news and opinion as they like.

- Terrorist use of the Internet is very vibrant. Websites appear, change format and disappear or simply change their addresses.
- Mechanisms do exist to monitor and regulate the Internet – '[it] is hardly an anarchy or regulation free'. Such mechanisms include ICANN, SIPS and ACTA. There are also numerous national surveillance tools used the world over.
- In order to combat this element of Web abuse, authorities are beginning to introduce a number of new measures. For example, eavesdropping technology is used in public access points and the European Union introduced a directive which will allow police authories to access users' traffic data, which compels every telephone company and Internet service provider (ISP) to save call and Internet records for up to two years.
- Government controls and their ensuing implications for society have left spectators lamenting the abuses of privacy and freedoms that governments can now legitimately undertake under the guise of protecting their citizens.
- Citizens can limit the visibility of their own digital environment. They can also make sure their information is safe by making sure their access to the Internet is safe too. Common sense must be applied when interacting over the Internet.
- The simple fact remains that we (both government and citizen alike) need to better monitor how the Internet is used and limit its capacity to be abused by Internet-savvy terrorists.

Notes

1 BBC Newsonline (2009) 'Obama Begins Cybersecurity Review', *BBC News*, 10 February, http://news.bbc.co.uk/go/pr/fr/-/hi/technology/7880695.stm.
2 Buckler, S. and Dolowitz, D. (2005) *Politics on the Internet*. Abingdon: Routledge.
3 Knight, A. and Ubayasiri, K. (2002a) 'eTerror: Journalism and the Internet', *Ejournalism* 2/1, http://www.ejournalism.au.com/ejournalist_v2n1.htm.
4 Scott, A. and Street, J. (2001) 'From Media Politics to E-Protest?', in *Culture and Politics in the Information Age*, Webster, F. (ed.) London: Routledge. pp. 32–51.
5 Bradbury, D. (2009) 'The Fog of Cyberwar', *Guardian*, 5 Februray.
6 Cukier, K. N. (2005) 'Who Will Control the Internet? Washington Battles the World', *Foreign Affairs* 84/6 November/December: 7–13.
7 Segoviano Monterrubio, S. (2005) 'Al Qaeda en la Red', *Papeles de Cuestiones Internacionales* 89, Primavera.
8 Matai, D. K. (2005) *Cyberland Security: Organized Crime, Terrorism and the Internet*. Oxford Internet Institute, University of Oxford, 10 February.
9 BBC Newsonline (2009) 'Obama Begins Cybersecurity Review', *BBC News*, 10 February, http://news.bbc.co.uk/go/pr/fr/-/hi/technology/7880695.stm.
10 Bradbury, D. (2009) 'The Fog of Cyberwar', *Guardian*, 5 February.
11 Conway, M. (2002) 'Reality Bites: Cyberterrorism and Terrorist 'use' of the Internet', *First Monday* 7/11 (November), http://firstmonday.org/issues/issue7_11/conway/index/html.
12 Painter, A. (2001) 'The Contagious Campaign (part 2)', in *Viral Politics*, Painter, A. and Wardle, B. (eds) London: Politicos Publishing. pp. 154–167.
13 Denning, D. quoted in Conway, M. (2002) 'Reality Bites'.

14 Denning, D. quoted in Conway, M. (2002) 'Reality Bites', p. 6.
15 BBC Newsonline (2005) 'Spammer Convicted of £1.6m Scam', *BBC News*, 16 November, http://news.bbc.co.uk/go/pr/fr/-/1/hi/england/cambridgeshire/4442772.stm.
16 Conway, M. (2002) *Reality Bites*; Weimann, G. (2004) *www.terror.net: How Modern Terrorism Uses the Internet*, United States Institute of Peace Special Report 116, March 2004, www.usip.org.
17 Rosenkrands, J. (2004) 'Politicizing Homo economicus' in *Cyberprotest – New Media, Citizens and Social Movements*, van de Donk, W., Loader, B.D., Nixon, P.G. and Rucht, D. (eds) London: Routledge. pp. 57–76.
18 Plunkett, J. (2005) 'French Bloggers Held after Paris Riots', Guardian Unlimited Special Reports, November, http://www.guardian.co.uk/story/0,11882,1638520,00html.
19 Weimann, G. (2004) *www.terror.net*.
20 Louw, E. (2005) *The Media and Political Process*. London: Sage Publications.
21 Conway, M. (2002) *Reality Bites*.
22 Lanzone, R. (2005) *Cyberjihad*. Indiana: AuthorHouse.
23 Weimann, G. (2004) *www.terror.net*.
24 Webster, F. (2001) 'A New Politics?', in *Culture and Politics in the Information Age*, Webster, F. (ed.) London: Routledge. pp. 1–13.
25 Knight, A. and Ubayasiri, K. (2002b) 'Reporting On Line: The Internet and Terrorism', *ON LINE opinion – Australia's e-journal of social and political debate*, http://onlineopinion. com.au/view.asp?article=1101.
26 Scott, A. and Street, J. (2001) 'From Media Politics to E-Protest?'
27 Weimann, G. (2004) *www.terror.net*.
28 Dahlgren, P. (2001) 'The Transformation of Democracy?', in *New Media and Politics*, Axford, B. and Huggins, R. (eds) London: Sage Publications. pp. 64–88.
29 Weimann, G. (2004) *www.terror.net*.
30 Ibid.
31 Conway, M. (2002) 'Reality Bites'.
32 Dahlgren, P. (2001) 'The Transformation of Democracy?'
33 McLuhan, M. (1964, 2002) *Understanding Media: The Extensions of Man*. London: Routledge.
34 Weimann, G. (2004) *www.terror.net*.
35 Stevenson, N. (2001) 'The future of public media cultures', in *Culture and Politics in the Information Age*, Webster, F. (ed.) London: Routledge. pp. 63–80.
36 Weimann, G. (2004) *www.terror.net*; Knight, A. and Ubayasiri, K. (2002b) 'Reporting On Line: The Internet and Terrorism'.
37 Kip Viscusi, W. and Zechauser, R. Z. (2003) *Sacrificing Civil Liberties to Reduce Terrorism Risks*, John F. Kennedy School of Government, Harvard University Faculty Research Working Paper RWP03-017.
38 BBC Newsonline (2007) 'UK Terror Tactics create unease', *BBC News*, 10 Novermber, http://news.bbc.co.uk/go/pr/fr/-/hi/uk/7088325.stm.
39 For an elaborative review of terrorist websites and their aims and objectives please refer to Conway 2002, Knight and Ubaysiri 2002a, Weimann 2004.
40 Kawamoto, K. (2003) *Media and Society in the Digital Age*. Boston: Allyn and Bacon.
41 Sunstein, C. (2002) *Republic.com*. Princeton, NJ: Princeton University Press.
42 The web analyst prefers to remain anonymous.
43 Plunkett, J. (2005) 'French Bloggers Held after Paris Riots'.
44 BBC Newsonline (2007) 'Internet Used to Target Extremism', *BBC News*, 31 October, http://news.bbc.co.uk/go/pr/fr/-/hi/uk/7070416.stm.
45 Weimann, G. (2004) *www.terror.net*.
46 Knight, A. and Ubayasiri, K. (2002b) 'Reporting On Line: The Internet and Terrorism'.
47 Ibid.
48 Ibid.
49 Sunstein, C. (2002) *Republic.com*.
50 Internet Corporation for Assigned Names and Numbers (ICANN) (2004) *Fact Sheet*, http://www.icann.org/general/fact-sheet.html.

51 BBC Newsonline (2005) 'US Retains Hold of the Internet', *BBC News*, 16 Novermber, http://news.bbc.co.uk/go/pr/fr/-/hi/technology/44441544.stm.
52 Cukier, K. N. (2005) 'Who Will Control the Internet? Washington Battles the World', BBC Newsonline 'US Retains Hold of the Internet', *BBC News*, 16 Novermber, http://news.bbc.co.uk/go/pr/fr/-/hi/technology/44441544.stm.
53 Klein, H. and Müller, M. (2005) *What to Do about ICANN: A Proposal for Structural Reform*, A Concept Paper by the Internet Goverance Project, 5 April, http://www.Internet Governance.org; Working Group on Internet Governance (WGIG) (2005), Château de Bossey, June, http://www.wgig.org/; Drake, W. J. (2005) *Reforming Internet Governance: Perspectives from WGIG*, ICT Task Force Series 12, Working Group on Internet Governace (WGIG).
54 Klein, H. and Müller, M. (2005) *What to Do about ICANN: A Proposal for Structural Reform.*
55 Cukier, K. N. (2005) 'Who Will Control the Internet? Washington Battles the World'.
56 Reporters Without Borders (2002) *Anti-terrorism Drive Threatens Internet Freedoms*, www.Think Centre.org, 12 September, http://www.thinkcentre.org/article.cfm?ArticleID=1724.
57 BBC Newsonline, 'US Retains Hold of the Internet'; World Summit on the Information Society (WSIS) (2005) *Tunis Agenda for the Information Society*, Document: WSIS-05/TUNIS/DOC/6(Rev.1)-E, http://www.itu.int/wsis/docs2/tunis/off/6rev1.pdf.
58 Kawamoto, K. (2003) *Media and Society in the Digital Age.*
59 Matai, D. K. *Cyberland Security: Organised Crime, Terrorism and the Internet.* p. 1.
60 Ibid. p. 2.
61 Conway, M. (2002) 'Reality Bites' p. 11.
62 Ibid.
63 Celeste, S. (2005) 'Want to Check Your E-Mail in Italy? Bring Your Passport', *The Christian Science Monitor*, October, 4 http://www.csimonitor.com/2005/1004/p07s01-woeu. html.
64 Gibb, J. (2005) *Who's Watching You?* New York: Conspiracy Books.
65 Celeste, S. (2005) 'Want to Check Your E-Mail in Italy? Bring Your Passport'.
66 Grossman, W. M. (2006) 'Will Logging Your Email Combat Terrorism in Europe?', *Guardian Unlimited Technology Section*, January, http://technology.guardian.co.uk/weekly/story/0,16376,1683944,00.html.
67 Ibid.
68 Gibb, J. (2005) *Who's Watching You?*
69 BBC Newsonline (2009) 'Anti-terror Tactics Weaken Law', *BBC News*, 16 February, http://news.bbc.co.uk/go/pr/fr/-/hi/world/europe/7892387.stm.
70 Raab, C. D. (1997) 'Privacy, Democracy, Information', in *The Governance of Cyberspace*, Loader, B. D. (ed.) London: Routledge. pp. 155–174.
71 Grossman, W. M. (2006) 'Will Logging Your Email Combat Terrorism in Europe?'
72 Gibb, J. (2005) *Who's Watching You?*
73 Loundy, D. (1995) 'Constitution Protects All Modes of Speech', *Chicago Daily Law Bulletin*, 11 May, accessed http://www.loundy.com/CDLB/Terrorism.html.
74 Loader, B. D. (1997) 'The Governance of Cyberspace', in *The Governance of Cyberspace*, Loader, B. D. (ed.) London: Routledge. pp. 1–19.
75 Williams, B. A. (2003) 'The New Media Environment, Internet Chatrooms and Public Discourse after 9/11' in *War and the Media*, Thussu, D. T. and Freedman, D. (eds) London: Sage Publications. pp. 176–189.
76 Gibb, J. (2005) *Who's Watching You?* p. 20.
77 Sunstein, C. (2002) *Republic.com.*
78 Reporters Without Borders (2002) *Anti-terrorism Drive Threatens Internet Freedoms.*
79 Weimann, G. (2004) *www.terror.net.* p. 12.
80 Lyon, D. (2004) *Surveillance after September 11.* Cambridge: Polity Press.
81 Loundy, D. (1995) 'Constitution Protects All Modes of Speech'; Celeste, S. (2005) 'Want to Check Your E-Mail in Italy? Bring Your Passport'; Reporters Without Borders (2002) *Anti-terrorism Drive Threatens Internet Freedoms.*

82 Fishenden, J. (2005) 'eID: Identity Management in an Online World', in *Proceedings of the 5th European Conference on E-Government*, Remenyi, D. (ed.) University of Antwerp, June 2005.

83 BBC Panorama (2008) 'You Can Run . . . but Can You Hide?' *BBC News*, 24 October, http://news.bbc.co.uk/go/pr/fr/-/hi/programmes/panorama/7685043.stm.

84 BBC Newsonline (2007) 'Cyber Crime Tool Kits Go on Sale', *BBC News*, 4 September, http://news.bbc.co.uk/go/pr/fr/-/hi/technology/6976308.stm.

85 Economist (2008) 'Identity Parade', published in *The Electronic Bureaucrat: A Special Report*, *The Economist*, 16 February.

86 Matai, D. K. *Cyberland Security: Organised Crime, Terrorism and the Internet.* p. 3.

87 BBC Newsonline (2009) '"Ministers 'Using Fear of Terror"', *BBC News*, 17 February, http://news.bbc.co.uk/go/pr/fr/-/hi/uk/7893890.stm.

88 Louw, E. (2005) *The Media and Political Process.*

89 Nixon, P. G. and Rawal, R. (2005) 'From e-Gov to we-Gov: Social Inclusion, Government and ICTs', in *Proceedings of the 5th European Conference on E-Government*, Remenyi, D. (ed.) University of Antwerp, June 2005.

90 Moore, R. K. (1999) 'Democracy and Cyberspace', in *Digital Democracy*, Hague, B. N. and Loader, B. D. (eds) London: Routledge. pp. 39–59.

Further reading

Dahlgren, P. (2001) 'The Transformation of Democracy?', in *New Media and Politics*, Axford, B. and Huggins, R. (eds) London: Sage Publications. pp. 64–88.

Gibb, J. (2005) *Who's Watching You?* New York: Conspiracy Books.

Weimann, G. (2004) *www.terror.net How Modern Terrorism Uses the Internet*, United States Institute of Peace Special Report 116, March, www.usip.org.

16 Ministry of Truth?
Perceptions of trust in E-Government

Paul G. Nixon

Summary

This chapter examines the links between trust and perceptions of ICTs and E-Government and how they may be affected by media coverage. The introduction of E-Government has often been heralded as the beginning of a bright new future, modernising government and its interactions with citizens. However, the very nature of most E-Government processes and procedures means that they do not always entail a harmonious and happy user interface. Facilitation of communication channels has little impact upon the quality of information provided.

Experiences of E-Government are not often shared and pooled in quite the same way that traditional experiences of government traditionally have been. Indeed, as many people are still to experience services and processes, particularly as newer interfaces are rolled out, often their first story of E-Government and governmental use of ICTs is that reported in the media. The press, particularly, though not exclusively, in the UK, tend to feed on bad news in their role as an organ to hold the government to account for their actions. The media thus present such stories with a higher profile than ones which reveal success. Indeed, one might argue that the relative lack of stories on E-Government is a silent testimony to its success. However, it could be argued that the nature of spectacular failures that are reported impinges upon the overall perceptions of the average citizen.

Introduction

This chapter examines the notion of trust with regard to citizen perception of E-Government. It draws upon some pilot interviews held in October 2008. Those pilot interviews were held to clarify issues and problems and to obtain a certain insight into the methodological minefields awaiting researchers in the subject area. One of the hypotheses seemingly warranting further explanation is whether the levels of citizen trust in E-Government are affected by media reporting on E-Government-related issues and, if so, to what extent. Does the publishing of articles that are critical of existing E-Government measures, which have negative and derogatory headlines such as 'Not fit for purpose: €2bn cost of government's IT blunders',[1] have a detrimental effect on public confidence that spreads throughout their relationships with government, but particularly in relation to online, E-Government-related activities? We return to this notion later in this chapter.

The E-Government narrative is, at first glance, seemingly awesome and seductively attractive. Sparkling and oh so modern, it should entrance people with its apparent advantages. Just as motherhood and apple pie were icons of a softer age, E-Gov, with its heady mix of youthful swagger and the sheen of modernity, catches the zeitgeist of contemporary society. It seems a no-brainer that people should be enthralled by its potential. The emergence and adoption of information and communication technologies (ICTs) into society in general is seen to have re-shaped the way we live our lives in every conceivable area. ICTs are often credited as aiding wealth creation and growth, stimulating intellectual development and re-defining our leisure and lifestyle. They create the potential for a revised 'Brave New World' of technologically aided, self-actualising human development. The development of the computer and its morphing from a large-scale, room-filling box into a miniaturised domestic appliance and, more recently, into a fully portable device coupled with the advent of the Internet, email and other opportunities facilitating Web-based services, has created a potential vision of government that 30 years ago was in the sole domain of science fiction writers. That said, we should remember that ICTs in government are not new; they have been in use for over 50 years.[2] While early use was largely down to mainframe computer usage, the later diffusion of personal computers enabled ICTs to be used by many or all government officials,[3] opening the way for the development of E-Government as we know it today.

This advance has been so rapid that, for those not at the cutting edge of technology, there is a danger of being left behind. Those without access to information – the information poor – can be excluded by a move towards a system of government operationalisation that may require a level of skills that some have yet to acquire. McNeal and Hale[4] identify in their research that while barriers such as motivation, limited access and lack of skills may be hindering citizen engagement via E-Government communication channels, there is also emerging evidence that 'e-government appears to be a double-edged sword, motivating citizen initiated contact of government for some (young and women) while magnifying existing gaps based on other factors'. When mentioning skills, they are talking not just of those who lack the technological skills to access E-Government services and are thus discouraged from engaging in online participation, but of more basic skills that may be lacking, such as general literacy or language skills. While their data is US-focused, it might not be too far a leap to suggest that similar problems could exist in Europe, particularly in areas of high ethnic minority density and also in those countries which are experiencing high levels of movement with the EU 27.

As Onora O'Neill said in her 2002 Reith lecture,

> Confucius told his disciple Tsze-kung that three things are needed for government: weapons, food and trust. If a ruler can't hold on to all three, he should give up the weapons first and the food next. Trust should be guarded to the end: 'without trust we cannot stand'.[5]

It is important that any E-Government system be inclusive if it is to win trust and acceptance from its citizens. Involving a range of stakeholders in the design and monitoring of E-Government is a prerequisite to success but not, one must stress, a guarantor. The most important conceptual leap that we need to make is that ICT use can in some sense shape our lives, but it is us as people – primarily, though by no means exclusively, via our elected representatives, the politicians – who need to understand and plan such changes in a way that is focused not solely on ICT-based solutions, but on people's needs. Kolsaker and Lee-Kelley[6] argue that we need to move toward a much more citizen-centric, value-oriented approach to E-Government development. Of course, as Bertot and Jaeger[7] note, producing citizen-centred E-Government implies that the government knows what users want. It then follows that users should drive or be significant contributors, through a meaningful consultation process, to the development process.

Along with a decline in public interest in traditional party politics, there is a feeling that government today is not what it used to be. A deep public mistrust hangs over politicians and public officials. Baldassare[8] posits the view that this is, at least in part, due to the fact that government is no longer perceived as having the answers to prevailing problems. Norris[9] confirms the rise of a more critical citizenry. In a sense, Baldassare is arguing that the 'tin man' of government has been found out by an increasingly educated and sceptical public. Certainly Tolbert and Mossberger[10] show how trust can be affected by events or policies, or presumably by the lack of them in certain situations, and that trust is indeed necessary for the stability of a political system.

The perception of government can often differ from the reality. As Rainey,[11] cited in Welch *et al.*,[12] observed, the public do not have perfect information and may be biased in their analysis of government performance; thus their perception of governmental activities may not be a fair or accurate one, but it is one they hold and no doubt propagate nonetheless. Shapiro[13] argues that expectations of information availability and dissemination have changed as an information culture has developed; citizens expect, and increasingly demand, access to information that may have previously been the (almost) sole domain of public officials. This, of course, can lead to issues of contestation. As Türksel[14] demonstrates, surveys show that there are sometimes differences of perception on E-Government issues between decision makers and stakeholders.

Mansbridge[15] describes how citizens' expectations of governments have risen and to some extent citizens view governments as having an almost infallible nature. Al-Omari and Al-Omari[16] argue that 'Governments can create trust . . . by convincing their customers that the same rigorous controls, which make government handling of traditional transactions trustworthy, also apply to online transactions.' However, this does seem to somewhat contradict the earlier point of Baldassare.[17]

Naturally, governments frequently, albeit understandably, fail to live up to these unreal expectations; this failure can reduce levels of citizen trust in government. E-Government, perhaps due to its technological underpinnings, can sometimes be perceived as having power, capabilities or potentialities that are hard to live up to in reality. This is the case particularly because, when push comes to shove, those systems are inherently dependent on human action and/or human design. Systems are thus subject to human fallibility and thus will not always live up to expectations, however realistic or unrealistic those expectations might be.

There would, however, seem to be a distinct schism between two (not necessarily always mutually exclusive) notions of what E-Government could, and/or perhaps should, be about. On the one hand, you have the notion of the Internet being used within E-Government as an information exchange, most normally top-down but also requesting or, for example, in the case of tax returns, demanding information online. On the other hand, you have the notion of the Internet facilitating a different type of government–citizen relationship with increased two-way dialogue, discussion and, to some extent, in the most extreme of readings, a re-distribution of power away from government to individual citizens. Welch *et al.*[18] note that previous research suggests that 'agencies are using the communication capabilities of the internet in a selective "one-way" communication strategy and foregoing a more complex "two-way" communication strategy'. Thomas and Streib's[19] research showed that people used the government websites more as a source of information than as a locus for transactions. However, as transaction opportunities available via E-Government sites increase one can expect that the number of people transacting online will grow – although one can assume that the use of online services for information purposes will also grow as many agencies transmute much of their previous paper-based information to online availability, and increasingly online availability will be the only source of such information.

Indeed, Welch *et al.*'s[20] own research concludes that while (in this case American) citizens see E-Government as delivering reasonably well in terms of transactions and transparency, there is still no real overall level of satisfaction with the potential interactive uses of ICTs within government. One might, albeit somewhat cynically, ask whether this is so different from the offline world of government.

Those organizations which are seen to provide, through the use of ICT-enabled E-Government, two-way communications channels embodying interaction, discussion, consultation and citizen involvement in many, if not all, stages of the policy-making process may benefit from an increased perception of trust. This could be due to their apparent openness, irrespective of whether the channels are themselves being fully utilised. The fact that such channels exist and are available to facilitate citizen engagement is often viewed as being a talisman of democratic engagement, and thus can help to reinforce the building of trust.

The rhetoric around E-Government is a buoyant one.[21] However, as Bonham *et al.*[22] point out, there are still challenges to be addressed. They stress E-Government's modern characteristics and posit E-Government as a re-energising tool of transformation for modern democracies. There is, of course, an assumption that people trust their government, but, as Norris *et al.*[23] comment,

> there is widespread concern that the public has lost faith in the performance of the core institutions of representative government and it is hoped that more open and transparent government and more efficient service delivery could help restore that trust.

Evidence from the OECD[24] appears to support this view that E-Government can be a tool for renewing trust between citizens and government. E-Government is seen by many[25] as a way of re-forging the bond between citizens and governments.

The Gartner model[26] set out four phases of E-Government:

- presence: establishing a Web presence for delivering basic information;
- interaction: enabling a citizen to request forms, etc. online;
- transaction: allowing a citizen to complete tasks digitally (e.g. licence applications, etc.);
- transformation: removing or re-engineering organisational barriers so that agencies are themselves changed, or even, in some cases, cease to exist, as the focus switches from agency-centric to customer-centric solutions.

In a UN report, E-Government is credited with being 'a transformation of public sector internal and external relationships through the use of information and communication technology to promote greater accountability of the Government, increase efficiency and cost-effectiveness and create a greater constituency participation'.[27] What seems to be missing here, as Hahamis *et al.*[28] note, is any discussion on the user perception in relation to trustworthiness of E-Government solutions.

The European Union, in its E-Government Action Plan for 2010, set out the following five pillars. (However, one can already see, from reports with headlines such as 'Credit crunch hits plans for DVLA's facial recognition database',[29] that any further developments are under tighter fiscal scrutiny because of the recent downturn in economic fortunes.)

- *No citizen left behind*: eGovernment will only really make a difference if everyone can use it. The Commission will work with Member States to make sure that by 2010 all citizens, regardless of gender, age, nationality, income, or disability will have access to a wide range of technologies such as Digital TV, PCs and mobile phones.
- *Raising efficiency*: Public services concern everybody – all 470 million citizens in the EU, 20 million firms and tens of thousands of administrations. Governments account for 45% of EU GDP, which has to be paid from taxes. Under the Action Plan, the Commission and the Member States will put in place a framework for benchmarking the impact of eGovernment in order get this process on track.
- *Implementing e-Procurement*: Government procurement represents 15% of GDP or about €1.500 billion a year. The Member States have committed to achieving 100% availability and at least 50% take-up of procurement online by 2010, with an estimated annual saving of €4-0 billion. . . .
- *Safe access to services EU wide*: When citizens travel or when they move they want easy access to services. EU governments have agreed to facilitate this process by establishing secure systems for mutual recognition of national electronic identities for public administration web-sites and services. The Action Plan foresees a full implementation by 2010. . . .
- *Strengthening participation and democratic decision-making*: 65% of respondents to the Commission's public consultation on eGovernment said that eDemocracy can help reduce Europe's democratic deficit. The Action Plan proposes to support experiments in the use of ICT for more effective public participation in policy making.[30]

However, as the Austrian Presidency of the EU noted:

> We face something of a dilemma: on the one hand, there is no formal, legal basis for mandatory coordinated EU action regarding the functioning of our public administrations. Put bluntly, nothing in the EU treaties obliges our administrations to work together in the area of eGovernment, at least not directly. On the other hand, however, if we do not act in concert, we could face a potentially embarrassing irony: that we erect electronic barriers to the exercise of those EU-wide freedoms of movement because of an exclusively national focus of our e-Government strategies, and this, precisely in the one domain – Cyberspace – that knows no natural borders![31]

European Information, Communications and Consumer Electronics (EICTA), which brings together the views of the European digital technology industry, also recognises the vital nature of trust in citizen–government relationships, whether on- or offline. As a consequence of this, in a report responding to the EU's i2010 proposals, they put forward the following four guidelines for building trust and acceptance (in E-Government) for citizens and business:

- Demonstrate that eGovernment solutions bring real benefits to citizens and business, ensuring inclusion of all citizens and improving their quality of life;
- Provide trust in eGovernment solutions, focusing on concerns over accessibility, relevance, effectiveness and respect for privacy;
- Seek public–private partnerships, from planning to implementation of the e-Government action plan; and
- Demonstrate that eGovernment contributes to increased citizen safety & security in Europe.[32]

Clift[33] put trust and accountability at the top of his list of seven goals 'to connect to e-government efforts and practices'. The other six are legitimacy and understanding; citizen satisfaction and service; reach and equitable access; effective representation and decision making; participation through input and consultation; and engagement and deliberation. But Clift's[34] vision of an E-Democracy requires many things, not least of which is a working two-way system of E-Government, which seems to be missing in many, if not most, E-Government scenarios on offer to citizens today. Why should this be? What are the barriers holding back on the move towards a more interactive form of E-Government? If we address the question of why the two-way potential of E-Government is yet to be, we can see the following:

- The technology is in, in historic terms, its early stages of development. One might foresee a greater use of the technology as it becomes more diffused and also easier to use.
- Present government organisations are not structured to deal with high levels of interactivity. While there is evidence of organisational restructuring that can be attributed to e-Governance and associated informatisation of the public sector, those changes appear to be incremental in their nature. Aldrich *et al.*[35] noted that

government systems are developed individually per department and thus lack the integration that might enable a more effective use of E-Government services. One can find little or no evidence of a root and branch restructuring of governance, but that is not to say that it might not take place in the future – although one cannot, as noted below, see a pressing desire for it from either the governed or those who govern.

- There is an element of institutional and bureaucratic control that is guarded by professionals and officials. Chou *et al.*[36] argue that the collective actions of public officials do have an impact on the development of E-Government efficiency.
- Keeping citizens at arm's length enables officials to, at least in part, determine how they work, on what they work and when they work. This agenda-setting role might be seriously challenged by a move to more interactive E-Government.
- The burning desire for two-way E-Government has yet to be established. Do citizens really want it? There is no discernible popular upsurge for participation that can be identified. There are calls from some for greater participation, but this has yet to move into a popular movement, thus politicians and officials have more immediate concerns.

Trust

The notions of trust and risk are important concepts when considering perceptions of E-Government. Societies, on any level, need trust in order to operate successfully.[37] Trust is needed not just in the technical capabilities of the E-Government process in question, but also in the systems and kit required to operationalise it and the organisation and the people responsible for it.[38] As Blakemore and Lloyd note, 'While investment in infrastructure and e-government service development is fundamental to service delivery, the governance characteristics of transparency and trust are critical in legitimating the investment and in creating the conditions for widespread usage of services.'[39]

The problem, of course, is that building trust is a very difficult concept with which to grapple. Why do we trust? Is there a magic formula for trust? If so, how does ICT use impact upon this? Let us state at the outset that the mere use of ICTs will not guarantee success even when those systems and processes have been successfully implemented into other governmental systems in differing organisations, regions or countries. Local political systems and cultures, as well as personal political championing of E-Government service provision, impact upon citizen perceptions – or so we would argue.

Thomas[40] identifies three types of trust:

- *Fiduciary trust*: where the relationships between citizen and bureaucrat are unequal and asymmetric. Based upon the work of early principal–agent theorists such as Spence and Zeckhauser[41] and Ross,[42] and in part derived from game theory, this trust shows the difficulties inherent in trying to get the public official or those working for agencies delivering services on behalf of what we traditionally recognise as the public sector (i.e. the agent) to act in the best interests of the citizen when the agent has an advantage, in terms of access to information, over the citizen and may indeed have different interests and goals from the citizen. Given that the bond of trust between agent and citizen may well be strengthened by the ability of the agent to use discretion when solving problems on behalf of a citizen, Welch *et al.*[43] observe that 'full scale electronic routinisation that reduces discretion . . . may work against fiduciary trust'.

- *Mutual trust*: relates to personal interaction between the agent and the citizen. Acting together can form mutual bonds of trust. This mutual trust of individuals can then also help to create fiduciary trust on behalf of the organisation. It can also lead to a strengthening of the third type of trust that Thomas identifies: social trust.

- *Social trust*: a form of social capital that is created and maintained via numerous social interactions which in turn inform and influence individual transactions in a symbiotic and dynamic process. Thomas[44] also saw social trust as supporting moral obligations inherent in fiduciary trust, as described above.

Parent *et al.*[45] argue that

> [i]ndividuals with a priori trust in government and correspondingly high levels of internal self-efficacy, will have these reinforced through electronic interaction with their governments. The reverse also holds: distrustful, low self efficacy individuals will not increase their trust irrespective of the medium of interaction.

Shah *et al.*[46] note that '[u]sing the Internet for exchange of information is associated with higher levels of interpersonal trust and civic participation'.

As citizens become immersed in Net technology in other areas of their life, their levels of acceptance of E-Government-based information and service delivery would seem to rise. They will find that the actions are intuitive and in many cases have added benefits such as removing the need to travel to government offices to perform routine tasks, thereby saving both time and money, and, perhaps equally important in these days of environmental concerns, resources.

One of the problems for E-Government is this increased interaction with and acceptance of the Internet. While, as noted above, this can help to create trust and acceptance of ICT-driven solutions, there are also associated problems that stem from such familiarity. Many people's experiences with the Internet relate to private sector commercial sites that have a great deal of money and time invested in their design and maintenance and can be constantly updated to take advantage of new developments in software and hardware. The customer, of course, pays for this level of service in the end. Therein lies the problem for government agencies as the pressure on them from government and from the general public is to reduce costs and not re-invest any potential savings in further cutting-edge technological solutions.[47] So, while expectations and demand levels are raised by the perceptions, mainly derived from experiences with commercial websites, of what is or is not an adequate interface with an organisation, the resources to be able to deliver such interfaces are constantly being driven down by the citizens' seeming and often contradictory wishes for small government and less government intervention.

The costs of building trust in E-Government could be viewed as an investment which may well bear fruit in relation to subsequent stages or operations. That is because, if deferred, the transaction costs borne by organisations in undertaking campaigns to re-build trust following failure or perceived failure in order to reassure doubters become what Fukuyama[48] argues is a type of hidden tax. However, there can be little doubt that there are winners and losers in terms of E-Government adopters, and that investment and the benefits (or losses) that accrue from it are not always distributed equally. This allows Nixon[49] to assert that '[it] may be said to resemble a type of "virtual klondyke", with some early adopters never fully recouping their investment while others strike it rich first time.' Certainly one can witness a dichotomy of views as to the purpose of E-Government, or at least Carter and Belanger[50] put it thus: 'Specifically, state government agencies should capitalise on the unique benefits of on-line services, promoting their use as a status symbol, and indicating the services' congruence with a citizen's lifestyle.'

Fighting distrust of E-Government

Elaborating slightly on Weckert's[51] four obstacles to online trust, one begins to see the difficulties of easily creating acceptance and creating confidence and trust:

- community values – shared positions and judgements are not always agreed;
- Internet context and roles – a lack of clarity about the limitations of our roles and possibilities of free action;
- disembodiment – lacking notions of identity and personality;
- security – a fear that somehow we will be compromised by engaging in ICTs and thus E-Government.

While there is not the space to comment extensively on these difficulties, they do perhaps demand a little further investigation. It is very difficult for governments to find agreements on shared values in this context. As with other political spaces and concepts, the idea of the information society, in which E-Government is grounded, is, as Webster notes,[52] a contested one. Technology is not a panacea; it is simply 'a tool that can aid us in improving society but it does not of itself provide solutions to questions such as inequality, power, democracy and justice'.[53] As Agre[54] suggests, the Internet tends to re-affirm existing offline political power and beliefs. McKnight *et al.*[55] point out that the trust given to online services has some correlation to the trust given to the institution promoting that online service in its offline 'persona'. Jaeger[56] notes that '[i]f these sources are often only presenting one side of an issue, citizens are being given the authoritative message that only one view is correct or acceptable on that particular issue'.[57] This can stifle debate and imply that only one viewpoint is socially acceptable.[58]

Nissenbaum[59] identifies difficulties of unfamiliarity or newness which are termed 'inscrutable contexts'. This is where our almost primeval fear of and reticence towards unknown situations lead us to distrust and/or be uncomfortable in using unknown systems and techniques such as those operationalised in aspects of E-Government service provision – although one might expect distrust of inscrutable contexts to disappear as individuals become more familiar with E-Government services. Indeed, as suggested earlier in this chapter, those who have been raised in the information age may consider E-Government to be the normal way to interact with government, rather than through other, more traditional means of communication.

Citizens want the same things from online and offline government in return for their trust. As Tassabehji and Elliman[60] point out, there needs to be a transparency that engenders trust and privacy issues need to be resolved to the satisfaction of society at large. The fact that this notion of satisfactory levels of privacy would seem to differ from country to country, and perhaps, one might dare to hypothesise, across the generations, would seem to offer the potential to be a fruitful area for future research. As the Austrian presidency of the EU concluded, 'A new privacy paradigm is required that reflects a realistic compromise between total privacy and total transparency.'[61] Perhaps governments need to reassure people as to what data is held on them and to what use or uses this data is put. Most people are reasonably comfortable with data being used for the purpose for which they believe that they had given it, particularly if they feel that they are getting something in return for their disclosure of data.[62] As I found in my interviews, people were less happy when that data was used across agencies for purposes that those people were unaware of and to which they had not knowingly consented. Also, while people trust individual professionals, they are less trusting of systems, particularly those which centralise data storage. As one respondent said,

> I trust my doctor to keep my information safe. I have a one on one relationship built up over 15 years but if he keeps electronic patient files on me and these are sent to hospitals or other agencies, I don't even know who I am trusting and they may not have the same standard of care towards my information.

There is a worry that function creep will take over. There already is some evidence of increased secondary legislation to facilitate data sharing.[63] This is particularly true of the attempt to introduce ID cards in the UK. The ID Card Act of 2006 specifically states that the data will be used for 'the efficient and effective provision of public services'.

The level of trust is based not just on real-life experience of data loss, but also on the fear of data loss. Just as in the realm of crime, where an individual's fear of crime is often worse than actual crime statistics would justify, others in the same area and presumably under the same threat feel no real fear, so in the field of E-Government some people are totally oblivious to the risks posed by data loss and potential abuse while others over-exaggerate the dangers. Often that fear is fed by eye-catching headlines and reports which, as noted earlier, sensationalise the impact of data loss and raise the fear of data misuse far above the actual danger. While I was writing this chapter, a number of headlines appeared, such as 'One official disciplined over data loss every day',[64] 'Virtual theft on the rise',[65] 'Government laptop scandal',[66] and 'Whitehall "loses computer a week"'.[67]

All of the above add to a public perception that the government cannot be trusted with data – though it is fair to say that, as with the first headline reporting a rise in virtual theft, such disquiet is not limited to the public sector. Certainly the evidence seems to suggest that media reports do affect people's views of government and the way in which government interacts with citizens. The British Computer Society

(BCS) report shows that, in its survey, when people were asked how recent media reports on data loss had affected their trust of government, 1 per cent said their trust had increased, 31 per cent said it remained unchanged and 66 per cent said it had decreased.[68] One problem is, of course, that the media are drawn to stories that are deemed newsworthy. Quite often those stories will be of a negative nature. 'No problems with E-Government' and 'E-Government working well' are headlines that are unlikely to be seen in the media.

Concerns over data privacy were identified in a recent survey carried out by Gallup on behalf of the EU.[69] Sixty-four per cent of citizens were worried that organisations may not be handling their data correctly[70] and 82 per cent were concerned that personal data transferred via the Internet was not sufficiently secure.[71] However, at the same time, organisations such as governments, health organisations and so on were among the most trusted organisations in terms of data protection; the public in the EU were much more sceptical about the private sector's ability to protect their personal data.[72] Of course, levels of trust varied across the EU 25, with Finland, Denmark and the Netherlands being the most trusting, while Greece, Romania and Latvia were much more doubtful in relation to data security in the public sector.[73]

The Gallup survey goes on to show that national data protection agencies in the EU 25 were relatively unknown, with only 28 per cent being aware of their existence.[74] While the report goes on to show that 82 per cent of EU citizens are in favour of a lessening of data protection rights in relation to data sharing between agencies and/or countries in an attempt to thwart terrorism,[75] there is some concern that data is being transferred, sometimes covertly, without the implicit agreement of an individual to a country such as the US, which offers lesser legal protection against prosecution to foreign nationals than to its own citizens.[76]

While there is some distrust of E-Government from a position of personal data security, many people are satisfied with their experiences when using E-Government services. In a survey carried out on behalf of the European Commission in 2004,[77] it was found that 62 per cent of people were very satisfied with their interactions in a range of services which were the subject of this study. The study went on to show that 75 per cent of respondents would recommend the service to people that they knew. Thus, those people become street-level champions for E-Government service diffusion and adoption.

Evidence from Europe seems to suggest a rather heart-warming and positive tale of a desire for humanistic values and interactions rather than a deep-seated mistrust of E-Government and ICT use. In a survey of E-Government user satisfaction[78] carried out in Slovenia, it was found that even among those respondents who were Internet users, 32 per cent of people did not use E-Government services to access information or communicate with a public official because they preferred traditional offline relationships. As Kiesler and Kraut pointed out, 'people generally feel less close to online communication partners than to those with whom they have formed real-world relationships'.[79] Thus many people are loath to trade in the traditional model of street-level bureaucracy, despite all its shortcomings, for interactions with a faceless computer screen in what Bovens and Zouridis[80] term 'screen-level bureaucracy'. Reddick's[81] research also notes the change from 'street level bureaucracies to system level bureaucracies'.[82]

This was also borne out in the pilot, unstructured interviews referred to earlier in this chapter where respondents said: 'I would rather deal with a human being than a machine' and 'I prefer to talk to someone. You can settle things without a constant exchange of emails or letters . . . Computers are fine for some things but when you have problems I find it just too impersonal.'

However, Accenture's[83] survey of American users seems to suggest the opposite. Accenture found in its survey that the respondents who were E-Government users preferred to deal with the government online rather than in person or via telephone. This apparent contradiction implies that there is both a cultural element and an experiential learning process which can impact upon citizen trust and satisfaction in relation to E-Government. It also shows us that E-Government development and adoption speeds are asymetrical,[84] and thus problematic for organisations such as the EU to operationalise and ensure interoperability.

Clearly it is important to include notions of human contact in any E-Government process. People must be comfortable using it – although one might argue that, as generations shift over time and most, if not all, citizens become instinctive and intuitive ICT users, those opinions may become less entrenched and there may be a more widespread acceptance of the technologies. Certainly one can make the case for that in terms of mobile phone saturation and use in many western countries. Even most former technophobes have joined the rush to adopt mobile phones and most people are comfortable with them, even if they may only utilise a fraction of their capabilities and features. However, it should also be noted that although new technology can aid government service delivery, there are times when human contact is a vital part of the system. For example, in terms of passport applications in the UK, while one can access the application form online in order to receive a shiny and new passport incorporating a chip which carries your biometric details (for more information see Chapter 10, this volume), you may still be required to attend a personal interview to verify your personal information and your identity.

Conclusion

It is clear that E-Government is here to stay for the foreseeable future until the next technological paradigm shape-shifts government into a new form. While trust in E-Government is not as high as it could be, the level of public disquiet is perhaps overstated – though this is, in part, contingent upon the media messages being delivered to citizens, as noted above. There is little doubt that trust is an issue that governments are seeking to address. Perhaps one way of doing this is through better explanation and training of how citizens can interact with government both in terms of accessing information and in terms of citizen input into service design and delivery. The future is bright for E-Government, but it should be developed without diluting democratic input.

Key points

- E-Government is here to stay, until superseded by a new technological leap. What we need to balance are the (sometimes) competing notions of efficiency, effectiveness and democracy.
- Trust is important in E-Government.
- Trust is much easier to lose than to gain.
- The success of E-Government depends upon the public's acceptance of it and their trust in it.
- Trust is affected by perception. Sometimes those perceptions can be wrong or ill-founded. This can lead to a lack of trust based on misperceptions. This is similar to the public perception or fear of crime often being worse than the reality of crime.
- A lot of people's perceptions of E-Government come not necessarily from direct experience of a given service or activity, but from the testimony of others (e.g. individuals or via media reporting).
- The media's sensationalist style of reporting can lead to misperceptions.
- Concentration needs to be given to the public relations image of E-Government developments as well as to technical feasibility.

Notes

1 http://www.guardian.co.uk/technology/2008/jan/05/computing.E-Government. All web links used in this chapter were active as of 21 November 2008.
2 Heeks, R. (2005) 'E-Government as a Carrier of Context', *Journal of Public Policy* 25/1: 51–74.
3 Yildiz, M. (2007) 'E-Government Research: Reviewing the Literature, Limitations, and Ways Forward', *Government Information Quarterly* 24: 646–665.
4 McNeal, R. and Hale, K. (2007) 'A Focus on Trust: Citizen–Government Interaction and the Internet'. Paper for Southern Political Science Association, New Orleans, 3–7 January 2007. p. 23. Accessed online at http://www.allacademic.com//meta/p_mla_apa_research_citation/1/5/4/0/6/pages154069/p154069-1.php.
5 O'Neill, O. (2002) *Spreading Suspicion*. Reith Lectures, London, BBC. Accessed online at http://www.bbc.co.uk/radio4/reith2002/lecture1.shtml.
6 Kolsaker, A. and Lee-Kelley, L. (2007) '"Mind the Gap II": E-Government and e-governance', in Wimmer, M. A., Scholl, H. J and Grönlund, A. (eds) *E-GOV 2007 LNCS* 4656. pp. 35–43. Berlin: Springer Verlag.
7 Bertot, J. C. and Jaeger, P. T. (2008) 'The E-Government Paradox: Better Customer Service Doesn't Necessarily Cost Less', *Government Information Quarterly* 25: 149–154.
8 Baldassare, M. (2000) *California in the New Millennium: The Changing Social and Political Landscape*. Berkeley, CA: University of California Press.
9 Norris, P. (1999) *Critical Citizens: Global Support for Democratic Governance*. Oxford: OUP.
10 Tolbert, C. and Mossberger, K. (2006) 'The Effects of E-Government on Trust and Commitment', *Public Administration Review* 66 (May/June): 354–369.
11 Rainey, H. (1997) *Understanding and Managing Public Organizations*. 2nd ed. San Francisco: Jossey-Bass Publishers.
12 Welch, E. W., Hinnant, C. C. and Moon, M. J. (2005) 'Linking Citizen Satisfaction with E-Government and Trust', *Government Journal of Public Administration Research and Theory* 15/3, July: 371–391.

13 Shapiro, A. L. (1999) *The Control Revolution: How the Internet Is Putting Individuals in Charge and Changing the World We Know.* New York: The Century Foundation.
14 Türksel, K. B. (2001–2002) 'Perceptions of E-Government in Turkey', *Turkish Public Administration Annual* 27–28: 41–57.
15 Mansbridge, J. (1997) 'Social and Cultural Causes of Dissatisfaction with U.S. Government', in *Why People Don't Trust Government,* Nye, J. S. (ed.). Cambridge, MA: Harvard University Press.
16 Al-Omari, H. and Al-Omari, A. (2006) 'Building an E-Government Trust Infrastructure', *American Journal of Applied Sciences* 3/11: 2122–2130.
17 Baldassare (2000) op. cit.
18 Welch, E. W., Hinnant, C. C. and Moon, M. J. (2005) 'Linking Citizen Satisfaction with E-Government and Trust', *Government Journal of Public Administration Research and Theory* 15/3, July: 372.
19 Thomas, J. C. and Streib, G. (2003) 'The New Face of Government: Citizen-initiated Contacts in the Era of E-Government', *Journal of Public Administration Research and Theory* 13/1: 83–102.
20 Welch, E. W., Hinnant, C. C. and Moon, M. J. (2005) 'Linking Citizen Satisfaction with E-Government and Trust', *Government Journal of Public Administration Research and Theory* 15/3, July: 371–391.
21 World Economic Forum, *The Global Information Technology Report 2007–08,* accessed online at www.weforum.org.
22 Bonham, M. G., Seifert, J. W. and Thorson, S. J. (2001) *The Transformational Potential of E-Government: The Role of Political Leadership,* 4th European IR Conference, ECPR, Canterbury, Kent. www.maxwell.syr.edu/maxpages/faculty/gmbonham/ecpr.htm.
23 Norris, D. F., Fletcher, P. D. and Holden, S. (2001) 'Is Your Local Government Plugged In?' Highlights of the 2000 Electronic Government Survey, p. 113, accessed online at http://findarticles.com/p/articles/mi_hb4325/is_200106/ai_n15078743.
24 OECD (2003) 'The E-Government Imperative: Main Findings', accessed online at http://www.oecd.org/dataoecd/60/60/2502539.pdf.
25 See, for example, Tapscott, D. (1997) 'The Digital Media and the Reinvention of Government', *Canadian Public Administration* 40/2: 328–345; or Clift, S. (2000) *The e-Democracy Book,* accessed online at www.publicus.net/ebook/.
26 Baum, C. and Di Maio, A. (2000) *Gartner's Four Phases of E-Government Model,* http://www.gartner.com/DisplayDocument?id=317292.
27 http://unescap.org/icstd/Pubs/st_escap_2342.pdf.
28 Hahamis, P., Healy, M. and Iles, J. (2005) 'Safety Net? Trust and E-Government', *Proceedings of the 5th European Conference on E-Government* (ECEG 2005) Academic Conferences International. pp. 119–130.
29 http://www.guardian.co.uk/politics/2008/nov/13/transport-economy.
30 http://europa.eu/rapid/pressReleasesAction.do?reference=IP/06/523. Original emphasis.
31 Austrian Federal Chancellery (2006) 'eGovernment for All Europeans', accessed online at www.egov2006.gv.at/egov4all.html. pp. 13–14.
32 EICTA EU, *E-Government Industry Declaration,* p. 3, accessed online at http://archive.cabinetoffice.gov.uk/egov2005conference/documents/proceedings/pdf/051125declaration_eicta.pdf.
33 Clift, S. L. (2004) 'E-Government and Democracy: Representation and Citizen Engagement in the Information Age', http://www.publicus.net/articles/cliftegovdemocracy.pdf p. 7.
34 Ibid.
35 Aldrich, J., Bertot, J. C. and McClure, C. R. (2002) 'E-Government: Initiatives, Developments and Issues', *Government Information Quarterly* 19: 349–355.
36 Chou, T. C., Chen, J. R. and Pu, C. K. (2008) 'Exploring the Collective Actions of Public Servants in E-Government Development', *Decision Support Systems* 45: 251–265.
37 Putnam, R. D. (1994) *Making Democracy Work: Civic Traditions in Modern Italy.* Princeton, NJ: Princeton University Press.

38 Camp, L. J. (2000) *Trust and Risk in Internet Commerce*. Cambridge, MA: The MIT Press.
39 Blakemore, M. and Lloyd, P. (2007) *Think Paper 10. Trust and Transparency: Pre-requisites for Effective E-Government*. http://www.ccegov.eu/Downloads/Paper%2010%20Trust,%20Transparency,%20Efficiency%20and%20e-government%20v2.3.pdf.
40 Thomas, C. W. (1998) 'Maintaining and Restoring Public Trust in Government Agencies and Their Employees', *Administration and Society* 30/2: 166–193.
41 Spence, M. and Zeckhauser, R. (1971) 'Insurance, Information and Individual Action', *American Economic Review* 61/2: 380–387.
42 Ross, S. (1973) 'The Economic Theory of Agency: The Principal's Problem', *American Economic Review* 63/2: 134–139.
43 Welch, E. W., Hinnant, C. C., and Moon, M. J. (2005) 'Linking Citizen Satisfaction with E-Government and Trust', *Government Journal of Public Administration Research and Theory* 15/3, July: 376.
44 Thomas, C. W. (1998) 'Maintaining and Restoring Public Trust in Government Agencies and Their Employees', *Administration and Society* 30/2: 166–193.
45 Parent, M., Vandebeek, C. A. and Gemino, A. C. (2005) 'Building Citizen Trust through E-Government', *Government Information Quarterly* 22: 720–736.
46 Shah, D. V., McLeod, J. M. and Yoon, S. H. (2001) 'Communication, Context and Community: An Exploration of Print, Broadcast and Internet Influences', *Communication Research* 28: 464–507; p. 491.
47 Stamoulis, D., Gouscos, D., Georgiadis, P. and Marrtakos, D. (2001) 'Revisiting Public Information Management for Effective E-Government Services', *Information Management and Computer Security* 9/4: 146–153.
48 Fukuyama, F. (1995) *The Social Virtues and the Creation of Prosperity*. London: Penguin.
49 Nixon, P. G. (2007) 'Ctrl, Alt, Delete: Re-booting the European Union via E-Government', in Nixon, P. G. and Koutrakou, V. N. (eds) *E-Government in Europe: Re-booting the State*. Abingdon: Routledge.
50 Carter, L. and Belanger, F. (2004) 'The Influence of Perceived Characteristics of Innovating on E-Government Adoption', *Electronic Journal of E-Government*, accessed online at www.ejeg.com/volume-2/volume2-issue-1/v2-il-papers.htmF.
51 Weckert, J. (2005) 'Trust in Cyber Space', in Cavalier, R. J. (ed.) *The Impact of the Internet on Our Moral Lives*. Albany, NY: New York University Press. pp. 105–108.
52 Webster, F. (1995) *Theories of the Information Society*. London: Routledge.
53 Nixon, P. G. (2000) 'Joined-Up Government: Whitehall On-Line', in Gibson, R. and Ward, S. J. (eds) *Reinvigorating Democracy: British Politics and the Internet*. Aldershot: Ashgate.
54 Agre, P. (2002) 'Real-Time Politics: The Internet and the Political Process', *Information Society* 18: 311–331.
55 McKnight, H. D., Choudhury, V. and Kacmar, C. (2002) 'Developing and Validating Trust Measures for E-Commerce: An Integrative Typology', *Information Systems Research* 13/3: 334–359.
56 Jaeger, P. T. (2005) 'Deliberative Democracy and the Conceptual Foundations of Electronic Government', *Government Information Quarterly* 22: 702–719.
57 Ibid. p. 709.
58 For example, in terms of views on terrorism, where challenging accepted views is seen as support for terrorists. See Chapter 15, this volume.
59 Nissenbaum, H. (2001) 'Securing Trust Online: Wisdom or Oxymoron?', *Boston University Law Review* 81: 101–131.
60 Tassabehji, R. and Elliman, T. (2006) 'Generating Citizen Trust in E-Government Using a Trust Verification Agent: A Research Note.' Paper presented 6–7 July 2006, at *EMCIS*, Alicante, Spain. Accessed online at http://www.iseing.org/emcis/EMCIS2006/Proceedings/Contributions/EGISE/eGISE4.pdf.
61 Austrian Federal Chancellery (2006) 'E-Government for All Europeans', accessed online at www.e-Gov2006.gv.at/e-Gov4all.html. p. 3.
62 BCS (2008) *Building Trust in E-Government*, accessed online at http://www.bcs.org/upload/pdf/dgs2008.pdf.

63 BCS (2008) *Building Trust in E-Government*, accessed online at http://www.bcs.org/upload/pdf/dgs2008.pdf.
64 Accessed online at http://www.telegraph.co.uk/news/3374341/One-official-disciplined-over-data-loss-every-day.html.
65 Accessed online at http://www.guardian.co.uk/technology/2008/nov/20/theft-in-virtual-worlds, 20 November, 2008.
66 Accessed online at http://www.thesun.co.uk/sol/homepage/news/article1955810.ece, 21 November, 2008.
67 BBC accessed online at http://news.bbc.co.uk/2/hi/uk_news/politics/7740593.stm, 21 November, 2008..
68 BCS (2008) *Building Trust in E-Government*, accessed online at http://www.bcs.org/upload/pdf/dgs2008.pdf.
69 Gallup (2008) 'Data Protection in the European Union: Citizens' Perceptions'. Flash Eurobarometer 225, available online at http://ec.europa.eu/public_opinion/flash/fl_225_en.pdf.
70 Ibid. p. 5.
71 Ibid. p. 5.
72 Ibid. p. 8.
73 Ibid. p. 8.
74 Ibid. p. 5.
75 Ibid. p. 20.
76 For more on this see http://www.statewatch.org/eu-dp.htm.
77 Top of the Web (2004) *User Satisfaction and Usage Survey of E-Government Services*. Ramboll Management for European Commission.
78 Vintar, M. *et al.* (2006) *Measuring E-Government User Satisfaction*, accessed online at http://www.fu.uni-lj.si/iiu/Clanki/MZS-eUprave-RazsirjeniPovzetekZaSplet-06-ANG(5).pdf.
79 Kiesler, S. and Kraut, R. (1999) 'Internet Use and Ties that Bind', *American Psychologist* 54: 783–784.
80 Bovens, M. and Zouridis, S. (2002) 'From Street-Level to System-Level Bureaucracies: How Information and Communication Technology Is Transforming Administrative Discretion and Control', *Public Administration Review* 62/2: 174–184.
81 Reddick, C. G. (2005) 'Citizen Interaction with E-Government: From the Streets to Servers', *Government Information Quarterly* 22: 38–57.
82 Ibid. p. 54.
83 Accenture (2004) *E-Government Leadership: High Performance, Maximum Value*. New York: Accenture.
84 Ebbers, W. E. and van Dijk, J. A. G. M. (2007) 'Resistance and support to Electronic Government, Building a Model of Innovation', *Government Information Quarterly*, 24/3: 554–575.

Further reading

BCS (2008) *Building Trust in E-Government*, available online at http://www.bcs.org/upload/pdf/dgs2008.pdf.
Blakemore, M. and Lloyd, P. (2007) *Think Paper 10. Trust and Transparency: Pre-requisites for Effective E-Government*, available online at http://www.ccegov.eu/Downloads/Paper%2010%20Trust,%20Transparency,%20Efficiency%20and%20e-government%20v2.3.pdf
Chadwick, A. and Howard, P. N. (eds) (2008) *Routledge Handbook of Internet Politics*. London: Routledge.
Ebbers, W. E. and van Dijk, J. A. G. M. (2007) 'Resistance and Support to Electronic Government, Building a Model of Innovation', *Government Information Quarterly* 24/3: 554–575.

17 Using E-Government for communication and co-ordination among regional international organisations

Preliminary insights from nascent interactions*

Vassiliki N. Koutrakou

Summary

This chapter presents preliminary conceptual arguments and insights pertaining to an innovative research project in progress. The project studies whether and how international organisations – particularly ones which represent major world regions (e.g. Europe) but also some consisting of countries of varied levels of economic performance (e.g. large parts of Africa, Latin America and South-East Asia) – utilise E-Government mechanisms, techniques and processes, not only within their own specific structures or to interact with their constituent institutions and member states, but also as a tool of communication with other international and non-governmental organisations for the purposes of information exchange, consultation or even co-ordinated action in matters of economic development and conflict.

What is argued here is that although evidence of actual take-up is scarce, by deploying E-Government at higher levels, sufficient benefits can be gained from the interconnectedness E-Government brings about due to its transnational nature. E-Government helps awareness and common action. It can thus aid existing domestic and international efforts to ameliorate conditions. It can eventually trickle down to an application at national level, involving individual citizens, even in areas where economic conditions have meant that the bottom-up approach has not materialised.

'Western' models of development are not necessarily applicable, in the same way or sequence, in the developing world, but this chapter examines how indeed different regional international organisations representing these regions are responding and sharing practice, and whether, and to what extent, they are endorsing this approach, utilising E-Government mechanisms and techniques for information, consultation and co-operation.

* Sincere thanks are due to the Europe Calling research teams at HEBO, Hague University for their help with the conducting of research, questionnaires and interviews.

Introduction

Seen in simple terms as a set of mechanisms and processes, based on the Internet and other information and communication technologies (ICTs), to enable the reform and modernisation of public administration and improve connectivity between governing bodies and the governed, one might mistake the potential of E-Government for a matter of mainly national significance. The majority of relevant literature is concerned with the numerous crucial issues arising at this level, such as citizen accessibility, the digital divide and participation, public trust and security, technological efficacy, versatility and management, political will, breadth and depth of actual government take-up, etc., presenting a host of prospective advantages and hindrances. Nevertheless, the vigorous advent of E-Commerce, and the take-up of related technologies by regional international organisations such as the European Union, has demonstrated that one, frequently overlooked, quality of E-Government is its inherent transnational nature.[1] Therefore, aside from enabling the governing-to-governed relationship, E-Government can be employed as a means for upgrading and enhancing interconnectedness between national, sub-national, international and trans-national bodies, as well as, of course, empowering individuals at local, regional and international levels. As such, it is an inextricable part of the process of globalisation, transcending geographical borders and depending as it does on some of globalisation's most crucial constituent ingredients.

Conversely, one manifestation of globalisation is not only a more interdependent world but, in parallel, a digitally interconnected one too. E-Government's most obvious role is that of servicing international business and linking the individual citizen faster and more directly with national, regional and local authorities, simultaneously modernising public administration networks and rendering them more responsive and transparent, and perhaps potentially playing a part in ameliorating the democratic credentials of institutions too.[2] However, less obviously perhaps, E-Government is increasingly permeating international, global and regional organisations, and their interactions with national and sub-national or non-governmental organisations, suggesting new implications and challenges for international relations. This dimension could be of particular use for regional groupings formed among developing or less developed countries, which are forever trying to be more in touch, achieve prominence and be better included, politically and economically, in the front line of international relations.

This chapter presents, in the context of existing specialist studies as well as newly acquired empirical evidence, some preliminary conceptual insights into whether and in what ways the European Union and other international organisations, particularly ones which represent major world regions consisting of a mix of some slightly better and some less well-developed countries (e.g. large parts of Africa, Latin America and Asia), utilise E-Government mechanisms, techniques and processes not only within their own specific structures or to interact with their constituent institutions and member states, but also as a tool of communication with other international and non-governmental organisations, for the purposes of information exchange, consultation or even co-ordinated action in matters of economic development and conflict.

Based on a research project in progress, this chapter examines the development of E-Government mechanisms that are feasibly applicable for use in the inter-relationship between major international regional organisations from parts of the so-called 'developing world' and the European Union and other regional, international or sub-national groups. This chapter examines this development in order to establish whether the trans-national use of E-Government as a communication, consultation or even co-ordination tool in this manner has the potential to be as beneficial as it is ordinarily expected to be at national level.

As the research is still ongoing, it is perhaps premature to claim final and conclusive findings. Nevertheless, it is important to acknowledge nascent trends and introduce discourse in this new area in the broad context of this book. It is therefore the primary aim here to set out certain conceptual premises and indicative early findings, which serve as an illustration of the potential contribution of E-Government in the manner in which regional international organisations interact in a multi-lateral world.

The international context and the European Union

E-Government is generally understood to be a network of tools, mechanisms, processes and procedures which are heavily dependent on the Internet, mobile and land-based telephony, videoconferencing and other available ICTs to streamline, modernise and interconnect public bodies at different layers of government with each other, as well as with citizens, businesses and other interested bodies. The aim is to achieve better and faster information provision and service delivery, and occasionally two-way interaction, as well as more efficiency of operation, directness, transparency and more widespread participation in public affairs, in fields as varied as taxation, health, education, political expression, justice, etc.

> Governments, across national boundaries and levels of government, have been found to share certain common beliefs about the practical benefits that e-government can produce, including reduced costs and increased revenue, economic development, reduced redundancy, increased transparency and accountability, and improved services to citizens.[3]

E-Government has been developing at a fast pace over the past 20 years, with Europe and North America being the front-runners. E-Government applications are more the result of feeling an obligation to embrace available technologies than strategically commissioning and developing them to plan; nation-states' authorities are pressed to appear to modernise and reform. E-Government is therefore pre-dominantly the result of national government initiatives, but it filters through to build more effective connections between different layers of government, thus empowering not only individuals, but also local authorities and pressure groups, even in regions where they have little tradition of being vociferous.

The United States and Canada can boast some of the earliest and best-developed E-Government models and commensurate examples of E-Democracy activity.[4] Through the NAFTA[5] connection, Mexico, the third and least wealthy member in the organisation, has benefited directly and indirectly in the growth of IT use not only in terms of commerce, but also right across the spectrum of the country's economy and public administration.[6] A cohort of state-driven E-Government systems have also been evolving across the whole of Europe over the past two decades, but the European Union has itself initiated overarching initiatives such as e-Europe, acting as what Manuel Baptista calls 'both a sub-set and a driver of government and public sector reform'[7] to ensure momentum, harmonisation and standardisation of inter-connectedness for the benefit of the member states and the improved visibility, transparency and efficiency of operation of the organisation itself and its own connectivity with the different layers of government and individual or group activity inside and outside Europe.[8]

The complex tree-like structure of the European Union has necessitated a two-pronged approach in the deployment of E-Government. From a political point of view, i2010 provides a framework for the support of public services for a European Information Society. From an operational viewpoint, the European Commission (EC) had to commit to the modernisation of its own administrative structures for the delivery of more efficient and transparent services for both its own staff and external stakeholders via the e-Commission Initiative. Just as crucially, the EC had to commit to the development of E-Governmental

> trans-European services that support the implementation of EU legislation, from internal market regulations to consumer and health policies, by facilitating the exchange of information between public administrations across Europe and by supporting the creation of on-line services for the benefit of businesses and citizens, through, for instance, the IDABC programme.[9]

The European E-Government i2010 vision focused on the basic benefits of cost-effectiveness, efficiency and the creation of public value. For example, at the turn of the century, the EC calculated that the cost of public procurement alone could drop by 5 per cent of the total by converting to electronic public procurement; these luring attractions of E-Government implementation are hard to ignore. Beyond the immediately identifiable practical benefits, however, the central objective has been to address the emerging needs of users as individual citizens, as customers and as diverse organisations, including governmental, local administrative, non-governmental, public and private actors. Figure 17.1 demonstrates the key actors which were identified by the EU's i2010.[10]

The websites, blogs and portals developed for the EU are some of the most consulted, by individual citizens with specific interests (e.g. scholars, researchers, lawyers, journalists, etc.) inside and outside the European Union; EU employees and politicians; a wide range of national member-state government actors; local authorities; businesses; civil society organisations operating in Europe; and a host of non-European actors seeking authoritative information and guidance on a variety of issues which directly or indirectly relate to EU activities. The europa.eu gateway acts as the main access point so that more and more EU official reports, declarations, opinions and other documents published by the European Commission, Parliament and other EU institutions are available online, regularly monitored, consulted and even lobbied electronically by a variety of individual or group actors internationally.

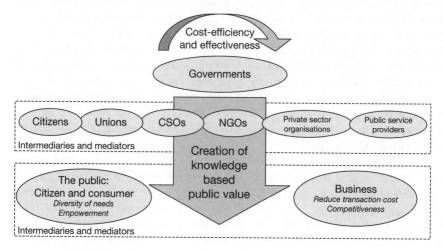

Figure 17.1 Actors involved in E-Government

Source: J. Berce, A. Bianchi, C. Centeno and D. Osimo (eds) (2006) 'Towards the eGovernment Vision for the EU in 2010: Research Policy Challenges', Institute for Prospective Technological Studies, European Commission, Joint Research Centre (DG JRC).

In addition, more and more EU officials and Members of the European Parliament increasingly maintain – though, as yet, not altogether extensively – one-way or even two-way interactive sites. These developments can have a huge impact on the business of the European Union, not only in terms of its domestic affairs but also in terms of its burgeoning international relations.[11]

A survey of Members of the European Parliament conducted for the purposes of this chapter revealed that two in three MEPs use E-Government techniques and mechanisms – primarily email, website consultation and occasional use of video conferencing – to keep communication lines open with their national governments, regional constituencies and home political parties, as well as with the media, lobby groups and other actors, though rarely with international actors. Furthermore, they consult other EU committees to inform themselves before Parliamentary debates or to prepare in their own involvement in policy committee work. There is some evidence to suggest that they also retrieve information from outside bodies, such as research institutes, think tanks and international and non-governmental organisation sites to gather information, though this appears to be much more limited (one in five at best) and much scarcer as yet for the purposes of actual consultation and interaction.

Projections for an i2020 envisage a government which is networked further as a result – though not exclusively – of E-Government. Projections envisage a government that combines distributed and centralised elements, an open, dynamic public sector which can be both personal and inclusive and is user-driven and more democratic. However, hardly any explicit provision is made for planned high-level use in the EU's interactions in the international arena.[12]

Nevertheless, just as e-interactions and e-services in government and business are becoming commonplace in North America and Europe, e-accessibility is becoming more widespread both by design – through centrally driven initiatives to make these available to more and more citizens – and by default – because citizens can ill afford to remain outside what is becoming a de facto way of dealing with business, banking, the state, etc. and therefore exercise their own initiative to join the information society. It could be argued, therefore, that issues of limited e-access for economic or political reasons are not necessarily an impediment to strategies of E-Government deployment as they can indeed add impetus to the enhancement of e-inclusion and involvement over time, and this would seem to have applicability and added relevance in the case of developing countries.

'With respect to international affairs, there has been extensive discussion about the need to include the private sector and civil society in structures and decision-making processes that traditionally have been the preserve of national governments.'[13] This challenge is particularly poignant in the developing world where, aside from the 'e-' element, government structures and procedures can vary greatly. They can vary from the range of regimes and their implications to the existence or lack of existence of civil society, and, of course, to the crucial issue of poverty and its repercussions in terms of access to basic services and, by extension, to expectations of widespread availability of telephony and the Internet. This is why modernisation of infrastructure through the support of the exportation and application of ICTs, in broad aid and trade programmes with developing countries such as the European Union's COTONOU Partnership with the African, Caribbean and Pacific (ACP) countries, is part and parcel of every initiative.

Figure 17.2, borrowed from Miniwatts Marketing Group's www.internetworld stats.com, displays the relative shares of Internet users per continent. It is immediately evident that, considering the relative population sizes, North America, Europe and parts of Asia (of which market leaders like Japan have a disproportionately high share) account for the majority of Internet use.

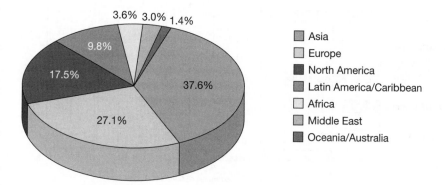

Figure 17.2 World Internet users, March 2008

Source: www.internetworldstats.com/stats.htm
Copyright © 2008, Miniwatts Marketing Group

Nevertheless, the histogram (Figure 17.3) which follows and which is also borrowed from the same source, actually demonstrates the growth in Internet use over the period 2000–2008. It clearly illustrates that laggards are fast embracing the new technologies and racing to close the gap.

The economy is the pace setter in this growth because economic competitiveness is underpinned by capitalising on revolutionary developments in science and technology, and knowledge and information is a key factor in this. The experience of leading countries in E-Government development shows that, despite shortcomings, single points of access provided via websites and portals, information sharing and interchange, integrated approaches to resources and service provision (i.e. joined-up government), improvement of administrative efficiency and arguably a certain amount of cost-cutting are some of the actual benefits which are already being reaped due the deployment of E-Government; these are very much the kind of benefits of which less developed countries are in great need.[14] Basic individual case studies, such as those depicted by Valentina Ndou, demonstrate that individual developing countries can and should 'pursue a more active role in the formulation of national policies and strategies to promote the information economy, to reap huge benefits in terms of economic and social growth/development'.[15] The strategies are inevitably based on successful experiences from developed countries, and their effective application in less developed countries is dependent upon the identification of key factors for adaptation and suitable implementation frameworks.[16]

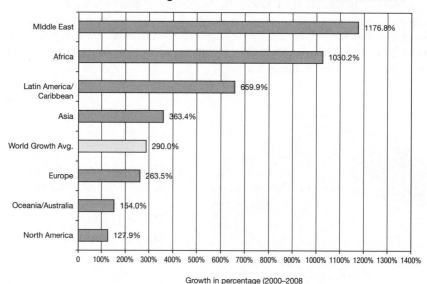

Figure 17.3 Growth of Internet users in the world between 2000 and 2008

Note: World Internet Users estimate is 1,407,724,920 for Q1 2008.
Copyright (c) 20087, Miniwatts Marketing Group – www.internetworldstats.com

The growth of the networked society has given rise to a multitude of inter-connections in all these regions and between different layers. Interconnections can be consultative, collaborative, contractual and designed to achieve common objectives.[17]

The following sections present brief overviews of E-Government developments in selected regions and corresponding dominant international organisations in South-East Asia, Latin America and Africa.

The aim is to attempt to gain insights regarding these developments and their potential to be used not only for domestic benefit, but also in the interests of their international relations.

E-Government status in selected world regions

As mentioned above, consultation of EU institutions by domestic and international actors using E-Government ICTs is fairly well established. However, whether and to what extent the reverse is true – that is, whether EU officials use E-Government mechanisms to communicate and/or interact with other international or non-governmental organisations – is much more difficult to ascertain. Moreover, even less is known about whether the Association of South-East Asian Nations (ASEAN), the African Union or MERCOSUR and other regional international organisations use E-Government mechanisms and techniques to inform themselves or consult or even formulate action in conjunction with other international or sub-national bodies.

South-East Asia

ASEAN, which dates back to the 1960s but re-focused and rejuvenated in the 1980s, consists of Singapore, Malaysia, Thailand, Brunei Darussalam, Cambodia, Laos, Myanmar, Vietnam, the Philippines and Indonesia. It is one of the most successfully integrated regional international organisations, second only to the European Union. One of its most significant, recent and innovative achievements is the so-called 'e-ASEAN initiative'. e-ASEAN has modernised the ASEAN infrastructure, facilitated the growth of electronic commerce and the liberalisation of trade in ICT products, promoted services and investments and enabled moves towards an E-Society in the region. The economic benefits of ASEAN have partially eclipsed, for a time, some of the fundamental politico-economic disparities between its member states. These disparities range from coping with a communist past to living with, to all intents and purposes, authoritarian regimes. This has happened while dealing with widely varying levels of economic hardship. This translates into equally varied levels of e-readiness and digital divide issues among the member states' populations, with, for example, Singapore at the top in terms of Internet access and Cambodia at the bottom in terms of Internet access.

The economic crisis of 1997 that stemmed the ascent of the 'Asian tigers' brought many of these problems back to the surface. The global economic recession of the end of the first decade of the twenty-first century has further prevented a reprieve. However, the connectivity which E-Government mechanisms and techniques can bring to an international organisation can flourish, even if e-access is limited due to persisting poor economic conditions at the grass roots of countries, because it is the connectivity between member states' authorities, as well as with other sub-national and international bodies, which is being primarily targeted, rather than the government-to-citizen connectivity. This is why all member states signed the e-ASEAN-Framework Agreement in 2000: to 'develop a broad and comprehensive action plan for an ASEAN e-space and to develop competencies within ASEAN to compete in the global information economy'.[18] 'Largely on the initiative of Japan, they also extended the project to the "plus three" states of China, Japan and South Korea.[19] Outside regional structures, but still within the region, the quasi-states of Hong Kong and Taiwan equally sought to become leading e-government players.[20] In the five years after 1997, only the hermit state of North Korea did not join the regional drive to put public sectors online.'[21] The other dominant regional grouping in the region, Asia-Pacific Economic Co-operation (APEC), has also jumped on the bandwagon of E-Government by participating in conferences alongside ASEAN, the OECD and other international organizations. However, APEC's very diversity – comprising states as varied as the ASEAN states as well as Australia, Japan and others – renders any cohesive action on the matter extremely difficult.[22]

A more concrete tool is ASEANConnect, a separate E-Government tool providing information digitally through a website, allowing the sharing of ideas and initiatives among organisations, as well as the evaluation of previous actions for the purposes of learning for the future.[23] From a technology point of view, ASEAN E-Government mechanisms and techniques still leave a lot to be desired, with much development and substantially more regular updating required. Nevertheless, it is a useful point of reference for the activities of the organisation, and for business and other interested actors who seek a first point of contact.

Although E-Government is also a great tool for communicating between member countries of an organisation such as ASEAN, different political views and worldviews can hamper the effectiveness of this process. Vietnam and Laos are still suffering from communist influence. Myanmar is occupied by military forces and has little contact with international actors outside the country. Therefore, examples such as the natural disaster of May 2008, when Myanmar suffered from a huge earthquake and the government refused any kind of help to start with, no matter in what form, illustrates that fundamental problems of international relations remain the same, irrespective of whether or not traditional or innovative methods of communication, consultation or co-ordination of action are employed.

Latin America

Latin America was, according to the International Telecommunications Union,[24] one of the regions of the world that most readily embraced telecommunications' privatisation. A quarter of all such privatisation happened in this region, leading to technological modernisation and improved accessibility. It is through this entry point that the informatisation of infrastructure and, consequently, E-Government began to flourish. Chile and Brazil, then Peru and Colombia, launched government initiatives to complement the mixed results of privatisation in promoting ICTs. These may have brought about a technological upgrade and a lowering of costs, but it was felt that they could not solve the extensive problems of accessibility and affordability in countries with high levels of poverty. Privatisation sometimes led to the simple replacement of public monopolies by private ones, but the climate of services' liberalisation encouraged mobile telephony and Internet-based services to carve out new sections of the market. All in all, the number of E-Government websites is still quite low in Latin America. They mainly act as providers of information and are centrally administered but not necessarily regularly updated. A few countries (i.e. Chile, Brazil, Colombia, Mexico, Peru and Ecuador) provide portals and limited online services. Indeed, although there are certain individual country studies,[25] detailed information on the region is scarce. However, a study carried out by Silvana Rubino-Hallman on Latin America and the Caribbean posits that even though there are fewer local government websites, they are better at providing actual online services than national ones. Perhaps this is because of local government's more limited and thus manageable remit.[26] The setting up of a basic information infrastructure and rudimentary linkages was key, but it was no easy task in a varied politico-economic terrain where, despite having enjoyed the longest period of democratisation in history over the past 15 years (with practically all countries having a democratically elected government in place), governments are still frequently seen as institutionally inefficient, sluggish and more than sometimes corrupt. Inevitably, however, not only had the new regulatory framework to contain specific state laws by the governments around the region, true liberalisation and private sector self-regulation, but it also came to rely on international organisations for the definition of norms affecting cyberspace.[27]

Studies and policy documents commissioned by the United Nations and other, more regionally specific international organisations (IOs) attempt to standardise the expectations and potential and regulatory environment of the ICTs used to deploy E-Government. In Central and South America, two of the dominant regional IOs are the Andean Pact and MERCOSUR. MERCOSUR, or Mercado Común del Sur, dates back to 1991 and is the fourth-largest trading bloc in the world. It comprises Argentina, Brazil, Paraguay and Uruguay. Since 1994 it has assumed a broader international status and formed a full customs union. MERCOSUR has a bilingual (Spanish and Portuguese) website which serves as a provider of increased cohesion and integration between its different organs. On the official portal of MERCOSUR, the section called 'who are we' contains a subsection with websites for all the institutions. In an interview for the purposes of this chapter, R. Souza, responsible for the organisation's website design, explained that most contact between the organs happens by email and the exchange of documents. The original documents are kept by the organ that produced them. When another organ needs a document, they request it by note and the document is emailed to them. Accordingly, the higher the use of Internet by MERCOSUR organs, the better and faster the communication between them seems to become.[28] Since the recent re-design of the website, more than 43,000 people visit the official website of MERCOSUR every week (compared to its previous rate of 5,000 per week).

The 40-year-old Andean Pact progressively created a free-trade area between its original four member states, Bolivia, Colombia, Ecuador and Peru, and then Venezuela. It aims for a common market and is concerned with regional integration for economic development, socio-economic growth, sub-regional solidarity, reduction of tensions and external vulnerability, as well as a better collective position for its member states in the international community.

The Andean Community has been developing an E-Government architecture to forward its aims. It is starting with a bilingual (Spanish and English) website, which serves as an information-provision site to interested parties from member countries and beyond. The website is about the organisation and its institutions, procedures, virtual library and archives. It also has news bulletins and official documents about the organisation's activities. This has been supplemented by E-CAN, a virtual space for meetings and facilitating working in community groups. Via this virtual space, telephone and videoconferencing, E-CAN enables communication between national, trans-national and sub-national groups within the Andean Pact. E-CAN has a view to increase the dynamics of co-operation while also reducing costs and delays and improving safety, reliability and ultimately the decision-making process. E-CAN has a view to eventually incorporate new actors in the Andean integration process.[29] In practice, interviews held during the current research project[30] – in particular the interview with Ruth Vasconez Estrella of Ecuador's Dutch Embassy – are already beginning to reveal that communication between states via E-Government – even in emergencies and crises, whether in response to conflicts or natural disasters – is practically absent. Rather, traditional diplomatic channels tend to be preferred. Within Andean, it seems to be recognised that E-Government is a good tool as a preliminary step in international relations because it costs less, provides speedy information exchange and is perhaps even tension-reducing as a preparatory mechanism ahead of face-to-face meetings. Despite this, it appears that the use of E-Government for actual policy consultation or policy co-ordination is some way off and would effectively require a change of paradigm in Latin American international relations.

Africa

The African Union succeeded the Organisation of African Unity (OAU) in combination with the African Economic Community (AEC) in 2002. The African Union consists of 53 African nations and seeks to achieve better co-operation among African nations in bringing about peace, security and economic development.

In a continent which suffers from 40 per cent illiteracy and a huge gap between the rich minority and poor majority, the telecommunications infrastructure is very fragile. Africa has 13 per cent of the world's population, but only 2 per cent of the world's telephone mainlines, 1.5 per cent of the total world number of PCs and 1 per cent of the world's Internet users.[31]

The technology in most African regions is slow and often outdated. This slows down the process of modernising what are often perceived as failing government systems in several African countries, and slows down much more communication among states. The importation of ICTs for the deployment of E-Government produces mixed consequences. On the one hand, it cannot resolve the poor individual accessibility issue, nor can it bypass the issue of the ill-afforded extra costs. On the other hand, it offers tried, tested and ready-to-apply models, which require adaptation to local needs and circumstances and promise a much-needed improvement to efficiency, accountability and transparency in African public administrations. Thus far, successes have been few and system failure has been common. As Richard Heeks puts it, 'the most obvious best practice will be customisation to match African realities ... E-Government solutions designed for one sector or country are being forced directly into a very different reality, creating failure'.[32] E-Readiness is also very different in different countries. Rolling out a diet of E-Government systems developed in the west is therefore not a straightforward solution for improving governance across the very varied African continent.[33]

It does, however, also tend to come with financial sponsorship from international bodies and 'Western-based' training for African operators, which in the long run is in favour of some semblance of international standardisation and has the potential to improve communication between African governing agencies and other international organisations, as well as strengthening sub-national and transnational civil society voices, thus far weak in much of Africa.

There is some evidence to show that on issues of economic and administrative development, there is a certain amount of E-Government use between different regional international organisations in Africa with the African Union, but also between these and non-African IOs, like the United Nations ICT Task Force and the United Nations Development Programme, the European Union, the World Bank and the G8, as well as other international actors. This usually consists of consultation, the organisation of strategy workshops and training schemes. One such example is the IST@frica workshops, funded by the European Commission and the Commonwealth;[34] another example is the annual Centre of Specialisation in Public Administration and Management (CESPAM) Executive Training Programme[35] to support E-Government activity in SADC countries.[36] Janet Kaya's assessment of the initiatives in East Africa, particularly by the three East African Community (EAC) member countries – Kenya, Tanzania and Uganda – shows promising results in terms of E-Government presence in the three countries. The three countries display well-developed government websites. They score differently, but encouragingly, in terms of telecommunication infrastructure and human resources (where Kenya does best) and actual interactivity (where Tanzania and Uganda perform better). Regional international organisations in Africa, including the African Development Bank, the Common Market for East and Southern Africa (COMESA), the Economic Commission for Africa (ECA), the Southern African Development Community (SADC) (mentioned above), the Inter-Governmental Authority for Development (IGAD) and the Economic Community of Western African States (ECOWAS), have websites containing information on their work and the activities of individual member states,[37] yet Mutula finds that 'wide disparities in E-Government exist within regional trading blocs in sub-Saharan Africa with Southern Africa far ahead of east and west Africa regions'.[38]

The New Economic Partnership for African Development (NEPAD), a scheme utilising G8 and African resources to implement economic and administrative reform across the African Union, has been in force since 2000 and has a dedicated ICT and E-Government dimension. The ITU is working closely with the African Union Commission, the African Telecommunication Union (the AU-specialised agency for telecommunications), the African governments and regional economic bodies such as

ECOWAS, SADC, UEMOA and COMESA, providing seed money, consultants and training and helping to implement projects and activities within the NEPAD framework. At the global level, a number of partnerships are already in place to assist in this. For example, the ITU and the European Union are implementing a US$995,000 project in partnership that is aimed at supporting the ECOWAS[39] countries to establish an integrated ICT market in West Africa in order to foster the development of related networks.

On political and humanitarian issues and issues of security and conflict, there is hardly any evidence thus far to indicate that there is any use of even the most rudimentary E-Government techniques for consultation, let alone policy co-ordination. Nevertheless, according to Mr Sabatohma at the South African Embassy in the Netherlands, 'a strong fast communication tool such as E-Government could prevent the escalation of major crises in African countries'.[40]

In the last few years there have been a few workshops in Khartoum and Addis Ababa to improve awareness on the crisis in western Sudan and the potential of technology to alleviate hardships. One such workshop, in 2003, was entitled 'The Sudan ccTLD Awareness Seminar'. It was a series of seminars and workshops to increase awareness about technological schemes such as the so-called 'Sudan ccTLD ".sd"' to strengthen links between individuals, civil society and outside actors, strengthening the Sudan Internet community with a view to alleviating suffering and improving understanding and assistance.

E-Government linkages between the EU and developing world regions

This section focuses on actual and potential linkages between regional international organisations and the ways in which E-Government methods can or do enhance linkages for the purposes of more efficient, better informed and even joint action.

The ASEAN website, available in English, is a very useful tool for an economic bloc only slightly smaller than the EU. ASEAN has important trade links with other regional IOs, businesses, the World Trade Organization (WTO) and so on. ASEAN's website is a potent one-stop shop for finding out about the organisation, keeping updated and seeking entry points for further contact. Information provision is, however, the predominant reason the website seems to be used. Nevertheless, the site has been diversifying. Since 2007, more focus has been given to the organisation's external affairs, with regular updates on ventures with neighbouring states and regional organisations, as well as on growing relations with the European Union.

The ASEAN Committee on Disaster Management (ACDM) is a committee that is responsible for crisis management of ASEAN member countries. It is composed of a team of experts who head various national agencies. Their purpose is to co-ordinate and implement regionally agreed activities in each and every member country. This co-operation forms part of the 2004–2010 ASEAN Regional Programme on Disaster Management (ARPDM). Within the ASEAN policy framework, one of the most important projects of the ARPDM, in collaboration with other international organ-isations such as the United States Department of Agriculture Forest Service, the Pacific Disaster Centre and the United Nations Office for the Coordination of

Humanitarian Affairs (OCHA), is the Establishment of an ASEAN Regional Disaster Management Framework.

This seems like the perfect area of regional organisation activity where E-Government methods and mechanisms could be exploited to facilitate and speed up proceedings and offer more cost-effective procedures.

The 26 December 2004 tsunami flooded parts of South-East Asia and caused the loss of approximately 300,000 lives and immeasurable infrastructural damage. It necessitated massive national and international help and co-ordination of efforts. The emergency response of the EU, trading partner of ASEAN, particularly in recent years through the ASEM (ASEAN–Europe Meetings), was very quick in terms of humanitarian assistance. The United Nations and other international bodies, as well as individual countries, were also responsive. However, co-ordination was riddled with problems and delays. These were exacerbated by difficulties on the ground (e.g. civil conflicts in which some of these areas, like Sri Lanka, are engaged). The use of websites by governments and organisations around the world to inform and collect monies for the tsunami victims took place in the months that followed. However, little use of any other E-Government-related techniques was evident in terms of consultation or co-ordination of action. Traditional channels of communication were preferred and considerable confusion was often apparent. So many actors (individual donor countries, IOs such as ASEAN and the EU, UN agencies, Red Cross, Crescent, NGOs, etc.) were acting in an uncoordinated way and on their own initiative. There were instances where it was unclear who was in charge of the dispensation of aid at any one time. This resulted in some 'first-in, last-out' aid rotting away unused, food and medical supplies parcels being re-packed and changing of donor logos in an effort by certain actors to score points and secure more of the credit.[41] There is scope in situations like these for E-Government mechanisms and techniques (which were absent in the above example) to improve responsiveness, transparency and efficiency in reconstruction work and the dispensing of humanitarian aid, while indirectly promoting dialogue, consultation and openness among local actors.

In Africa, the Regional Impact of Information Society Technologies in Africa (IST-Africa) is a multi-stakeholder initiative that has been financially supported by the European Commission since 2005. Its purpose is to reduce the digital divide in sub-Saharan Africa by promoting dissemination and exploitation of European IST research results in the region and developing training modules for E-Government, E-Health, E-Learning and ICTs for Agriculture so as to strengthen national and pan-African capabilities, facilitate EU–ACP networking and highlight IST exploitation and international co-operation. The construction of Africa One, an undersea fibre-optic cable which will connect African states to the global backbone and to each other. is an example of trans-African activity in this area that is currently in progress.

Some measures are being taken by sub-regional organisations, such as SADC or COMESA. SADC has developed a model law pertaining to telecommunications, which has been approved by the majority of its members and has become a legally binding document. The formation of the Telecommunication Regulators Association of Southern Africa (TRASA), which acts as a forum for regulators in the region to exchange information and experience, is another project. COMESA has initiated the ComTel project to develop terrestrial tele-communication links between neighbouring states within the group, [and] harmonize and upgrade the cross-border information systems in transport, customs, import/export and trade.[42]

Despite e-access being still low in Africa, there is clearly considerable effort being expended to create E-Government linkages between states and some sub-state actors within regional organisations and the AU, but also between African regional organisations themselves and between these and other IOs like the UN, G8 and the EU, which often act as sponsors as part of broader development initiatives. As Von Haldenwang argues,

> development cooperation can use E-Government as a means of supporting partner countries in devising and implementing political and administrative reforms and in improving market-oriented frameworks. Beyond the immediate benefits of the new technologies, E-Government should be taken as an instrument to promote good governance and to strengthen reform-oriented actors in politics and civil society.[43]

Yet the scope thus far mostly has to do with infrastructure upgrade and general development issues rather than the addressing of conflict or political and human rights issues.

In Latin America E-Government linkages also seem to be mostly for economic development reasons, and more specifically for the facilitation of trade links.

On the official portal of MERCOSUR, the section called 'who are we' contains a sub-section with a list of 12 links to websites of other organs. These include, for example, 'MERCOSUR educational', 'MERCOSUR health', 'sub workgroup no. 7 "industry"' and 'meeting of ministers of justice of MERCOSUR'. All of these websites contain documents and information related to the organ in question. Its website designer, R. Souza, explains that, as MERCOSUR is working with a lot of content, some organs are independent of the secretariat of MERCOSUR and have separate websites. It is the responsibility of the organs to maintain and update these websites, but any changes made must be sent to him for approval because he is responsible for the layout. So in this case, E-Government cohesion between the secretariat of MERCOSUR and the other organs seems more evident and centralised – indeed, coming down to one person effectively – than for instance, the much bigger operation of the EU's europa website.

The EU has supported MERCOSUR and gradually strengthened trade ties with it since the creation of the organisation in 1991. This interaction has helped to reinforce and improve the common market of MERCOSUR, but MERCOSUR has also experienced its fair share of trade difficulties due to the EU Common Agricultural Policy's prohibitive tariff barriers, the Latin American 'dollar-banana' issue, etc. Early, informal political co-operation between the EU and MERCOSUR was later institutionalised through the framework agreement and the joint declaration, establishing ongoing political dialogue, and in this, the websites of the two organisations have served as mutually beneficial information databases for officials and operatives, but little else.

When it comes to interactivity between MERCOSUR and other international organisations, Souza mentioned that there is a lot of communication between MERCOSUR and ALADI (Associação Latino-Americana de Integração or LAIA, Latin American Integration Area, as it is more commonly known in English).[44] As the main goal of ALADI is to integrate Latin-American countries into a common market to achieve economic growth, ALADI frequently communicates with other international organisations in the region (e.g. MERCOSUR and the Andean Community of Nations) in order to achieve eventual integration. According to Souza, ALADI frequently visits the official website of MERCOSUR to look for information, and vice versa. In short, the use of E-Government mechanisms and methods appears to facilitate, to some extent, interactivity and awareness between these two organisations, and shows signs of doing so even more, in future.

The website of the Andean Community acts as an even richer information source for different sectors and bodies. Sectors and bodies can visit the website and often request information by email to the General Secretariat of the Andean Community. The website is more appealing, used more extensively and is designed to involve the public. Therefore, the website scores better than the other Latin American organisation websites in the E-Government interactivity stakes. However, Elmer Díaz, responsible for the Andean Community's website, posited when interviewed that governments of member states are the 'principal visitors' of the website.[45] It is possible to subscribe to the daily news bulletin produced on the website, and 'many people subscribed to this service are civil servants of the different entities of governments', so again we see that the primary use is an information retrieval tool.

A reason for not being able to detect a significant amount of interactivity between international organisations is the poor showing, still, of Internet connectivity within Andean and MERCOSUR nations. Internationally, the role of E-Government has led to a positive reception towards MERCOSUR and the Andean Community. European Commissioner Liikanen, giving a speech to the MERCOSUR–EU Business Forum (MEBF), praised the co-operation between the European Union and MERCOSUR on issues of E-Government, and the benefits that it produces – namely, increased trade and co-operation.[46]

Conclusion

It is clear that if E-Government has potential as a consultation tool for regional international organisations in the developed world and, especially, the developing world, this potential is nowhere near being fulfilled yet. Nevertheless, one can pause at certain pointers which emerge so as to ascertain the importance of this potential.

The regions examined are very different in every way: geographically, anthropologically, strategically and economically. They are also very different in terms of their level of economic development and exposure to ICTs: South-East Asia enjoyed a period of economic success, particularly in the 1990s, before being hit by the 1997 slow-down; Latin America lagged behind as some countries experienced enormous chasms in affluence and poverty among their populations; and Africa comes in last with the greatest challenges to meet by way of catching up with Europe and the more developed world.

The first point that has been argued in this chapter is that, although the above conditions do not bode well for achieving universal e-access in those regions in the near future, these very conditions and consequent needs create an even greater opportunity and urgency for the deployment of E-Government mechanisms and procedures, albeit at higher levels. Deployment at higher levels implies that one should concentrate, for the time being at least, on the benefits which can be gained from the interconnectedness E-Government can offer due to its trans-national nature, between countries, regions and international and other organisations, where the issue of access is either solved already or more easily solvable. The purpose of this line of attack is to tackle problems of regional economic development, aid, political dialogue and conflict, as well as to encourage wider awareness, the exchange of best practice and closer consultation and collaboration. This may, in turn, help existing domestic and international efforts to ameliorate conditions. The benefits thus eventually trickle down to individual citizens.

This appears a top-down approach perhaps, but for its inclusion of the much-needed empowerment of civil society as one of those high-level actors, and one which, it is argued, is suitable to these situations, working alongside a host of other existing, more bottom-up initiatives. This leads to the second point that has been argued in this chapter. By adding momentum to the standstill and kick-starting improvements, this high-level E-Government approach cannot help but domino to involve grassroots citizens in time. This approach is very different to that dominating the rolling out of E-Government in Europe, North America and generally more developed regions, but in every other area of development it has been shown time and time again that Western models of development are not necessarily suitable and applicable – or at least not in the same way or sequence – in the developing world.

The third issue that has been argued in this chapter is how indeed different regional international organisations representing these regions are responding in practice, and whether, and to what extent, they are endorsing this approach and utilising E-Government mechanisms and techniques for information, consultation and co-operation.

The research project is still in its early stages and therefore definitive answers cannot yet be given. However, it is already sufficiently evident that regional IOs in the developing world are embracing existing and emerging ITCs, more often than not imported by the 'west', and adapted however possible, in an attempt to apply E-Government mechanisms and procedures which can primarily help them to raise awareness and efficiency in dealing with economic development in their respective regions. Actual reforms in the public administration of their member states and political consultation come a poor second, with conflict-related sensitivities and perhaps a lack of realisation of the potential benefits or eagerness to change being the more obvious factors.

It has also become evident that Internet access and even access to telephony is a much greater problem in these regions. However, as argued above, although this can be perceived as a fundamental problem in developing E-Government on a national level, it does not have to be so in terms of trans-national, inter-organisational and inter-regional and international use of E-Government to tackle issues of broader interest. Indeed, one could argue that where in developed countries, as in the European Union, the rolling out of E-Government took place hand-in-hand with increasingly widespread citizen access to the Internet and assorted ICTs, in a partially bottom-up way, in developing countries it is possible that increased use of ICTs at higher levels is likely to have the benefit of filtering down to improve national public administrations, contribute to better economic development and, consequently, eventually improve individual citizens' e-access. This can work in tandem with related approaches like how to manage knowledge in E-Government in developing countries through the creation of virtual communities, given the resource limitations of several of these countries, where enterprise solutions may not be suitable.[47] Indeed, the world economic recession of the end of the first decade of the twenty-first century bodes poorly for any prospects of additional widespread public economic resources becoming available in Europe or North America, much less in developing countries in the short to medium term, and this may add extra poignancy to this type of approach.

What seems undeniable is that, in studying the websites and, where available, the forums provided, and taking into account the experiences of the persons interviewed, E-Government techniques are currently used for little more than their informational capacity, are seldom two-way and act as a front-runner to more traditional channels of contact. In terms of utilising these means and technologies, there is little evidence of interactivity or actual consultation and hardly any evidence of co-ordination of action in everyday or even crisis situations thus far. Although one cannot generalise, many developing countries need to make considerable sacrifices to develop and maintain E-Government architectures, even with outside sponsorship, when the domestic pressing needs are many, so the benefits need to be crystal clear and tangible to warrant the diversion of resources. It is safer, therefore, to apply these readily imported technologies to technocratic matters in order to improve general awareness and attract business interest, rather than entrust them with radical reforms. However, there are clearly opportunities for E-Government to be used more extensively for consultation and co-ordination purposes in cases of natural disasters and humanitarian aid at least, for political co-operation where feasible and for responding to international conflicts.

The World Economic Forum is starting to use ICTs in its efforts not only to inform via websites, but also to attempt to co-ordinate and consult with state actors and international and non-governmental organisations in identifying potential conflict hotspots through webcasts, videoconferencing, etc. alongside traditional means like real-life meetings. Whether this kind of potential is better realised and being considered for the future certainly merits further investigation.

Key points

- Aside from enabling the governing-to-governed relationship, E-Government can be employed as a means for upgrading and enhancing interconnectedness between national, sub-national, international and trans-national bodies.
- Consultation of EU institutions by domestic and international actors using E-Government ICTs is a fact, yet the reverse is less well established.
- Developing regions in Africa, South-East Asia and Latin America are very different geographically, anthropologically, strategically and in terms of their level of economic development and exposure to ICTs.
- Although disparities and economic challenges do not bode well for achieving universal e-access, they create an even greater opportunity and urgency for the deployment of E-Government mechanisms and procedures, albeit at initially higher levels.
- High-level E-Government deployment in developing regions can domino to involve grassroots citizens in time.
- Bottom-up E-Government deployment in Europe and North America may not be similarly applicable in developing countries in the short term.
- ASEAN, MERCOSUR, the Andean Pact, the African Union and other regional international organisations are developing E-Government capabilities to optimise the domestic management and activity of these organisations.
- The European Union, the United Nations, the G8 and so on often sponsor E-Government innovation initiatives in developing regions.
- In terms of utilising these means and technologies, there is little current evidence of interactivity or actual consultation and hardly any evidence of co-ordination of action in everyday or even crisis situations thus far.
- The potential for E-Government mechanisms and techniques to act as a consultation tool for regional international organisations in the developed world and, especially, in the developing world to address issues of conflict and development is still mostly untapped, but it is a very real growth area.

Notes

1 Norris, D. F. and Lloyd, B. A. (2006) 'The Scholarly Literature on E-Government: Characterizing a Nascent Field', *International Journal of Electronic Government Research*, 2/4: 40–56.
2 Bozinis, Athanasios, I. (2007) 'Bozinis, Internet Politics and Digital Divide Issues: The Rising of a New Electronic Aristocrats and Electronic Meticians', *Journal of Social Sciences* 3/1: 24–26.
3 Jaeger, Paul T. (2003) 'The Endless Wire: E-Government as Global Phenomenon', *Government Information Quarterly* 20: 323–331.
4 West, Darell M. (2005) 'State and Federal E-Government in the United States', Brown University, September, http://www.InsidePolitics.org/egovtdata.html; see also http://www.insidepolitics.org/egovtdata.html.

5 The North American Free Trade Agreement has been in force since 1994.
6 Ibarra-Yunez, Alejandro (2004) 'NAFTA as a Vehicle for Regulatory and Institutional Convergence in the North American Region – Mapping the New North American Reality', IRPP Working Paper Series, no. 2004-09g, Canada.
7 Baptista, Manuel (2005) 'E-Government and State Reform: Policy Dilemmas for Europe', *The Electronic Journal of e-Government* 3/4: 167–174.
8 Nixon, Paul G. and Koutrakou, Vassiliki N. (2007) *E-Government in Europe – Re-Booting the State*. Abingdon: Routledge.
9 European Commission (2008) 'eGovernment Factsheet – European Commission – Information Strategy', 19 December 2008
10 Berce, J., Bianchi, A., Centeno, C. and Osimo, D. (eds) (2006) 'Towards the eGovernment Vision for the EU in 2010: Research Policy Challenges', Institute for Prospective Technological Studies, European Commission, Joint Research Centre (DG JRC).
11 Koutrakou, Vassiliki N. (2004) *Contemporary Issues and Debates in EU Policy – The European Union in International Relations*. Manchester: Manchester University Press.
12 Berce, J., Bianchi, A. *et al.* (2006) op. cit.
13 MacLean, Don (2004) 'Herding Schrödinger's Cats: Some Conceptual Tools for Thinking about Internet Governance', Background Paper for the ITU Workshop on Internet Governance, Geneva, 26–27 February.
14 Lee, Sang M., Tan, Xin and Trimi, Silvana (2005) 'Current Practices of Leading E-Government Countries', *Communications of the Association for Computing Machinery*, 48/10, October: 99–104.
15 Ndou, Valentina (Dardha) (2004) 'E-Government for Developing Countries: Opportunities and Challenges', *The Electronic Journal on Information Systems in Developing Countries* 18/1: 1–24. The survey covered Argentina, Brazil, Chile, China, Colombia, Guatemala, India, Jamaica and the Philippines.
16 Chen, Y. N., Chen, H. M., Huang, W. and Ching, R. K. H. (2006) 'E-Government Strategies in Developed and Developing Countries: An Implementation Framework and Case Study', *Journal of Global Information Management* 14/1: 23–46; see also Heeks, Richard (2006) *Implementing and Managing eGovernment: An International Text*. London: Sage.
17 Castells Manuel (1996) *The Rise of the Network Society*. Oxford: Blackwell.
18 www.aseansec.org.
19 The principal actor being the Japan Ministry of Foreign Affairs (2000).
20 The Hong Kong Information and Technology Broadcasting Bureau (2002) was one of the actors later involved.
21 Holliday, Ian (2002) 'Building E-Government in East and Southeast Asia: Regional Rhetoric and National (In)action', *Public Administration and Development*, 22: 323–335.
22 Banerjee, Indrajit (2007) *The Internet and Governance in Asia: A Critical Reader*. Singapore: Asian Media Information and Communication Centre (AMIC).
23 Wescott, Clay J. (2001) E-Government: Enabling Asia-Pacific Governments and Citizens to Do Public Business Differently, Asia Development Bank E-Government Workshop, 26–27 April, as part of Combating Corruption in Asia-Pacific: A Distance Learning Program for Knowledge Sharing and Capacity Building.
24 International Telecommunications Union (2001) 'America's Telecommunications Indicators 2000'. Geneva.
25 Lau, T.Y., Aboulhoson, Mira, Lin, Carolyn and Atkin, David J. (2008) 'Adoption of E-Government in Three Latin American Countries: Argentina, Brazil and Mexico', *Telecommunications Policy* 32: 88–100.
26 Rubino-Hallman, Silvana (2002) *E-Government in Latin America and the Caribbean. Reinventing Governance in the Information Age*, XVI Concurso de Ensayos y Monografías del CLAD sobre Reforma del Estado y Modernización de la Administración Pública 'Gobierno Electrónico'. Caracas.
27 Items International and Hernán Moreno Escobar (2007) *E-Government architectures, technical and political situation in Latin America*, United Nations Publication LC/W.129 Copyright © United Nations, April 2007.

304 *Koutrakou*

28 Mr Ricardo Souza, personal interview, 8 November 2007.
29 http://secgen.comunidadandina.org/ecan/.
30 Of particular interest, among others, was the interview given by Ruth Vasconez Estrella, in charge of consulate affairs, Embassy of Ecuador, The Hague, the Netherlands.
31 Kitaw, Y. (2006) 'E-Government in @frica, prospect, challenges and practice'. Retrieved 15 May 2008. http://people.itu.int/~kitaw/egov/paper/E-Government_in_Africa.pdf.
32 Heeks, Richard (2002) 'E-Government in Africa: Promise and Practice', *Information Polity* 7: 97–114.
33 Kalu, Kalu N. (2007) 'Capacity Building and IT Diffusion: A Comparative Assessment of E-Government Environment in Africa', *Social Science Computer Review* 25/3: 358–371.
34 See: IST@frica, E-Government Workshops for the SADC Region, Botswana, 2006–2007, supported by the European Commission and the Commonwealth Secretariat.
35 See: CESPAM Executive Training Programme workshop for: 'SADC Regional Consultation on National E-Government Readiness', Report on Proceedings Gaborone, Botswana, April 2004. Also: CESPAM Executive Training Programme workshop for: 'Planning for E-Government in SADC Countries', Maputo, Mozambique, 19–21 November 2003.
36 SADC, the Southern African Development Community, comprises the countries of South Africa, Mauritius, Botswana, Lesotho, Swaziland and Tanzania.
37 Polikanov, Dmitry, and Abramova, Irina (2003) 'Africa and ICT: A Chance for Breakthrough?', *Information, Communication and Society* 6/1: 42–56.
38 Mutula, Stephen M. (2008) 'Comparison of sub-Saharan Africa's E-Government status with developed and transitional nations', *Information Management and Computer Security* 16/3: 235–250.
39 The Economic Community of Western African States (ECOWAS)
40 Interview with Mr Sabatohma, Consular Affairs, Embassy of the Republic of South Africa, The Hague, April 2008.
41 Interviews with 'Solidarity' NGO officials, and officials of the Greek Ministry of Foreign Affairs, Humanitarian aid division.
42 Polikanov, D. and Abramova, I. (2003) op. cit.
43 Von Haldenwang, Christian (2004) 'Electronic Government (E-Government) and Development', *The European Journal of Development Research* 16/2: 417–432.
44 Rooted in a 1960 agreement between seven countries – Argentina, Brazil, Chile, Mexico, Peru, Paraguay and Uruguay – all aiming for a higher degree of economic integration through expansion of their own domestic markets. ALADI was officially created and expanded on 12 August 1980 with the signing the Montevideo Treaty.
45 E. Díaz, responsible for Andean Community website: personal interview, 20 November 2007.
46 Liikanen, Erkki (2003) Speech at the Vth Plenary Session of MERCOSUR European Business Forum (Brasilia), Oct. 2003, *EU@UN*, retrieved 22 October 2007 from website: http://www.europa-eu-un.org/articles/en/article_2968_en.htm.
47 Wagner, Christian, Cheung, Karen, Lee, Fion, and Ip, Rachael (2003) 'Enhancing E-Government in Developing Countries: Managing Knowledge through Virtual Communities', *The Electronic Journal on Information Systems in Developing Countries* 14/4: 1–2.

Further reading

Molnár, Szilárd (2007) *E-Government in the European Union*, publication of coursebook supported by European Commission DG Education and Culture, via the Leonardo da Vinci and NETIS programmes. Budapest.
Holliday, Ian (2002) 'Building E-Government in East and Southeast Asia: Regional Rhetoric and National (In)action', *Public Administration and Development* 22/4: 323–335.
Cocchiglia, Michele and Vernaschi, Silvia (2006) 'E-Government for Development: Rhetoric and Reality', *Journal of E-Government* 2/2, April: 2–18.

Gascó Hernández, Mila (ed.) (2007) *Latin America Online: Cases, Successes and Pitfalls*. Hershey, PA: IRM Press.

Kamel, Sherif (2009) 'Building the African Information Society', *International Journal of Technology Management* 45/1–2: 62–81.

IPTS. (2007) *The Future of E-Government: An Exploration of ICT-Driven Models of E-Government for the EU in 2020*. Seville: European Commission.

European Commission, DG INFSO (2007) *Bringing Together and Accelerating E-Government Research in the EU: E-Government Evolution towards 2020*. Brussels: EU Commission.

Misuraca, G. (2007) *e-Governance in Africa, from Theory to Action: A Handbook on ICTs for Local Governance*, IDRC/Africa World Press, July.

Conclusions

Paul G. Nixon, Rajash Rawal and Vassiliki N. Koutrakou

There can be little doubt that, as in so many facets of our lives, the Internet has, at least in part, changed the way in which we interact with governments at all levels. It has moved on from being some bizarre technical toy to becoming an accepted part of mainstream life in many countries. The first conclusion we can draw is that, at least for the foreseeable future, Internet-enabled government will play a role in the delivery of services in a bundle of practices and procedures that is commonly described as E-Government. The shape of E-Government and the component parts of it will no doubt change. As technologies develop and morph, there will be changes in the appearance, structure and operability of E-Government. As services are increasingly outsourced to other agencies and providers, the nature of government is changing subtly, and it will continue to do so for the foreseeable future. The nature of E-Government is in turn influenced by this new dynamic.

We need to accept a need to change government and the culture in which it operates. Public acceptance of technologically backed changes is key to success. As Frissen *et al.*[1] point out, there will be a need for harmonisation and inter-operability within the EU member states' systems of E-Government. How will the changes implied by that be accepted by a range of disparate publics? Government styles and cultures (thankfully!) differ between EU member states and the necessary homogenisation of systems still seems some way away. It is fair to say, nevertheless, that the EU has made some progress, particularly in areas of identity management. Examples include EU-badged passports and common driving licences – although these are controlled and issued by each individual state. Homogenisation would require a single accepted position for all member states to move towards and it would also require political actors of vision to foster its development, and the conviction to persuade a doubtful public of its value. But we should not rule out the possibility of change, for – leaving aside death and taxes – change is the one constant in our modern society.

We can quite clearly see that generations will grow up unaware of life before the Internet. Indeed, we must remember that while the ARPANET, a forerunner of what we know today as the Internet, was developed in 1969, the World Wide Web, developed by Tim Berners-Lee, was only launched to the public in 1991. Thus, this being in some terms the year '*anno Internet*' 18, one can argue that the Internet has only just begun its adult life and is not yet maturely developed – although, while not wishing to reify the technology, it could also be argued that one day the Internet will wither and die and be replaced by a different, as yet undiscovered, technological solution.

But clearly, as Dutton[2] suggests, the Internet has come of age. It is an accepted technology that pervades many areas of modern society. Its usage straddles generations, social groupings and issues. Already, as Dutton[3] has shown, there is a case for terming the Internet the 'Fifth Estate'.

There can be no doubt that the move towards mobile Internet usage via mobile telephony – a technology that facilitates text-based or SMS service provision and has deep penetration levels in most of Western Europe – and the development of other portable devices will encourage usage of E-Government services on a 24/7 basis, the user thus being able to determine where and when to access required services. Indeed, some services which are far more suitable to mobile technology (e.g. paying for car parking spaces, etc.) are already operative.

As Codagnone and Osimo[4] point out, the composability of future services is a key target to drive up usage. This re-design and re-interpretation of service interfaces is vital if uptake is to be maximised – though, as Margolis and Moreno-Riāno[5] note, the evidence suggests that this opening up of services and greater public involvement is not yet being achieved and a shift towards E-Government may in fact close down some channels of involvement between legislators, officials and the public, particularly on a face-to-face level. Moreover, Montargil argues that the increase in the technical interactivity dimension does not necessarily imply increased real citizen participation. Also, states appear keener to roll out these technical advances in fields relating to revenue than other services, which leads to scepticism regarding its potential for improving transparency and accountability in the eyes of citizens.[6] Certainly we can envisage that there will be more emphasis on developing interactive and discursive elements of government on the Internet. This of course is dependent upon governments being able to free themselves from the shackles of the knee-jerk need to control and legislate and to become a partner in the dialogue between citizens, groups, etc., trust citizens, to listen and hand back some of the power to their public constituencies. Letting go of power is often alien to governments and their officials, but it can create solid and stable future relationships built upon mutual trust.

Of course, as noted above, government is increasingly outsourcing its activities. This perhaps brings efficiencies and opportunities in a scenario similar to the notion of 'planning gain'. Governments may offset part of the research and development costs of E-Government by piggybacking their services on commercial sites and portals, the owners of which pay for the upkeep and development of technological solutions. This can allow officials to get on with the tasks of developing and implementing policy and reducing costs to the taxpayer. Outsourcing can also bring about issues of quality control and security. Lodge notes that there can be potential problems when outsourcers in turn outsource part of their task or project to a third or subsequent party who may not be in accord with the values and vision underpinning the contract as envisaged by its original designers. This is also clearly the case in matters as sensitive as E-Health (as seen in Savvides and Koutrakou[7]).

As Blakemore *et al.*[8] state, the creation of citizen-centric government poses a great challenge for governments. Perhaps they need to see it less as a challenge and more as an opportunity to transform government–citizen interactions. Networked government is here to stay. The only question is: Who has the power and influence? To the average citizen, organisational forms of government are of less interest than the notions of efficiency, effectiveness and equity. These are the key elements that they seek from government, be it offline government or E-Government. There is evidence of some governments already developing potential ambient intelligent environments, including aspects of E-Consultation. Of course the danger comes when we simply try to replicate offline government services online. This can lead to policy silos and a lack of co-ordination or joined-up thinking between differing arms of government, however wide the definition. While a normal avenue of development, such an approach does not utilise the full potential that ICTs offer us. In a sense, we have to unlearn the past in order to develop or transmute those services into ones that are more relevant to our needs today. There is no doubt that a big bang approach of total change is impossible and unwanted by most people. We will see more gradual, although radical, changes taking place over time. As technology and the willingness to engage in using it develop, we will see the development of information and services that could actually take the load off some existing services which may be already overstretched. Savirimuthu[9] has shown how the development of dispute resolution mechanisms and/or solutions can take some of the pressure off an overburdened legal system.

As both O'Donnell *et al.*[10] and Nixon[11] have shown, one of the problems in relation to unlocking the potential of E-Enabled consultation or discursive possibilities facilitated by ICTs is the public's distrust of government and, perhaps to a lesser extent, the level of trust, which does fluctuate, in the technology itself. Trust is affected by perception and perhaps the media have been too quick to condemn the efforts of government to transform itself in the information age. Perhaps we need to return to the much-derided age of spin in order to sell E-Government to a somewhat sceptical public. The two-edged nature of trust has been evidenced quite clearly by Lips *et al.*[12] when they spoke of the development of identity management systems both producing trust, by authenticating transactions and transaction histories, and causing concerns over potential human rights abuses and misuse of the data. These worries are amplified by Lodge,[13] who has pointed out that citizens not only are worried by the use of biometric and other data by agencies which they know use their data, but also worry that the data may be shared with those that they do not know, thus denying them the potential safeguards under any form of freedom of information act that may be in force in a given country.

It is not just the information of individuals that is at risk. Governments are also prone to attacks from those seeking to appropriate or steal information for their own purposes or from those who seek to disable or hamper government activities via cyber attacks, as Rawal[14] has described. Cyber attacks do not just affect small states. Emerging evidence suggests that large states are also under threat from cyber espionage. A recent report[15] shows the perceived lack of readiness by the US Department of Homeland Security to secure US information from competitor countries such as China. This was amplified by the Commission for Cyber Security, which issued a report[16] that has led the newly installed President Obama to call for a thorough review of US cybersecurity.[17]

When asked by a journalist what the most likely thing to blow government off its chosen course was, former British Prime Minister Harold Macmillan replied 'Events, dear boy, events.' At the time of writing, we can see the aptness of these words demonstrated once more as the present financial crisis throws up a degree of uncertainty. Businesses and governments are faced with a time of doubt and a lack of clarity. As Margolis and Moreno-Riãno[18] have pointed out, in times of financial insecurity, people's focus sometimes drifts from enhancing democracy towards satisfying more primeval security needs. In many people, the need for employment and its pecuniary and socio-psychological benefits supersedes any desire to re-engineer the government–citizen interface.

The financial crisis offers governments and international and non-governmental organisations enormous challenges and opportunities. There are those who read the financial crisis as leading to a retrenchment of government expenditure, with the focus shifted away from E-Government development and other policy issues towards economic regeneration, employment and wealth creation. Under such a view, E-Government projects will be either abandoned or put on the back burner and new developments thus be thwarted or delayed. Another view is that those very same financial constraints can lead to an increased dependence on E-Government as the constraints dictate that governments seek to streamline and modernise governance. E-Government can also act as a vehicle for broader consultation and co-ordination worldwide and for addressing conflict and economic development issues more efficiently, as Koutrakou has posited.[19] In order to save in the long term, it may be necessary to spend in the short term. This would have the potential benefits of possible long-term savings in expenditure, while the short-term expenditure could play a part in reflating economy and society alike, both directly and indirectly, by creating the conditions that facilitate future wealth creation and engagement, which can in turn fund the next generation of developments in E-Government.

Of course, forecasting future developments in technology is an endeavour which is fraught with difficulty. Predicting the future is not easy, given the lack of perfect knowledge of future events and developments, but there are certain indications that allow us to determine short-term trends that seem to influence how the future of E-Government may develop. There can be little doubt that the availability of so-called 'Web 2.0' technologies, coupled with rising general computing literacy and associated skills and competencies, will, potentially, enable a transformation of government–citizen interfaces. Web 2.0 technologies offer the potential for dynamic re-invention of interactions. Such technologies offer the potential for a much more inclusive and citizen-centric form of interaction. These will be interactions that are shaped by users. By that we mean in part by users both within government (using the widest sense of the word to include officials and so on) and those who must communicate with government. Both groups will have their own perspectives on and goals of what they wish to achieve via the technology. One has to accept that, at times, those range, of goals may be competing ones. Petrakaki[20] has discussed the potential consequences of officials' behaviour and accountability in an increasingly Internet-reliant government machine. Edwards[21] and Misuraca *et al.*[22] have offered tangible examples in different European contexts (i.e. the Netherlands, Switzerland, Norway and the United Kingdom). The notion of power is not removed from such relationships by the introduction of E-Government-based services, procedures and communication. It still exists and will perhaps always remain a contested area.

There is of course another area of contestation that migrates from offline to online activity. This is the clash, faced by many officials day after day, between rigidly applying rules and exercising discretion in individual cases, which can, however well intentioned in each case, lead to perceptions of diverse and unfair or unequal treatment. One must also remember that discretion in the implementation phase will also impact upon future E-Government use just as it does today in both the online and the offline encounters between government and the governed. Discretion empowers street-level – or perhaps in this case keyboard-level – bureaucrats to deviate from the original conception of policy applications and to interpret them in a way that may, in however small a way, contradict or contrast with the rules or the original intentions of the policymakers.

Web 2.0 developments will further intensify the notion of partnership in government. Differing stakeholders in all sectors (i.e. public, private and, increasingly, third sector) will combine in ever-changing coalitions with others to produce a coherent whole as the public and private do not disappear or break down, but continue to blur or become fuzzier. This means that the clarity of what is or can be defined as government is, due to the diasynchronic nature of change, ever more opaque. A challenge for government is to determine not only the structures and organisational forms necessary to achieve their goals, but also how to deal with the vast amount of information flowing through and around the system.

The problems faced by those who will move forward with E-Government developments are not necessarily ones that can be solved by technology alone. Given that most people would agree that governments should be based on democratic principles, and that democracy was not perfect prior to the adoption of E-Government, why should we assume that those problems will be solved by technology? The problems, on the whole, are those of human interactions; we must look at changing such human interactions in order to find a solution. The Internet has a role to play, but it is we who must harness technology to change the world. For it to be a more democratic and equitable place to live, we need to change first. It is a challenge for governments to use all means, including technology, to create conditions where all sections of society feel they can participate in that change. Governments need to spend more time listening to what their people want and be prepared to step back and hand back power in order to empower their citizens to utilise technology to create a better, more citizen-centric and trusted form of government.

Notes

1 Frissen, V. *et al.* (2007) *The Future of E-Government: An Exploration of ICT Driven Models of E-Government for the EU in 2020.* JCR Reports, Brussels. Accessed online at http://ipts.jrc.ec.europa.eu/publications/pub.cfm?id=1481.
2 Dutton, Chapter 1 this volume.
3 Dutton, Chapter 1 this volume.
4 Codagnone and Osimo, Chapter 3 this volume.
5 Margolis and Moreno-Riãno, Chapter 5 this volume.
6 Montargil, Chapter 4 this volume.
7 Savvides and Koutrakou, Chapter 11 this volume.
8 Blakemore *et al.*, Chapter 2 this volume.
9 Savirimuthu, Chapter 8 this volume.

10 O'Donnell *et al.*, Chapter 7 this volume.
11 Nixon, Chapter 16 this volume.
12 Lips, Chapter 9 this volume.
13 Lodge, Chapter 10 this volume.
14 Rawal, Chapter 15 this volume.
15 United States Government Accountability Office (2008) *Critical Infrastructure Protection: Testimony to the House of Representatives.* Accessed online at http://www.gao.gov/new.items/d081157t.pdf.
16 CSIS Commission on Cyber Security (2008) *Securing Cyberspace for the 44th Presidency.* Accessed online at http://www.csis.org/media/csis/pubs/081208_securingcyberspace_44.pdf.
17 BBC News (10 February 2009) http://news.bbc.co.uk/2/hi/technology/7880695.stm.
18 Margolis and Moreno-Riãno, Chapter 5 this volume.
19 Koutrakou, Chapter 17 this volume.
20 Petrakaki, Chapter 6 this volume.
21 Edwards, Chapter 13 this volume.
22 Misuraca *et al.*, Chapter 12 this volume.

Further reading

Frissen, V. *et al.* (2007) *The Future of E-Government: An Exploration of ICT Driven Models of E-Government for the EU in 2020.* JCR Reports, Brussels. Accessed online at http://ipts.jrc.ec.europa.eu/publications/pub.cfm?id=1481.
Lanvin, B. (2008) 'Where is E-Government Going in 2020?' Paper presented to OECD 2008 E-Leaders Conference 'The Future of E-Government – Agenda 2020', http://www.oecd.org/dataoecd/42/57/40304889.pdf.
Nordfors, L., Ericsson, B. and Lindell, H. (2006) *The Future of E-Government.* Vinnova Reports. Accessed online at http://www.vinnova.se/upload/EPiStorePDF/vr-06-11.pdf.

Index

Italic page numbers denote references to figures/tables.